Higher Learning, Greater Good

Higher Learning, Greater Good

The Private and Social Benefits of Higher Education

WALTER W. McMAHON

The Johns Hopkins University Press

Baltimore

© 2009 Johns Hopkins University Press
All rights reserved. Published 2009
Printed in the United States of America on acid-free paper

Johns Hopkins Paperback edition, 2017
9 8 7 6 5 4 3 2 1

Johns Hopkins University Press
2715 North Charles Street
Baltimore, Maryland 21218-4363
www.press.jhu.edu

The Library of Congress has cataloged the hardcover edition of this book as follows:

McMahon, Walter W.
    Higher learning, greater good : the private and social benefits of higher education /
Walter W. McMahon.
        p. cm.
    Includes bibliographical references and index.
    ISBN-13: 978-0-8018-9053-6 (hardcover : alk. paper)
    ISBN-10: 0-8018-9053-5 (hardcover : alk. paper)
    1. Education, Higher. 2. Higher education and state. 3. Education—Economic aspects.
4. Education—Social aspects. I. Title.
    LB2324.M39 2008
    378—dc22

                    2008015481

A catalog record for this book is available from the British Library.

ISBN-13: 978-1-4214-2403-3
ISBN-10: 1-4214-2403-7

Special discounts are available for bulk purchases of this book. For more information,
please contact Special Sales at 410-516-6936 or specialsales@press.jhu.edu.

Johns Hopkins University Press uses environmentally friendly book materials, including
recycled text paper that is composed of at least 30 percent post-consumer waste, whenever
possible.

With my love to Carolyn,
whose encouragement and support have been vital,
and to our children, Lynn, Vicki, Christopher, and Jennifer,
who are all benefiting from higher education
in the ways discussed here

CONTENTS

PREFACE TO THE 2017 EDITION

Since this book first appeared, I think that there are no major changes that need to be made to the substance of the analysis. If anything, the political upheavals that have occurred in the United States, the United Kingdom, and, potentially, the European Union make the analysis about the skill deficits, their sources, and their implications even more pressing.

There are updates to the rates of return and comments on the stability of the trends that are pertinent, however. Since 2005, the unadjusted social rates of return to associate degrees (p. 187) have essentially held steady at 13.5% for males and 13.1% for females, as they have for bachelor's degrees at 13.0% and 10.9%, respectively. Adjusted both for ability bias, net of measurement error, as well as for longitudinal trends, they are currently 10.0% and 11.8% for associate and 11.6% and 9.6% for bachelor's, respectively. These updates affect none of the conclusions.

There has been no diminution of the upward secular trend in the college earnings premium earned by bachelor's graduates over high school graduates. This is when a 1989 starting point is used for measuring the secular trend that has the same 5.3% unemployment rate as the ending point in 2015–16. This reveals a constant upward longitudinal trend of 1.3% per year on average for males and females. This contrasts with arguments by some that the trend in the college earnings premium has flattened recently. The latter occurs only if you include the cyclical upsurge in the college premium during the 1982-89 sharp recovery from the recession in 1982. Interestingly, the trend in the college premium for graduates with master's, Ph.D., and professional degrees is now wider than at the bachelor's level, averaging a 1.65% increase per year from 1989 through 2016. This pattern of the education premium moving upward from primary education in the poorest countries to secondary to college and now to graduate levels as countries develop is typical of the pattern I have observed working in many developing countries over the years.

T HIS BOOK sets forth a modern human capital approach to higher
education policy in the United States but also in other developed
OECD member countries. It emphasizes the nature, measurement,
and valuation of the private and social benefits of higher education—with
special attention to the non-market private and social benefits, direct and
indirect effects, and short- and long-term effects—all in relation to the
total investment costs. This includes drawing on the theory and analysis
of sources of endogenous development, economic efficiency, and market
failure to identify current higher education policy gaps and devise solutions. With respect to the latter, the book seeks a balanced consideration
of viable policy options.

Unfortunately, much of current higher education policy seems to be
asleep at the switch. For one thing there are massive skill deficits generated by globalization and technical change. These skill deficits explain
why real income has not risen for Americans who have not gone to college
since 1980. At the same time, the real income of college graduates has
risen 57% since 1980. These premiums are stable or even wider during
recessions. Higher education policy has not responded in significant ways
to the 64% of Americans with lower skills who are socially and economically being excluded from the benefits of economic growth. Similar trends
toward widening inequality and domestic skill deficits are apparent in the
European Union, although access to higher education has been expanding
more rapidly there. There is an obvious political backlash in the United
States and the European Union in the form of protectionism and other
policies that go beyond seeking a level playing field and that are not conducive to sustained growth.

Higher education policy initiatives also have not responded with anything approaching a unified voice. They have not joined with K–12 to try
to secure the kind of state-level education finance reform and state fund-

ing needed. They have not reached across the public-private and university-community college divides to stress their complementary roles and common overall mission. The U.S. Department of Education and state boards of higher education have not articulated the value of the important private non-market benefits relevant to more efficient private investment by students and their families. Instead, they seem content to put up with the market failure. Some leaders turn to increased privatization and some writers stress that this can aid internal efficiency, while both largely ignore external efficiency. Both are necessary to achieving overall economic efficiency as well as the greater good. National commissions have focused only on the rising tuition and institutional costs, and some of their members conclude—based only on this—that there is overinvestment. The recent commissions largely ignore that the costs must be related to the returns to be able to reach such a conclusion. Others have been equally guilty of looking only at the benefits and ignoring rising costs.

As globalization expands, national policies are moving toward protectionism instead of eliminating the skill deficits that would enhance the comparative advantage in human capital that is now slipping for the United States and the European Union. Some fair trade with protections for working conditions, the environment, and a level playing field are reasonable. But taking the lead with high export subsidies, increased tariffs, and tax subsidies normally supports inefficiencies and inequities, and limits growth. In this environment of pressing needs calling for a response, higher education policy is unique in being able to offer a solution that simultaneously contributes positively to growth. Other policy options tend to limit growth and eventually lower tax revenues in one way or another.

The second major factor that has motivated the writing of this book is that higher education policy research tends to be very slow in incorporating recent research in modern human capital theory. Yet the new research has powerful policy implications. This is paradoxical since higher education institutions themselves take pride in being at the frontier of new knowledge. For example, there are dramatic advances in the analysis of the economic value of human time. These are crucial to separating the earnings benefits from the non-market private and social benefits of higher education without overlap, and hence to valuing the total outcomes of higher education. These distinctions are not apparent in most of the higher education literature or in most of the publicity about the wider benefits of learning. For another example, there are major advances in endogenous growth theory, which is the conceptual basis for the knowledge-based economy. This has important implications for complementarities between graduate education and research at the research universities. Again, this is not a central tenet of most higher education literature. It has implications for how higher education externalities raise growth and development later. There is related research on the analysis of endogenous development that identifies specific non-market externalities as distinguished from aggregate externalities as part of the dynamic development process. The analysis of the dynamics of this process is in contrast to a few studies that conclude that higher education does not contribute to growth and therefore there are no externalities. But these studies tend to eliminate the interaction between higher education and new technology, as well as ignore the indirect effects. Both may be appropriate when considering immediate impacts but are not appropriate over the medium term or longer run as will be shown later. As a final example, there have been advances in measuring and valuing non-market private and social benefits of higher education. These reveal a source of market failure, again with implications for higher education policies. Both looming policy gaps and these new developments in modern human capital theory and their implications are key motivations for this book.

Much higher education policy is very inward looking, focused on internal campus management. But there are also important internal campus academic policy implications. For example, privatization trends that neglect the value of non-market private and social benefits of education lead to internal distortions in the allocation of funds. This includes undervaluation of the contributions of fields where patents are not possible, since patents permit private capture of the benefits. That is, some fields such as law, political science, and constitutional law contribute to civic institutions, the rule of law, and political stability, which feed back through indirect effects to set the stage for the next round of growth and development. Other fields such as English and mathematics nourish other disciplines but also are vital to earnings directly by contributing to what most graduates do every day. Foreign language and international affairs contribute to trade and hence to growth. In these fields the short-term monetary returns are usually not high and patenting is not possible. If the contribution of these fields to growth and development were more adequately measured and valued, this would likely lead to them getting more attention and support because of this contribution and would probably lead to a smaller distortion of academic priorities. As it stands, standard rate of return studies based only on earnings by field are largely ignored, as they should be. If a provost, for example, looks only at market rates of return by field he would dramatically expand the MBA, business, and engineering programs; scale down mathematics, education, and the social sciences; and terminate all humanities and fine and applied arts programs immediately. Estimating the non-market benefits can not only help to reveal the contributions of these fields to the quality of life and the greater good but can also help to bring internal campus academic policy into better balance.

THIS BOOK OWES A MAJOR DEBT OF GRATITUDE to the Spencer Foundation, which funded much of the research through a major research grant and many of the research assistants who contributed to its completion. Although the research reported here was made possible in part by this grant, the data presented, the statements made, and the views expressed are solely the responsibility of the author. The earliest origins were in reports for the University of Illinois that utilized tracer study data on the earnings of Illinois graduates to compute standard private and social rates of return and compare them to the same rates computed from nationwide data. The author is indebted to Sylvia Manning, then vice president for academic affairs, and to Larry Faulkner, then provost of the Urbana Champaign Campus, for support of these studies (McMahon, 1998a, 1998b). This led later to the Spencer Foundation grant in which King Alexander was a co-principal investigator. King contributed significantly to earlier draft reports to Spencer. Since then the manuscript has undergone a major reorientation, reflects extensive additional research, includes additional chapters, and has been completely rewritten. I owe King, a dear friend, who is now president of the University of California at Long Beach, an enormous debt of gratitude. This includes the inspiration for including higher education in the OECD countries as part of the analysis, for earlier analyses of the market rates of return in Chapter 3, and for an important policy thrust that the reader will discover in Chapter 7.

Others also have been particularly helpful. Elizabeth Appiah contributed as a research assistant to the analysis of costs, and later while teaching at the University of Maryland at Baltimore to the re-estimation of the private and social market rates of return. Wendy Cunningham, now at the World Bank, contributed to the adaptation of the computation of national rates of return to a program for estimation of rates of return that are campus specific based on local tracer study data that is available on the author's website. My longtime friend George Psacharopoulos has always been a good sounding board. I would also like to thank Stanley Ikenberry for his useful tips on emerging national higher education policy issues and his moral support. Jason Dunick and Micah Pollak, PhD students in economics supported by the Spencer Grant, were very helpful respectively with data collection and with the estimation of the growth equations in Appendix D. Liza Bordey, a PhD student in agricultural economics, has been extremely helpful in working closely with me on the valuation of the non-market private and social benefits in Appendixes C and E. Last, but by no means least, I am deeply grateful to an earlier referee for the Johns Hopkins University Press for his insightful and useful comments, as well as to Larry Leslie for his enthusiastic reactions and very thoughtful suggestions that were the result of his careful reading of the entire manuscript. None of the persons mentioned is responsible for the conclusions or the final result, for which the author bears sole responsibility.

My deepest debt of gratitude is to my dear wife Carolyn, for her encouragement, response to my occasional request for advice, and sustained moral support.

CHAPTER ONE

What Is the Problem?

Trickle down does not work when two-thirds of the population
does not have the necessary skills.

W. MCMAHON

T HE DEGREE OF PRIVATIZATION of higher education has been increasing since 1980, and even more sharply from 2001 through
the present. As public funding of higher education per full-time
student has declined, tuition has risen 29% in real terms net of increases
in financial aid since 1996 at public institutions according to the College
Board (2007a). For public and private institutions alike, the funding of
federal and state student financial aid in real terms on a per student basis
has not kept up, even with the 2007 increase in the maximum for Pell
Grants of $260 to $4,310 for 2008 (ibid.). At public institutions this increase in tuition has made up for only about one-fourth of the decline in
state funding. The net increase in costs to families has been accompanied
by a reduction in participation by lower-income groups and minorities,
as well as increased reliance on student loans at both public and private
institutions. This shift of the costs to students and their families is an
important aspect of the privatization of the financing of higher education
I discuss further in this book.

Similarly, research funding at the research universities is increasingly
financed by firms and Internet courses financed totally by individuals.
This includes privately financed organizations housed in university foun-

dations, as well as support of research the results of which can be patented and therefore the monetary benefits captured privately. It includes rapid expansion of Internet courses such as those offered by the University of Phoenix as well as privately owned for-profit colleges, both of which normally have a strong vocational slant. Together this powerful trend constitutes what has been called the de facto privatization of higher education.*

Although a vast literature now has emerged in higher education about this and other related financing problems facing higher education policy, little analysis has been done on the degree of privatization that is economically efficient. If control of higher education is to be fully relinquished to private markets, then there needs to be analysis of the extent to which there may be market failure leading to distortions. In order for any market, including higher education markets, to work efficiently, there must be relatively complete information in the possession of students, families, and higher education policy makers. If there is poor information available to the average citizen and politicians about the value of the non-market private and social benefits of higher education, then poor investment decisions and policy decisions will result. An economic value can be placed on the benefits of higher education to better health and to longevity beyond income valued in terms of their income equivalent that are just as legitimate as the value placed on the earnings benefits, for example. But the problem is that although families and students are well aware of the increases in earnings following completion of a college degree, as shown by many studies, they are only very vaguely aware of the value of the non-market benefits beyond earnings that enhance the quality of life.

An implication is that as privatization of higher education proceeds, private investment by families and students will be insufficient to be economically efficient. It is possible that privatization has not proceeded far enough outside of the United Kingdom in Europe, at the one extreme. There higher education expenditure per student is under half what it is in the United States. The result is that a major source of additional financing, the private support of families able and willing to pay (coupled with need-based financial aid), is not tapped and there are insufficient resources to sustain the quality of higher education in many European countries. In

*Lyall and Sell (2006). See also Bok (2003).

Greece, for example, the Constitution mandates that tuition must be free, and expenditure per student of $4,700 is less than one-fourth the $20,500 average in the United States (Psacharopoulos, 2005).* But as privatization proceeds, if there is poor information about the value of the private non-market benefits, total private investment still may be insufficient. If there is poor information about the specific social benefits available to voters, then again there is market failure, the level of public investment is not economically efficient, and the greater good is not served. That there may be underinvestment is suggested by the fact that about 80% of each age group now finish high school in the United States, but only 27% finish college, a large 50 percentage point gap leading to the National Center for Education Statistics (NCES) estimate that four hundred thousand pre-pared young people annually now do not go to college. It is also strongly suggested by the fact that 64% of the population that has only finished high school has seen no increase in their real earnings since 1980, whereas the real earnings of college graduates continue to rise sharply, as we will see in Chapter 3. Of course, the opposite can also be true. If the costs are too high and rising in relation to the true private and social benefits, then the social rates of return will be low. This implies that more are going to college than can benefit from it, or else that there is internal inefficiency, or both. There is overinvestment at the current cost levels in this case. The policy remedies are to reduce costs and/or to invest less.

There are three main kinds of policy implications:

- First, what is higher education's mission in globalizing knowledge-based economies, when examined in the context of the race between the contributions of research creating new knowledge and the need by the rest of the population to acquire the skills necessary to keep up?
- Second, what is the level of total investment in higher education financed by both private and public sources that is economically efficient for growth and broader development?

*Total expenditure per student is, for example, $20,500 in the United States, $12,400 in Australia, $11,000 in Germany, $9,000 in France, $7,000 in Portugal, and $4,700 in Greece. Citations to scientific publications are 70% in the United States, 30% in the rest of the world. Of the best 20 universities in the world, 17 are in the United States, 2 in the United Kingdom, and 1 in Japan. The first continental European Union university appears at rank 39. See Psacharopoulos (2005, pp. 5, 6, 10).

- Third, how far should the degree of privatization in the financing of public and private higher education continue to go if higher education is to be economically efficient in serving the greater good?

These are the main themes of the chapters that follow.

The Goals of the Book

The intended audience for this book is higher education policy makers within universities and government, scholars and graduate students, and members of the general public interested in higher education policy issues. That is, it is directed to a general audience, not to economists or technical specialists. The book, however, does seek to maintain a standard of analysis that gains the respect of and is of interest to professional economists and specialists.

The main goals of the book, with key terms defined further in Chapter 2, are:

- To develop a systematic comprehensive and cohesive conceptual framework for analyzing contemporary higher education policy and for devising solutions for major policy gaps such as those identified above.
- To emphasize the nature, measurement, and valuation of the private and social benefits of higher education, with special attention to the non-market private and social benefits beyond income, direct and indirect effects, and short- and long-term effects, all in relation to the total investment costs.
- To consider the true costs of investment in higher education, all in relation to trends in the returns. These include tuition costs to families, which have been rising faster than inflation; the level of public support; institutional costs, which also have been rising; and forgone earnings costs, which rise over the lifecycle but over time have been flat.
- To employ endogenous growth and endogenous development theory and related empirical research to obtain new insights into higher education policy. Endogenous growth and endogenous development are the conceptual basis for the knowledge economy

and for higher education externalities, all defined further in Chapter 2. They are a critical basis for evaluating growth equation research and for the analysis of the dynamics of indirect effects, all basic to social benefits and to higher education policy.

- To consider the theory and evidence of market failure due to lack of information about the nature and extent of social benefits and positive externalities as well as the private and social non-market benefits of higher education. Efficient markets require all participants to have complete information.

This comprehensive modern human capital approach applied to the analysis of key issues related to higher education policy gaps seeks to replace the "familiar, but curious, economics of higher education" (Clotfelter, 1999, p. 3) with a coherent framework easily accessible to the general reader. Beyond isolating major gaps in policy, it is useful in devising policy options leading to solutions.

Higher Education in Globalizing Economies: What Does a Human Capital Perspective Add?

Bringing a modern human capital perspective to higher education policy issues is revealing. It deals with not just the narrowly defined economics of job markets and earnings, as some mistakenly interpret human capital to be. This is an important part of the story. But the uses of human capital and human capital outcomes include the use of human capital at home and in the community during leisure-time hours. Time spent at home uses human capital in producing non-market private satisfactions like better health, greater longevity, and greater happiness very important to the household's welfare. And time spent in the community or in helping others uses this same human capital to generate social outcomes that benefit others and future generations. These include contributions to the operation and development of civic institutions vital to democracy, human rights, political stability, and the criminal justice system necessary to civic order. Neither these private non-market benefits nor social benefits are basically job-related but are specific contributions of human capital to "living a life," as W. E. B. DuBois said. A modern human capital perspective includes these leisure-time uses of human capital in household production that have a strong foundation in economic theory, thanks largely to Gary Becker. These include the uses of human capital in the community that serves the public interest. Both private non-market effects over the lifecycle and the benefits to society are, or should be, central to discussions of academic policy.

Human capital theory also provides the conceptual basis for adding the non-market returns to the market returns and for valuing the non-market benefits. Human capital used in the workplace generating earnings, and then used at home or in the community during leisure-time hours generating non-market benefits, cannot be used by any individual in more than one place at the same time. So the non-market returns are separate and discrete from the market returns. All that is necessary is that in measuring the non-market benefits there must be a control for the market benefits, usually by including per capita income or earnings in the regression. This is not always done, but unless it is there will be double counting when the benefits are added up in order that they may significantly affect policy.

This simultaneously provides the basis for placing an economic value on these non-market outcomes. The monetary values of these non-market outcomes are just as legitimate as the monetary value of the earnings outcomes from higher education. Say that the non-market outcome is better health. The income equivalent value of the increment to better health is calculated based on the average behavior of large numbers of individuals. The income coefficient in the regression shows how much more health the "typical," or average, individual will buy given additional income. The education coefficient shows how much health an additional year of education will produce after controlling for income. And the ratio of the education to the income coefficient gives the income-equivalent value of the improvement in health produced by the additional year of education. Using this measurement technique attributable originally to Haveman and Wolfe (1984), each non-market outcome of higher education is measured, valued, and comprehensively added up, as I explain further and implement in Chapters 4 and 5.

Beyond this, a human capital formation perspective offers insights into how to better interpret the rising costs of higher education. Institutional costs get almost all of the attention, but they represent only about half of the total investment by families in higher education at public institutions. Many of the discussions conveniently omit forgone earnings costs, which are approximately equal in size to institutional costs and are a legitimate part of the total investment. Institutional costs have risen, as is very well known. But forgone earnings costs have not risen in real terms since 1980. This is because the earnings of high school graduates, which are the best measure of the earnings forgone by parents (since parents pay most room, board, transportation, and clothing costs while the student is in school), have *not* risen in real terms. This means that the description of rising institutional costs distorts the true investment cost increases in higher education. The true economic increase in investment costs is, therefore, less than what is normally believed.

Considering forgone earnings costs, it then also becomes apparent that a considerably larger fraction of total higher education costs is borne privately than is frequently thought. Tuition and fee costs to students and their families definitely have risen very sharply, especially at private institutions and less so at public institutions. This is largely because state support per student in real terms for institutional costs, and for student financial aid, which also helps private institutions, have both fallen. Room and board costs have also risen, although less rapidly. Overall, the public share of the total investment in a college education has fallen for the average student. So tuition and fees have risen largely because of this, and by definition the privatization of higher education financing has increased. But still total costs have not risen as sharply as the tuition and fee component.

A human capital perspective sheds new light in other ways on higher education policy as the following chapters demonstrate. It focuses on the more ultimate outcomes of higher education over the lifecycle of graduates, including how their activities affect society, the more ultimate bases for higher education accountability. A new perspective also comes from considering the full values of these outcomes in relation to their costs. This reveals whether higher education investment is below, at, or above its optimum. New perspectives also come from considering the impacts from investment in academic research, which is linked in human capital theory with the embodiment of new knowledge through graduate education at the master's, PhD, and professional levels. This link has implications for which levels of higher education are most significant for growth in each state and hence for which state investment policies are most conducive to the state's growth and development, as we will consider in

Chapters 6 and 7. There are also implications for the broader mission of higher education policy and for the mission of each campus. A human capital perspective has implications for campus-level academic policy relating to the allocation of resources among disciplines and for the questionnaires used by campus tracer studies following graduates. Finally, a human capital formation perspective also has implications for the standard higher education policy issues of access, affordability, accountability, and privatization.

In summary, the human capital approach addresses three main themes:

- the emerging new mission of higher education in knowledge-based growing and globalizing economies
- whether the current rate of total investment in higher education is above or below optimum
- the search for criteria for the amount of privatization that is optimal

The objective is to use a more rigorous modern human capital approach to the analysis of higher education benefits in relation to their costs and to higher education policy. This should take the valuation of higher education's private and social non-market benefits and a more adequate social rate of return to a higher level. But there are still gaps in knowledge. Higher education's social benefits and the timing of their impacts over time are seriously under-researched. But the existence of unknown elements is typical of any active field. New research brings more to light virtually every day. In the meantime, current economic models can be deliberately stretched to make them relevant to higher education policy.

It is important to stress again that this book is directed to a general audience, not to economists or technical specialists. I assume that the reader has an intelligent interest in higher education policy, including an interest in how higher education relates to the economy and society on which it depends. The book assumes very little or no prior knowledge of economics. Higher education leaders and their staff must explain to legislators and the public what the private and social benefits are, what overall economic efficiency means, and what the implications of market failure are in clear, straightforward, and non-technical, terms. The few technical economic terms used are those basic to higher education policy. And these few crucial terms such as *human capital, education externali-*

ties, market failure, and *endogenous growth* I define and discuss in Chapter 2 or at the point where they are used extensively.

As mentioned, the primary focus of this book is on higher education policy in the United States. But in the United Kingdom, the European Union, and other developed countries in the Organization for Economic Cooperation and Development in Paris (OECD), including Canada, Australia, New Zealand, Japan, and South Korea, the technology, globalization, and privatization impacts are similar. So the basic analysis of human capital formation and of the private and social benefits applies, although the policy context differs somewhat. The latter is largely because there is more decentralization of higher education in the United States than in the European Union, private families contribute much more to higher education costs in the United States and South Korea than in continental Europe, and the United States has a much more extensive community college system set up for lifelong learning where students live at home and transfer to four-year colleges later. However, the basic similarities in the situation facing higher education in the developed countries do not extend to the radically different conditions in most of the poor countries. Most important is the lack of basic education throughout Africa, South Asia, and the Caribbean. Also there are low tuition policies that therefore benefit primarily the wealthy, few student need-based grant and loan programs, almost no two-year community college programs, and very serious problems with emigration of college graduates. All of this is very different in the United States, Canada, South Korea, and most of the European Union. So education policy priorities need to be quite different in developing countries. Therefore, the decision was made not to include higher education policy in developing countries within the scope of this book, except by tangential reference here and elsewhere. So although the primary focus is on U.S. higher education, most of the analysis—including the analysis of human capital and endogenous development, of market failure, of where the comparative advantage lies, and of the implications of globalization for higher education policy—also applies to the United Kingdom, Canada, and the European Union. I will note differences from the United States occasionally where they are relevant.

In summary, a modern human capital perspective offers many insights for higher education's mission in sustaining the technological frontier at the research universities and in the leading regions that can retain the high-tech graduates without forgetting the follower unskilled persons and follower regions that are not at the frontier. Valuation of the private and social benefits relative to costs also offers insights into whether private and public investment in higher education is above or below optimum, and into how far the current trend toward privatization should go. There have been other recent contributions to higher education research that address the problems of higher education, including accountability, access, and affordability, as well as the de facto privatization of public universities in *The True Genius of America at Risk* by Lyall and Sell (2006). However, this book seeks to further develop a systematic and comprehensive modern human capital framework for addressing these and related issues and investigating the new implications for higher education policy. This includes greater emphasis than the earlier books on policy gaps and potential solutions.

Public Funding Is Declining: Is This Appropriate?

The United States spends several hundreds of billions of dollars annually on higher education, and even more is spent in the other developed nations taken together. Is it not reasonable and important to ask, "What do we get for that very considerable investment?" It is a question that is asked by legislators, parents, students, and the general public, not just by economists and those in higher education. It is a difficult question to answer, however. Half-hearted attempts that answer the question with anecdotes, or that contain a hidden agenda, or that are not rooted in a careful analysis of the process of human capital formation and its impacts on society are sometimes worse than saying nothing at all.

The implications of this question for higher education policy are striking.

- The first overarching policy question is, "What are the new needs and opportunities for higher education policy in modern globalizing economies?"
- The second fundamental question is, "Should we invest more in higher education, including both public and private funds, or should we invest less?"

- The third key question and policy issue is, "Should the current trend toward privatization within universities and colleges continue, and if so, how far should it go?"

Public universities and colleges in the United States enroll 77.6% of all students, with private nonprofit and private for-profit enrolling the rest. The private for-profit institutions grew from 2% of the full-time students in 1995 to 8% in 2005, the latest data available from NCES as of April 2008, all at the expense of public four-year institutions since the shares of the public two-year and private four-year institutions held steady (College Board, 2007b, p. 22). There was a 17% decline in constant dollars in state funding per full-time equivalent student from 2001 through 2005, followed by a partial recovery in 2006. But at $6,695 per full-time student this still remains 4% below the 1985–86 level (ibid., p. 23).

From the point of view of the institutions, this decline in state funding has not been fully offset by increases in tuition and fees. Net funding per student at public institutions after the tuition and fee increases was down sharply by 9% from 2001 through 2006. Private colleges and universities are also feeling the stress. They rely heavily on publicly funded state and federal student grants and on subsidized student loans. They have raised tuition even more sharply with the wider gap funded privately. One result has been a steady and substantial increase mostly since 2001 in non-federal student loans (College Board, 2007a, p. 3). So private colleges and universities are also part of the trend toward increasing privatization of funding sources.

PRIVATIZATION

How far the trend toward privatization should go depends primarily on the extent to which higher education generates social benefits that are above and beyond the private benefits to the student and his or her family. The trend toward the "entrepreneurial university" is unmistakable (Kirk, 2003) as is the trend toward de facto privatization as indicated above and discussed further by Lyall and Sell (2006). Sometimes this issue generates more heat than light. The position at one extreme is that higher education programs should be privatized and forced to cover their full costs, otherwise they will not be efficient. At the other extreme is the position that the market should have no role whatsoever, that the academy should be exempt.

Those who support privatization suggest that this competition would force greater efficiency. There is, however, little attention given to defining what economic efficiency in higher education really means, and then using the term properly. Instead, the term *efficiency* is thrown around with wild abandon.

Efficiency includes the externalities involved in serving the public good. That is, it includes both internal efficiency (related to unit costs) and external efficiency (how well the outcomes relate to social benefits expected by society). Economic efficiency therefore requires a balance in the degree of privatization that is optimal. Some is essential, but carried too far the interests of the greater good and future generations can be in jeopardy. Considering the low earnings in some fields, such as primary school teaching, and how much lower the demand for teachers would be if there were no publicly supported schools, it should be relatively obvious that there are benefits to future generations and that the social benefits are not absolutely zero. So insights are needed on how the size of the social benefits relative to the private benefits can be estimated. If they are not zero, purely private markets are economically inefficient. In the answer to these subtle questions lies guidance to such questions as "How far should tuition increases go in relation to public and/or gift and endowment support?"

The chapters that follow suggest a more rigorous conceptual framework that should offer new insights for achieving true economic efficiency. The concepts involved can also be applied in a more qualitative way to academic policy judgments program by program. The result is a new perspective on the degree of privatization campus-wide, and program by program, that is optimal. Perhaps this will be of help to higher education leaders seeking to explain and parents seeking to understand policies relating to rising tuition, fees as a percent of college costs, and growing privatization of research funding.

Some bemoan "vocationalization." This is characteristic of the private for-profits and of Internet courses. It is also an outcome of the squeeze put on the humanities, social sciences, and physical sciences as students "vote with their feet" and migrate toward vocationally oriented fields that offer the highest starting salaries. The basic rationale for public support is the ratio of spillover public benefits to others in the society and future generations, all relative to the private benefits enjoyed by the individual for which he or she is willing to pay. It is sometimes said, perhaps somewhat mindlessly, that since college graduates earn so much, essentially all of the benefits of higher education are private. In some circles this is viewed as the conventional wisdom. This is an issue that cries out for greater scrutiny.

For one thing, there are sources of market failure in higher education markets that cause fully privatized markets to be inefficient. For example, there is poor information about what the non-market private benefits really are and also about specifically what the public benefits are. Where there is poor information, private markets fail, and the result is economic inefficiency. In contrast, there is relatively good information about the contribution of a college education to earnings. This is not only about the differences among academic fields where there is ample evidence that students do "vote with their feet." The better information about earnings is also evident in the awareness of how two-year associate degrees contribute to employability and higher earnings, and in the major premiums four-year college graduates can command in job markets in most years.

But the story is different for awareness about the non-market private benefits. Most students do not know how much more each year of college will contribute to their longevity, to their health, and to their happiness and quality of life. This contribution of education for "living a life" was stressed in the earlier quote from W. E. B. DuBois, but the specifics of these benefits are poorly understood and therefore probably significantly underestimated. But there is now current research on these specifics, and my best estimate in Chapter 4 will show that the non-market private benefits beyond income are actually slightly more valuable than the contribution of college to earnings.

The implication is that the poor information leads to underinvestment in education. The efficiency of higher education markets could probably be increased if colleges and universities would mail out a one-page sheet to high school juniors summarizing the specific benefits for a typical graduate. Alumni also could help. Better information about the private benefits would help the high school students and the families of alumni to make more rational investment decisions and to make higher education markets work better.

The knowledge about the nature and scope of the social benefits of higher education is even worse. This is in spite of the fact that it is intuitively obvious that some of the earnings and quality of life of graduates is due to the education of others, including prior generations. For example, there are earnings and the quality of life benefits from living in a democratic society with substantial human rights due in part to the fact that college graduates serve on civic boards, commissions, and juries, as well as contribute financially to many nonprofit civic institutions. The crime rates are lower as well when more young men attend community colleges, and are motivated to finish high school and to continue their education. State criminal justice system costs are lower, as are state health and welfare costs, and tax receipts are higher. These social benefits of education do spill over to benefit taxpayers in the wealthy suburbs.

Students also benefit from the education of their parents. It is obvious that how far students are able to go in school is due in part to the education of their parents, which helps to finance the education. Parents who are college graduates also contribute to the cognitive development of their children, as I will measure and evaluate in Chapter 4. Beyond this, one of the largest social benefits unique to higher education is from the wider diffusion of new knowledge. This raises the productivity of those with less education within the firms in which these graduates are employed, but also benefits the family at home, neighbors and friends, and civic organizations to which the graduate contributes time. Without this diffusion of knowledge, most of the results of new research are likely to remain inaccessible.

But the lack of specific knowledge about these social benefits is another source of market failure likely to lead to underinvestment. Poor information effects are then compounded by the fact that the spillover benefits to others are externalities that individual students and their families generally do not have the incentive to finance. This is another potential source of underinvestment in higher education and the greater good is then not served. Student grants and loans and state institutional support is likely to be lower than it would otherwise be if there is poor information about what the social benefits are and their value. The money goes to prisons and state health care without recognition that these costs are high due to insufficient prior investment in education. State budgets become dominated by rising Medicaid, welfare, and prison system costs. State sales and income tax receipts, in turn, drop because taxpayers have insufficient earning capacity due to limited education. The squeeze on higher education budgets is part of a vicious cycle.

A better known source of market failure is the failure of private capital markets without government guarantees for the financing of student loans. This is also due to poor information. Lenders do not know whether individual students will succeed, or whether they will repay, and students from poor families especially are unable to provide collateral, so the risk is too high and if they lend at all it will only be at high rates. So to make these markets work better, government guarantees the loans, thereby eliminating the lender's risk of repayment, and provides subsidies to the banks for their administration. I discuss the issues involving the latter in Chapter 7. In the United States these are the subsidized Stafford Loans, and the unsubsidized Stafford Loans that are not means-tested; the two are about equal in terms of the fraction of total higher education expenses that they finance. Together these accounted for about one-third of all higher education funding, public and private, in 2007 (College Board, 2007a, p. 3). These have grown but only very slightly in real terms since 2001. Pell Grants, which account for a much smaller share (about 10%), have not grown at all (ibid.).

When government grants and loans to students are under-funded, perhaps due to inadequate awareness of the net benefits and perhaps due to other factors, the result is that access to higher education is restricted to below the optimum. In fact, enrollments have grown much more slowly in the United States than in the European Union, Canada, or South Korea. Another observable result is increasing inequity. As the percent of college costs covered falls, poorer students and minorities are increasingly unable to attend. The net price, which is tuition and fees less grant aid, has risen from 1992 to 2004 to 39% of family income for low-income and 22% of family income for low-middle-income groups at public four-year institutions, and at private nonprofit institutions to 68% and 39% of family income for these low- and low-middle-income groups (College Board, 2007b, pp. 18–19). There is the potential loss to society of the talents of many bright young people who come from families who have limited means. There is also a reduction of minorities and an increase in the percentage of students from higher-income families on campus (National Center for Education Statistics, 2006). Although the failure of capital markets is partially corrected by federal guaranteed student loan programs and federal and state grants, when these loan programs and grant programs receive insufficient public support the results are underinvestment and inequity in access, leading to greater inequality in the income distribution later.

With state financing of institutions and student grants falling to about 20% of the total funds for higher education expenses, and private costs for tuition, fees, and loans rising, the supply of two- and four-year college graduates is not keeping up with the rising demand for those with more skills, as I will show in Chapter 3. Since 1980 there has been a growing surplus of persons with insufficient skills, and a rising demand in jobs requiring college-level skills. Privatization also means that inequality in access to higher education increases at a time when inequality in the distribution of income in the United States and the OECD is increasing. So higher education policy does not appear to be responding to these needs.

Increasing privatization beyond some optimum point also has implications for the kind of curricula that are offered. Rather than allocate most resources to producing the "educated citizen," there are pressures to expand curricula that are cash cows. These include MBA programs, master's of science programs in finance and in information technology, and other vocationally oriented curricula in four-year residency and Internet programs that make profit or at least pay their own way with fees. High economic return fields should expand where earnings in relation to costs are high. This is not the problem. But what is happening to the level of support for fields that educate students more broadly, including some courses for these otherwise highly vocationalized students, as the public sources of funding are cut?

Expanding online Internet degrees furthers vocationalization and privatization rather dramatically. This began in major ways with the phenomenal growth of courses offered by the University of Phoenix, which is now having some major difficulties according to *The Chronicle of Higher Education,* and is now being actively expanded by most universities. But almost all of these online programs have a heavy job-training orientation. Persons lacking in strong self-motivation, which may be most potential students, and courses in the humanities, the social sciences, and the arts are likely to be squeezed out. Producing the educated citizen and the social benefits that flow from that are likely to suffer.

Privatization that goes too far also has implications for the kind of research that gets done. Private funding of research affects the rate at which knowledge in different fields expands. As research universities seek support for research, the types of research that can be patented and therefore privatized or that lead to profitable consulting raise faculty salaries in these fields. Sometimes the universities themselves also profit from the patents. This access to outside money in these fields leads to lower teaching loads and reallocation of campus resources toward these fields, which in turn results in larger fractions of faculty time spent on research, more research assistants, more labs, and faster progress in the development of new knowledge in these patent-oriented commercially financed fields. At the same time, in other fields where many of society's most acute problems lie, such as political science, education, psychology, sociology, economics, and social work, for example, there is far less outside and hence less internal matching support.

Privatization also has impacts on university management. Entrepreneurial universities increasingly market their research through research parks to acquire private financial support. They write exclusive contracts with firms to provide soft drinks, food, computers, housing, and other things that offer profitable opportunities for firms. Some universities offer exclusive contacts with students. Privately funded and often politically motivated think tanks support selected faculty and pre-selected research projects whose conclusions are to their liking. They support publications that are not subjected to external peer group review and that therefore tend to pollute the literature with one-sided arguments that profess to be scientific when they are not and therefore undermine the objectivity of the scientific method in the minds of the public. Campus ethics training and ethics policies about research sponsorship affecting results are efforts to counter this. But it is not apparent given the external funding nationally how well they succeed. These trends are viewed as desirable by some in order to produce cost-efficiency, as necessary for survival by others, and as selling the university's soul by still others.

THE LEVEL OF TOTAL EXPENDITURE ON HIGHER EDUCATION

Should total investment in higher education, both public and private, be larger or smaller? South Korea, the United States, and Canada are at the very top in total public and private investment in higher education as a percent of gross domestic product (GDP) (McMahon, 2006b, Table A-5). South Korea's economy has been growing the fastest and it is increasing the international patents it acquires far more quickly than any other country. Part of the reason for this high level of investment is that both the United States and South Korea tap private sources of funding from families especially far more than does the European Continent, South Korea even more so than the United States (ibid.) But no criteria exist to be able to say what the total level of investment in higher education should be. The economic criteria apply to determining whether there should be more or less investment than at present, and hence whether investment is below or above optimum. But they do not pinpoint the level at which total investment is at the optimum level of economic efficiency. If the social rate of return were measured properly, and it is higher than the average return obtainable on other investments or on other uses of tax funds, usually taken to be about 10% in real terms, then more should be invested if society is to be economically efficient in achieving faster economic growth and development. If the real return is less than 10%, then less should be invested. Using this as a guide, it is necessary to keep rechecking every five years or so to avoid overshooting the unknown optimal level. Alternatively, using growth equations with macroeconomic time series data, which is not easy to do given the limited number of growth observations over time available for any one country, then those investments (for example, human capital versus physical capital) or other policies (for example, fostering trade) that are shown to contribute the largest amount per dollar invested and most significantly to growth should be emphasized to attain faster per capita real growth, and those that do not work should be cut back or dropped.

Everything turns, however, on measuring the total benefits of higher education, private and social, and their costs. The measurement and valuation of the private non-market benefits include the contribution beyond income to own-health, spousal health, children's health, children's schooling, children's cognitive development, happiness, and longevity. The social benefits include contributions beyond income by higher education to the operation of civic institutions essential to democracy, human rights, and political stability, as well as contributions to the operation of the criminal justice system, to crime reduction, to poverty reduction, to environmental sustainability, and to the creation and dissemination of new knowledge. After each of the contributions of higher education is considered (as we will do in Chapters 4 and 5), then the value of each contribution must be estimated and added up. Then total private and social benefits can be related to the cost of the investment in human capital, and a much firmer basis for whether too much or too little is being invested in higher education becomes available.

With respect to equity, the maximization of happiness in the society also turns on whether higher education policies reduce or increase the degree of inequality in income at later ages and hence on the kind of society most desire for the nation's future. Whether inequality should be reduced or not, however, is a philosophical and religious question, and is not pure economics. Yet this very standard position among economists now must take into account the new research on the economics of happiness. The latter has produced cardinal measures of happiness, making relevant again Henry Sidgwick's classic utilitarian solution requiring some redistribution for the maximization of total social welfare (Layard, 2006). But philosophical questions aside, it is important to note that reducing the effects of imperfect capital markets with guaranteed student loans and providing means-tested Pell Grants both operate to reduce inequality below what it would otherwise be. But they simultaneously provide for investment in human capital with social rates of return that are relatively high, as I will demonstrate. In the case of human capital investment there is therefore frequently no tradeoff between efficiency and equity as there normally is in welfare programs. Instead, policies that promote equity to reduce inequality in future generations can simultaneously be very efficient in yielding relatively higher private and social rates of return. In the unique case of investment in human capital, investment that reduces inequality can also be efficient and promote growth so that efficiency and equity are complementary.

The problem with adding up the value of the private and social benefits is that although there is a huge volume of current research, especially on the private benefits, it is in very narrowly defined bits and pieces. It must be organized within a coherent framework. Care must be used not to double count the behaviors that contribute to final outcomes and other studies that focus only on the final outcomes, as well as to double count the non-market benefits measured in ways so that they overlap the earnings benefits of higher education. These forms of double counting are common if one were to make any attempt to add up the benefits reported in many studies such as those by the College Board (2007) or others. The task is made more difficult because frequently research is conducted and ideas are implanted in the general awareness in ways that are misleading to coherent higher education policy. For example, the jobs created in a local community as a college or university spends its budget on local salaries are not benefits of higher education from the point of view of the nation as a whole, although they are sometimes dubbed as such. Dollars spent locally that come from parents or that have been collected in taxes reduce parental expenditures in other communities. There is a concomitant loss of jobs and short-term benefits in those other localities. Impact studies can sometimes be useful in explaining the impact on the local people and helpful in relating to the local community. But for higher education policy the positive local impact and negative statewide impact cancel out. The net benefit of higher education measured in this way is zero, unless one chooses to use tunnel vision.

To cite another important example of fallacious counting, the health benefits of higher education are substantial. These include the health benefits from the purchases of doctors' services, drugs, and health care financed by the higher earnings due to higher education. To add these health benefits to the earnings benefits double counts the earnings benefits that contribute to better health and is very misleading. To cite a third example, to add up improvements in overall health due to education and the effect on behaviors that contribute to this better health (such as reduced smoking, less obesity, and so forth) again double counts overlapping effects. So great care must be used. And although there are hundreds of studies, those that do not control for the income effects of education and those that examine overlapping behaviors cannot be used to inform higher education policy.

HIGHER EDUCATION IN GLOBALIZING ECONOMIES

The endless onrush of technology and globalization are powerful trends likely to continue into the indefinite future. This is a sound basis for higher education policy. New technologies internal to the education system, such as the use of computers by faculty and in instruction or Internet instruction, have some promise in increasing effectiveness, but are as likely to raise costs as to lower them and similar to televised instruction, which turned out to be a fad, are unlikely to be a panacea. The impacts of technology on the economy and the kinds of skills and numbers of graduates required are much more important to higher education's mission. When combined with the impacts of globalization as higher-paying but medium- to lower-skill manufacturing jobs are outsourced internationally, these powerful forces are together much more likely to determine higher education's future.

The vital contribution of the research universities to advancing the technological frontier is the other key part of the race in modern knowledge-based economies. The impact of the new knowledge and technologies on productivity is a major source of the need for the upgrading of skills in the rest of the population through lifelong learning by community colleges and four-year institutions. Not only do the more highly educated earn more, but also new technology lowers the demand for the unskilled. This relative surplus of the less skilled prevents increases in their real earnings, and immigration by mostly lower-skilled workers in the case of the United States further restrains wages but by the best estimates available only a small 4 to 6%. Although higher education enrollments have been rising in the United States and the European Union, the demand for college graduates has risen relatively faster. So the relative earnings of college graduates have risen virtually everywhere.

The contribution of research universities in training new researchers as well as in producing new knowledge conducive to growth is shown by recent research to vary depending on how close the state or major city in which they are located is to the technological frontier. For the United States, the United Kingdom, and other developed countries to continue to lead, the funding of academic R&D and of advanced graduate education that trains the researchers for industry and government is essential. For those states at or near the technological frontier, this is shown to have a very high growth payoff by Aghion et al. (2005). The main reason is that the advanced graduates more frequently find employment in these technologically advanced regions. For those states (or countries) farther from the technological frontier, which Aghion et al. define as those with lower per capita income, the investment found to have the largest growth payoff is in two- and four-year college degree programs. These graduates generally remain within the state and do not migrate to the extent master's and PhD graduates do to the high-paying high-tech centers. Investment in increasing high school graduation rates also has a very high payoff, reducing state welfare, Medicaid, and criminal justice system costs as well as increasing state sales and income tax revenues, all of which is of great spillover benefit to higher-income families in the suburbs in new research summarized by Levin (2006).

Exacerbating the effect from new technologies are the effects from freer trade and international job outsourcing. U.S. jobs, mostly lower-skill but also those that can be handled over the Internet, are outsourced to Mexico, China, Vietnam, India, Taiwan, Indonesia, and Latin America. Similarly U.K. and European Union jobs are outsourced to Turkey, Eastern Europe, China, and the Far East. The jobs lost from freer trade in the industrialized economies are primarily middle- and low-skill manufacturing jobs in textiles and other manufacturing, and clerical jobs from car rentals to publishing that can be outsourced over the Internet. The result of freer trade is fast-growing demands for higher-skilled persons in the country from which the outsourcing is occurring, and increases in the excess supply of persons with lesser skills. This is especially apparent in states such as South Carolina and others, where textile and manufacturing jobs have been outsourced.

Although some businesses are recruiting from abroad persons with high skills, including doctors and nurses, the largest numbers of immigrants are in the lower-skill categories. In the United States these immigrants come mostly from Mexico, Central America, and the poorest Caribbean nations and compete for lower-middle and lower-skill jobs. In the European Union immigrants come from Turkey into Germany, from North Africa into France and the Netherlands, and from Pakistan, India, and other former British colonies into the United Kingdom. Although these immigrants earn more than they did back home, the competitions for low-skill jobs and with those citizens who have a high school education or less further holds down these wages.

As a result, the real earnings of lower-skilled workers without more than a high school education have not increased since 1980, and by some measures have fallen. This has also contributed to the increase in the inequality in the distribution of income. The 64% of the population that have seen no increase whatsoever in their real income constitute a silent majority, but the less well-educated poor appearing on television following Hurricane Katrina revealed an important aspect of the situation to a wider nationwide audience. The 43 to 57% increases enjoyed by those with a college degree since 1980 have sometimes been attributed to the extraordinary increases received by the top 1%. But when this 1% is deleted, large percentage increases for college graduates remain. The pattern is the same in European Union nations, where there has been a remarkable increase in wage inequality since 1980 (Faggio et al., 2007). There the percentage with a high school education or less is larger.

This means that a large proportion of the population is not enjoying the fruits of economic growth. This group is increasingly excluded both economically and socially. It is leading to a protectionist backlash both in the United States and in the European Union. In the United States, for example, there is the movement for fair trade among workers, joined by firms feeling pressures from imports, and leading to political pressure for protectionist tariffs, subsidies for firms that do not outsource, quotas, and opposition to additional free trade initiatives following the North American Free Trade Agreement (NAFTA) the Latin American Free Trade Agreement (LAFTA), and the founding of the World Trade Organization (WTO). There is also political pressure for more intensive policing of U.S. borders, ejection of illegal immigrants, and penalties on firms that hire immigrants. In the European Union similar forces are causing protectionist reactions. They include French farmers pressing for protection and sustained subsidies under the Common Agricultural Policy, votes in France and the Netherlands against the new European Union Constitution incorporating Eastern Europe, and opposition to the proposed admission of Turkey to the European Union.

But what is the basic problem? It is the lack of sufficient college-level skills empowering the left-out majority to join in the benefits of economic growth. This is the first piece of the new mission for higher education in this changed environment. The higher education policy implication involves a major national initiative supporting lifelong learning for adults at community colleges and more rapid expansion of access for the next generation to two- and four-year associate and bachelor's degree programs at public and private higher education institutions.

The other part of the new mission involves sustaining the race between new technology and its need for ever-increasing skills. This means increased support for research and for graduate education that trains the new researchers at research universities. This is also essential since the United States is losing its lead and comparative advantage both in research and in human capital to places like South Korea, China, and Canada. As Thomas Friedman has put it, the world really is flat (Friedman, 2007)! But what enables the United States and leading OECD countries to remain competitive in a world where trade, outsourcing, and capital movements all flow toward a flat common equilibrium is their R&D and stock of highly skilled people. These persons will largely remain in these countries at the technological frontier where the pay premiums can be paid. But as China, South Korea, and even India and parts of the European Union surge ahead, without more serious attention to its higher education system and research universities, the United States runs the serious risk of losing the main source of its comparative advantage in a globalizing knowledge-based world.

Government support is essential to initiate the process. But this then must and will be supplemented by families as more students enroll since this enrollment automatically generates private investment in the form of forgone earnings, tuition, and fees. With both public and private investment increasing by roughly equal amounts this means that the proportion of public to private investment is not necessarily changed. With a growing economy both public and private sectors are larger, and this would be true within higher education as well as economy-wide. But due to this partnership with families in investment in higher education the *relative* size of the public sector vis-à-vis the private sector is no larger.

The Need for Proposed Solutions

This role of higher education in economic development is not ignored by policy makers or key leaders among the public. They do recognize that higher education makes significant contributions to economic growth and development. However, higher education enrollments in the United States are growing more slowly than elsewhere, and the number of jobs in computer engineering are six times the annual number of graduates. China and India are plunging ahead in these fields, while public funding in real terms at state and federal levels in the United States continues to decline. There are many higher education policy pieces documenting this problem. But little attention has been directed to finding viable solutions.

Instead, most campus and state policies tend to be oriented to internal campus management. There is little attention to the human capital formation that connects graduates and each discipline to the current needs of the society. There is enormous attention to costs and accountability, accompanied by piecemeal privatization, and a major trend toward hiring large proportions of low-paid adjunct faculty who are often less well qualified and yet teach large classes and courses on the Internet. The new Spellings Commission Report (2007), according to President Bennett of Earlham College, "wants to improve higher education on the cheap" (Bennett, 2007, p. B7). A lot of the higher education literature is preoccupied with the competition with other institutions for students and for prestige. It is of course true that when academic departments and colleges excel, their contribution to graduates and to the society is larger. But this is not a substitute for the lack of cooperation among public research universities and community colleges or between public and private nonprofit institutions in seeking the support necessary for the common mission of serving society's needs. Broader state policies for economic development often do not stress the basic and higher education system of the state as the centerpiece, which is strange in modern knowledge-based economies, but instead stress various kinds of tax subsidies that can sometimes subsidize inefficiency and can often be cancelled out by the actions of other states. This need for better cooperation within the higher education community on higher education policy includes articulating the connection between insufficient access to two- and four-year programs and the rising inequality in earnings and in the distribution of income later. In fact, I will suggest in Chapter 7 that there is considerable potential in dramatically raising public awareness of the connection of inadequate education to criminal activity and prison costs, to high public assistance costs, to high state Medicaid costs, and to the loss of state sales and income tax revenues. All of these would reduce the fiscal pressure on the states and be of substantial benefit to higher-income taxpayers who are paying higher tuition and whose children attend college. But this message requires cooperation between higher education policy makers and K–12. There is a huge disconnect with the public's awareness of how higher education serves the public good.

There is also recognition among policy makers of the problem that both economic growth and growth in access to higher education in the United States are slower than in China, South Korea, and even the European Community. South Korea is number one among all OECD nations in math scores and number 2 in science scores of fifteen-year-olds whereas the United States is number 23 on both (data for other countries is presented and discussed in McMahon, 2006b). This contributes to a far larger proportion and absolute number entering engineering and science fields in South Korea. The percentage increase in international patents received by South Koreans and the per capita growth rates are both many multiples of those in the United States (ibid.). A much higher proportion of the younger generation in South Korea is entering college; 47 to 52% of persons ages twenty-three to thirty-four have completed college in Japan and South Korea respectively, whereas only 39% in this group have completed college in the United States; rates in Canada equal those of Japan (ibid., Table A-2). But U.S. higher education institutions, legislatures, Congress, and the public seem to be complacent. U.S. commissions and some state boards of higher education seem preoccupied with a narrow and basically incorrect definition of college costs (Chapter 2). Universities have turned to privatization in search of revenue. So although there is vague awareness of the eroding of the U.S. comparative advantage in human capital and research, potential solutions are not given wide attention. So as a result this has led to no action.

It seems quite possible that if there were more specific information about the non-market private and social benefits of higher education, and their value in relation to their costs, the degree of market failure would be reduced and necessary private and public financial support would be forthcoming. This did happen at the World Bank earlier when the (market) returns to education in relation to the costs were extensively documented. As a result of this evidence from heavier investment in physical capital projects, the fraction of the World Bank budget devoted to education and education sector-wide concessional loans worldwide increased dramatically.

Addressing the above issues with possible solutions is something national commissions have failed to do. The U.S. National Commission on the Cost of Higher Education (1998) focused exclusively on institutional costs, and ignored the trend in forgone earnings costs, which even at that time was flat. It also ignored the trends in the market returns, some of which are easily measurable and were available even at that time, as well as the many non-market private and social benefits. In the United Kingdom, the National Committee of Inquiry Into Higher Education (1997) was only slightly better. And the Spellings Report (2007) is probably worse. To be accountable to the public and to find ways to save costs are commendable goals. But a more meaningful analysis must define costs properly, and not think of accountability only in terms of costs but instead in terms of costs relative to outcomes. It also must consider intermediate outcomes such as graduation rates and learning as measured by tests at graduation for analytical ability and the like that measure these on a value-added basis. The Spellings Report supports value-added, but offers no practical means of how to measure it, such as the measure I propose in Appendix A. And finally, these commissions should consider more seriously the more ultimate private and social benefits of higher education in relation to their costs. These include how these longer-term benefits change in value over time, how they are related to the new knowledge produced by research, and how they relate to the full cost of investment in higher education paid by parents and society.

Since these national reports, new insights have been offered by research on non-market private and social benefits and on higher education externalities as they relate to the dynamic process. These terms are defined in Chapter 2 and the measures presented in Chapters 4 and 5. Since T. W. Schultz's earlier *Investment in Human Capital* (1971), his *Investment in People* (1981), and his augmentation of the classical Solow (1956) production function with human capital, there has been a great deal of important research on endogenous growth theory and empirical tests. This includes work on endogenous growth models by Lucas (1988) and Romer (1990) that establishes the great importance of education externalities (that is, spillover social benefits) as well as the crucial role of higher education in the training of research scientists. Empirical endogenous growth research includes tests by Barro (1991, 2001b), Barro and Sal-I-Martin (1995, 2007), McMahon (2002, 2007a), Mattana (2004), Keller (2006a, 2006b), Jamison et al. (2007), and others. The interaction of academic research with higher education and their joint outcomes pioneered by Griliches (2000) also offers very important insights into how human capital formation and research are entwined in generating growth. Rosen (1975) pioneered the embodiment of new knowledge created by research in human capital followed by the gradual obsolescence of both unless there is replacement investment (lifelong learning). There are a few dissenters such as Pritchett (2000, 2006), Acemoglu et al. (2005a, 2005b), and Lange and Topel (2006) that exclude these dynamic technology effects. Their choice of a conceptual framework that employs a static view with the control variables that this static view implies leads to the conclusion that higher education is not a significant player and that externality effects do not exist. These studies and those that they choose to survey also exclude the indirect effects that feed back and affect growth later.

Not included in these national reports are also new tracer studies of higher education graduates that develop the impacts of the private and social non-market benefits of higher education over their lifecycles (for example, Bynner et al., 2003) and other studies issued by the Center for the Wider Benefits of Learning, such as that by Green and Little (2007). Together all of the foregoing constitute the research base for the catch phrase "the knowledge-based economy." This line of research is a major source of new insights relevant to higher education policy.

Since the book's objective is to bring a modern human capital perspective to higher education policy, it should be noted that human capital concepts have revolutionized other fields in economics. Labor economics is now dominated by human capital analysis. In labor market analysis it has largely replaced the earlier historical and institutional approaches. The field of economic growth has been heavily influenced, if not revolutionized, by endogenous growth models, defined as models for which there is an internal joint analytic solution for the rate of investment in human capital and the rate of economic growth. These models incorporate human capital concepts and have been followed by many empirical tests. Home economics is another field that has been transformed. Most home economics departments have now reoriented themselves to focus on human resources and are dominated conceptually by Becker's household production functions. The latter feature the use of human capital in the home, and these departments no longer teach much cooking, sewing, and other household management without a strong conceptual framework.

Education policy departments in colleges of education have also been affected, partly because the economics of education has been revolutionized to become human capital analysis. The trend in higher education finance courses, especially but also in education organization and leadership courses, is toward bringing in more economics, and central to this is the analysis of human capital formation, public-sector economics, and market failure. And there are other examples. But older approaches and tangential lines of analysis continue to exist. These include historical-descriptive approaches, the screening hypothesis, Marxist perspectives, and over-educationists. But they largely provide more detailed institutional description, illumination of limited side effects, and outlier views that occupy the fringes.

New human capital insights are needed for quantifying research outcomes of the research universities as well. This is because in graduate education, new research worldwide to which the faculty have access is embodied in master's and PhD students through graduate courses and research experience in such a way that it is almost impossible to disentangle the impacts of the new knowledge on the economy from the impacts of the graduates who disseminate it and the means of adapting it. This interdependence stressed by Griliches (2000) long ago is now captured formally in Romer's (1990) endogenous growth model.

But currently much of the publicity about the impacts of academic research is anecdotal. This is useful for descriptive richness, but it is not sufficiently objective or scientifically based for purposes of higher education policy. To isolate the benefits of research in relation to the costs is important for the financing of higher education. To be sure, it is more important for research universities than for two- and four-year colleges. But it has implications for the latter as well. For one thing, the embodied new knowledge created through the interaction of graduate education and research at the research universities becomes a major source of learning by students at two- and four-year colleges as these colleges hire new faculty who come from the research universities. Research productivity by the faculty in relation to the costs is a major determinant of faculty salaries at the research universities and some other places, and is the major determinant of the perceived quality of higher education institutions offering graduate work. In the United Kingdom, for example, recent measures of institutional research productivity have impacted the funding of campuses and departments throughout the nation through the Research Assessment Exercises. The latter now are the basis for about 28% of all higher education funding there. Sponsored research that is all on a peer group review basis and that is a good means of evaluating the quantity and quality of past and prospective research productivity now supports over 50% of the budgets at leading U.S. public and private research universities.

Relevant to both research and education outcomes, new insights also are being generated by the new work on social capital and on happiness, and on the relation of higher education to both. The concept of social capital has now reached the point that measurement is possible. Social capital has earlier been defined by sociologists as social networks that link to information or cultural capital (Bourdieu, 1986; Coleman, 1988). They include trust , but it also has come to be measured as social cohesion. The latter has been shown to increase with the reduction of inequality, as well as with more education, although there are not always controls for per capita income (see Green and Little, 2007; Helliwell and Putnam, 1999). The spring European Commission (2006, pp. 5–6) recognized this interdependence between education and social cohesion in its progress report, which concludes "that education is critical to develop the European Union's potential for competitiveness and social cohesion . . . (and requires) reforms to achieve both efficiency and equity."

Happiness also has emerged as a policy theme, particularly in the United Kingdom. This has occurred as links between measures of happiness by psychologists and per capita income have been developed by economists such as Layard (2005, 2006) and others. Happiness has been measured by the intensity of brain waves involving pleasure and shown to correspond closely with responses on questionnaires to what causes pleasure. This is a cardinal measure that permits, once again, interpersonal comparisons of utility. It is linked to the economic outcomes of higher education since happiness increases as income increases up to $60,000 for a family of three, where it flattens out. Considering this, Layard asks, "As we get higher and higher income why aren't we all that happy?" One implication of Layard's work is that the diminishing marginal utility of per capita income in producing happiness beyond about $20,000 per year, or $60,000 for a family of three, suggests that wider access to community colleges that would raise the graduate's and hence the family's income closer to $60,000 would increase not only social cohesion but also total happiness. If these points ever should get wider attention, they have important implications for higher education policy.

A human capital formation perspective provides other kinds of insights on financing issues. If public financing were to take the lead with increased student grants or increased institutional support, then as private families automatically increase their investment as they contribute forgone earnings costs and some tuition, this also increases saving by the family. The family refrains from consumption (the definition of saving) to simultaneously invest in the future through their support of higher education. Since total saving and investment, both public and private, are critical to the nationwide economic growth process, this is crucial for achieving faster growth and development.

The later European Commission (2006) and to some extent the U.S. Department of Education Spellings Report (2007) both take a broader view that includes social benefits and avoids the narrow distorted focus of the earlier U.S. Department of Education Commission (1998) that only looked at rising institutional costs. The American Council on Education's Commission (2007), focusing on *Solutions for Our Future,* takes a much more vigorous view, stressing the private and social benefits. Given this new wave of interest in both the United States and the European Union, the time would seem to be opportune for this more rigorous and deeper analysis of the value of the private and social benefits of higher education, and how they relate to society's new needs and to the costs. This in turn has implications for how higher education and research affect economic growth as well as the quality of life and the public good.

Barnett (1992, p. 216) some time back observed that "society is not prepared to accept that higher education is self-justifying and it wishes to expose the activities of the secret garden." If this exposure occurs in a comprehensive and rigorous fashion, there is a better chance that the "age of disenchantment" and the "new age of privatization" can be brought into better perspective. Government policy makers, higher education leaders, and the public do want to know how higher education serves the public interest. And legislators, taxpayers, parents, and those without sufficient skills to participate are all asking questions and posing problems to higher education leaders for which these leaders are having difficulty in providing answers and solutions. If there are to be new directions, both new insights and new evidence are needed. It is hoped that this book can contribute to these new directions.

Higher Education and Economic Development

Why is higher education so closely scrutinized? It is not just because of rising tuitions and higher institutional costs. Historically, it is also because economic development has become a driving force transforming the character of higher education institutions worldwide.

This began in the United States with the "land grant act" (the Morrill Act of 1862) signed by President Abraham Lincoln. It broadened the role of higher education beyond training priests and civil servants to include engineering, agriculture, and business, making higher education more relevant to the broader needs of society. It was extended by the Hatch Act of 1887 to fund research, and the second Morrill Act of 1890 to further fund public institutions and black colleges. Federal funding of research grew dramatically during World War II, and the GI Bill of 1944 led to a vast expansion through the federal funding of enrollment by many veterans.

This was so successful in providing an engine of economic growth and development that it spread to Britain as the Robbins Commission created a nationwide system dubbed the "red brick universities." They now are among the best in the world. This pattern of institutions with a broader scope and a clear development mission spread throughout Europe and the Far East, revolutionizing the role of higher education worldwide.

The vast expansion in the United States of two-year community colleges in the 1960s carried this relation of higher education to development a step farther. Now 38% of all higher education students are enrolled (National Center for Education Statistics, 2005), amounting to 53% of all undergraduates in the United States. These colleges are very effective in relating higher education to local labor markets and to economic development in their local communities and regions, as I show using the rate of return evidence. This is especially so because most of those who finish two-year degrees remain in their local communities, and because 55% of the students in many of these colleges are engaged in lifelong learning, as overage students who have come back to upgrade their skills. The Federal Higher Education Act of 1965 and Education Amendments of 1972 supported this while also firmly expanding higher education's role to address poverty and equal opportunity by providing need-based Pell Grants and supporting student loans.

Governments worldwide have been slower to expand two-year polytechnics that allow students to transfer to four-year institutions, need-based financial aid programs, and student loan programs than has the United States. But this is coming, and many countries have moved and will continue to move in this direction. Governments throughout the European Union are deeply concerned with lifelong learning, for which two-year institutions where students can live at home or work part-time are well adapted. The European Union and countries throughout the industrialized world are actively investigating new ways to assess institutional effectiveness, taking into consideration the wider social benefits of learning, the importance of lifelong learning for the upgrading of skills, and the economic development impacts of their existing higher education institutions (Burke and Serban, 1998; Gilbert, 1999; European Commission, 2006).

The financing problem is that higher education is not seen by political leaders as "the" solution. Tax cuts are another solution often advocated. They clearly stimulate private demand and are very helpful to a cyclical recovery. But their supply side effects on human and physical capital formation, which are important to longer-term productivity growth, are much more controversial among economists. Localized tax breaks to attract firms to one locality are another solution frequently employed. But these have a very localized focus since they attract firms away from some other locality and therefore cancel out nationwide. They also can subsidize inefficiency and special interests, which is not conducive to longer-term productivity growth. Tax cutting that stimulates local demand can be confused with longer-term investment that raises productivity (including the investment in human capital) and is crucial to long-term sustainable growth.

There are other competing policies to higher education as "the" solution to achieving growth. Freer trade does aid growth. But an export strategy can only succeed if the nation has a well-educated, skilled labor force. This strategy of early investment in education was very successfully employed by Japan, then later by South Korea, Taiwan, Hong Kong, and Singapore, enabling these nations to free themselves from exporting extractive raw materials and instead to export increasingly high-tech manufactured goods and services (Wood, 1994). So free trade is not "the" solution without considerable prior investment in education. For the more advanced countries, prior investment in higher education aids high-tech exports.

Increasingly, the relation of education to the development of civic institutions and democracy is being recognized as important to development. Poorly functioning democratic processes and, worse, authoritarian regimes prone to corruption and instability and the civil wars related to them have not been conducive to growth in Africa, Haiti, Latin America, the Middle East, and elsewhere. A major factor, however, that undercuts authoritarian rule and corruption is the elimination of illiteracy on which it feeds, so badly needed in Africa and many poor countries. (See McMahon, 2002, Chapter 7, for a survey of the literature, scatter diagrams showing the patterns worldwide, and a discussion of some of the main determinants of democratization and human rights.) At the more advanced stages of development in the United States and European Union, the leaps upward in the degree of democratization and human rights are less pronounced. But still there are many problems and imperfections in the effectiveness of democratic processes that can stand refinement. At some point the expansion of two- and four-year college education among the population becomes important to this continuing development (see McMahon, 2007a for some of the impacts of inadequate education in the poorest states). Some do challenge the effect of education and income growth on democratization such as Acemoglu et al. (2005a, 2005b), but use methods that rule out significant results, as I explain in Chapter 5. In other work by Glaeser et al. (2004), impressive impacts from policies supporting growth and widespread education emerge. In South Korea and Taiwan, authoritarian regimes supported universal education and export-oriented growth from 1950 onward, and in 1980 in both places democracy emerged. In Pakistan, most of the labor force is still illiterate, there has been little growth, and dictatorship by the army prevails. Latin America also offers powerful empirical evidence. Thirty years ago all countries there were authoritarian. Now, with most persons finishing secondary-level education, and significant growth, all are democracies, albeit fragile ones. In places such as Iraq, imposing democracy without these education and per capita growth preconditions seems problematical.

There are other aspects of development apart from growth and democratization. By far the largest number of countries in the world are authoritarian. And this should begin to suggest that although education, including some higher education, may not be "the" solution, without this most of the alternatives without education fail.

The relation of higher education to development is undercut within the academy by those who hold to the exclusive scholastic view. They argue that higher education is not to serve society but instead depends on their department selecting the most able privileged few. The problem is that this is too narrow if applied to the higher education system as a whole; different higher education institutions and individual departments within each have different and complementary roles. Community colleges, four-year liberal arts colleges, and research universities all have different missions. Historically there has been an evolution from a few centers of scholastic excellence toward a vast system of higher education that contains hundreds of institutions. Most institutions when they were young were not prestigious. But they did serve the needs of their time. Although some departments or colleges remain selective and small, nationally higher education enrollment has expanded in the United States by 61% since 1980 alone. It continues to increase at a rate of 3.2% annually. Worldwide student populations are estimated to reach 100 million by the year 2010 (UNESCO, 2005). The more selective high-quality programs train faculty for other institutions. And these other institutions serve regional needs. The system works together to act as major nationwide engine for creating new knowledge, transmitting new and existing knowledge, and encouraging knowledge-based growth.

So, how fast should this continuing expansion go for development? And what is an economically efficient and equitable level of privatization as governments and families share the costs?

What's New and Interesting?

This book builds on previous studies of the private and social benefits of higher education. But it also seeks to update, provide in-depth analysis, systematize, and extend these studies.

Some of the most notable earlier studies that include attention to private and social benefits are Bowen's *Investment in Learning* (1977) and T. W. Schultz's *Investment in Human Capital* (1971) and *Investing in Peo-*

ple (1981). More recently there has been Leslie and Brinkman's *The Economic Value of Higher Education* (1988), McMahon's *Education and Development* (2002), and Pascarella and Terenzini's *How College Affects Students* (2007, 1991). My earlier work does not focus on higher education, or on the United States or the European Union. Most of the others do not relate the outcomes of higher education in a comprehensive fashion to the total investment costs, include research, or focus on the implications of newer human capital–related research for higher education policy.

Lyall and Sell's (2006) *The True Genius of America at Risk* documents very nicely the broad sweep of the privatization trend in the United States, as does Slaughter and Leslie's *Academic Capitalism* (1997), which traces the impacts of privatization. But neither gets into the valuation of outcomes, or the externalities, or the implications and potential of both of these for higher education policy. The new European Commission's *Efficiency and Equity in Education and Training Systems* (2006), the U.S. Department of Education's Spellings Report (2007), and the American Council on Education's (2007) Commission Report *Solutions for Our Future* list many economic and social outcomes, as well as consider access and accountability. Paulsen and Smart's *The Finance of Higher Education* (2001) is a good collection of readings that supplements other aspects of higher education finance. These are all complementary with this book. They deal with many of the same issues. But none provides a comprehensive human capital conceptual framework for the economics of higher education, for valuing the outcomes and relating these to the costs, or an in-depth systematic analysis of the dynamic process by which higher education affects society. The interaction of human capital formation with academic research outcomes, and the distinction between short- and longer-term impacts of education, are also issues addressed only in this book. It is also unique in providing a more comprehensive modern human capital approach to higher education policy.

What Follows?

Chapter 2 defines and explains key concepts vital to higher education policy and education finance. These start with human capital and externalities and include market failure in higher education markets, embodiment of new technology as human capital is formed, and endogenous growth as the conceptual basis for knowledge-based economies. Major current higher education issues are then considered from a human capital perspective, such as access, affordability, accountability, and de facto privatization, leading to new insights. These issues are seen to have a common source.

Chapter 3 considers the market returns to investment in higher education, including jobs, earnings, and growth. The current and forecasted needs for college-educated higher-skilled, and lower-skilled workers by occupation and by industry are considered. This is followed by analysis of the data on the trends in earnings at each education level, and the trends in higher education costs. New private and social rates of return by degree level and their trends are calculated and discussed. These are compared to the evidence on earnings relative to costs in the United Kingdom, European Union, and other OECD countries.

This chapter also considers the empirical evidence on the relation of higher education to economic growth in macroeconomic data. Some of the studies in the literature are very confusing to the uninitiated until it is realized that some eliminate the role of technology and higher education's interdependence with this as well as indirect effects whereas others do not. Some also are focused on relatively short-term five-year impacts whereas others take the buildup over time into account. The hypotheses that there is over-education and screening models are also examined. The implications of the trends in market-measured returns for higher education policy remain the main focus.

Chapter 4 considers the non-market private benefits of higher education. It identifies, measures, and values each of these non-market benefits more comprehensively than heretofore. How these and other non-market outcomes are valued in monetary terms is explained, arriving at income equivalent values of each that are just as legitimate as the estimates of the earnings increment outcomes. These non-market private benefits include education's contribution beyond income to own-health, spousal health, child health, child education, fertility rates, longevity, and happiness. When these private non-market benefits are not understood by students and their families, there is market failure and underinvestment.

Chapter 5 considers the social benefits of higher education. These also are identified, measured, and valued. The distinction between public goods and indirect effects, and how both are externalities, is explained. Although conceptually the logical relevance of externalities is clear and essentially universally accepted, there is controversy about the meaning of the empirical evidence. So the conceptual framework and the nature of the dynamic process must be explained and addressed since differences in this is the source of most of the controversy about the interpretation of the empirical evidence.

The social benefits of higher education beyond income include benefits to the operation and development of civic institutions, including democratic processes and the rule of law with their effects on human rights and political stability. They include effects on the reduction of poverty and can include effects on the reduction of inequality. The social benefits include lower crime rates and criminal justice system costs, lower health care and public assistance costs, greater social cohesion, indirect effects on the sustainability of the environment, and benefits through the interdependence with research to the diffusion of new knowledge.

The economic value of these social outcomes is estimated, as are the externalities, and included as part of the total value of the benefits from higher education. The fraction of the total benefits that are externalities has vitally important implications for the degree of privatization that is optimal.

Chapter 6 considers the returns to academic research in relation to the costs. This is important to research universities. But the embodiment of new knowledge and its rate of obsolescence are also vital to higher education policies in those institutions that are involved in lifelong learning such as community colleges.

The main studies of the rates of return to research are considered first. These include the costs of the failed experiments if they are to be relevant to policy. New techniques are badly needed for estimating the more ultimate returns to research, since much of the literature is anecdotal. These techniques must include the returns to research in the social sciences, humanities, law, business, and other fields that do not have patent or private market outcomes. The cost-effectiveness of research in different fields can be measured, as I will show. But it is important to try to go the next step. This chapter therefore considers how the concept of the embodiment of new knowledge in human capital as it is formed through graduate education and research training has promise. The rate of embodiment, and rates of obsolescence of human capital, can be studied and calculated.

Chapter 7 considers the implications for new higher education policies at the national, state, and campus levels. There are different policies appropriate to different problems. For example, if there is poor information about private non-market benefits, the policy remedy is to get higher education markets to work better by seeing that better information is provided. This policy does not involve any significant amount of additional public investment. Instead, with better information the private investment by students who are not now transitioning from high school and their families would be closer to optimal. For the social benefit outcomes and new sources of human capital obsolescence the policy implications are different. At the campus level there are implications for providing better information about outcomes, using student time more efficiently, encouraging fields that do not have the benefit of patents, evaluating value-added, and evaluating the degree of privatization, among others.

Chapter 8 summarizes conclusions from the preceding chapters and looks at the overall role of higher education in providing for the public good. It is hoped that this suggests new potentials for achieving more efficient and equitable levels of financing, both private and public, in support of higher education's new mission as it serves society's changing needs.

CHAPTER TWO

Challenges Facing
Higher Education Policy

Societies entrust the conserving, transmitting, rectifying, and
expanding (of knowledge) in significant part to universities . . .
Universities are entangled with the world, but must never lose the
capacity . . . to focus on the more enduring truths.

LYALL AND SELL (2006, P. 52)

THIS CHAPTER BEGINS with a review of basic human capital concepts vital to higher education policy. It then considers the standard current higher education policy issues from a human capital
perspective and the implications. It introduces some tools and draws on
empirical evidence, but it does not develop the analysis in depth or present
the detail to be found in later chapters.

Basic Concepts Important to Policy

To consider the implications of a modern human capital approach to
higher education policy, a few basic concepts must be defined and briefly
discussed. These are concepts that are central to higher education policy,
essential to understanding that policy, and in line with the main themes
of the book.. These concepts include human capital, the market versus
non-market benefits of higher education, market failure in higher education markets, and the embodiment of new knowledge and skills in stu-

dents. A diagram is presented that helps to distinguish the direct from the indirect effects of education, and defines and discusses externalities. A few other concepts, such as social rates of return, dynamics, and endogenous growth, are defined more precisely in later chapters before they are used extensively.

HUMAN CAPITAL

Human capital is the knowledge, skills, and attributes acquired by investment in education and health throughout the lifecycle. It does not include the innate value of a human being apart from acquired productive skills. Knowledge and skills are acquired through formal education in school and in college, but also through additional learning and support from the home, including preschool; the amount of on-the-job training by firms, which is usually correlated with prior education; and lifelong learning in community colleges or elsewhere.* Where the parents' education is limited, as it is in poor neighborhoods, and if the students come from broken homes, the unit costs of education are significantly higher. But the value-added by the school is also proportionately larger.

However, these productive human capital skills are not just used on the job. They are carried home with the individual, and affect the productivity and value of his or her time there. They are also used and are productive during time spent in the community. Household production using human capital at home and in the community is the basis for the private non-market benefits and for the social benefits of higher education respectively. And these benefits are discrete, because the human capital of any individual cannot be used in more than one place at any time. Human capital is a bedrock element in the "ownership society"; it belongs only to the individual until death.

---

*Sometimes movement in location is considered to be an addition to the individual's human capital. However, in this book the additional earnings in the new location will be regarded as a property of the location, not of the individual. The jumps in productivity reflect the civic and other institutions and environment at that new location that are partly the result of the education of others at the new location and hence are education externalities. Rauch (1993) uses the effect of the average level of education of others in the standard metropolitan statistical area (SMSA) as a measure of education externalities, based on Lucas's (1988) concept, so they and others also make this distinction.

As people retire and die, their human capital must be replaced. About 65% of the total human capital formation in each cohort of new student graduates is really replacement investment, replacing those who retire and die.* This replacement investment alone does not increase the average education level in the community. Therefore, this 65% of all new graduates is not reflected in measures of the stock of human capital such as average educational attainment of the population. This important point will arise later in Chapter 3 when we consider growth equations that study the relation of higher education to growth, as well as in this chapter in connection with the rate of obsolescence of human capital.

MARKET VERSUS NON-MARKET BENEFITS

Market benefits are the additional earnings due to higher education from the use of human capital that is productive on the job. The value is determined in labor markets and hence the term *market benefits*. These are sometimes called economic benefits but this terminology is inaccurate for the reasons indicated below. Earnings are the largest fraction of income, accounting for about 70% of national income, and interest, rent, and profits (which can also be affected by human capital) accounts for the rest. For wealthier individuals, most of their income is from dividends, interest, and capital gains, which include profits, and not from earnings. The earnings from raw unimproved labor, such as wages for the totally unskilled, account for very little, so almost all of this 70% of national income is due to earnings from human capital. But human capital also is used by individuals to improve their returns on financial assets and on rental properties, and to earn profit. So in addition to earnings, a fraction of dividend, rent, interest, and profit income is also attributable to human capital. Since standard rates of return are based exclusively on earnings, this fraction must be added as part of the non-market private returns when seeking correct rates of return (see Chapter 4).

The non-market benefits of human capital arise as the same human capital used on the job is carried home and used by the individual in combination with market goods to improve the productivity of time at

*For example, of the 2,398,000 persons who died in 2004 according to the U.S. Census, about 839,000 had bachelor's degrees. There were 1,288,000 bachelor's graduates in 2004. So on this basis, about 65% of the latter replaced those who died.

home or in the community. These private non-market benefits of higher education to the individual include lower infant mortality of children, better own-health, better spousal health, greater longevity than high school graduates, and a higher score on the happiness index developed by psychologists. They arise as the college graduate modifies his or her behavior to manage diet, exercise, reduce smoking, care for children, counsel his or her spouse on health matters, and choose activities that avoid disease and accidents. It does not take health education: a mother who knows to take the temperature of her child and see a doctor if it is high contributes to better child health.

The term *non-market benefits* is used rather than *non-economic benefits*, which appears in some of the higher education literature. This is because economics always has included the analysis of non-market phenomena. The classic example going back at least to 1719 is that of a Robinson Crusoe one-man economy. Robinson allocated his time among saving (as he withdrew some of his time from consumption), investment (as he invested his time building a hoe), work supporting consumption, and leisure. These are the basic elements of economic decisions. There is no money or markets involved at all; only time is being allocated among alternative ends. Consistent with this, Becker's (1965) classic on the theory of the allocation of time analyzes the productive use of time in the home. The value of this time is increased by investment in human capital. Time allocated to the production of human capital has a return in the future, but this return is partly in the form of earnings and partly in the form of non-market benefits from the use of time not spent in the labor market.

This is fully consistent with the most widely accepted definition of economics, which is "the science which studies human behavior as a relationship between ends and scarce means which have alternative uses," by Lionel Robbins in his *An Essay on the Nature and Significance of Economic Science* (1945, p. 16). This does not limit economics to the study of markets or monetary valuations, but includes the study of the allocation of time. So market or monetary versus non-market or non-monetary benefits of higher education are both more correct than economic versus non-economic benefits when distinguishing between the earnings benefits and the benefits to the quality of life from higher education.

So much for earnings as (labor) market benefits. What about economic growth? Adding up all earnings (70%) plus interest, rent, and profit gives aggregate national income. This is equal to gross domestic product (GDP), ignoring extremely small items that reconcile the two in the national accounts. Expressing this in constant prices and in per capita terms, it can be interpreted as also referring to a typical individual or household. The average rate of change in this real per capita GDP over at least a five-year period, which is necessary to remove the transitory effects of business cycle fluctuations, is the per capita rate of economic growth. Growth regressions then are estimated using data for the Organization for Economic Cooperation and Development (OECD) countries in Appendix D, where this is the dependent variable and the rates of investment in human capital and of investment in physical capital are included to reveal the net effects of investment in human capital on per capita economic growth. Over time the relative contribution of human and physical capital to growth depends not just on the size of the coefficients, which are the return to each, but also on which has been increasing more rapidly. The rate of economic development is a broader concept that includes the non-market aspects of development affecting the quality of life and the public good.

MARKET FAILURE

Market failure is the failure of higher education markets to produce an economically efficient result leading to optimal investment in higher education. There are three classic sources of market failure that are present in higher education:

- The lack of accurate information on the part of students and their families
- The presence of social benefit externalities that benefit others and future generations
- Monopoly that distorts markets

If any of these distort higher education markets, full privatization will not produce an economically efficient solution. The only practical way to reduce the inefficiency that results is through public intervention to try to make the markets work better. Public-sector failure also must be considered. It is very serious in authoritarian countries in Africa and in failed states like Somalia, for example. But the degree of public-sector failure is relatively small in the United States and other developed-country OECD democracies. Just because some individuals may be displeased is not evidence of public-sector failure; with any group decisions some displeasure is inevitable.

With respect to poor information as a source of market failure, the evidence is that students are quite well informed about the effects of college and choice of field on their earnings. At this level competition among higher education institutions and among fields works. There is a lot of information available about the characteristics of different colleges and universities. Some of it is provided by government employees, such as high school counselors, and some by the College Board. Federal Pell Grants, most state grants, and student loans are quite portable. In this environment it is hard to make a case that any public institutions or private institutions have a monopoly. There is a small degree of monopoly power geographically in some local higher education markets, such as among local community colleges where the student needs to live at home or near his or her work, and some due to institutional differentiation. But it is small. Within institutions, there is also a lot of evidence that students are aware of the differences in earnings and in job market demands among different fields and that they "vote with their feet." There are placement offices in virtually all colleges and universities that publicize job openings, average starting salaries, and starting salaries by field, and reams of information available on the Internet. So competition among institutions, and among curricula within each institution, works well, at least when it comes to earnings, vocations, and job market–related outcomes.

The problems with market failure become more acute when it comes to the non-market outcomes and the relation of higher education to the public good. On these fronts the evidence suggests that the information is vague and sometimes nonexistent. With respect to the private non-market benefits, they may be underestimated in relation to the size of the market benefits. Students are known to be aware that college increases their chances of meeting a more suitable mate, that some fields such as music are more likely to yield relatively larger private non-market benefits than others, and that their higher education is likely to increase their chances that they may be of some service to the community and to society (McMahon, 1984b). But when probed, there is very little specific knowledge of what the benefits to their longevity, health, or happiness are. Students also may be somewhat myopic. Studies reviewed in Chapter 4 find evidence that more education tends to make persons more far-sighted, but those who drop out of high school or do not go on to college may be more myopic and as a result invest too little in their own human capital formation. This is a more serious problem in very young students, but their parents tend to make the decisions in their behalf and support completion of grade school, middle school, high school, and sometimes the early college years. To the extent that either the private non-market benefits of higher education or the benefits in the more distant future are underestimated, markets fail and there will be underinvestment.

There is also market failure contributing to underinvestment because capital markets are very imperfect in financing investment in human capital. This is largely because banks have very poor information about any given student's capacity or willingness to repay and because students from lower-income families are unable to provide collateral. So lacking collateral, banks will not lend or will lend only at exorbitant rates. The remedy is government guarantees to reduce the risk, possible since the government knows the graduation rates and earnings outcomes of larger groups of students and is able to spread the risk, as well as use the tax system if necessary to collect. Some certified universities can now lend directly to students, although there is political opposition to cutting out bank intermediaries to realize the savings.

The social benefits are the remaining major source of market failure in higher education. Since social benefit externalities spill over to benefit others in the community or future generations, the individual has no incentive to invest since he or she cannot capture the benefits. I define and discuss externalities further below. Research generates major externalities, as is well known and not controversial. But education externalities are harder to demonstrate in macro-data and more controversial. In micro-data, however, there are many examples. It is well known from National Center for Education Statistics (2005) data that college graduates contribute a larger percentage of their time and money at each given income level to civic institutions than do high school graduates at the same income level. This potentially contributes to more effective civic institutions and improves the quality of life for others. These civic institutions include such nonprofit organizations as the Urban League, the city council, the courts and justice system, the YMCA, the United Way, Family Service Agencies, community orchestras, and many others that depend heavily on college graduates and their volunteered time and money. These create a quality of life in the community that benefits others, and also set the stage for the next round of growth and development in the community.

EMBODIMENT, VINTAGE HUMAN CAPITAL, AND OBSOLESCENCE

Higher education embodies knowledge, research skills, and understanding. At K–12 levels, the skills that are embodied are very basic ones, such as reading, writing, arithmetic, and the received wisdom. In higher education, there is embodiment of more advanced analytical capacities as well as understanding of how to use the new technologies. This new knowledge can be created at research universities but also includes the emerging new knowledge in each field worldwide with which the faculty at research universities is in close touch as they publish. That is, non-proprietary research is widely shared worldwide and faculty have very strong incentives to keep up with the latest within their fields.

The result is that human capital formation embodying recent knowledge creates more recent vintages of human capital. Older vintages in the labor force become gradually more obsolete. One reflection of this is that age-earnings profiles peak and start to decline after about age fifty-five, although there are additional reasons for this. The exceptions are in professions where there are strong incentives to keep up, such as for MDs who locate in larger group clinics, faculty at research universities, and many business and government research scientists. But generally recent bachelor's graduates and others who replace those who are retiring are of more recent vintages. They carry the new knowledge and technologies into the labor force, are more productive after a short period of learning on the job, and command an earnings premium in the job market.

Human capital in many environments can become obsolete. It becomes more obsolete in academic fields where the new research is plunging ahead than in others (Rosen, 1975). It also becomes more obsolete in some working environments than in others: it is known, for example, that doctors in larger active clinics have a stronger incentive to keep up than most solo practitioners. Much human capital also becomes obsolete when there are huge technology shocks or globalization shocks, as discussed exten-

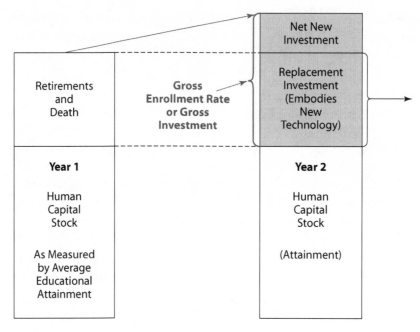

Figure 2.1. Stock versus flow measures of education.

sively in this book. And finally, human capital also becomes obsolete when there are massive changeovers from centrally planned to market economies, as has occurred in the ex-Soviet economies because the transition economies require very different kinds of business and farm management skills. Overall, far too many bachelor's graduates whose human capital was flexible like putty during the formative college years fail to engage in lifelong learning. As a result, their human capital becomes hardened clay, typified by the Joe-six-packs watching a great deal of entertainment television. That is, putty turns to clay unless there is replacement investment in human capital through lifelong learning.

These human capital concepts of embodiment, vintage human capital, and obsolescence have important higher education policy implications. Apart from those for the importance and needs for lifelong learning, a crucial implication flows from the fact that part of higher education's effect is not just from the education but from the new technologies. Investment in human capital and gross enrollment rates are both flows that add to the stock of human capital in the population. as illustrated from Year

1 to Year 2 in Figure 2.1. Of this gross investment, about 65% is replacement investment in human capital that takes the place of those who retire or die as mentioned earlier. A measure of the change in the stock from Year 1 to Year 2 picks up only the net new investment increment shown; the replacement investment cancels out. But it is not just the net new investment component, which is relatively small, that carries with it the effects of new technologies; it is also the replacement investment that has been ignored when only a measure of the stock level is used, such as average educational attainment. Unless the reader is wary, studies that exclude the effects of replacement investment and of technical change on non-market private and social outcomes of education (as in Pritchett, 2006) underestimate the significance of higher education for development.

Illustration of Externalities in Relation to Private and Social Benefits

Figure 2.2 illustrates the market and non-market benefits, both private and social, and their relation to indirect benefits and externalities. Each have different implications for higher education policies. In the figure, the private benefits of human capital formed through higher education are shown in row A and the private non-market benefits are in row B. The social benefits appear in row C. The social benefits are sometimes defined to be the sum of the private and external benefits (for example, Lange and Topel, 2006, p. 461). In this book we will regard the social benefits as

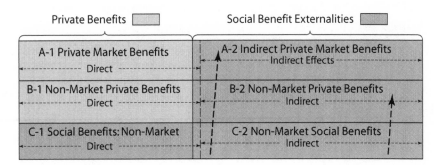

Figure 2.2. The benefits of higher education. Dashed arrows assume that all of the indirect effects from social benefits are eventually enjoyed by someone. *Source:* McMahon (2006a).

being largely concerned with the external benefits that are the "public goods" in row C plus the indirect effects in the column on the right composed of A-2, B-2, and C-2. There is considerable vagueness in the literature about what the indirect effects are and what the public goods aspects of education are, a vagueness that this discussion should help to clear up.

MEASUREMENT

When measuring the non-market benefits of higher education it is important to make sure that they do not overlap the market benefits. Otherwise if the market and non-market benefits are added in order to get the total benefits in a way that is relevant to higher education policy, there is double counting of the market benefits. For example, is the better health and greater longevity of college graduates compared to that of high school graduates simply the result of the higher earnings used to purchase better health care? Yes, of course, in part. So if one adds up the contributions to earnings and the contributions to better health and longevity, the market returns to higher education are double counted and the total effect of higher education is exaggerated. So the effect of higher education on health measured in this way cannot be used for policy guidance. The same principle applies to social benefits. If college graduates contribute more of their earnings to civic institutions than do high school graduates, is this because they have higher earnings? Yes, of course, in part. So it is necessary to measure the effect beyond earnings by measuring the additional contributions to charities by college graduates at each given income level.

There is a very simple solution to this measurement problem. It is to control for per capita income by including per capita income in the regression equations when either the private non-market benefits or the social non-market benefits is the dependent variable. Then there is no overlap between the market and non-market returns, just as there is not for any individual who uses his or her human capital on the job, or at home, but not both places at the same time. Figure 2.2 therefore illustrates the separation between the market benefits in row A and the non-market benefits with a discrete line, and only those studies will be considered as relevant to measuring the total benefits and relating them to policy that include a control for per capita income. Fortunately, most studies do this that are surveyed by Michael (1982), Grossman and Kaestner (1997), McMahon

(2004b), and Grossman (2006) as well as in this book. But it is important to recognize that this control is not imposed in much of the research reported on non-market outcomes. There is nothing wrong with reporting overlapping outcomes so long as it is recognized that their policy relevance is limited.

INDIRECT BENEFITS

Indirect benefits from higher education occur when the effect from higher education comes through its influence on another variable. For example, if higher education improves health, and then this improvement in health contributes to earnings, the latter increment to earnings is really due to an indirect benefit from education. The indirect effect on earnings can also come from the prior education of earlier generations that contributed to institutions and a stable society with trust and social capital where people can be more productive. It is important to note that these indirect effects on earnings (and growth) overlap earnings, as shown in section A-2 of Figure 2.2. Part of everyone's earnings is due to indirect effects and/or the education of others. This point is very important to consider because it sometimes is casually asserted, without much thought, that the earnings of higher education graduates are so high that virtually all of the benefits must be captured privately, in which case there are no externalities. This assertion is wrong because each individual's earnings are partly the direct effects of his or her education, and partly the indirect effect coming from the education of others in the community and their contributions to available knowledge and civic institutions as well as the education of others in future generations. As I will show, this can be measured. The reverse side of the coin is that just as these contributions come indirectly through other variables and from others, the college graduate also makes contributions indirectly through other variables that benefit others and future generations. Given this more highly productive environment, immigrants and migrants from other localities earn more than they could with the same education in their earlier locality.

Some of the benefits of higher education in a given locality spill over and benefit the income of those with a high school or primary school education. Empirical evidence to this effect can be found in Moretti (2004). His estimate is that a 1 percentage point increase in the supply of college graduates in a community raises the wages of high school graduates by 1.6% and those of high school dropouts by 1.9%. Without endorsing the precision of this estimate, since there may be external shocks raising all labor demand, it clearly does suggest that the benefits of having college graduates in the community to the earnings of others is positive and possibly substantial. We consider the evidence for the specifics of the these indirect effects later in this book. These include benefits to earnings that come indirectly through lower crime rates, better health, better child education and cognitive achievement, lower fertility rates leading to lower per capita poverty, better civic institutions and greater political stability, and the more difficult to measure contribution of higher education to the diffusion of technology in all fields.

EXTERNALITIES

Externalities are the benefits of education to others in the society and in future generations. They are the sum of the public goods benefits in row C of Figure 2.2 and the indirect benefits in column 2. The indirect benefits will be measured in Chapter 5 as the benefits "from others," but these should logically be about equal to the benefits "to others."

Social benefits that are public goods (or close to that, since almost no examples exist of pure public goods) are goods or services where the consumption by one does not limit the consumption by others. An example would be National Public Radio or Television; an additional listener tuning in does not limit the enjoyment of others who are listening. Romer (1990) calls these public goods "non-rivalrous" to distinguish them from "rivalrous" goods or services such as, say, a parking place where the use by one car eliminates use of the same space by another. The parking meter enforces the exclusion principle, excluding those who do not pay from using the space, which is characteristic of all goods and services in the private sector. Other examples of public goods related to higher education are the benefits of democracy and political stability, essentially freely available to all. Higher education is partially a public good, as symbolized by its contribution to the greater good and future generations yet unborn. But it is also partly a private good, as reflected in its contribution to earnings and research contributions to patents.

Indirect effects of education are overwhelmingly externalities. This is because this is the main way those who invest in education benefit others, including future generations. Lucas (1988) makes the further point that these effects are not anticipated and are taken for granted by those who invest. Because each individual's investment in higher education has such a small effect on the average level of education in the community, it is generally ignored.

To measure total externalities, this book will sum up the direct social benefit public good effects in C-1 in Figure 2.2 measured by the Haveman and Wolfe (1984, 2007) method I discuss in Chapter 5 and the indirect effects of education on the private market and non-market benefits in A-2 plus B-2 of Figure 2.2. This assumes that all of the indirect effects from the social benefits become private benefits to some individual, as shown by the black dashed arrows in Figure 2.2. Then a new basis has been provided for measuring higher education externalities. The Haveman-Wolfe method does not capture all of the indirect social benefits that cumulate over time.

Philosophically it can be argued that social values that are included in the direct social benefits (C-1), such as democracy, equality, or the state, have a separate existence from their utility to individuals in this or future generations. This view is rooted in the organic view of the state as the custodian of values that are beyond their utility to individuals, a view historically identified more with continental philosophy in Europe and influential historically in the continental public finance literature. This can be distinguished from Jean-Jacques Rousseau's social contract and the idea that the state and its values are rooted in a social contract with individuals. The latter, however, is today probably the dominant view, certainly in the more individualistic view characteristic of English and American political philosophy. So the view is taken in this book that these direct social benefits (in C-1) are of direct benefit to individuals, and their value will be added as part of the total. The outcome of this philosophical discussion about who benefits, however, has no effect on the total value of the social benefits of higher education.

POLICY IMPLICATIONS

As a brief reminder of the policy implications, the value of the social benefits as a percent of the total benefits is a guide to the fraction of public financing that is appropriate if economic efficiency is to be achieved and the greater good served. This assumes that there is good information about the non-market benefits that will allow private markets to work properly; if there is not, the policy remedy is a different one.

This is a guide to the degree of privatization that is appropriate. If the indirect effects from higher education are zero, and if there is perfect information and equity, all of which are unlikely, then higher education should be fully privatized for economic efficiency. In fact, it is extremely unlikely that indirect effects are zero by anybody's measure. But keeping in mind that private investment includes forgone earnings reinvested in human capital formation, the value of the direct social benefits plus the value of the indirect effects estimated later in Chapter 5 will offer a guide to the degree of privatization that is optimal. We will consider other policy implications later in the book.

A Human Capital Perspective on Current Major Higher Education Policy Issues

A human capital perspective offers some new insights on the standard higher education policy issues widely discussed in the literature. These include declining public support, access, affordability, accountability, and, following on the above, privatization.

DECLINING PUBLIC SUPPORT

There is a serious problem for public institutions as lower per student institutional support and net student financial aid in real terms lead to tuition increases. This is the major source of the trend toward de facto privatization and the entrepreneurial university. But it is also a serious problem for private institutions since they depend heavily on tuition being underwritten by publicly supported Pell Grants and state student grants and student loans. Tuition at private institutions has risen much more in absolute terms than tuition at public colleges and universities. Both public and private universities also depend heavily on state and federal research grants. These trends are extensively documented in Lyall and Sell (2006). Privatization is less serious in continental Europe in the sense that public support of institutional costs is much larger as a percent of the total than in the United States, and expenditure per student remains significantly lower (McMahon, 2006b, Table A-5; Psacharopoulos, 2005).

This trend generates other kinds of internal stress. Higher average user fees are achieved in part by greater emphasis on and more rapid expansion of professional programs that are more market-oriented. Firms are willing to help support some students for those programs that yield the high earnings later and are cash cows, and students are encouraged to borrow more. The research that firms are willing to finance is also more commercially applicable to applied research, as compared to basic research, often in engineering and biomedical fields. Profit-oriented research creates stress for scholars who are committed to the unlimited search for truth and its free dissemination.

Since the institution has a motivation to help maintain quality in the more profitable fields, the corollary is relatively less research and student support in fields where the benefits are more indirect. Fields such as teacher training, the social sciences, and social work serve the nonprofit sector that serves the society at large. In fields such as English and math, where instruction precedes vocational programs, teaching assistants tend to be used very extensively because of the lower costs. Too many PhD candidates are admitted and graduated where there are few jobs in the private sector, keeping faculty salaries low nationwide and hurting the quality of undergraduate programs. Other fields that are heavily dependent on public support to maintain quality include the education of teachers, and even the training of research scientists in the physical and social sciences.

Total state tax appropriations per full-time equivalent student for public universities and colleges in the United States has been constant at about $7,000 from 1980 to 2000 in constant 2007 dollars, declined to $6,200 in 2005, and since then has increased to $6,700 (College Board, 2007b, p. 23). Pell Grants per student have increased somewhat, but the problem is that they now cover a smaller fraction of the costs for admissible students from poor households. In absolute terms Pell Grants leave a wide gap of about $4,000 between annual college costs to the student and his or her total sources of support. Some chancellors have been trying to raise money from private corporations to try to fill the gap for at least a few students. State grants have not helped with this problem because they have been trending away from need-based aid that often also uses a merit criterion toward purely merit-based aid. The result is that for students from poor and middle-income families, financial aid increases have not been large enough to compensate for the increases in tuition. So in spite of the human capital formation analysis of labor markets in Chapter 3 that documents the deficit in college-level skills, these students are being squeezed out.

The stress on institutions is also quite severe in other ways. The real unit costs of retaining faculty and staff are rising in real terms although appropriations per student have not risen. Health care costs for academic and nonacademic staff, another cause of rising institutional costs that colleges cannot control, have also continued to rise, and even more rapidly than tuitions have increased. The declining public support coupled with these sources of rising unit costs have been the main source of the increase in tuition and fees that continues to exceed the rate of inflation. This is in spite of extensive cost cutting that has led to the employment of a much larger proportion of adjunct faculty with lower qualifications teaching large classes. Funds for athletics and for construction are generally compartmentalized and are not used for academic instruction. The same is true for funds appropriated by legislatures for construction. So although athletic and construction budgets grow, full-time faculty are reduced. This has been going on for some years so there is no buffer left and quality suffers. This is occurring as human capital models show that there are high and rising social rates of return and high and growing needs for the more highly skilled and educated workers, both documented in Chapter 3.

ACCESS

Declining public support per student in real terms is a major source of the second very troubling policy issue, restricted access. The higher net tuition restricts access of minorities and students from low- and low-middle-income families the most, where the price elasticity of demand is the highest. Net tuition after financial aid in constant dollars has risen an average of 29% per full-time equivalent student since 1991 in the United States. But it has risen closer to 60% in Illinois, Kentucky, Maryland, Nebraska, Connecticut, and Tennessee, and an average of 90% in Oregon, Texas, Hawaii, and Montana (Wright, 2004). When this is put in the perspective of falling real family income in the middle class, the concerns with access can be seen as legitimate.

Tuition, fees, and total charges to families of students in the lowest income quartile at public four-year institutions rose from 40% of family income in 1980 to 72% of family income in 2005 (College Board, 2004b, Figure 8, p. 18). At private institutions for students in this lowest income quartile, they rose from 30% in 1980 to 180% of average family income in 2005! (ibid.). This is leading to the exclusion of many able students from middle- and lower-income families to the point where participation rates for students from families with income averaging $88,675 are 85% and these same rates for students from families at $35,000, including community college enrollments, are about 50%—a 35 percentage point difference (College Board, 2004b, p. 17). This problem is particularly acute for admissible students from low-income families at private colleges and at public and private research universities. The exclusion of larger percentages of blacks and Latinos leads to decreasing diversity. This is as the population as a whole becomes more diverse. Student loans have increased dramatically, but so have student bankruptcy filings.

From a human capital point of view, this increases rather than reduces the skill deficit that exists in this segment of the population. It also increases rather than reduces the amount of economic inequality. The income, dividend, and estate tax cuts from 2000 through 2006 have disproportionately aided higher-income families, while increases in regressive social security taxes going back to 1982 and in gambling taxes have fallen disproportionately on lower-income families. These have contributed to rising inequality in the United States; it is not just the inequality in the financing of the basic education system augmented by these trends in higher education financing. Rising inequality also has occurred in the larger European economies since 1980. Considering the supplies and demands for human capital, both the United States and the European Union have been affected by rising automation, international outsourcing, and immigration, all of which have led to greater skill premiums in job markets for college graduates and rising inequality in earnings. Now in 2008 higher unemployment rates are exacerbating these same trends.

AFFORDABILITY

The affordability of a higher education for students from the middle class is also a major current higher education policy issue. It is important from a human capital perspective because the families supporting these students generally have a high school education or less. As documented in Chapter 3, they have had no increase in their real earnings on average since 1980 due to the impacts of automation and of international outsourcing that are adverse to the kinds of human capital skills they possess. Their capacities to finance increasing tuition and fees without comparable increases in real terms in per student need-based financial aid is limited. This is the group more than others that has been forced to rely on subsidized Stafford Loans, unsubsidized Stafford Loans, Federal Parent Loans, and Non-Federal Student Loans, all rising dramatically since 2001, especially the latter. Together these student loans accounted for over one-half of all funds used to finance higher education expenses in 2007 (College Board, 2007a, p. 3)! Enrollment rates among lower-middle ($35,000–$65,000) and upper-middle ($65,000–$89,000) income groups have not increased since 1995 (College Board, 2004b, Figure 11, p. 17). Students from middle-income families are working part-time jobs; 50% from the low-, lower-middle-, and upper-middle-income groups are borrowing; and students from all income groups are currently carrying historically high levels of student debt (College Board, 2007a, Figure 4a, p. 13).

A problem from a public finance perspective is that this middle class is the group that public higher educational institutions historically have depended on for public institutional support. They have willingly offered this support because the state universities and community colleges are institutions that benefit them. As net tuitions rise so that the net benefit for the middle class gets smaller, their continuing support may be muted.

In summary, fundamental to the access and affordability issues is the stagnant and falling real incomes of the middle class. The skill deficits contribute to the rising inequality and related increases in criminal justice system costs, state health care and Medicaid costs, and public assistance costs, as well as restricted growth in state taxes, which are often regressive, all of which contribute to the squeeze on higher education budgets. This has also been a source of restrictions on need-based aid available for use at private institutions. These powerful technological and trade forces affecting the human capital stock ultimately underlie the political demands not just for access and affordability, but also for accountability.

The fourth widely discussed higher education policy is accountability. Much of the attention in the commission studies such as the Spellings Report is to unit costs at the public institutions, although the absolute tuition increases and the per student costs are both much higher at private institutions (U.S. Department of Education, 2007; College Board, 2007b, p. 10; National Center for Education Statistics, 1996–2007, Tables 39 and 43). The pressure for accountability results from rising tuition, which in turn reflects increasing institutional unit costs and falling public support. But it also comes from the economic pressure that places middle-class families and public budgets under stress.

Institutions should be expected to be accountable. Internal efficiency is clearly a part of overall economic efficiency. But the costs also need to be defined correctly. And the educational outcomes, including the more ultimate outcomes, need to be better defined for which institutions are to be held accountable. In both instances a human capital perspective has a very major role.

Consider first the measurement of the costs. Rising institutional costs have been the focus of much of the debate, as in the Spellings Report (Burd, 2007, p. 3). This is fine as far as it goes. But institutional costs represent only about half of the total investment costs of human capital formation. The other portion includes the cost of the student's time. This is normally measured by forgone earnings, measured by the earnings of high school graduates who did not go to college. A crude approximation of forgone earnings are the room and board costs of students at college, although these are sometimes higher when parents support a luxurious lifestyle and sometimes lower when students scrape along to make do. When these costs are not considered, higher education accountability policies are distorted.

Room and board costs are sometimes added to institutional costs, and this results in a somewhat better measure of the true investment in human capital formation. They only capture the out-of-pocket costs and students' parents are likely to be more aware of these than they are of the true economic costs. But it is basically the time spent at school rather than spent working in a job that is the true economic cost.

Forgone earnings costs have been falling in real terms. This is because they are determined by the real earnings of high school graduates, which have been flat since 1980 and falling since 2001. They fall much more sharply in recessions when the employment opportunities for those with a high school education or less are worse. Forgone earnings costs rise when the length of time it takes full-time students to complete a degree increases, and it typically now takes 4.5 to 5 years to complete a 4-year degree. But even with this increased inefficiency, the true total costs of human capital formation through higher education have not been rising as fast as institutional costs alone might suggest. In fact, since forgone earnings costs are roughly about the same as institutional unit costs at public institutions, the percentage increase in institutional costs is roughly halved by the decline in forgone earnings costs adjusted by the increase in the time-to-degree. However this cost-effectiveness calculation works out for any type of institution, using a modern human capital perspective reveals that exclusively focusing on only institutional costs is not legitimate.

So part of the costs that need to be considered for accountability is the cost of the student's time. Campus policies affect the amount of time it takes for a student to obtain a degree. Since the late 1960s there have been trends toward increasing the length of the Thanksgiving, Christmas, and spring breaks; eliminating attendance requirements campus-wide; and lowering the semester credit hour requirements for full-time status. All of these are likely to reduce the time-on-task, which is well known in the research to be related to the learning and the human capital formation that occurs. They probably together with other factors contribute to the lengthening time-to-degree that is approaching 4.5 to 5 years. These would be included in reviews of accountability using a human capita perspective and an appropriate definition of costs.

Another aspect of costs that helps define whether rising costs do or do not reflect internal inefficiency is that many of the major sources of rising institutional costs are due to external market forces over which institutions have little or no control. Faculty salaries are determined in a competitive nationwide academic labor market specific to each academic discipline, and most but not all salaries are closely related to what is paid in the private sector. If colleges and universities do not pay salaries comparable to those paid in these fields, faculty leave for elsewhere or the private sector, faculty human capital is lost, and quality suffers. Low-cost part-time and short-term adjunct faculty and academic professionals cover the classes, but in this major instance, cheap higher education leads to less human capital formation. Increased utility prices and increased health insurance costs are also driven by largely external factors.

There are aspects of costs that campuses can control. These include the restriction of offerings of advanced courses that enroll too few students. Campuses can seek better competitive bids from suppliers, and not give priority to supporting high-cost local businesses. They can manage inventories more efficiently, such as high-cost excessive inventories in the chemistry department that have opportunity costs for the funds that are tied up. They can utilize the latest technologies to manage costs. Technology, however, adds significantly to instructional costs at the same time that it contributes to somewhat more effective learning and research. Those without direct experience with instruction often seize technology as a silver bullet, but it can be overrated as a cost-savings device. One of the more promising devices for increasing accountability defined primarily as internal efficiency are the tests that seek to measure the value-added since entering ACT test scores in the form of learning outcomes such as analytical ability and capacity to adapt knowledge within each field being offered by the Rand Corporation to campuses. Accountability for value-added and a major suggestion for how to measure it is considered further in Appendix A.

External inefficiency and its relation to the more ultimate private and social benefits of higher education is also part of accountability. Measuring these outcomes requires a modern human capital approach, which will be left to Chapters 4–6. But an example or two might be useful. It is possible to have 100% internal efficiency, but to be externally inefficient, and hence not achieve economic efficiency. If the social benefits generated by certain fields are discounted, as the current U.S. Department of Education website does by not including them as fields important to the nation, then accountability defined as economic efficiency is not served. The department did this by singling out for-profit institutions in commission meetings as "more efficient" without considering their heavily vocational focus (Ashburn, 2007, p. 3); by defining "high need" fields to exclude the social sciences, English, history, the humanities, and medical education (ibid., p. 5); and by calling for a "restructuring" of financial aid programs that could mean no net new money at a time of human capital skill deficits (Bennett, 2007, p. 1). Another example of how accountability relates to human capital outcomes is that in some fields too many high-cost PhD candidates can be admitted simply because they reduce the costs of under-graduate instruction by serving as teaching assistants in the large required courses and populating the advanced seminars taught by full-time faculty. These fields such as English are vital. But when there are eight hundred applicants for every position offered, this is a symptom that too many are being produced at high unit cost (except for their teaching) and of exter-nal inefficiency. An important part of the education of graduate students is learning as apprentices in teaching, but if carried too far quality and external efficiency suffer. Similarly, faculty teaching large classes is not economically efficient if the quality of the human capital outcomes falls along with the unit costs.

Accountability has focused too much on a very narrow definition of productivity as instructional units (IUs) and research units (RUs—such as articles published) and too little on the more ultimate outcomes. There has been some improvement recently in the shift toward outcome mea-sures such as persistence, graduation rates, and value-added in learning that use tests at graduation of analytical abilities, as discussed above. These are better measures of productivity and closer to ultimate human capital formation outcomes than, say, IUs. But although there is a role for more immediate short-term productivity measures, accountability needs to be defined and measured in terms of the more ultimate benefits to the graduate and his or her service to society. Analogously, it would be foolish to evaluate automobile production only in terms of the number of panels or rivets installed on the production line without reference to whether the automobile would run free of continuing service. IUs fail to take into ac-count what is being learned by the student, and whether what is being taught is up to date, reflecting advances in knowledge and a faculty mem-ber who is current on his or her topic. Consider, for example, two oncolo-gists who prescribe cancer treatments in office visits of equal length (that is, IUs equal). But one is less up to date on the more recent research find-ings about appropriate treatments, so his patient dies. Are they equally "productive"? Consider also the size and value of the contributions of higher education to earnings, better health, longevity, civic institutions, democratization, political stability, lower crime rates, and the wider dis-semination of ideas and technologies. These can be measured in terms of the value-added by the institution, which is the ultimate accountability relevant to economic efficiency.

This includes an illustration of the importance of the effects of the embodiment of new knowledge when considering productivity as it relates to accountability. It therefore reveals the fallacy of the "cost disease" when this widely misused concept attributable to William Baumol is applied to human capital–intensive activities. The cost disease applies to lower-skilled service industries where technology has not brought about greater efficiency. The idea is that salaries are rising, and technical change is not applied, so unit costs rise. Most of the economy is now services; manufacturing is down to only about 12% in the United States. Where services are not human capital–intensive, say, in delivering mail, salaries go up, costs go up, and postage rates go up. But this concept of the cost disease does not apply where the services are human capital–intensive, such as they are for faculty and physicians. Here being up to date with the new knowledge and technologies and how to use them is everything.

The faculty and the doctors that are most up-to-date are more productive in creating new human capital and knowledge through teaching, research, and the physician's role of creating better health. And the faculty and physicians that are more productive in this way earn a premium in the job market for these skills. Salaries should not be higher than competitive markets dictate. But markets for most faculty are national and international and are extremely competitive. It is therefore a misapplication of the cost disease concept to apply it to this situation. The costs are higher, but the human capital outcomes are larger and more valuable. So if the outcomes were measured properly, the true unit costs are no higher and may in fact be lower. New technology is being applied to the human capital formation process but not basically through use of computer hardware or other technologies involving physical capital as is typical in other industries. Mindless application of the cost disease concept overlooks the role of the flow of new knowledge constantly being embodied in faculty and doctors and passed along as it is embodied in student and patient outcomes. Whenever the cost disease concept is applied to higher education, it is best to be wary.

PRIVATIZATION

The fifth important current policy issue, and one on which a human capital analysis offers a major new perspective, is the trend toward increasing privatization of higher education. I introduced this issue in Chapter 1, but it must not be overlooked.

De facto privatization has been defined here as increases in the percentage of funding that comes privately from students, their families, and firms relative to the public funding of institutions, student grants, and research. It is occurring gradually at public institutions as tuition increases without comparable increases in public institutional support or student aid. It is occurring at private nonprofit institutions as well through lower support from student Pell Grants and larger dependence on student loans. It is occurring at for-profit institutions, which now serve 8% of all students, grow more rapidly mostly at the expense of four-year public institutions and with the growth of Internet instruction based on fees (College Board, 2007b, p. 22). It is occurring in the trend toward privatization of research funding symbolized by rapidly expanding research parks and privately funded institutes within colleges and foundations. The trend toward privatization also includes entrepreneurial universities that sell large amounts of television advertising to firms for athletic events and contract for exclusive rights that allow companies to market their brands to students. The overall result is that a higher percentage of the total investment costs in instruction and research are borne privately by families, students, and firms.

I touched on the implications of these trends in Chapter 1. In brief summary, they include vocationalization of degree programs; less basic research and more applied research leading to patents, research, and dissertation support, where recipients are picked who will produce outcomes advancing certain political views; and decreased support for instruction and research in public service areas. Bok (2003) details other impacts from the commercialization of higher education and Slaughter and Leslie (1997) and Leslie et al. (1999) identify impacts on research in the United States and the United Kingdom especially. Although there is more total funding per student than there otherwise might be, when a larger percentage is private the support for students from middle- and lower-income families has tended to decline. A lower percentage of high school graduates from these groups go on to college, reflected in the lower rate of growth in enrollments in the United States than in the European Union. This trend is occurring in spite of the major skill deficits increasingly denying access by the middle class and lower-income groups to the benefits from economic growth (College Board, 2004b, p. 17; National Center for Education Statistics, 2006).

Privatization is motivated largely by the view that those who benefit should pay. In human capital analysis part of the benefits clearly is private. Privatization also is motivated by the desire to reduce the disincentive effects and avoid the political unpopularity of taxes. The strength of these effects involves lifecycle models and research in public finance. Privatization is also motivated by the hope that this increases efficiency. But this usually means internal efficiency. External efficiency, which includes externalities, is also required for economic efficiency. So whether or not increased privatization continues to be workable in achieving optimal levels of investment depends on the value of the externalities that benefit society and the future relative to the value of the private benefits. The latter is an issue only human capital analysis can address. Economic efficiency also needs markets that work, which entails good information. Information about the benefits from human capital formation also requires a human capital analysis, as well as consideration of the degree of market failure.

This trend toward privatization is not unique to higher education. It is part of a broader array of issues in the United States and the United Kingdom in particular that encompasses public broadcasting (for example, the Public Broadcasting Service [PBS] and the British Broadcasting Corporation [BBC]), passenger rail service (for example, AMTRAC and the privatization of British Rail), postal services, health insurance, and social security. For example, in the case of public broadcasting, PBS raises 41% of its funds from private sources even though 90% of the listeners contribute nothing. The latter are free riders whose contributions can be obtained only through the tax system. That is, public broadcasting is an example of a public good in that the exclusion principle does not work as it does in private markets where those individuals who do not pay are excluded. There have been proposals to privatize social security in the United States and the United Kingdom, following the partial privatization in Chile with varying degrees of success. The basic education system would be partially privatized by vouchers, enabling parents to send their children to private and religious schools. So higher education is not alone. But the principle is the same in each of these public services. How far privatization should go to achieve economic efficiency depends on the value of the social benefit externalities relative to the private benefits. Some privatization results in more resources, but if it goes too far the greater public good is not protected.

Beyond privatization but related to it, the new fundamental challenge to higher education policy is from the combined impacts of automation, freer trade, and immigration, which all operate to create major skill deficiencies in the labor force. When 64% of the population have a high school education or less, and have real incomes that have been flat or falling since 1980 so that they are not sharing in the gains from growth, there is a major problem. The evidence from standard human capital analysis is that the social rates of return for two- and four-year college degrees are high and rising, much higher in the United States than the standard benchmark of 10% real return for the alternative use of funds. The huge skill deficit, and the evidence to back it up, is the new additional major higher education policy issue to add to the standard list of access, affordability, accountability, and privatization.

The United States was the leading and dominant country in the world after the end of World War II largely because of the size of its economy. But China, the Far East, and the European Union are quickly coming to the fore while the relative size of the United States is beginning to shrink. Modern economies are now largely knowledge-based, which is accompanied by the growth of the service sector as manufacturing diminishes. The comparative advantage of the United States in the world is due to its larger human capital stock nurtured by its superior higher education system, not its unimproved cheap labor or even its physical capital as manufacturing shrinks. But as higher education enrollment rates increase faster in Canada, the Far East, and the European Union, this human capital advantage is rapidly shrinking. The United States is running the serious risk of falling behind as the leading economy; some of its other leadership roles will be affected as well. If current trends continue, historians of the future writing about the weaker relative position of the United States will likely cite the loss of its human capital advantage and note that higher education policy was asleep at the switch.

These Current Issues Have a Common Source

Many agree that access, affordability, accountability, and privatization are key current policy issues facing public higher education (St. John and

Parsons, 2001; Heller, 2001; Bok, 2003; Lyall and Sell, 2006). Some might even begin to add major skill deficits. However, all of these policy issues have a common underlying major source: the decline in real per student public funding.

Declining public funding is partly due to stagnant or declining real per capita income of the majority of the population in each state. This contributes to a partially stagnant tax base. It is also due to rising costs for the criminal justice system, public health, Medicaid, and public assistance, which squeeze state budgets. These costs rise partly because of insufficient investment and inequity in basic education, which, in turn, contributes to the next round of this vicious cycle. And declining support is also partly due to poor information about the non-market external benefits of basic and higher education and how they set the stage for future development as they cumulate over time.

If the current higher education policy problems are to be properly addressed, then the stagnation of the tax base also needs to be addressed. This requires analysis of the contribution of two- and four-year college degrees to earnings and growth, and hence to tax receipts. It also requires analysis of how higher education externalities also contribute to growth, tax receipts, and the reduction of income inequality that is the source of state welfare costs. The higher-income residents of the suburbs who normally have more human capital and also pay more taxes need to be made more aware of how education in the poor districts and expansion of community colleges benefits them. Those who pay more get more. But part of what they get is in the form of lower state welfare and criminal justice system costs and hence state taxes lower than they would otherwise be. Lower tuition at public institutions also benefits them.

New technologies and more highly skilled graduates also help business. But businesses also tend to be aware of skill deficiencies. The stagnation of the tax base requires diffusion of the newer and more advanced skills to a larger fraction of the labor force. Some of those with inadequate skills have skills that have been made obsolete by automation and international outsourcing. Many could benefit from lifelong learning programs, which community colleges are well set up to provide. Many community colleges already have a majority of non-traditionally aged students. Reaching this group will require the dissemination of information about the benefits of postsecondary education and a further lowering of the economic barriers for adults as well as for students from middle- and lower-income families whose parents have not attended college. Community colleges are particularly good at linking to local job market needs and to employers with joint programs (McMahon, 2004a). The research universities need to understand how this is also in their interest and take a leadership role. A major new higher education intervention is required.

The chapter has now come full circle. Starting with the declining public support per student and privatization trends, it has considered human capital perspectives on access, affordability, and accountability. It has suggested that declining per student public support is a source of rising tuition that triggers the other issues, including de facto privatization. It has suggested that a major source of the underinvestment is poor information about the private and social non-market outcomes of higher education, about the nature and scope of national skill deficits, and about external benefits among citizens and policy makers.

To provide specific information about the national skill deficit and the private and social non-market outcomes of higher education, all in relation to costs, are key objectives of the chapters that follow. If universities, community colleges, and K–12 could formulate a common policy response, the support for addressing national skill deficits and underinvestment that are also higher education's problem might well constitute a critical mass.

CHAPTER THREE

Higher Education and Economic Growth
Jobs, Earnings, and the Skill Deficit

> Losing jobs is painful. So let's be sure people are educated so that
> they can fill the jobs of the 21st century.
>
> PRESIDENT GEORGE W. BUSH

THE KEY QUESTION for this chapter is, Does higher education contribute significantly to jobs and to economic growth? And if so, what is the evidence? What are the powerful underlying economic trends to which higher education policy must respond, and how much does higher education contribute in relation to its rising costs?

The increased earnings available to an individual after completing college are relatively well known. But there is less awareness of the basic trends affecting job openings, earnings increments, and contributions to economic growth. And there is very little awareness of these trends in earnings and growth outcomes in relation to current higher education costs. Transitory fluctuations in job markets do occur. But they are not very important for developing higher education policy because investment in a college education is a long-term one. It should not be evaluated on the basis of short-term transitory factors. It will yield monetary and non-monetary returns throughout an average lifecycle of about forty-five years in the labor market and twenty or so years in retirement thereafter. Many physical capital investments in the private sector have a time horizon considerably shorter than the fifty to sixty-five typical for human capital.

From society's point of view, higher education's contribution is to the more basic longer-run supply side of the growth processes. It also contributes to the improvement of skills among the middle class and students from poor families. These are both relatively longer-term processes and not transitory.

Higher education's contribution to economic growth is raising new issues in the research literature. In particular, why are the social rates of return to investment in two- and four-year college degrees based on micro-earnings data consistently high and also higher than the contributions of higher education to economic growth in some studies using macro cross-country data? That is, the evidence of higher education's contribution to growth based on micro-earnings data, especially in the United States, is solid and very strong, whereas the evidence based on macro-data is much more conflicted. Is it because the number of years of postsecondary education matters less whereas quality matters more? The recent research says that quality matters (Hanushek and Wobmann, 2007). But it also says that increasing the number of years of education at current quality levels also matters.

Are the contributions of higher education to growth found in the macro-data smaller because there has been a decline in the number of students enrolling in science education? This pattern is common to the United States and other Organization for Economic Cooperation and Development (OECD) countries since the mid-1990s, but science education is dramatically higher in South Korea. This is a serious problem. But the potential impact of this alone on growth is not really detectable. Fast-growing countries like South Korea have dramatically increased enrollment rates across the board (McMahon, 2006b). The fact is other fields also contribute to growth and development in the medium term if the feedback effects as education operates through intermediate variables are taken into account (McMahon 2006a). Furthermore, there are hopeful approaches for reversing the decline in science majors. For example, an OECD study of sixty programs in nineteen countries finds that the introduction of a new lower-cost entry-level "science year" that is not called remedial but that offers math, science, and analytical/quantitative social science courses helps able students from poor high schools to recoup and is leading to many more students choosing science. Another determinant of science enrollments can be seen in South Korea, where both math and science scores for fifteen-year-olds are at the very top of the list essentially world-wide. With these proficiencies, many more students choose science and engineering careers in college.

The positive contribution of higher education to economic growth based on macro-data that is found in the mainstream of economic studies is challenged by Pritchett (2006). He suggests that there are diminishing returns to additional education past high school and that any contribution of education to growth in general is doubtful. But this is based on his and some other studies that fail to take the indirect effects of higher education on growth into account. Pritchett also introduces a variable for time in his regressions and in studies he cites. This does away with the interaction with R&D and embodiment of new technologies and hence eliminates higher education's role in contributing to the diffusion of new technologies. However, Benhabib and Spiegel (2006) study and emphasize this diffusion effect.

Another challenge to higher education's role in economic growth is the over-education argument. It was popularized by Freeman (1976) during an earlier recession. Even though it turned out to be mistaken, the argument is still alive and well in some quarters. I will address the over-education issue later in this book.

The role of higher education in economic growth is not an arcane abstraction, but instead it has empirical substance. There are powerful basic forces at work such as the onrush of new technologies displacing many workers from good manufacturing jobs as well as from lower-skilled jobs as they are automated. But this simultaneously is opening up major earnings advantages for those who have more advanced skills. Freer trade, which contributes to growth, is also displacing jobs in textile and other manufacturing industries and making things worse for those with a high school education or less. So the growth benefits flow to those with a college education. A huge nationwide skill deficit has emerged. I develop the empirical evidence for these effects further below.

Higher education is in the center of this race between developing new technology, much of it through R&D at the research universities, and providing the labor force with the skills necessary through two- and four-year college programs if the rest of the population is to keep up. Furthermore, this double role and the positive contribution of both its parts to growth and development are unique to higher education. There are other policies, such as protectionist trade policies, slowing down R&D, and subsidizing firms that do not outsource (and may be less efficient), which run the serious risk of slowing growth. Higher education policy is unique in being able to provide solutions to the need to stay on the frontiers of new technology, address skill deficits, and also reduce inequality while simultaneously supporting faster economic growth.

The United States, the United Kingdom, and other developed OECD countries all are being affected by the same powerful forces of new technology, increasing globalization, and immigration. All of these countries have much more human capital than the poor countries, and maintaining and increasing this stock will enable them to maintain their position and their comparative advantage over places with cheap unskilled labor. All of these countries face languishing tax bases and public assistance costs higher than they would otherwise be because of the skill deficit. All are also facing a looming protectionist and voter backlash. When there are too few college graduates, both the tax base and the number providing political support for higher education budgets suffer.

Fortunately, there is evidence relevant to these issues. My intent is to consider the evidence in a balanced fashion, and in a way that is clear and interesting to the reader.

Knowledge-Based Earnings and Growth

Demand for the highly skilled workers has been rising faster than the supply of college graduates in the United States and most other OECD countries. So as job growth in skilled occupations requiring two to four years of college has risen, real earnings for this group have risen 49.5% and 48% respectively in the United States since 1980. Social rates of return that do take rising institutional costs into account have also risen significantly in the United States and continue to rise as I will show below. At the same time the demand in the occupations typically employing persons with a high school education or less, roughly 64% of the U.S. population, has risen more slowly. There is currently an excess supply of those without appropriate skills. The result is that real earnings of this group have stagnated since 1980. These are also the persons in the lowest three-fifths of the income distribution (Mishel et al., 2005, Figure 1G, p. 61). As I will demonstrate below, the social rates of return at the high school level have remained flat. These persons constitute a very large group. Many are in smaller towns and rural areas, although many are in the middle-class neighborhoods of larger cities. They are not participating in the benefits of economic growth and are being increasingly economically and socially excluded.

The main reason for this is that graduates in command of the more recent technologies in most fields are in higher demand by employers and have an earnings advantage in the job market. This is well known and has been frequently studied since Bartel and Lichtenberg (1987) documented it earlier. In contrast, the failure of demand to grow in occupations requiring a high school education or less reflects the fact that this group is increasingly displaced by automation, imports, and international outsourcing. The result is an excess supply of persons with limited skills. Although college enrollments have been increasing in the United States and in other OECD nations, numbers of graduates have not increased fast enough and the number without college has diminished too slowly. So the excess supply of the lower-skilled has grown. Immigrants from Mexico (and from Turkey, India, Pakistan, and Africa in the European Union) have increased this pool. The result is large numbers with skill deficits. Given that financial aid for students from lower-income families has not kept up with the size of this pool, and state support for institutions has fallen, this is a major higher education policy gap.

There are exceptions to this pattern of technology, trade, and immigration favoring the more highly educated. But most of it is anecdotal. Unemployment of PhDs in Silicon Valley followed the bursting of the technology bubble, for example. But this was transitory. Another is the international outsourcing of some medical procedures (medical tourism) and some jobs requiring college-level skills in bookkeeping, publishing, or telephoning, where these can be channeled over the Internet or satellite phones. But a few anomalies like this do not stand up against the overwhelming weight of the evidence produced by repeated nationwide surveys of the U.S. labor force and other systematic evidence.

SKILLED WORKERS EARN MORE

Higher education creates a larger stock of productive human capital skills. So these skills are in demand. Employers are willing to pay more, and also *to continue to pay more* if these skills are genuinely productive of revenues for the firm. This simple point as well as reviews of the available empirical evidence lead to the clear conclusion that there is little in the data that supports "job market signaling" (which implies that human capital is not productive) as an explanation for the observed returns to schooling (Lange and Topel, 2006, p. 505). It also rejects a "diploma effect" that suggests that it is not the skills that are productive. Degree holders have a diploma and earn more than those who have dropped out and do not have a diploma. This is not a fake diploma effect, because those who have a diploma have more human capital. Graduates who have completed all degree requirements with a satisfactory grade point average have acquired more human capital than those who have not, some because of unsatisfactory grade point averages that indicate that they did not learn much. The diploma holders with more human capital are more productive in the judgment of employers and are therefore worth more. Diploma holders from a prestigious college may earn more, but the quality of their education may have been better. If it is not, employers will eventually in most cases recognize that they are not more productive.

The rising demand for highly skilled workers and the slackening demand for low-skilled workers with only high school or less are shown in Figure 3.1. In the right-hand panel, as new technology creates a rising demand for those best able to convey and adapt new knowledge, demand is rising. Since demand for college graduates is increasing faster than supply, average earnings for males and females have risen in constant 2007 dollars from $43,740 in 1980 to $66,363 in 2007 (U.S. Census, 1980, 2007).* This is an increase of 48% in real terms since 1980. The average increase for those with a two-year associate degree is a very similar 49.5% since 1980 (ibid.). The real increase is faster for females (73%) than for males (37%). Even if the top 1% is removed where the increases have been larger, the real increases for college graduates are very substantial.

There has been an increase in the number going to college in this same period, as is shown by the increase in the quantity supplied from 1980 to 2007 in the right panel of Figure 3.1. But this increase was not large enough to dampen the 48% increase in real earnings. Currently, 27% of

---

*This compares those with high school or less with those with four years of college or more. It eliminates those with one to three years of college and those with associate degrees.

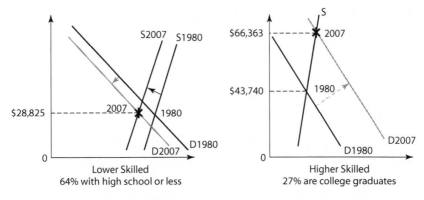

Figure 3.1. The demand for college graduates is rising faster than supply. High school graduates earn 43% of what college graduates earn. This gap continues to widen, as it has since 1980. *Source*: U.S. Census (2007, 1980).

the population have four years of college or more, and about another 9% have a two-year associate degree. Together this means that about 38% have college-level skills in the United States, a minority of the population (McMahon, 2006b, Table A-2).

THOSE WITH LOWER SKILLS EARN LESS

From 1980 through 2007, the demand for persons with a high school education or less and lower skills fell in relative terms, as shown in the left panel in Figure 3.1. They made up 64% of the labor force in the United States, and a somewhat higher percentage than this in the European Union. Their real earnings remained nearly constant in real terms at $28,825 in 2007 as shown, less than a 1% increase since 1980 (U.S. Census, 1980, converted to 2007 prices). The real earnings of males who have completed only one to three years of high school fell 10% since 1980 (ibid.). This understates their true plight. This is because this U.S. Bureau of Labor Statistics data only includes those with earnings, and proportionately more high school dropouts are unemployed or have become discouraged workers and left the labor force so they are therefore not included in this earnings data. Many with a high school education or less have become part of two-earner families partly because of this economic pressure. Nevertheless, they are falling behind in the race against technology. In 1980 they earned 72% of what college graduates earned, but in 2007 earned only 43% of that amount.

The falling demand for those less skilled can be attributed to automation in manufacturing and agriculture and international outsourcing of jobs associated with freer trade. The supply of lower-skilled workers has shifted to the left, as shown in Figure 3.1, as more have gone to college. It would have fallen faster if there had not been immigration. Recent estimates are that this immigration has restrained earnings growth in this group by about 5% below what it would otherwise have been so it is a factor, albeit a minor one.

The conclusion that real earnings for lower-skilled, less well-educated workers that make up a majority of the population have remained flat for a quarter of a century has major implications.

THE EVIDENCE BASED ON SPECIFIC JOB MARKETS

There is another relevant kind of evidence based on specific job markets. As secular economic growth occurs or even as more transitory economic recovery from a recession takes place, the demand for workers rises and more job openings are created. The U.S. Bureau of Labor Statistics analyzes the thirty occupations that are growing the fastest currently and are expected to continue to do so from 2006 through 2016 (U.S. Bureau of Labor Statistics, 2007, Table 6; see also Table 3.1). All thirty occupations growing fastest percentage-wise, except for home health care, medical, and pharmacy aides, require a community college or four-year college education or more. For the thirty occupations accounting for over half of the numerical growth in jobs, 11 are designated by the U.S. Bureau of Labor Statistics as requiring an associate degree or more (ibid., Table 5). And for the thirty occupations expected to account for over two-thirds of the numerical decline in jobs, twenty-eight out of thirty are lower skilled, requiring only on-the-job training after high school (ibid., Table 8). Of course skill requirements for these lower-skilled occupations also tend to be upgraded over time. So although it can be said that the largest number of openings are expected to be in the larger occupations replacing those who retire that are lower skilled and do not require a college education (for example, food preparation, retail sales, office clerks), it is also true that these are not the fastest growing. The largest number of jobs is also expected to be in larger but less-skilled occupations, including stock clerks, hand packers, and farm workers even those these occupations are not growing (ibid., Table 8). But even if there were a dramatic increase in access to postsecondary education, there will continue to be a very large number of persons with a high school education or less, and probably a continuing surplus, for many years.

This pattern of continuing change can be illustrated graphically and more dramatically in Figure 3.2. Almost all of the occupations in which job openings are growing the fastest percentage-wise typically require two or four years of college education, as indicated in the column on the right. These fastest-growing occupations account for over one-third of all of the new jobs becoming available. More specifically, the four fastest-growing occupations in Figure 3.2 require four or more years of college. They include medical and physician assistants, network and computer system analysts, computer software engineers, and computer systems analysts. The next fastest-growing occupation is health care aides, needed to attend to an aging population in the United States, but also in Europe and Japan. This typically requires no college and only some on-the-job training. So it is an exception to the pattern, but also one where an increasing number of jobs are occupied by immigrants. Following this in Figure 3.2, a two-year associate degree or more is needed for eleven of the remaining fastest-growing occupations. These include medical records technicians, physical therapist assistants, computer software engineers, veterinary technologists, and dental hygienists. No college and only some on-the-job training is needed for the remaining five fast-growing occupations. These again are largely personal services needed because of an aging population. Overall, at least two years of college is needed for three-fourths of the fastest-growing occupations.

Figure 3.3 shows the U.S. Bureau of Labor Statistics forecast by broader industry groupings and in terms of the numerical number of new jobs as distinct from the percentage growth rates. Estimated education levels are not as homogeneous within these groups because the classifications are not skill-based and the types of jobs within each group are broader. Nevertheless, again the largest increases are expected in the professions such as medicine, law, teaching and research, librarianship, and architecture,

TABLE 3.1 The Thirty Fastest-Growing Occupations, 2006–16 (in thousands)

Occupation	Occupational group	Employment 2006	Employment 2016	Change Number	Change Percent	Education needed[a]
Network systems and data communications analysts	Professional and related occupations[b]	262	402	140	53.4	Bachelor's
Personal and home care aides	Service occupations[c]	767	1,156	389	50.6	On-the-job training (OJT)
Home health aides	Service occupations[c]	787	1,171	384	48.7	OJT
Computer software engineers	Professional and related occupations[b]	507	733	226	44.6	Bachelor's
Veterinary technologists	Professional and related occupations[b]	71	100	29	41.0	Associate
Personal financial advisors	Management, business, and financial[d]	176	248	72	41.0	Bachelor's
Makeup artists, theatrical and performance	Service occupations[c]	2	3	1	39.8	Postsecondary vocational
Medical assistants	Service occupations[c]	417	565	148	35.4	OJT
Veterinarians	Professional[b]	62	84	22	35.0	Professional degree
Substance abuse counselors	Professional[b]	83	112	29	34.3	Bachelor's
Skin care specialists	Service[c]	38	51	13	34.3	Postsecondary vocational
Financial analysts	Management, business, and financial[d]	221	295	75	33.8	Bachelor's
Social service assistants	Professional[b]	339	453	114	33.6	OJT
Gaming surveillance officers	Service occupations[c]	9	12	3	33.6	OJT
Physical therapists	Service occupations[c]	60	80	20	32.4	Associate
Pharmacy technicians	Professional	285	376	91	32.0	OJT
Forensic technicians	Professional	13	17	4	30.7	Bachelor's
Dental hygienists	Professional	167	217	50	30.1	Associate
Mental health counselors	Professional	100	130	30	30.0	Master's

Substance abuse social workers	Professional	122	159	37	29.9	Master's
Marriage counselors	Professional	25	32	7	29.8	Master's
Dental assistants	Service[c]	280	362	82	29.2	Associate
Computer systems analysts	Professional	504	650	146	29.0	Bachelor's
Database administrators	Professional	119	154	34	28.6	Bachelor's
Computer software engineers	Professional	350	449	99	28.2	Bachelor's
Sports writers	Service[c]	18	24	5	28.0	OJT
Environmental protection technicians	Professional	36	47	10	28.0	Associate
Manicurists and pedicurists	Service[c]	78	100	22	27.6	Postsecondary vocational
Physical therapists	Professional	173	220	47	27.1	Master's
Physician assistants	Professional	66	83	18	27.0	Master's

[a]An occupation is placed into one of eleven categories that best describes the postsecondary education or training needed by most workers to become fully qualified in that occupation. For more information about the categories, see Occupational Projections and Training Data, 2006–7 edition, Bulletin 2602 (U.S. Bureau of Labor Statistics, February 2006) and Occupational Projections and Training Data, 2008–9 edition, Bulletin 2702 (U.S. Bureau of Labor Statistics, February 2008).

[b]Major occupational groups 15-0000 through 29-0000 in the 2000 Standard Occupational Classification (SOC).

[c]Major occupational groups 31-0000 through 39-0000 in the 2000 Standard Occupational Classification (SOC).

[d]Major occupational groups 11-0000 through 13-0000 in the 2000 Standard Occupational Classification (SOC).

for which generally five years of higher education or more are required. These "professional and related" occupations are expected to add 6.5 million jobs by 2012, which is also the largest in absolute numbers.

The service occupations shown in the second row in Figure 3.3 require

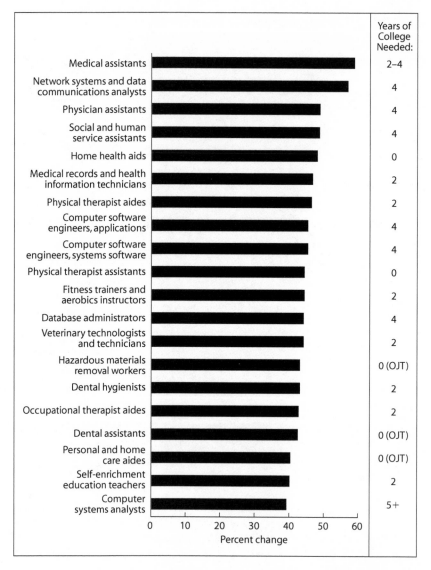

Figure 3.2. Percent change in employment in occupations projected to grow fastest, 2002–12. *Source:* U.S. Bureau of Labor Statistics (2005, Chart 7).

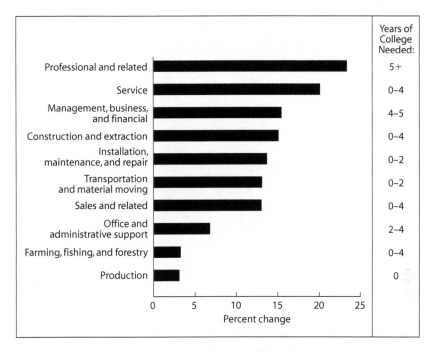

Figure 3.3. Percent change in total employment by major occupational group, 2002–12. *Source:* U.S. Bureau of Labor Statistics (2005).

zero to four years of college since they include services outside the professional range, from relatively low-skilled health care aides to the human capital–intensive services of systems analysts. These service occupations are expected to enjoy the second largest percentage growth but also the second largest numerical gain, 20.1%, or 5.3 million jobs. A number of these are social and human service assistants, medical records specialists, and so forth that require two years or more of college. But 2.7 million of these new jobs, about half of the total, are in food preparation and home health care support that do not require college and depend only on on-the-job training.

However, almost all of the additional 2.4 million management, business, and financial service jobs, which are the third fastest-growing in both absolute and percentage terms (15.4%), will require 4 or more years of college. There then follow the 4 next fastest-growing occupational groups. These include construction and extraction occupations (+15 %, or 1.1 million jobs), installation and repair (0.8 million jobs), transportation (1.3 million jobs), sales (2 million jobs), and office support (1.6 million jobs). But although only some of this last group require 2 to 4 years of college, its 6.8 million numerical total is considerably smaller than the 11.5 million increase in the three fastest-growing industries that do require college-level skills.

The occupations that are expected to decline are also very revealing. Projected job loss is concentrated quite dramatically in the very low-skill occupations. Essentially, all of these occupations overwhelmingly employ only persons with a high school education or less. The exception is travel agents, which is a very small category. The numerical decline in the numbers of farmers, ranchers, and farm workers is a continuation of the very long-term process of technology displacements in agriculture, and an example of the automation I discussed earlier. The decline in employment in manufacturing is having major impacts in the industrial states. The 10% continuing annual decline in textile and apparel industries is another example with major impacts, for example, on places such as South Carolina, where the international job outsourcing is documented by Klein et al. (2003, p. 130). And the decline in the jobs for word processors, stock clerks, order filers, secretaries, postal clerks, and telephone operators all reflect displacement by new computer and cell phone technologies.

EARNINGS TRENDS OVER TIME REFLECT THESE JOB TRENDS

The increasing percentage and number of jobs for higher-skilled labor are reflected in steady trend in the increasing real earnings over time for two- and four-year college graduates in contrast to the constant real earnings of high school graduates from 1980 through the present as shown in Figure 3.4. This pattern of job and earnings growth is also reflected in increasing social rates of return to investment in higher education, rates that take the rising institutional costs into account, as I will discuss shortly. It is important to consider the trends in social rates of return because they consider rising institutional costs in a way that is more relevant to policy than just looking at the rising costs alone. Non-market benefits must also be included, but I will consider these benefits later.

Since these earnings trends reflect strong underlying basic forces from technology and globalization, they are very likely to continue for the foreseeable future. Therefore, they provide a sound basis for formulating

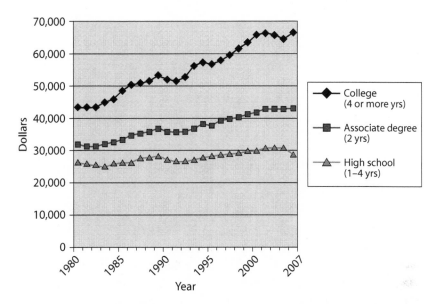

Figure 3.4. Earnings of college graduates, 1980–2007, in 2007 dollars. *Source:* U.S. Census (1970, and earlier issues).

longer-term higher education policy. Short-term fluctuations, including the surge in the job markets for graduates in 2006 and 2007, and also a transitory cyclical dip in 2008–9 are not a sound basis for policies relating to long-run investment in human capital.

The trends in real earnings over time illustrated in Figure 3.4 also show that the real earnings for high school graduates or less remained essentially constant under $30,000 from 1980 to 2007. At the same time the real earnings of 4-year graduates increased from $43,740 to $66,363. The trend in the earnings of those earning 2-year associate degrees has also been steadily upward. The earnings in the earlier period from 1980 until 1990 are not strictly for 2-year associate degrees since the U.S. Census only began reporting 2-year degree earnings separately in 1991. So before that Figure 3.3 reports earnings for those with 1 to 3 years of college, rather than 2-year degree holders. However, male and female associate degree holders earned on average $40,312 in 2007, one-third more than high school graduates, and males finishing bachelor's degrees earned over $75,000. Transitory dips can be seen during the 1992 and 2001–2 recessions, and in 2008–9. But these are all temporary and relatively small.

The long-term payoff for finishing college is about $1.1 million in future dollars. Over time, the upward trend involving the increase in the real earnings of both male and female four-year college graduates was steady and persistent from 1980 through 2007, as shown in the two top lines of Figure 3.4, whereas the earnings of high school graduates were relatively flat.

ARE THERE DIMINISHING RETURNS TO FOUR OR MORE YEARS OF COLLEGE?

If access to higher education were to be increased, much of this increase would occur at the two- and four-year college degree level. Reducing the 64% with a high school education or less and increasing the 36% with two years of college or more can be expected to start to narrow the widening gap between college and high school graduates. This would eventually begin to lower the high rates of return to investment at the college level. This can be seen to have occurred in South Korea, where the increase in enrollment rates at the college level has been much larger than in the United States (McMahon, 2006b). But this is a very slow long-run process. It has taken twenty-eight to thirty years since 1980 for the gap to widen. It is likely to take this long or longer for the inequality gap to narrow to what it was before.

The True Investment Costs of Higher Education

"Jobs" and "earnings" growth alone are not enough to serve as a basis for higher education policy. Tuition costs and institutional costs have risen as well. Their relation to job growth in higher-skilled occupations and earnings growth must be considered in relation to both institutional costs, which have been rising, and forgone earnings costs, which have not.

The most meaningful way to do this is to express earnings in relation to the total investment costs as a standard social rate of return. This has the distinct advantage that it can be compared directly to the total rate of return on alternative investments. These include the alternative use of tax funds by taxpayers and the alternative use of funds by students and their families. Standard social rates of return are limited, however, because they are based only on earnings and relate only to pure economic growth effects.

Final policy judgments must also consider the non-market social benefits that accrue in addition to money earnings and economic growth effects.

DEFINITION OF THE COSTS OF HIGHER EDUCATION

The true economic costs of higher education include not just institutional costs but also the value of the student's time invested in human capital formation. The size of the latter is approximately equal to institutional costs per student at public institutions, and a little less than the institutional costs per student at private institutions. These opportunity costs are usually not borne by students, some of whom enjoy a good living standard while in college. Instead, they are normally borne by parents as they cover room, board, clothing, transportation, and incidental costs while the son or daughter is in college. This parental support constitutes saving by these parents as they forgo their own consumption, which is the economic definition of saving. They simultaneously invest these amounts saved in human capital formation in the education of their children. This saving is automatically induced by the student's enrollment, and is over and above financial saving in the narrow sense. Amounts saved and invested in human capital formation are just as important as financial saving to economic growth because the human capital formation it finances contributes directly to growth.

The cost of the college student's time and hence his or her forgone earnings is estimated using the average earnings of a high school graduate of the same sex as the amount that the college student could have earned. So for higher education policy to be relevant to economic growth it is not institutional costs but also forgone earnings costs that represent the total investment and must be related to increments in earnings or jobs to obtain criteria relevant to economic efficiency.

Political decisions by states tend to focus too exclusively on institutional costs and on tuition and fees since these require out-of-pocket expenditure. Some studies include room and board costs, and this is somewhat better. Both out-of-pocket and other forgone earnings costs affect family income and borrowing constraints for the financing of human capital formation are most serious for middle- and lower-income families. Since state support of public institutions, federal Pell Grants, and state financial aid in the United States have not kept up on a per student basis

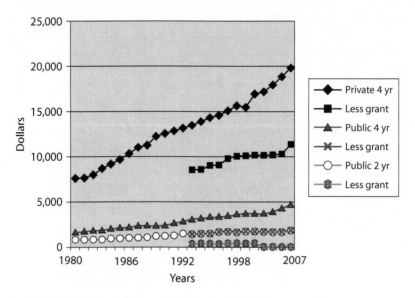

Figure 3.5. Tuition and fees, 1980–2007, before and after average grant, in constant 2003 dollars. *Source:* College Board (2007b, pp. 10, 17).

with tuition increases, students from poor and minority households are being excluded disproportionately.

Trends in Tuition and Fee Costs to Families. Tuition and fees have increased 46% per student at private institutions in constant dollars and 56% at public 4-year institutions since 1980. They have increased a somewhat smaller 32% per student at U.S. public 2-year institutions, as shown in Figure 3.5. The absolute increases have been consistently higher at the private institutions, but in recent years the percentage increases have been higher at the public 4-year institutions given that the base at public 4-year institutions ($6,185 in 2007–8 prices) is only about one-fourth what it is at private institutions ($23,712) (College Board, 2007b, p. 10).

Net tuition and fees after allowance for financial aid waivers and grants also have increased but somewhat more slowly. This is because per student grants have also been increasing. But they have not increased fast enough to keep up with tuition and fee increases. In real terms, the increase in net tuition and fees has been 33% at private 4-year institutions and 26% at public 4-year institutions since 1993, with no net increase at public 2-year institutions (College Board, 2004b, pp. 16–17). Actual tuition and fees net of financial aids is about half the sticker price at private institutions, and less than half the sticker price at public institutions.

However, what is more important is the total tuition and room and board costs net of grants relative to a student's family's income. One student in college means that a family where the parents have a high school education would be spending 82% of its income for a child at a private institution and 33% of its income for a child at a public 4-year institution (see Figures 3.6 and 3.7). If the student goes to a 2-year institution, average costs are still 25% of family income (see Figure 3.8). Since these percentages are high, college expenses must be financed with loans, plus a shift toward two-earner families, and unfortunately, through a lower percentage going on to college from high school wage earner families. When parents have 4 or more years of college, the real burden of college costs relative to their higher income is significantly lower, as can be seen in Figures 3.6, 3.7, and 3.8 respectively. At private 4-year institutions, net tuition and room and board costs on average are 32% of family income in single-earner families. At public 4-year institutions they are 13% of income where the parents are college graduates, and 10% of income

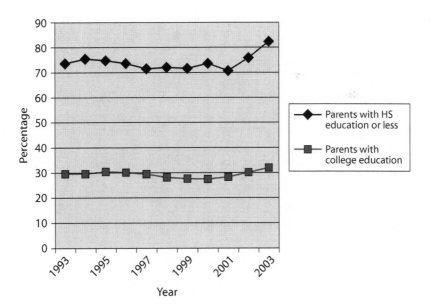

Figure 3.6. The net cost of private four-year institutions as a share of family income.

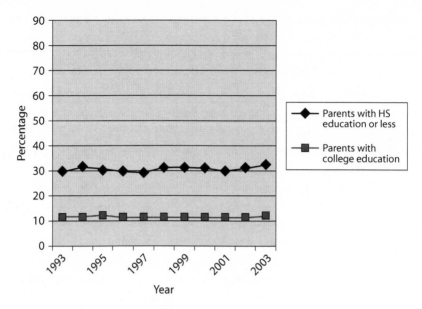

Figure 3.7. The net cost of public four-year institutions as a share of family income.

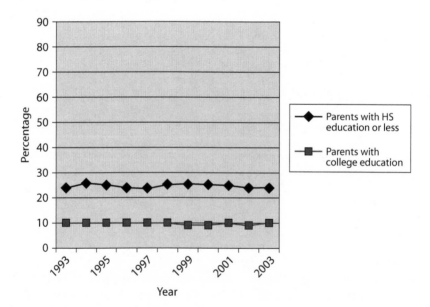

Figure 3.8. The net cost of public two-year institutions as a share of family income.

respectively at 2-year public institutions. These out-of-pocket costs of college are a much more manageable burden if the parent is a college graduate. This is a major reason why over 75% of the children who are high school graduates coming from these families go on to college, whereas less than 50% of those with family incomes below $35,000 go on. The latter average includes multiple-earner families (College Board, 2004b, p. 17).

Trends in Total Costs. Table 3.2 is quite revealing. It shows that institutional costs per student have gone up in real terms by 70% at private institutions and by 60% at public institutions since 1980. But it also shows that forgone earnings costs as measured by the earnings of high school graduates have gone up only 14%. (The real earnings of those with less than a high school diploma have been falling, so the earnings of both groups have been essentially flat.) Table 3.2 also shows that these forgone earnings costs are about equal to institutional costs at public four-year institutions, and a little less than institutional costs at private colleges (as seen by comparing columns 1 and 2 to column 4 in Table 3.2). So the total investment costs of a bachelor's degree from a human capital formation perspective have gone up 41% at private institutions and 34% at private and public four-year institutions. *This is less than the 70% and 60% increases in institutional costs, and also less than the 57% increase in the real earnings of college graduates during this same period.* This puts the average increase in college costs into better perspective. Looking forward, it also suggests that we should expect to find the narrow social rate of return based only on earnings for completion of a four-year college degree to be trending upward since 1980.

Trends in Rates of Return to Higher Education and Growth

Putting the earnings benefits and costs together is one of the more important calculations reported in this book. The narrow social rates of return to higher education are found not only to be relatively high in the United States but since 1980 have been trending upward over that time when calculated by the same methods. The rates of return to secondary education over the same period have remained relatively flat. This pattern reflects the high and rising demand for two- and four-year college gradu-

TABLE 3.2   Investment in Human Capital through Higher Education
(in constant 2005 prices)

Year	Institutional Expenditures per Student in FTE			Forgone Earnings (HS Grad's Earnings)	Total Investment Costs of Higher Education		
	Private 4-Year (1)	Public 4-Year (2)	Public 2-Year (3)	(4)	Private 4-Year (5)	Public 4-Year (6)	Public 2-Year (7)
1980	23,442	18,509	6,794	24,420	47,862	42,929	31,214
1981	23,454	18,382	6,612	23,854	47,308	42,236	30,466
1982	23,461	18,848	6,673	23,379	46,840	42,227	30,052
1983	24,736	19,299	6,859	23,349	48,085	42,648	30,208
1984	25,769	20,599	7,677	23,929	49,698	44,528	31,606
1985	27,188	20,546	7,657	24,093	51,281	44,639	31,750
1985	28,714	21,689	7,990	24,275	52,989	45,964	32,265
1985	30,910	22,468	8,090	25,260	56,170	47,728	33,350
1988	31,719	22,638	8,142	25,653	57,372	48,291	33,795
1989	32,129	22,952	8,304	25,805	57,934	48,757	34,109
1990	32,905	23,166	8,181	24,856	57,761	48,022	33,037
1991	33,365	23,172	8,250	24,546	57,911	47,718	32,796
1992	34,045	23,530	7,922	24,407	58,452	47,937	32,329
1993	34,210	24,135	7,996	24,804	59,014	48,939	32,800
1994	34,858	24,675	8,441	25,288	60,146	49,963	33,729

1995	36,749	25,468	8,640	26,114	62,863	51,582	34,754
1996	37,357	25,533	8,908	26,333	63,690	51,866	35,241
1997	37,688	26,107	9,085	26,613	64,301	52,720	35,698
1998	38,014	26,562	9,258	27,072	65,086	53,634	36,330
1999	38,000	27,005	9,485	27,557	65,557	54,562	37,042
2000	37,828	27,648	9,832	27,326	64,154	54,974	37,158
2001	37,885	28,037	10,073	28,286	66,171	56,323	38,359
2002	38,294	28,403	10,245	28,350	66,644	56,753	38,595
2003	38,787	28,831	10,387	28,286	67,073	57,117	38,673
2004	39,293	29,215	10,536	28,000	67,293	57,215	38,536
2005	39,786	29,667	10,755	27,800	67,586	57,467	38,555
Percent change, 1980–2005	70	60	58	14	41	34	24

SOURCES: Column 1: National Center for Educational Statistics (1996, Table 43, p. 97); columns 2 and 3: National Center for Education Statistics (2000, Tables 48 and 50) (1980–84 are from the source for col. 1); columns 1–3 are converted to 2004–5 constant prices using the Consumer Price Index; column 4: Mean of male and female high school graduate earnings in 2003 prices converted to 2005 prices using the Consumer Price Index. 2004–5 are estimates based on preliminary U.S. Bureau of Labor Statistics data.

NOTE: The specific recent costs used in the social rate of return calculations are shown in the spreadsheet formulas downloadable from the website at McMahon (2008). They differ somewhat from the above because they weight public and private costs to correspond to the earnings data, they are for educational and general expenditures/FTE rather than total institutional costs/FTE, and foregone earnings costs are based on the earnings of the youngest 18–24 year age group only. The website will be updated occasionally.

ates. But these social rates of return now also include the rising institutional costs.

This fact is not in dispute, but it has been overlooked by those who have focused primarily on costs (for example, U.S. Department of Education, 1998, 2007) and by others who have suggested that there are diminishing returns to investment in education over the lifecycle, which implies that rates of return for higher education will be lower than rates of return for primary and secondary education (Heckman and Klenow, 1997; Carneiro and Heckman, 2003). The latter is very true in poor countries, where universal primary and secondary education have not been achieved. It is also true in corrupt authoritarian countries, where poverty, corruption, and control by elites tend to result in serious underinvestment in basic education. More recent work by Hechman et al. (2008) does show that the rate of return for finishing high school as compared to dropping out is extremely high (52%, ibid., p. 12 and Table 2a), but this reflects the penalty borne by dropouts. The problem with the earlier Carneiro-Heckman analysis is that it focuses on the rising forgone earnings costs over the lifecycle as one moves from preschool to primary to secondary to higher education levels. These low costs at early ages make investment in primary, kindergarten, and even preschool education very advantageous. Without denying that investment in education at these levels in developed countries is extremely important, such an analysis ignores the facts that forgone earnings costs based on earnings of the less well-educated over time have been flat or falling, and that the earnings of college graduates driven upward by new technologies have been high and rising. The supply of college graduates has increased, but the demand has increased faster.

The assumption that there are diminishing returns to education at the more advanced levels reappears in work by some based on macro nationwide and cross-country data. Pritchett (2006), for example, cites the "stylized fact" of the slowdown in rates of growth in the OECD countries since 1972. This did occur, but when he links it to the expansion of access to higher education during the same period, the conclusion becomes debatable. He concludes from this alone that there has been diminishing returns to education, and that it cannot be argued that the increase in education contributed to growth. The problem is that he does not control for other factors adversely affecting growth. The effects of higher education may well have been positive, as concluded by Keller (2006b), but not strong enough to overcome other adverse factors. During the earlier part of the period, when higher education in the European Union was not expanding as rapidly, these adverse effects included the worldwide oil price shocks in 1973 following the Yom Kippur War and inflation followed by rising real interest rates in the United States. These were widely recognized in the literature at the time as the source of the productivity slowdown. Throughout the entire period there has been rising life expectancy in the European Union and the United States, contributing to rising social security and health care costs, and slower growth. The higher public costs related to this support of consumption through social security is identified by Barro and Sala-I-Martin (2007, 1995) as a drag on growth in their regressions. And in the growth equations fitted for this book based on OECD panel data, life expectancy, for which Barro's social security costs are a proxy, clearly is slowing growth in these more developed countries (see Appendix D). The expansion of access to education continues to contribute to growth when there are controls for these other adverse factors (McMahon, 1984a; see also Appendix D). There was also remarkably rapid per capita growth in East Asia from 1960 through 2007, fueled in significant part by the expansion of education (World Bank, 1993; McMahon, 1998d, 2002, Chapter 3; Keller, 2006b). Growth slowed during the 1997–98 financial crisis in East Asia, during which time education would not have been expected to contribute to growth in studies of that region that did not control for this crisis (Barro, 2001a). But since then growth there has resumed, and overall education's contribution to growth in East Asia is generally regarded as very highly significant (Keller 2006b).

STANDARD SOCIAL RATES OF RETURN TO HIGHER EDUCATION IN THE UNITED STATES

First, social and private rates of return need to be distinguished clearly.

Social rates of return are formally defined as the rates that discount the stream of net increments to earnings before taxes over the lifecycle that are attributable to higher education back to their present value and equate them to the total investment costs of higher education, which include institutional costs plus forgone earnings costs. The first important point is that the costs include total institutional instructional costs per student. Where institutional costs include costs other than instructional costs, as is often the case, the rates reported are understated, as has been stressed and illustrated earlier by Leslie and Brinkman (1988). The second important point is that they do not include the value of the non-market private and social benefits beyond earnings. Therefore, standard social rates of return understate the true return for this reason as well. I will refer to them in this book as narrow social rates of return, as they are termed in the recent literature, because they are based only on earnings. The third key point is that these social rates of return, whatever their failings, are the rates that are relevant to public policy, and to whether more or less should be invested by governments and by families to achieve economic efficiency.

Private rates of return are formally defined as the rates that discount the stream of net increments to earnings after taxes over the lifecycle that are attributable to higher education back to their present value and equate them to the private investment costs of higher education to students and their families, which include net tuition and fees after grants or tuition waivers plus forgone earnings costs. Private rates of return do not reflect the public tax costs or the costs to donors. Private rates of return are relevant to private decisions by students and their families about whether or not it is profitable for them to invest. They are not relevant to public policy because they ignore public costs.

The social and private rates of return reported in this book are computed using the "full method" directly from the U.S. Census earnings and National Center for Education Statistics institutional cost data. This is a mathematical calculation of a pure internal rate of return and is directly comparable to a rate of return computed on any other financial investment. The social rates of return, including the rising institutional costs and the comparability with other investments, are major advantages of using the full method and in general of rate of return benefit/cost analysis. Ability bias, which is sometimes referred to as self-selection bias, is assumed to be almost entirely cancelled out by measurement error. The latter occurs when measuring the number of years of education, which respondents tend to overstate when reporting their own education, or which governments overstate when reporting their own enrollment rates. This neutralization of ability bias by measurement error is a well known research result since Griliches and Mason (1988), and it has been confirmed more recently in studies of large samples of identical monozygotic

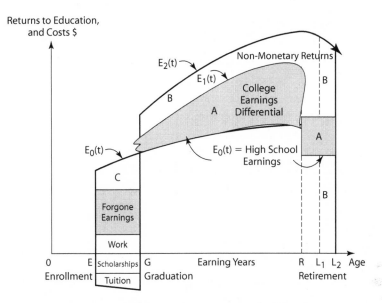

Figure 3.9. Investment in education and returns over the lifecycle.

twins by Rouse (1999), Behrman and Rosenzweig (1999), and others. It applies to two- and four-year college degrees, but exceptions in some situations must be made such as at the PhD level. Additional research on ability bias and how best to handle it is discussed further in Appendix A. The methods used in all calculations are discussed in McMahon (1991) and in Arias and McMahon (2001), and the spreadsheets containing the earnings data, cost data, and formulas can be downloaded from my website (McMahon, 2008).

A brief illustration of how social and private rates of return are calculated will help to explain their meaning and why they have different policy implications. The earnings of college graduates in excess of the earnings of high school graduates over the lifecycle is the "college earnings differential" in Figure 3.9. The use of the graduate's human capital during leisure time hours raises the productivity of time used to produce final outcomes in the household or in the community, yielding additional non-monetary returns up to and after retirement (Area B). Since college graduates live longer than high school graduates, there are additional non-monetary benefits, as shown to the extent that the college education increases the longevity of college graduates ($L2 > L1$).

To calculate a private rate of return, the private investment costs are shown during the college years in Figure 3.9 from enrollment (E) to graduation (G). These private investment costs include the forgone earnings costs as shown, as well as tuition and fee costs. But these must be reduced by part-time work since this is not time invested in human capital formation. They also must be reduced by Pell Grants or other subsidies, and do not include institutional costs. Then, as indicated earlier, the private rate of return is that rate that equates the discounted present value of the college additions to earnings to these private costs. The earnings should be after taxes so that the benefits are purely private, but frequently as later below in the PURE study the before tax earnings are used. Doing so then forces the social rate to be lower than the private rate since the costs in the denominator for the social rate include subsidized institutional costs and the public costs of student aid. Since the true total social rate of return includes the non-market returns beyond earnings, these can be added to earnings and to the narrow social rate since the costs of producing these returns, which are in the denominator, for the benefit/cost calculation is the same for both the market and the non-market returns.

STANDARD SOCIAL RATES OF RETURN IN THE UNITED STATES

The narrow social rates of return based on earnings for those who complete two-year associate degrees in the United States are a high 16%, as shown in Figure 3.10. They are up from 11% in 1995. This compares to a 10% rate of return for high school graduates, which has been flat or falling slowly since 1995. In fact, when the shifts in cross-sectional age-earnings profiles are taken into account, as they must be, the resulting "dynamic" rates of return for completion of four years of high school has fallen from 12.56% in 1967 for males to 10.23% in 1995 (Arias and McMahon, 2001, pp. 133–34)! Compared to those who drop out after tenth grade, Heckman et al. (2008, Table 2a and Figure 2) find that the private rate of return for white males who finish high school has risen from 20% or so in 1967 to 52% in 2000. This indicates that both preventing high school dropouts and completion of an associate degree are very good investments. For public tax funds they yield a better return than the 10% or so in real terms that the taxpayer could earn on average on alter-

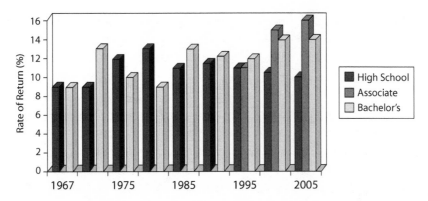

Figure 3.10. Rates of return to investment in secondary and higher education in the United States. *Sources:* Data for 1967–85 is from McMahon (1991, p. 287); data for 1990 is from Arias and McMahon (2001, p. 134); and data for 1995–2005 is based on new calculations by the same "full" method based on U.S. Census Current Population Surveys (2006). The U.S. Census only began reporting earnings of associate degree holders separately in 1991.

native uses of the taxed funds. Similarly, it is a good investment for the family since the private returns on alternative investments of their funds in stock mutual funds over the long run, for example, is close to 10% in real terms. In savings accounts or CDs, their return would be a lower 3 to 5% after subtracting the inflation rate. The 16% real social rate of return for completing an associate degree when computed by the full method is lower than the private rate of return since if the student has a Pell Grant or other scholarship, the latter lower the costs to the family, which are in the denominator. Private rates are lower for twelve to fourteen years when completion of an associate degree is not a criterion, as in Heckman et al. (2008). The 16% still understates the true social return because it is based only on earnings and does not include any non-market private or social benefits.

At the bachelor's degree level the social rates of return for males and females average 12% in real terms. This is up from 9% in 1967 and 1980 to 12% in 1995 and 12% in 2005–6, as shown in Figure 3.10. Compared to the standard 10% benchmark, this is a high real return that also underestimates the true return, which would include both the continuing upward shifts in the cross-sectional age-earnings profile for college graduates (that adds about 3 percentage points) as well as non-market benefits beyond earnings. The benchmark average total return *after correction for inflation* normally used for such comparisons again is 10%, the average return on longer-term investments representing roughly comparable risk.

Social rates of return change only very gradually over time. This is because the new graduates each year affect only earnings in the first few years of the lifecycle and do not affect earnings in cross-section data, which includes many earners who are farther along over the entire forty-five years in their lifecycles before retirement. Starting salaries are very misleading because they reflect transitory cyclical factors. But long-term trends of increased earnings do gradually raise rates of return, and a long-term decline would operate eventually to lower rates. Continuing secular declines in the demand for those with a high school education or less, as well as even sharper declines in the 1980 recession, for example, are lowering social rates of return at the secondary level, and this combined with the secular rising real earnings for college graduates leads to continuing increases in the social rates of return for two- and four-year college graduates in spite of temporary fluctuations and the rising institutional costs.*

INTERNATIONAL COMPARISONS OF HIGHER EDUCATION
RATES OF RETURN

Other developed countries close to the technology frontier have the capacity to retain highly educated workers. In these countries the rates of return to investment in higher education are also relatively high and rising, al-

---

*Analysis of human capital policy by Carneiro and Heckman (2003) has not taken into account the decline in demand for the lower-skilled workers and the rising demand for higher-skilled workers that is causing the rates of return on investment at the college level to be higher. Focusing on the costs, and the lower forgone earnings costs at primary and preschool levels, they stress that the returns to investment at the lower levels of education is the most advantageous. This is true as far as it goes, and there should be greater attention to these very young education levels (see Carneiro and Heckman, 2003, pp. 7–8). But before arriving at wider policy prescriptions than that, the rising demand for highly skilled college educated workers in the industrialized countries needs to be considered. Where there is essentially universal basic education, as in the United States and the OECD countries, there is almost a fixed constraint on further expansion of primary education, for example. This is not true in Africa or South Asia, however. Carneiro and Heckman do recognize that final policy conclusions must consider the current level of public investment in basic education, as well as the spillover social benefits (2003, p. 10).

though they generally are not as high as in the United States and there is some brain drain. In most continental European Union countries tuition is lower and most institutional costs are covered by the government, although some additional cost sharing is a trend (Johnstone, 2004). This heavy dependence on tax sources means that the total resources per student that are available are smaller, there is a growing sense of austerity in higher education, admissions to the more elite public institutions are more restricted, and a growing private sector is picking up some of the slack and the overall result does not serve the needs of the economy as well. Psacharopoulos (2005) suggests that lower expenditure per student is accompanied by more central control, and that both of these contribute to lower quality.

An exception is the Nordic countries, the Netherlands, and Denmark, where the public share at the more elite institutions is high and admission is more restricted, which maintains high quality. But many graduates enter public service jobs and the standard social rates of return tend to be lower. Apart from this, the farther a nation or region is from the technology frontier, as in the ex-Soviet eastern bloc, the lower are its salaries for educated workers and the larger the brain drain due to emigration (Aghion et al., 2005). So although OECD labor markets are experiencing technology impacts similar to those in the United States, the social rates of return for higher education are somewhat lower, but generally higher in the more advanced European Union countries.

STANDARD SOCIAL RATES OF RETURN IN OECD COUNTRIES

Psacharopoulos and Patrinos report social rates of return for higher education worldwide computed by the full method (Psacharopoulos and Patrinos, 2004, Table 1A.1 and 1A.7). They are therefore more comparable to the social rates of return for the United States. This sometimes includes postgraduate degree programs where the standard narrow social rates of return everywhere are lower. As illustrated in Figure 3.11, they find 13.5% for Spain (1998), 6.5% for the United Kingdom (1998), 7.8% for Denmark (1994), 5.5% for the Netherlands, 13.4% for Japan (1994), 16.3% for Australia (1994), 15.5% for South Korea, and a lower 5.5 to 9.2% for the Scandinavian countries (1994). They report no computations of social rates of return for France or Germany. However, the private rates

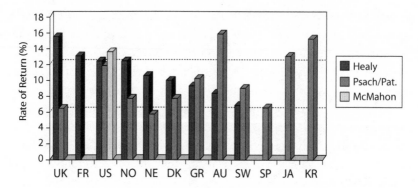

Figure 3.11. Social rates of return to investment in higher education in OECD countries. *Sources:* Data from Psacharopoulos and Patrinos (2004, Table A1); Healy and Istance (1998, Table A4.3); and Ryoo et al. (1993).

of return to private investment in higher education are a very high 20% in France, reflecting the high tuition subsidies there, and 10.5% in Germany. They report low social rates of return of 5.7% in Greece, but the higher education system is over-expanded with free tuition, low expenditure per student, and problems with morale. A low social rate of return indicates that the net returns are low and suggests a need to improve policies encouraging efficiency before there is additional new investment.

In another extensive study of standard social rates of return in the OECD countries computed by the same methods, Healy and Istance (1998, p. 113) report estimates for some but not all of the above countries. They report social rates of return for investment in a university education in 1995 averaged for males and females computed by the full method as shown on the left bar for each country in Figure 3.10. They are 15.9% for the United Kingdom, 12.6% for the United States, 10.1% for Denmark, 8.6% for Australia, 12.5% for Norway, 10.7% for the Netherlands, 9.5% for Germany, 13.4% for France, and 6.8% for Sweden.*

Where the earnings of higher education graduates are trending upward, the longitudinal earnings data will produce higher rates of return than those shown above computed from cross-section data. Arias and Mc-

---

*Their social rates of return for Portugal are so high (27.7% for a university education) that I have not included them in Figure 3.10.

Mahon (2001) compute social rates for the United States that take these trends into account. This point is developed again by Heckman et al. (2008). When this is done, rates of return at the college level are about 3 percentage points higher than those shown, whereas high school rates of return are about the same or a bit lower. That is, as technology and globalization trends continue, as graduates approach, say, age forty-five, their earnings will be higher in real terms than the earnings reported by persons age forty-five today that appear in the standard cross-sectional data. Therefore, assuming these current technology and globalization trends continue, which seems likely, the social rates of return shown in Figure 3.11 are conservative, and the true narrow social rates of return are about 3 percentage points above those shown. But these still do not include the non-market benefits from higher education beyond earnings.

PRIVATE RATES OF RETURN

Rates of return have also been computed for the OECD PURE study and are shown in Figure 3.12 (PURE, 2001, p. 80). The problem, however, is that they are not comparable to the above because they are *average* rates

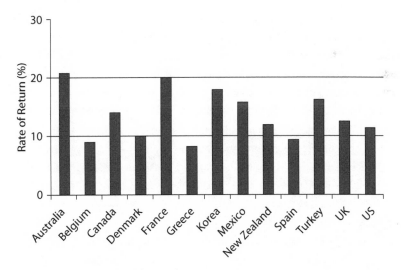

Figure 3.12. Private rates of return to investment in higher education in OECD countries.

of return over all education levels and apply to the twelve years of education received by the average person. They are not marginal rates specific to higher education. They are also *private* rates of return, and do not take institutional costs into account. They can be expected to be, and are, higher for those countries where higher education is heavily subsidized and tuition is especially low, such as Australia and France as seen in Figure 3.12. Nevertheless, they range from 4% in Sweden to 12 to 14% in the United Kingdom and Ireland (see PURE, 2001).

Figure 3.12 suggests that the incentives provided to students for going on to college coming not just from the job market but also from public subsidies to higher education are strongest in Australia, France, and South Korea. The incentives provided by the private rates are not quite as strong in the United States or the United Kingdom. This is true even though the recent evidence on social rates of return is that the social rates are high and the growth benefits from additional public investment in higher education are also relatively high in the United States and the United Kingdom.

Higher Education and Growth: The Evidence from Macro-Data

In the worldwide economy the technologically advanced nations, firms, and research institutions lead with the creation of new knowledge at the frontiers. They do this primarily through their investment in R&D, not just at the universities but also elsewhere in research that faculty at the research universities are in touch with, and through human capital formation and acquisition of graduates at the more advanced master's and PhD levels. The leading firms and universities are able to invest in new research and pay very well to retain the most skilled individuals. These aspects are central to Romer's (1990) endogenous growth model. I will also address them further in Chapter 6, which deals with the interdependence between university-based research and graduate education as they relate to growth and development.

This, however, sets up a race between the new technology, which makes some of the existing human capital obsolete, and forces the follower firms and members of the population to proceed at a heightened pace to acquire the skills necessary to keep up. In terms of the empirical size of the impact of new technology versus its diffusion, it is almost certainly the diffusion of the new knowledge through human capital formation that has by far the greatest impacts. Discoveries of 150 years ago, such as the steam engine or bicycle-trailers, still have not penetrated most of rural Africa, where over 80% of the population live, many of whom are illiterate. With few exceptions, new discoveries in microbiology or computer design, for example, that are published in advanced journals cannot be accessed, adapted, or applied given the complexity of modern technology without very considerable education and training (Benhabib and Spiegel, 2006). Largely because of lags and inadequacies in this diffusion of knowledge, which the Lucas (1988) endogenous growth model features, the rich countries are getting richer while the poor countries fall ever farther behind. Similarly, college graduates in the rich countries are doing very well while those with a high school education or less are increasingly excluded economically and socially. Although human capital formation and its role in the diffusion of knowledge is the focus of the Lucas endogenous growth model, the Lucas and Romer models make clear that education is central to knowledge-based growth and both make explicit provision for the very important role of education externalities.

This is not to say that education, or even education linked with R&D, is the only cause of economic growth in the logic of the growth process. Other institutions also contribute. But institutions such as democratization, the rule of law, and political stability are themselves heavily dependent on education becoming more widespread. These other institutions reflect education externalities (see Glaeser et al., 2004; McMahon, 2002, 2007a). Free trade and trade openness, when put into growth equations, are also found empirically to be determinants of economic growth after including investment in physical and human capital formation and in R&D. But success in an export-oriented growth strategy after a country passes the undeveloped stage of having only raw material and cheap labor exports is well known to be a function of human capital formed through education (Wood, 1994). To this extent exports are also ultimately dependent on education and therefore another instance of an education externality. Even physical capital investment as a percent of gross domestic product (GDP), and the fertility rate and hence the control of excessive population growth that retards Africa, are both significantly affected by education. So even these sources of per capita growth can be interpreted as reflecting education externalities.*

THE EMPIRICAL EVIDENCE

In the theoretical endogenous growth models, higher education is central to both the creation of new technology and its diffusion, and generates externalities, all of which are central to the growth process. In the microeconomic data, much the same story of relatively high narrow social rates of return and hence significant contributions of these investments to growth emerges. This much is generally not disputed. But the evidence based on macroeconomic data is much more mixed. Empirical studies that eliminate the impacts of embodied technologies and indirect effects and do not control for external shocks generally find that the evidence in macro-data for education and education externalities affecting growth is limited (Pritchett, 2006; Lange and Topel, 2006). Those that consider the dynamic process and indirect effects generally find much more significant effects in the macro-data from education and education externalities (Keller 2006a, 2006b; Jamison et al., 2007; McMahon, 1998d).

Anecdotally, in the United States the GI Bill in the late 1940s following World War II led to a major surge of investment in higher education. This has been widely regarded as contributing very substantially to the major surge of economic growth that occurred in the 1960s. But there were also other policies involved and the sample is small. In cross-country panel data for the developed countries we see that basic education as well as higher education contribute significantly to growth. However, in developing countries, although some higher education is essential, too much investment in higher education can detract from growth. For one thing,

---

*Other common policies designed to encourage economic growth include special tax breaks. These are offered to induce firms to locate locally. They have been very successful for some tax shelters such as Luxembourg and Andorra. But for states within the United States they invite countermeasures by other states. So the effectiveness of tax breaks from the point of view of the nation as a whole cancel out. They also can result in subsidizing producers that are less efficient in competing by other means. However, as one country or one state increases their investment in education, it is less likely that other states will retaliate since they are not hurt. Other states may even benefit because fewer persons with inadequate skills emigrate to larger cities in the other states, and because the states increasing their investment in education have rising per capita income and become better trading partners.

higher education is more conducive to out-migration. Krueger and Lindahl (2001, p. 1130), for example, conclude that "[overall], education . . . is positively associated with subsequent growth only for countries with the lowest level of education." But they do not clearly distinguish between basic education, which is well known to be very important for growth in the poorer countries, and higher education. The expansion of higher education is likely to be more important in developed countries because they are closer to the technological frontier where there is the strongest market for high skills and little emigration, and because basic education there is nearly universal. But Pritchett concludes that investment in higher education even in developed countries has a dubious impact (Pritchett, 2000, 2006). Pritchett's study, however, includes dummy variables for time, which largely exclude higher education's role in the diffusion of technology. He and others he cites use controls for trade, democratization, and fertility that include indirect effects from education that feed back positive effects on growth over time if allowed to do so.

Evidence for the Developed Countries. Among the studies that find significant effects from higher education on growth in developed countries, Keller (2006a, 2006b) explains per capita growth based on panel data for 1960–2000. She uses gross enrollment rates lagged ten years as a measure of additional education inputs. Enrollment data is not perfect and contains some measurement error as Krueger and Lindahl (2001) point out. But data on educational attainment is not perfect either, and gross enrollments include the effects from the embodiment of technology in the 65% or so of the graduates who replace those in the labor force who are retiring. She includes rates of investment in physical capital as a percent of GDP and controls for trade openness, democratization for fixed effects, and uses individual country dummies to control for culture and ethnicity (ibid., Models 4–8, Table 8). There then is a side analysis of indirect effects of education through trade, democratization, and other growth determinants. Her results show that increased higher education enrollment rates after ten years have a positive and highly significant relation to ten-year per capita growth rates (Models 5–7, Table 8, $R^2 = 0.49$–0.63). Increased secondary education enrollment also has a significant positive short-term effect on growth in the developed countries, although the coefficient for secondary education (0.02) is smaller than her coefficient for higher education (0.10) and not as highly significant.

Evidence for the U.S. States. There is other evidence based on data for U.S. states. Moomaw et al. (2002) find that investment in education as a percent of gross state product (GSP) is a highly significant determinant of per capita real growth for 1977–97. They include investment in physical capital as a percent of GSP. But they had to estimate the latter by allocating nationwide gross private domestic investment to each state based on *the state's in-place capital stock* since state-level data on investment in physical capital does not exist. They use five-year periods, so four periods for each state times 50 states means n = 200. They also control for lagged per capita income. The negative coefficient they obtain for the latter in their Table 4 reveals *conditional* convergence, even though the absolute gap between the rich states and the poor states is widening. The implication is that the poor states could catch up, but it is conditional on them pursuing appropriate policies such as increased investment in education, among other things, in the growth equation (McMahon, 2007a). Moomaw et al. control for state-level fixed effects, which they say account for a large part of the total variation (Table 1). In Table 2, $R^2 = 0.63$ and the coefficient for investment in education as a percent of GSP is a highly significant determinant of growth (with t = 7.2–7.9). The relation of investment in physical capital to growth is negative, however. This is quite possibly the rust belt effect, in that it is really the existing stock of physical capital that is being measured, and not new investment. Their variables are in logs so a 1% increase in investment in education as a percent of GSP is interpreted as a 0.8% to 0.9% increase in per capita growth. This suggests a very substantial impact. Other evidence supporting the positive effect of education on per capita income and growth based on panel data for U.S. states is in Roenker and Thompson (2003) and Bhatta and Lobo (2000).

Evidence Concerning Levels as Well as Growth Impacts. Returning to studies of growth, based on a panel of cross-country data for 1960–2000 for sixty-two countries, including all of the most developed countries, Jamison et al. (2007, Table 5) find a positive and highly significant relation of the level of education (educational attainment) to the level of per capita income. The undefined technology component over and above the contributions of physical and human capital stock to the level of per capita income is then shown to be related to the quality of education. The latter is measured by math test scores. The argument is that this as well as openness in trade then contribute to the diffusion of technology and the capacity to innovate and hence to economic growth. So the total contribution of education composed of its quantity and also its quality to the level of per capita income plus to the growth of per capita income is very substantial. So theirs is really a dynamic context since it allows for education's role in the diffusion of technology over time. The less significant effects from education on growth found by Pritchett (2006) are under conditions where this role of education is excluded.

Evidence Relating to the Diffusion of Technology. To explore the dynamic feedbacks on growth from the indirect feedback effects over time, a growth equation estimated for OECD countries is used to simulate the effects of changes in education investment for the ten states in the U.S. Deep South (McMahon, 2007b). Using starting positions determined by the data for all variables specific to each state, modest increases in investment in education above what they would otherwise be are used to boost gross enrollment rates. After a lag, this has a net effect of increasing per capita income in these states that is above and beyond the effect of other factors. The states that pursue this policy catch up with where the U.S. average is by 2040. This is a demonstration of conditional convergence, and suggests the importance of education policy to growth and development. The simulations incorporate the indirect effects from education as they set the stage for each new round of growth.

One qualification to this result must be mentioned, however. The model's predictions depend on the states in question employing policies that will increase enrollment rates. This includes increasing need-based financial aid that often also involves a merit criterion or increasing institutional support that lowers tuition and fees. Studies show that purely merit-based student financial aid with no need criterion does not increase statewide college enrollment rates because the recipients of merit aid generally will attend college anyway (Cornwell et al., 2003). State student financial aid in Louisiana, Mississippi, Georgia, and a growing number of other states is purely merit based. Although this helps maintain middle- and upper-class support for publicly supported financial aid, policies that increase enrollment rates such as increased institutional support or the addition of perhaps a more widely defined need criterion to purely merit-based aid would be necessary to obtain the effects predicted by the model on economic growth and development. This suggests that the relevance of higher education policy to growth also depends on how that policy is designed.

Another perspective on the effectiveness of technology diffusion through human capital formation is offered by Aghion et al. (2005), as was mentioned in the introduction. They study higher education's effect on growth based on data for the forty-eight continental U.S. states for 1947–2005, and whether investing in graduate education at research universities or investment in, say, expanding two-year community college enrollments is more advantageous. They measure a state's investment in education by investment expenditure on education as a percent of the state budget, and second by educational attainment, which is a measure of the stock of human capital, not a flow of additions to the stock. Neither distinguishes investments in education by level of education. But this problem is somewhat reduced by the fact that given their focus on investment in undergraduate versus graduate levels, the total education budget that states allocate incorporates the difference in cost among levels.

Aghion et al. find that "people with research degrees are particularly prone to migrate," whereas "increases in four-year and two-year college spending have a statistically significant effect on a state's number of residents with baccalaureate degrees and lower postsecondary attainment" (ibid., pp. 34–35). That is, undergraduates largely remain in the state where they get their degrees, whereas postgraduate degree holders do not. Based on this they find that additional education spending for postgraduate master's, PhD, and professional degrees and the more expensive four-year college degrees is more growth enhancing for states that are at the technological frontier, which they define as the highest per capita income states since this is where most of the higher-paying jobs are for these advanced graduates. They find further that investment in two- and four-year college degree programs is more growth enhancing for states that are farther from the technological frontier, which they define as the middle and lower per capita income states (ibid., p. 39). That is, research-level and best quality baccalaureate education are useful for innovating; lower cost per student two- and four-year postsecondary education is useful for imitating.

In terms of growth impacts, for states farther from the technological frontier, Aghion et al. find that each additional thousand dollars per person of additional education spending on postgraduate degree programs raises the state's per capita growth rate by only 0.093 percentage points, whereas the same amount of additional spending on undergraduate four-year college degrees raises the state's per employee growth rate by 0.198 percentage points. Spending this same amount on two-year college degrees raises the state's per employee growth by a dramatic 0.474 percentage points. That is, there is a tremendous economic advantage for the poorer states if they concentrate their limited resources on two- and -four-year degree programs. For the highest per capita income states at the technological frontier, investment in higher education at the graduate level is relatively much more productive. There a thousand dollars of additional spending at the postgraduate level raise the state's per capita growth rate by 0.269 percentage points, much higher than the 0.093 in poorer states.

Higher education's role in facilitating innovation at the technological frontier and in dissemination of the technology and new knowledge among those in the race seeking to keep up is a fascinating subject. I will explore it further in Chapter 6 on the relation of investment in research and embodiment of its results through graduate education, which in turn becomes a major vehicle for the diffusion of the new knowledge essential to development.

Over-Education?

If investment in higher education and research are to be increased to support economic growth and development, the issue raised by skeptics who suggest that there is "over-education" in the labor force, or at least in some parts of it, must be addressed. This comes from those using the "manpower requirements" approach but also stressing the screening hypothesis, which suggests that human capital is not productive.

MANPOWER REQUIREMENTS AND OVER-EDUCATION

The basic concept of over-education in the manpower requirements approach starts by defining the education requirements for each type of job. A farmer needs to have only a certain education level to perform her or his role adequately, a janitor another, a truck or bus driver another. Although most who engage in manpower requirements planning do seek to allow for the changing educational requirements as technological change occurs, the basic fact is that the education level demanded by the market in each and every occupation has risen continually and at a rate that is very difficult to predict. Janitors were normally illiterate early in the history of the United States and European Union countries, and still are in the poor less developed countries. But in the United States now they are called building custodians, and most have high school and even college degrees. They can do many things in maintaining and protecting buildings that the illiterates before them could not do, can see what needs to be done and do it on their own, and have more responsibility and more equipment to operate and maintain. Hence, they are more productive. Each four-story building has one custodian at most, and no longer has ten janitors, many sitting around not knowing what to do, as is very common in the poor countries. The same is true for truck drivers, bus drivers, and those who deliver express letters and parcels. More education allows them to be more productive with capacities to perform accounting functions, operate complex computerized technologies, use mobile phones to communicate with their offices and save time, and, in the case of bus and truck drivers, relate to bus passengers and freight customers. Each now tends to have a dramatically better education than runners and teamsters had historically.

The U.S. Bureau of Labor Statistics estimates the education level typical of each job category, with results such as those shown earlier in this chapter. This procedure is very useful in studying current job markets and the directions of trends in the demands and supplies of broader types and levels of skills. It is also useful in the broad planning of capital investments, such as for the building of teacher training institutions or hospitals. Here demographic trends are known and longer-term planning is essential. But it is misleading and almost useless when applied to narrowly defined occupations such as individual types of engineers or other narrowly defined manpower requirements. These applications ignore the response of students in selecting their majors, and shifting from one field to another while in college in response to the earnings and jobs available, which are the much more close-in market signals. The latter are much more efficient than central planning using manpower requirements, as was typical of the Soviet bloc countries and is still fairly widely used today in some developing countries such as South Korea. Such requirements make little provision for substitution, not just before graduation but also after graduation, where the average graduate now changes jobs and sometimes even moves into related fields several times during his or her career.

Rising educational requirements over time due partly to changing technology are very obvious not just for custodians and bus, truck, and delivery drivers but for also for farmers. Farmers to be successful must now know how to buy, operate, and maintain very complex machinery; operate global positioning systems while applying fertilizer in the right mix for each spot; know soil and plant biology; know about health care and nutrition for their animals; operate on futures markets; apply sophisticated bookkeeping and tax accounting computer software; and know how to market their products in response to world prices. The education levels and skills that teachers need to have also have increased dramatically and continue to increase as time passes. In graduate schools the number of published articles required of new PhDs and faculty has risen sharply, and each new MD has massive amounts of new research and technology to master that were not required of patient-friendly, homeopathic physicians who made home visits. A manpower requirements planning approach has great difficulty in predicting over longer periods of time the impacts of new technology and the changing supplies and demands within each narrowly defined occupation with any precision. Nevertheless, the manpower requirements approach predicting over-education still occupies a niche in the academic literature. It seems better to calculate the rates of return, and then to recalculate them later as demands and supplies change. It is difficult to take into account the changing productivity of human capital as job demands respond to changing technologies, and analyses that attempt to predict based on unchanging education requirements can be misleading, as in Rothstein (2002).

THE SCREENING HYPOTHESIS AND OVER-EDUCATION

The screening hypothesis, and its variant the "diploma disease" hypothesis, suggest that human capital is not productive. They instead propose that it is screening for the innate ability of the individual, or in the case of the diploma disease the reputation of the college and its old-boy network, that leads to better salaries after graduation and not the productivity of skills acquired while in school. Nobody denies that these effects can operate in isolated instances. It is instead whether they have much empirical relevance to the broader scope of the main things that occur in schools and colleges that is at issue. If human capital is not productive, then there are cheaper ways to do screening than the billions invested in colleges.

A key conceptual point is that *employers will not continue to pay for additional educational qualifications if the knowledge purchased is unproductive.* Some taxi drivers are very bright, but they do not have the necessary skills to be effective in sophisticated occupations. Employers are better close-in judges of the marginal revenue productivity of the workers they hire, and could give cheap tests to taxi drivers if it were only IQ that they were buying. A diploma or a degree also is not just a school label but also indicates that the student has completed courses in the field in which he or she is graduating with a sufficient level of understanding indicated by a passing grade point average. Therefore, he or she has more human capital than those who drop out, or than those who went to colleges of lower quality. Coming to the conclusion of over-education based on either of these hypotheses requires some downplaying of how employers actually behave.

It is not just in the United States but also in the United Kingdom and European Union that the issue of over-education is brought forward by the skeptics. They maintain that education provides only for screening, sorting, and sifting rather than creating human capital that is productive. Some screening for innate ability, of course, occurs at the PhD level and in selecting entrants to medical schools. But this is far less relevant for the higher education system as a whole, or for most of higher education, which is at the two- and four-year undergraduate levels. That higher education does not create productive skills is also unbelievable for any who have tried to read a typical PhD dissertation in, say, microbiology, mathematics, or economics, or to review National Science Foundation Grants, or to read National Cancer Institute research studies that oncologists must read. One U.K. study designed to test this screening hypotheses by persons who thought screening was a good hypothesis concludes that the "data did not confirm the predicted negative relationship between schooling and innovation or creativity in the workplace" (Little and Singh, 1992, pp. 197–98). Nevertheless, screening may be a more prominent feature of the British system, with its eleven-plus exam and the education system's stronger emphasis on tracking. But it is very hard to believe that even those with very limited ability do not have the quality of their life improved by learning productive skills. Much wider access to higher education in the United Kingdom since the Robbins Report suggests that its significance is also less at these levels.

In the United States, at the postsecondary level, different types of higher education institutions clearly have different roles and missions. In the United States most states now seek to guarantee all high school graduates access to some higher educational institution. So screening for admission to higher education in general is irrelevant. Rank in the high school class does have an effect on which institution the high school graduate can attend. And once in college, whether it be two- or four-year, academic grades act as a major incentive for students to study, to work hard, to learn, and to develop human capital. Grades for the purpose of selecting those with innate ability normally have a relatively minor role for most of a child's career from primary school through two or even four years of college. From this point of view the assessment function assesses how much human capital each student possesses and allocates students among institutions or among jobs later based on this. Only very rarely at undergraduate levels in the United States at least are students screened completely out of the system. The main logical argument against the screening hypothesis, however, remains that few employers are likely to be so out of touch with their own bottom line that they continue to pay higher wages after an initial trial period to those with a college degree, including a PhD, even though they are unproductive.

VOCATIONALISM AND OVER-EDUCATION

In the United States the over-education argument has recently been linked to the complaint that higher education has become prone to excessive vocationalism, producing too many narrowly educated vocationally oriented graduates. One implication is that there should be a larger liberal arts and public interest role (Grubb and Lazerson, 2004). This is a serious problem and consistent with the analysis of the social benefits of higher education I present in Chapter 5. But to say that excessive vocationalism constitutes over-education even though employers are willing to pay for these graduates, and without estimating the value of the social benefits is a non sequitur.

This is not to say that there are not instances of over-education that involve producing too many graduates. This happens at PhD levels in a few fields, and in particular geographical areas following economic shocks. For example, in Silicon Valley after the high-tech bubble burst in 2000 many PhDs were left unemployed. But this was transitory and mobility and economic recovery have gradually taken care of this. There is also the possibility of localized over-education within specific vocations, as suggested by the anecdotal evidence offered by Rothstein (2002, pp. 1–6). The first job of each graduate may not be as closely related to the graduate's major as one might hope, especially in liberal arts. But this first job is very seldom the final one, and liberal arts majors with a broader background are more able to adapt to where the jobs are. It is the job five to seven years later that is much more indicative of the graduate's permanent age-earnings profile.

Formal education is well known to increase the chances of selection by the employer for additional on-the-job training (Mincer, 1962). This reduces the seriousness of any disconnects between the majors selected by graduates and employers' needs. But overall, in spite of some localized over-education and under-education in specific job markets, it is very hard to escape the fact that the overall demand for higher-skilled workers is rising faster than the supply. This basic trend is apparent both in the United States and in the European Union (PURE, 2001).

JOB MARKET SIGNALING AND THE EMPIRICAL EVIDENCE

The job market signaling model traces its roots to Spence (1973). His model emphasizes not so much the activities of schools and colleges as it does equilibrium in the labor market. His model has positive returns to schooling absent any productivity effects of schooling. In this sense it is the same as signaling and the diploma disease in that they all imply that education is wasteful and therefore that there is over-education. In Lange and Topel's (2006) review of the extensive literature that this has generated, they conclude that "there are few convincing tests of job market signaling. (There is) even less evidence that allows us to quantify the contribution of human capital relative to job market signaling" (ibid., p. 488). They conducted some very extensive tests of their own. They note that "in the US between 1940 and 2000 aggregate measures of human capital are highly correlated with productivity . . . This strong positive link between productivity and education is problematic for adherents of the Job Market Signaling model . . . our review of the available empirical evidence on Job Market Signaling leads us to conclude that there is little in the data that supports Job Market Signaling as an explanation of the observed returns to schooling" (ibid, pp. 504–5).

CONCLUSION: OVER-EDUCATION AND THE SKEPTICS

There is little or no basis for concluding based on manpower requirements planning, screening, diploma disease, or job market signaling hypotheses that overall over-education exists. The increasing education of custodians, bus drivers, express delivery persons, farmers, teachers, doctors, faculty, researchers, and others is not over-education. Instead, it is the higher productivity of the human capital skills embodying the new technologies that raises the demand for these skills in relation to their supply as their productivity is recognized by employers and the market. A mechanistic assigning of manpower requirements for narrow degree specializations or occupational categories for more than a few years also can be and is misleading. The screening, diploma disease, and signaling hypotheses all deny the productivity of human capital; exaggeration of the scope to which they apply cannot be supported by the evidence. The prediction of over-education, if carried beyond isolated instances, is debatable at best.

Instead, the evidence suggests that new technology created by investment in R&D and embodied in human capital through higher education is highly productive and commands a premium on the job market as a result. The effects from new technology or knowledge and the effect from the human capital formation cannot be cleanly separated (Griliches, 2000). The evidence suggests that the process of embodiment of technology through human capital formation is vital to the diffusion of the technology and hence to economic growth (Phelps, 1962; Griliches, 2000; McMahon, 1991, 2007a; Keller, 2006a, 2006b; Heckman et al., 2008).

Conclusions

There are significant increases in the earnings of college graduates over those of high school graduates of the same age and sex that persist throughout their lifecycles. These increments have been growing very significantly since 1980. They are amounts that cannot be attributed to differences in innate ability (see Appendix A). They also cannot be attributed to screening or job market signaling. Employers are unlikely to continue to pay for diploma or screening effects that do not convey the presence of productive human capital. And there is no empirical evidence for job market signaling that also implies that schooling is unproductive that stands up. Suggestions that there is over-education based on manpower requirements planning which do not adequately take into account the increasing productivity of human capital as technology advances and the increasing educational requirements in each occupation are also debatable at best.

The micro-data for individual earnings strongly suggests a major contribution by investment in higher education to economic growth. Beyond this there is a huge skill deficit as revealed by the higher current and expected growth in jobs that require two- or four-year college degrees or more. In the United States the earnings of college graduates have grown by 48% since 1980 in real terms while the earnings of high school graduates have remained flat. Also very important is the fact that the narrow social rates of return for associate degree graduates of 16% and for four-year college graduates of 14% as well as the high returns for reducing high school dropouts are well above the 10% available on alternative investments. These are all in real terms, and there is clear evidence that this type of investment has a substantial growth payoff. The rates of return to postsecondary education also take rising institutional costs into account, and offer strong evidence that conclusions by some that there is over-education based only on rising college costs are badly misguided. In fact, the true narrow social rates of returns are about 3 percentage points above those just cited when the upward shifts in the standard cross-section age-earnings profiles of college graduates are taken into account.

The evidence on the relation of investment in higher education to growth in the United States and other developed OECD countries is harder to interpret, but with care it becomes more clear. A few researchers have imposed controls that eliminate the interaction between higher education and technology as well as the indirect effects of education on growth. Largely as a result of this, they find few or no effects from higher education on growth, and few or no externalities. But once the interaction between higher education and technology is included, along with the indirect effects from education on growth, more robust relations between higher education and growth appear in the data for the United States and other developed OECD countries.

Europe invests only about one-third of what the United States does in higher education and until 2007 was growing more slowly. But this is partly due to an aging population (see Appendix D), and partly due to lower total investment because tuition is more highly subsidized and public support through taxes is hard to come by. That is, with less cost sharing with parents and less need-based grant aid higher education has less per student and is more austere. In the United States the ten southern states invest less in education and also have been growing more slowly (except Florida, which attracts retirees). Studies suggest that increasing enrollments in two- and four-year degree programs would help the most. But states such as Louisiana, Mississippi, and Georgia that now do not attach a broadly defined need-criterion to their merit-based grants do not increase statewide enrollment very significantly with their merit-based programs and it is very hard to show that these programs aid growth. Studies also suggest that higher-income states gain somewhat more from investment in graduate programs, assuming that there are job markets that encourage graduates to locate there.

This chapter has focused on the relation of higher education to jobs, earnings, and growth. There are, however, many private non-market benefits to individuals and substantial social benefits to the society and future generations from investment in higher education. So narrow social rates of return must be corrected to approach true social rates of return as the value of the private and social non-market benefits are addressed in the chapters that follow.

CHAPTER FOUR

Private Non-Market Benefits of Higher Education and Market Failure

There is no education that is just for earning a living; it is also for living a life.

W. E. B. DUBOIS (1973, P. 84)

HIGHER EDUCATION has become so expensive to students, their families, and governments that it has become essential to articulate what they are getting for their investment. An important part of these benefits are private non-market benefits that positively affect each graduate's quality of life in ways other than just income. These are to be sharply distinguished from social benefits, which spill over to benefit others in the society other than just the graduate in question and that contribute to the greater good. But to place an economic value on social benefits, it is also necessary to estimate the economic value of the private non-market benefits since some indirect effects feed back and increase these private non-market benefits for others later. These indirect effects are part of the social benefits I will discuss in Chapter 5.

Private non-market benefits are generated as the graduate uses his or her human capital during the seventy-two hours or so each week that he or she is not at work or sleeping and is therefore time spent at home and in the community. The productivity of this time is increased by higher education with the result that there are benefits to the individual's private well-being as well as benefits to others in the community and future generations. These very important products of higher education are often overlooked because they are poorly understood. And yet they can be measured, and are vital to improving the quality of the individual's life throughout his or her lifecycle, including the value of time after retirement. They are benefits that must be measured in a way that controls for income so that they are truly benefits other than income, especially if the measures that result are to be relevant to higher education policy. They include better own-health as measured by health status, greater longevity, better-educated and healthier children, smaller families with less poverty, increased probability of having a college-educated spouse, and greater happiness. All of these things now can be measured. With respect to happiness, for example, psychologists have devised effective ways to obtain cardinal measures of brain waves, which increase in intensity in response to enjoyment and positive satisfactions. This is a cardinal, not ordinal, measure. Based on this, economists find that happiness increases with income but only up to about $20,000 per capita, which means up to $80,000 for a family of four. Education obviously contributes to income, and through this to happiness up to these levels. But the evidence is weaker that education contributes further to happiness beyond this income level.

I refer to these as the non-market private benefits from education because this is the way they are known in the research literature. Their value can be measured by techniques developed by Haveman and Wolfe (1984, 2007), Wolfe and Zuvekas (1997), and Wolfe and Haveman (2001, 2003). The process is laborious because the effect of education on the quantity of each non-market outcome first has to be determined, then the value of this has to be measured, and then all the individual values have to be added up. The values are legitimate measures of how much the typical individual would pay for the health or other non-market benefit, that is, their income equivalent value, and directly comparable to the estimates of the net earnings benefits.

The best prior estimates by Haveman and Wolfe are that the total value of these non-market benefits is equal to or greater than the value of the market benefits. Grossman and Kaestner (1997) and Grossman (2006) estimate that the education benefits to health and longevity alone are equal to or greater than the benefits of education to income. Some of these benefits come from basic education, but most continue to increase as the result of years spent in college. Based on these thoughtful estimates by others, it follows that if the value of the non-market benefits of higher education is equal to the market benefits, then the total return on investment in higher education is about twice the standard narrow rates of return based on earnings alone. If the narrow rates of return are used by families and governments when deciding whether or not to invest, then they underestimate the true return and there is underinvestment.

But there is a more basic reason for considering what these private non-market benefits from higher education are. There is evidence that public information about these private non-market benefits is quite poor and is not as good as the information about market benefits. The same point can be made about the non-market social benefits considered in the following chapter. As an example, most stories in the press talk about what has happened to the earnings of new college graduates each year, but they very seldom mention the benefits of education to better health, longevity, and quality of life. As another example, students can be observed "voting with their feet" as they move toward higher-paying fields such as MBA programs, computer engineering, information science, law, medicine, and accountancy. Many avoid lower-paying fields such as teaching, social work, and the humanities. To be sure, not all students do this. Many excellent college students choose lower-paying fields and seek public service, as well as music and the fine arts, even though the rates of return in the latter fields are often negative. But most do not do this. Given the freedom to choose, at the margin large numbers are attracted to the higher-paying fields. To offer a third example of poor public information about non-market returns, in focus groups for a nationwide survey for *Solutions for Our Future*, American Council on Education (2007) interviewers found that respondents were very aware of higher education benefits to earnings, jobs, growth, and international competitiveness. When prompted, they agreed that there were specific private non-market and societal benefits from higher education. But they never came up with them on their own.

The result of this poor information is that the markets for higher education fail to work efficiently. This is a second reason that there are distortions and underinvestment. The implication is that there is a higher education policy gap at the national, state, and campus levels. Better information needs to be provided to students, families, and the public about the non-market benefits in order for higher education markets to function efficiently. Also, legislative leaders need to be informed about this source of market failure. There is a clear public interest in seeing to it that full and accurate information is provided so that markets work. There are many precedents. The Securities and Exchange Commission, for example, is one of many public initiatives that requires firms to provide full and accurate information, in this case so that the securities markets can work efficiently. Government even enforces full and accurate disclosure quite vigorously, as Kenneth Lay and Jeffrey Skilling of Enron found out. Colleges and universities and the American Council on Education do try to provide some public education about the private and public non-market benefits, but they do so in ways that overlap the market benefits, that do not include valuations, and that are not very systematic. The U.S. Department of Education maintains a website that lists a few isolated outcomes. But the Spellings Report (U.S. Department of Education, 2007) was confined to the traditional access, affordability, quality, and accountability issues, and only in its final draft squeezed in a little about the private and social benefits. Neither the website nor the report addresses the basic issue of market failure due to poor information. The report does not recommend that better information be provided by the U.S. Department of Education or others. So the information remains relatively poor, and the market failure as a source of economic inefficiency persists.

There is a third reason for considering non-market outcomes more seriously than in the past. As universities get farther away from their standard ways of doing business, including trends toward the Internet, privatization, and vocationalization accompanied by declining public support, there is need for documenting the non-market social benefits. Otherwise privatization per se cannot be said to increase economic efficiency. Private markets do work, but only where there is relatively good information about outcomes and where externalities that serve the public good are given public support. But the latter is the subject of the following chapter.

How Can Non-Market Benefits of Higher Education Be Measured?

Lest some feel that we are setting out to measure the unmeasurable, it is important to briefly consider in more depth how the important non-market outcomes of higher education are measured. It may also be that some are less familiar with regression methods. But these and the related statistical controls are basic to all fields, including lab experiments in physics, astronomy, epidemiology, and the social sciences where data analysis is involved. They are not unique to the measurement of the non-market returns to education. Also, different readers will have different degrees of familiarity with what is known. So it is necessary to consider how the non-market outcomes of higher education are measured, and how they are valued. Valuation in monetary terms goes a step beyond measurement of the quantity of various outcomes. But this is an essential further step because these monetary values must be obtained before the quantities of the non-market outcomes can be added up. Only after their total value is obtained can they be added to the earnings benefits and the result related to the costs of higher education. Then higher education policy makers, families, and the society are in a better position to determine whether further investment in higher education is warranted.

GROSS VERSUS NET EDUCATION BENEFITS

Many of the contributions of education to health, longevity, happiness, democracy, and social capital that are the most widely reported are gross outcomes in the sense that they are reporting the benefits of education that result from higher income as well as the effects that are over and above the income effects. So one must be careful.

The gross non-market outcomes of higher education such as better health, which may in part be due to higher income, are legitimate non-market benefits. The improvements in health due to better health care and diet made possible by higher income is part of the better health made possible by higher education. But these gross non-market health benefits are not very relevant to higher education policy. This is because their value cannot be added to, or separated from, the value of education's income benefits. If they are added, as they often are implicitly, then the income benefits of higher education are double counted. The total benefits include this overlap and overstate higher education's true benefits, which is not legitimate.

To overcome this problem, while measuring the quantity of the non-market benefits of higher education we need to control for income by including per capita income in the regression. The result will be the net non-market benefit, whose value can then be legitimately added to the income benefit. An alternative is to measure education's net contribution by considering how large education's contribution is at each income level. A second very important reason to include per capita income in the regression is that this also is the best representation of the total value of all market goods that are used in household production of final outcomes as required by the logic of the household production function I discuss below. A third reason, also important, is that when per capita income is in the regression, this then provides the coefficient on the income term necessary for valuation of the non-market benefits, as I will show later.

These three reasons for including per capita income in any regression measuring net non-market outcomes each are so powerful that the research studies that do not do this will be ignored, especially when attempting to value and add up the total benefits in a way that is relevant to higher education policy. The result then can be related to the cost of obtaining these benefits. There is, however, an exception. Sometimes the only studies that exist of particular non-market outcomes do not control for per capita income. So to be comprehensive when surveying non-market outcomes, these studies will be mentioned in such cases. The reader must be cautious and recognize that we are looking at the income benefits as well. If these non-market benefits then are added to the income benefits, the result is overstated. Warnings will be issued, however, since relevance to higher education policy is a major theme of this book.

THE RATIONALE USED TO MEASURE
NON-MARKET OUTCOMES

The rationale for the measurement of the productivity of human capital created by higher education in producing non-market outcomes is the household production function based on Becker's (1965, 1976) theory of the allocation of time. For this and related work he received the Nobel Prize in Economic Sciences. The theory expresses the logic of the process by which human capital is used in the home or the community during time not spent at work to combine education-enhanced time with market goods, such as time spent reading a book or watching television, to produce final satisfactions. Human capital increases the productivity of each hour of this non-market time, and hence its value. The individual with a college education, for example, may use market-produced goods such as a book, a television, or a computer purchased with his or her income to learn by reading, or watching, say, the *Leherer NewsHour,* or looking up health information on his or her computer to produce final outcomes that enhance health and participation in community life. A high school graduate may have purchased the same television and computer, but uses them mainly for watching drag racing or for gaming. Lifelong learning is well known to be highly correlated with the amount and quality of prior education, and this lifelong learning occurs not only through on-the-job training but also at home. Such continued learning facilitates behavior conducive to better health and the development of civic institutions, among other benefits, as is evident from extensive research.

A household production function is shown in Equation 4.1. It shows more clearly how market goods and human capital–enhanced time are used to produce the final outcomes that are the non-market as well as income-generated ultimate benefits of higher education. It is the main rationale for measurement of these benefits using multiple regression equations, which are usually linear or log-linear approximations based on it in the very extensive literature. Examining it facilitates a clearer understanding, and is essential for any potential researchers who may wish to advance the knowledge of non-market education outcomes. Specifically, it expresses the final satisfactions, Z, of a typical household or individual as dependent on market-produced goods as represented by income, Y, combined with the individual's human capital, H, enhanced by education. The latter is used during only a fraction of the week, $1-\mu$, spent in household production at home or in the community. These two inputs, Y and $(1-\mu)$H, are inside the parentheses expressed as $Z(\ldots)$.

The productivity of these two inputs inside the parentheses is augmented by the education of others in the community, including those in prior generations shown outside the parentheses. This could be from many things—from useful information available on the Internet, to jobs and/or commodities available through trade, to the benefits of stable democratic institutions. These are education externalities to the extent that education has contributed to their existence in the community. It is useful to simplify these symbolizing their net effect as H_β, reflecting the average level of education in the community. The latter is analogous to the way Lucas (1988) simplified these external effects in his production function for market outcomes and has led to many research studies using this average level, although our consideration of what these externalities are will seek to go far beyond this. The household production function for a typical household or individual is:

(Eq. 4.1) $Z = Z(Y, (1-\mu)H) \, H_\beta$

Specifically, and in summary, Z on the left represents final satisfactions produced by a typical individual, $(1-\mu)$ is the fraction of total hours each week spent at home or in the community (μ is the fraction spent at work), H is the stock of human capital or raw labor time augmented by education, and Y is market goods as represented by income. H_β outside the parentheses defined by $Z(...)$ are education externalities that enhance the efficiency of the individual's time.

The data used to estimate the regression equations based on the above is most often micro-data for individuals, which in turn is usually a cross section across individuals, some of which are younger and some older, including individuals with different backgrounds. The data, however, is sometimes macro cross-country or interstate data reporting aggregates of individuals but expressed in per capita terms. In the latter case, the household production function is interpreted as applying to this per capita average as relating to a typical individual. The data used to estimate household production functions is occasionally longitudinal data for individuals, as is the National Bureau of Economic Research (NBER)–Thorndike sample that followed up individual World War II servicemen over many years, or aggregate time series data in per capita terms. But this longitudinal dimension is more difficult to come by because it takes a long period of years to collect. In any event, each of these types of data offers somewhat different perspectives on the same phenomena, and often one type of data can be more helpful in revealing effects that are not revealed well in the other types of data.

As a regression equation is specified for estimation from the data based on Equation 4.1, it can be seen that controlling for Y removes the effects of the market goods on the non-market outcomes. Also, since the market goods are purchased largely by income due to education this simultaneously avoids double counting the market returns to education. The multiple regression equations that appear in most studies are linear approximations of the above household production function expressed in per capita terms. Since any individual's human capital cannot be used both at work and in the home or community at the same time, logically there is not an overlap between the contributions of human capital due to education used on the job and the contributions of this same human capital used at home or in the community, and these separate contributions of human capital therefore can be added up if they are measured properly.

SEPARATING HIGHER EDUCATION FROM BASIC EDUCATION OUTCOMES

Just because basic education contributes to a particular higher education outcome, such as longevity, does not mean that higher education does not. Normally, the contribution of each year of education continues into the college years, although sometimes it diminishes and sometimes it increases.

Longevity, for example, is a roughly linear function of years of schooling. That is, a year of education at the secondary level adds as much to longevity as a year of college. So in cases like this the net contribution of a four-year undergraduate education can be measured directly. The case is strengthened further when a specific study exists, such as one done by Grossman of health status that will be cited later, that considers a large sample of males and controls for health status as of the date of high school graduation. Any additional contribution to better health then has to be due to additional years spent in college.

However, there are cases where the effects of education are nonlinear. Criminal behavior is one. Retention in high school until graduation that keeps young males off the street and under supervision is known to reduce crime rates, for example, and the first two years of college may have a similar effect. But completion of the third and fourth years of a college degree does not appear to have as much of an effect in reducing crime rates as does increasing high school retention rates. Diminishing marginal returns also seem to exist for the production of happiness as measured by psychologists. More income and more education both are known to contribute to greater happiness. But this is true only up to a point. As indicated, international data shows that individuals with per capita income over about $20,000 per year or $60,000 for a family of three are not on average much happier (Layard, 2005, pp. 32–34). But these diminishing returns at higher education levels do not mean that higher education contributes nothing to reducing violent crime or to increasing happiness.

Another approach to measuring the net contribution of higher education to the production of, say, better health is to include both basic and higher education separately in the regression (while also controlling for income). Then the coefficient for basic education and the one for higher education measure the contribution of each to better health. The problem, however, is to find a dataset where primary education is not universal. If the data studied is characterized by universal primary education, there is no variation in this variable and its contribution to better health will show up as zero, even though obviously this is not true. Primary education as compared to no education not only contributes to better health, but also is essential to entering secondary and higher education levels. So consideration of the nature of the database is essential.

A third approach is to use microeconomic longitudinal data that follows individuals and re-interviews them over longer periods of time. This is expensive and such data is hard to come by. However, the study by Grossman (1975) is an excellent example. He used the NBER-Thorndike longitudinal sample of 9,700 males, all of whom had graduated from high school, and controlled for their income and also for their health in high school (and their scores on mental tests). Grossman found that after they had reached middle age, additional years of college education had a positive and significant net effect on their health status. That is, he found that the favorable effect of years of education on health persists after high school and clearly the college years also help to produce better health.

Finally, throughout this book I speak of the non-market benefits of higher education with full knowledge that some of these benefits can be negative. The best example is the contribution of higher education to white-collar crime, or crimes that require advanced skills. These negative benefits must be included. But they are rare, and are overwhelmingly offset by the positive benefits. In the case of crime rates, the number of white-collar crimes is small compared to the large number of violent crimes and even larger number of simple property crimes. That is, overall crime rates are known to be reduced by universal high school and community college attendance even though there are some educated criminals. The economic value of the social loss due to white-collar crime is much harder to estimate, although in principle it would be possible to estimate the specific value of each white-collar and violent-crime loss. Valuation of non-market benefits, both positive and negative, raises separate issues I will address later.

Overview of Private Non-Market Benefits

An overview of the main non-market benefits of higher education is given in Figure 4.1. The market benefits are at the top of the figure, then come the private non-market benefits, and finally come the social (or public) benefits.

Moving from left to right, standard accountability measures used in higher education that tend to be more immediate come first. These include instructional units, numbers of graduates, graduation rates, increments in test scores, and time-to-degree. These are useful especially when they are more outcome oriented (such as increments in test scores and graduation rates) because they are readily available and immediate. But they can be and are often misused since they are relatively narrow (for example, instructional units) and reflect neither quality nor the ultimate outcomes of the higher education process.

Moving to the right in Figure 4.1, as graduates go through their life-cycles they use their human capital to learn through experience on the job, at home, and in the community and the short-term outcomes of higher education indicated in the first main column are generated. These include such things as jobs, earnings, less smoking, less obesity, and greater civic participation. Most information about these impacts of college is based on research that uses data from tracer studies that re-interview graduates five to twenty years later. Most campuses conduct similar tracer studies, but the information collected normally does not include objective outcomes and extend what is known, so these tracer studies are far below the potential of what each campus could learn about the impacts of its programs, resulting in another serious higher education policy gap. Other studies use microeconomic cross-section and panel data and still others use macro cross-country data to estimate household production functions.

Moving farther to the right in Figure 4.1, these shorter-term specific outcomes map into more general medium-term outcomes. They also interact with one another. In a very real sense each phase of short-term out-

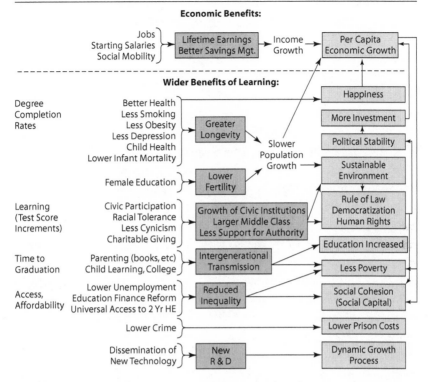

Accountability Measures	Shorter Term Benefits	Medium Term Benefits	Longer Run Impacts on Growth and Development

Economic Benefits:

Jobs
Starting Salaries
Social Mobility
Lifetime Earnings
Better Savings Mgt.
Income Growth
Per Capita Economic Growth

Wider Benefits of Learning:

Degree Completion Rates

Better Health
Less Smoking
Less Obesity
Less Depression
Child Health
Lower Infant Mortality
Greater Longevity
Slower Population Growth
Happiness
More Investment
Political Stability

Female Education
Lower Fertility
Sustainable Environment

Learning (Test Score Increments)

Civic Participation
Racial Tolerance
Less Cynicism
Charitable Giving
Growth of Civic Institutions
Larger Middle Class
Less Support for Authority
Rule of Law Democratization Human Rights
Education Increased

Time to Graduation

Parenting (books, etc)
Child Learning, College
Intergenerational Transmission
Less Poverty

Access, Affordability

Lower Unemployment
Education Finance Reform
Universal Access to 2 Yr HE
Reduced Inequality
Social Cohesion (Social Capital)

Lower Crime
Lower Prison Costs

Dissemination of New Technology
New R & D
Dynamic Growth Process

Figure 4.1. Mapping accountability and short-term benefits into impacts on growth and development.

comes sets the stage for the next round of development over time. Some non-market outcomes, such as better health, feed back and enhance earnings and pure economic growth as time passes. Each higher education outcome can be traced from the shorter-term impacts on the left to the medium-term outcomes in the middle column, and these in turn can be mapped logically into still more general and longer-term impacts in the last column. The latter are standard development goals for which there are standard economic development measures for most states and all countries.

To illustrate this mapping from specific short-term micro-outcomes into longer-term more general impacts, less smoking, less obesity, and other specific effects of higher education on healthier lifestyles lead to better overall health and also to lower fertility rates. Both of the latter in turn contribute to faster per capita growth, to greater longevity, and to slower population growth rates, and in developing countries the latter especially puts less pressure on forests, wildlife, water resources, and other aspects of environmental sustainability.

There are many interactions among these various higher education outcomes as time passes. So the dynamic process can only be represented by a system of difference or differential equations. Such systems are very common. They are used to plot and control the trajectories of every orbiter and each space capsule from launch to landing, for example, on Mars. Similarly, the time path of the impact of each higher education outcome can be plotted over time in a way that takes the side impacts from other higher education outcomes into account. When this is done, the short-term impacts of higher education are seen to be insubstantial, and then to build up over time, so that in twenty-five or forty years or so they can be seen to be very substantial (McMahon, 2007a). The precise effect of education on each outcome depends of course on the precision with which each outcome equation is estimated as well as on the underlying rationale of the process. But this will always be true. The very important point that the medium- and long-term impacts of education (including higher education) are much larger than the short-term one- to five-year impacts is now established but not well known.

The public benefits of higher education appear farther down on Figure 4.1. These are benefits to others, the society at large, and future generations, about which I will say much more in Chapter 5. The same mapping from narrowly defined specific outcomes to more general outcomes as part of an interactive dynamic process applies. For example, college graduates contribute more of their time at each income level and a larger percent of their income to civic institutions than do high school graduates; they are also more racially tolerant, less cynical, and are less prone to unquestioning support for authority. These college-induced behaviors and attitudes map into increasing degrees of democratization and stronger judicial processes protecting human rights. Democratization is a very long, slow process, and evidence for education's contribution generally cannot be found in micro-data or data that extends over less than forty years. But there is strong evidence for the net contribution of education to democratization in cross-country and long-term data, and this in turn is highly correlated with improvements in human rights and in political stability. So although the evidence is very weak or nonexistent that democracy contributes to either economic growth or reduced inequality, there is evidence that democracy contributes to political stability and the rule of law, as shown by the arrows in Figure 4.1, which in turn contribute to growth. Democracy also can contribute to the democratization of education, which in turn reduces inequality. So perhaps this gives a feel for the interactions among education outcomes and for the dynamics of the process.

Reduced inequality that would eventually follow a higher education policy supporting a major expansion in Pell Grants, thus vastly expanding access to two-year community colleges for capable students from lower-income families, is known to contribute to social capital, social cohesion, and trust (Preston and Sabates, 2005; see also Figure 4.1). School finance reform in U.S. states that reduces the vast inequality in expenditure per child among local school districts because of overdependence on the property tax would also reduce inequality and contribute to greater social cohesion. Public support for universal preschool education, a cost-effective policy as shown by Heckman and Masterov (2007), might well do the same thing. Beyond this, higher education policies that reduce inequality in skills and earnings could even contribute to the pursuit of greater happiness as measured by both psychologists and economists. This is because each additional dollar of benefit to a family of three whose income is still below $60,000 per year increases their happiness. To the extent that this is paid for by those with incomes over $60,000, since the latter have diminishing marginal productivity of income in producing happiness, there is a net gain in total happiness.

Finally, an extremely important higher education outcome last but not least in this overview is higher education's contribution to the dissemination and advancement of technology and new knowledge, as illustrated at the bottom of Figure 4.1. This complementarity of research and higher education impacting economic growth and non-market development relies heavily on the concept of embodiment of new knowledge and new technologies in human beings as human capital is formed. That is, new knowledge and technology has little or no effect on economic productivity or the productivity of time spent at home and in the community unless it is disseminated and unless continuing developments can be accessed and adapted. Journal articles reporting technical research findings will only lie on library shelves and collect dust unless they can be read and understood, and the results used in a way that depends dramatically on there being human capital skills embodied in people. This is a very important reason that the use of technologies on which economic development in the West depend has not spread to Africa beyond narrow aspects of a few urban environments.

Each new group of bachelor's, master's, and PhD graduates embodies recent knowledge and skills and constitutes a new vintage of human capital entering the economy. The evidence is overwhelming that employers are willing to pay a premium for these more up-to-date skills (Bartel and Lichtenburg, 1987). It follows that most of these skills are also productive at home and in the community. So they increase the productivity of human time in generating non-market benefits of education. The older vintages of human capital become increasingly obsolete and provincial, as is true for most bachelor's graduates. In some professional fields and occupations there is pressure to keep up with new developments and therefore replacement investment in human capital and lifelong learning is essential. For example, there are incentives for university faculty teaching graduate students to publish, which is not possible unless the faculty member follows recent developments in the field closely, and there are requirements for physicians and other professionals to take short courses to keep their credentials up-to-date.

The other aspect of this complementarity of higher education with research is that industry and government depend on higher education to train PhDs, who then conduct the research and development for these firms and governmental agencies. That is, new technological and organizational discoveries in firms, government, and universities through investment in R&D performed in these places generally do not occur without a constant supply of new PhDs, given the complexity nowadays in microbiology, electrical engineering, economics, and other fields if useful advances are to occur. Higher education's role is unique in this dynamic growth process.

Overall, the marginal products of higher education are its contributions to the development goals, shown in the last column of Figure 4.1. The internal efficiency of higher education is one important aspect of economic efficiency, but it can be very misleading because it is possible to be extremely efficient in producing something nobody wants. Efficiency in contributing to these private well-being and public good development goals, which are higher education's ultimate outcomes, all in relation to their costs, are the true basis for efficiency in higher education and for accountability.

The Evidence Concerning Private Non-Market Benefits

There are surveys of non-market private benefits such as the one by the College Board (2007). It refers to non-market private benefits as non-monetary benefits, but these are the same thing. Other surveys go more deeply into the professional literature, such as Wolfe and Haveman (2003), Grossman and Kaestner (1997), and Grossman (2006). But the latter do not focus on higher education outcomes and are largely confined to health outcomes. They do not address happiness, for example, and consider very few of the social benefits. A more comprehensive survey of the recent research on private non-market outcomes follows.

As to whether there is market failure due to the lack of information on the part of students and their parents on non-market outcomes, there is one nationwide study of why families invest in higher education that asks about potential effects of college on own-health, longevity, child health, community service, and earnings (McMahon, 1976, 1984b). Econometric estimates of a simultaneous equation investment-demand and supply-of-funds model provides evidence about the degree of significance of these non-market influences in affecting college investment decisions. I will also cite these findings where relevant in the following discussion. The evidence about the non-market private benefits of higher education that follows lays the groundwork for the economic valuation of these outcomes later, and hence for a more comprehensive appraisal of the degree of market failure.

BETTER HEALTH

The evidence is overwhelming that each additional year spent in college contributes to increasingly better health and, in due course, to greater longevity. Those at the top of the education distribution live seven or more years longer in Western economies, for example. "This finding emerges whether health levels are measured by mortality rates, self-evaluation of health status, or physiological indicators of health, and whether the units of observation are individuals or groups," according to Grossman (2006, p. 33), who has done the most in-depth studies of this literature over many years (1972, 1975, 1997 [with R. Kaestner], 2000, 2006). "A very significant portion of this schooling effect cannot be traced to income or occupation" (2006, p. 33). The causal connection is clear: the increased education comes first and the improvements in health come later, not the other way around, a key element of causality. There are also extensive controls for other possible effects on health status in all the studies discussed here, such as controls for income (and hence effects from purchased health care or diet), for ability (and hence for the possibility that it may be only those with higher IQs that choose healthier lifestyles), for parents' education, and for the degree of health status upon completion of high school (and hence for the reverse causality hypothesis that better health causes more schooling). All uncertainty can never be eliminated but the point would seem to have been reached where the burden of proof has shifted to any who might wish to claim that a causal connection running from more and better education to better health does not exist.

Much of this health benefit due to education is due to a greater capacity to choose healthier lifestyles and the inducement of more future-oriented behavior. There is a clear connection, for example, to the extent that an individual stays informed about health matters (Hyman et al., 1975). There is also evidence about smoking behavior and about exercise patterns from very large samples. Specifically, 1.6 fewer cigarettes are smoked per day for each additional year of schooling, and the typical individual exercises 17 minutes more per week for each additional year in college. This would suggest that after 4 years of college bachelor's graduates smoke 6.4 fewer cigarettes and exercise 68 more minutes per week than high school graduates. Of those who actually smoked, college graduates were about twice as likely as high school graduates to have quit (Pierce et al., 1989). College-educated individuals are also less likely to be obese. These are specific improvements in lifestyles that have important effects on overall own-health.

Some of the effect of education on health is the result of further education causing individuals to value the future more highly. Time preference is difficult to measure, but Becker and Mulligan (1997) suggested a more concrete way to measure it (that is, as the logarithm of the ratio of consumption between consecutive time periods). The strength of the effect on health that is channeled through time preference is important for informing the kinds of education policies likely to be most effective, as Grossman (2006, p. 76) points out. That is, the endogeneity of time preference may suggest that education policies that encourage future-oriented behavior, including simply increased Pell Grants supporting more in college beyond high school, may be more effective in the long run than more specific education interventions designed to discourage cigarette smoking, alcohol abuse, or the use of illegal drugs. The reductions in the schooling coefficient when health knowledge from such courses is included is relatively small, from 5 to 20% according to Kenkel (1991). But the lack of precise knowledge of what percent of education's effect is channeled through time preference, which is the basis for earlier reservations by Fuchs (1982) and Stacey (1998, p. 54), is not very relevant here because this issue does not undercut the basic proposition that further college education contributes to better health.

Another aspect of the effect on behaviors affecting health is that higher education facilitates wiser and more frequent use of health care services. This may be part of staying better informed about health maters, as I mentioned earlier. For example, if college graduates recognize symptoms earlier and see the doctor who has their health records and get the problem taken care of in a timely fashion instead of waiting until it becomes an emergency and going to the emergency room followed by costly hospital stays this can save on health care costs and also be conducive to better health. There is evidence that college-educated individuals make more frequent doctor visits than the less educated (Cobern et al., 1973). But part of this is an income effect that must be removed if the net health effect is to be relevant to higher education policy. When this is done by controlling for per capita income, there is still evidence that the college-educated make greater use of health services (Bowen, 1977), hopefully partly in the more cost-effective ways mentioned.

All of these improved health-related behaviors contribute to better overall health status. But education's contribution to healthier behaviors and to health status should not be added to arrive at the value of higher education's contribution to better health because the obvious overlap would result in double counting. Considering what health status measures, self-rated health has been shown to reflect the degree of physical mobility, mental health, ease of respiration, and the presence of pain by Wagstaff (1986). Surveying 132 studies of the impact of education on own-health, Grossman (2006), who is very alert to the controls for per capita income, concludes that the value of education to own health is about 40% of the market value of the benefits from education. Twenty-two of these studies of the impacts of education on own-health will be itemized later. But as mentioned previously, the most definitive study of college versus high school contributions is by Grossman (1975), who uses the large NBER-Thorndike longitudinal sample that follows up on World War II veterans who had completed high school. He was able to control for health status in high school, parents' schooling, income, job satisfaction, and ability test scores. So the net health effect is due to a college education and not to basic education, income, IQ, or the other factors that might reasonably be expected to contribute to health. In his words, "my finding is particularly notable because all the men graduated from high school. Hence it suggests that the favorable impact of schooling on health persists at the higher levels of schooling" (Grossman, 2006, p. 602).

If this value of the own-health benefit at 40% of the market returns holds up (about which more later), then all standard market return–based, narrow, private, and social rates of return are underestimated by at least 40%. Furthermore, students do not seem to be aware of this. A large nationwide survey of students that asked them about their expected non-market returns finds that the effect on better health on their college investment decisions is not significant, whereas expected market returns are very highly significant. This differential effect was true separately for white males and for white females (McMahon, 1984b), as well as for black males and for black females (McMahon, 1976). There were not only controls for expected market earnings but also for ability and for parents' income and education. This is dramatic evidence consistent with the hypothesis that there is poor information possessed by students about the health benefits of education, which implies that this is a major source of market failure leading to underinvestment in higher education. Together with other evidence, this suggests that private markets for higher education are inefficient and a case for government and educational institution intervention to provide better information as governments do in agricultural, financing, and securities markets so that private higher education markets work better and this inefficiency is corrected.

It is one thing to have better health, which also contributes to happiness as I show later, and another to live longer, for which there is no evidence of any contribution to happiness, at least in the way happiness is currently measured (that is, per year). Longevity, or life expectancy, is longer when mortality rates at earlier ages are lower. So longevity and mortality are mathematically related and are not independent, which prevents their value from being added up as separate private non-market benefits.

Considering mortality, Grossman's (1975) study of the NBER-Thorndike sample that was discussed earlier concludes that each additional year of college lowers the probability of death between the ages of 32 and 46 by 0.4 percent. This translates for the number of years the average undergraduate spends in finishing a bachelor's degree into a 1.76% reduction in the probability of death in any given year. Based on standard mortality tables, this indicates that the lifespan of the average 2-year associate degree graduate is increased by about 2.25 years, and the lifespan of the average bachelor's graduate is increased about 4.5 years. The average PhD graduate can expect to live about 8.5 years longer than the high school graduate. This is a pure non-monetary private benefit since the income effect has been removed with controls. In view of the strong advantages of the large NBER-Thorndike longitudinal dataset, and the care with which Grossman controls for health status upon leaving high school, per capita income, and ability, this permits a focus on the causal net effect of years spent in college on longevity. This is the strongest result in the current literature. It is also consistent with studies by sociologists who find longevity to be highly correlated with socioeconomic status without analyzing this into the separate income and education effects on longevity. They conclude that those in the top socioeconomic status live on average at least seven years longer.

Deaton and Paxson (2001) confirm the importance of schooling to mortality after controlling for family income using both 1976–96 U.S. Current Population Survey and National Longitudinal Mortality Study data. It is interesting that the effect of income in lowering mortality becomes weaker and the effect of years of schooling becomes stronger for males as the length of time between 1980 and the year of death increases. This could be because poor health has a weaker effect in lowering income moving forward (Deaton and Paxson, 2001) but also because income can actually have a harmful effect on health after a point with schooling held constant because higher-income people may consume larger quantities of things harmful to their health, such as alcohol and rich foods (Fuchs, 1982; Grossman, 1972). However, the beneficial effects of more education appear to swamp possibly adverse income effects. In another study, Lleras-Muney (2005) finds that an additional year of schooling lowers the probability of dying within the next ten years by 3.6 percentage points. She studies cohorts from the U.S. Population Censuses of 1960, 1970, and 1980 using instrumental variable techniques. She uses as instruments compulsory education laws that are unlikely to be correlated with unobserved determinants of health, while also controlling for state of birth and other characteristics at age fourteen. Taken together, these studies provide substantial evidence that completing two or four years of college contributes significantly apart from the income benefits to better health and hence quality of life, reduced mortality rates, and increased life expectancy, increasing longevity by about one year for every additional year spent in college, including years spent in graduate school.

CHILD HEALTH AND INFANT MORTALITY

It is common knowledge that as a larger percentage of mothers acquire more education, especially at the secondary and postsecondary levels, they read the parental health guidance books, check out issues with their doctors and on the Internet, and are more cognizant of how to reduce infant mortality and improve their children's overall health. The research indicates that this does not depend on having specific courses in health fields, only on having more years of formal education. For example, parental knowledge acquired through higher levels of education allows mothers and fathers to know that when a child has a fever it is wise to check with a doctor or phone the duty nurse, feed their children more nutritious foods, and immunize their children at the proper times.

Again, there is a relationship of years of postsecondary education to behaviors that are in turn conducive to better overall child health. Grossman and Kastner (1997) and Grossman (2006) and other studies he surveys find a robust relationship between the education of the mother and the health of her adolescent children (oral health, obesity, anemia, etc.).

This relationship includes better health of infants (neonatal mortality, low birth weight). This suggests that not only do many college and university graduates benefit from better health, but their children are healthier as well.

Lower infant mortality rates are closely associated with higher female primary, secondary, and postsecondary education enrollments in cross-country data (McMahon, 2002). This evidence holds after controlling for per capita income, which also reduces infant mortality, suggesting that nationwide effects are broadly consistent with many microeconomic findings (see McMahon, 1997, 1998a, 2004b; Grossman and Kaestner, 1997; Grossman, 2006). Strauss et al. (1993) find that the strong positive effects of college education on adult health just discussed have multiplier effects on children's health, including lowering infant mortality. Frank and Mustard (1994) find in their study that education enables individuals to acquire knowledge on better nutrition that is associated with a decline in child mortality rates and also with increased life expectancy. The evidence also indicates that children who received better nurturing during childhood are healthier and do better in adult life.

CHILD EDUCATION

A basic proposition in human capital and endogenous growth theory is that generally children have more education than their parents. Probably everybody reading this has more education than their grandparents had. Education is a dynamic process within families and within societies over generations (Lucas, 1988).

But the problem is to sort out how much of this is due to the parents' income and their capacity to finance college for their children, and how much is due to the influence of the parents' education in helping their children establish longer-run goals and to prepare for college. Controlling for income, Ermisch and Francesconi (2000) estimate that the impact of a mother's education alone raised the probability that her daughter in the United Kingdom will have a vocational (associate) degree by 25%, more than additional family income raises this probability (18.7%); in all, the mother's attainment of a degree contributes as much as about £1,500. Angrist and Levy (1996), Murname (1981), and Edwards and Grossman (1979) all report roughly similar findings for families in the United States.

The education of the mother appears to have a far more significant effect on college attendance than the education of the father if the influence of the father's education through higher family income is removed. Controlling for family income, McMahon (1984b) finds that the mother's education is always more significant than the father's education as an influence on the decision by white males and white females to attend college. This conclusion is based on two-stage least-squares estimates of an investment-demand and supply of funds model estimated for a large nationwide sample of potentially college-bound students and after controlling for family income as reported by the parents. The author also found that for black males the parents' education was a highly significant determinant of college attendance with similar controls, whereas for females from the lowest income quartile the parents' income was insignificant. But overall, for all of these groups the availability of Pell Grants and student loans, as well as the parents' income (or lack thereof), were of overwhelming importance (McMahon, 1976).

Evidence that this effect of the mother's education is intergenerational over several generations within families and therefore consistent with both endogenous growth models and the perpetuation of poverty is offered by Blau (1999) and Powers et al. (2008). Based on this research it can be estimated that an increase of 4.8 years in the grandfather's schooling is worth $4,008 in permanent income due to its influence on the better education of the grandchild, and an increase of 3.6 years in the grandmother's schooling is worth about $2,692 in permanent income due to her intergenerationally transmitted influence on the education of her grandchild.

In both of these studies by the author, these benefits of college to the students in the form of the better health and better education of their children and grandchildren was found to be insignificant as a determinant of enrollment (McMahon, 1976, 1984b). Since there are very real benefits of this type, the fact that students are myopic or poorly informed so that they do not realize and act on this when making college investment decisions suggests again that poor information is a source of significant market failure in higher education markets.

There is extensive evidence that fertility rates and family size decline continually as women become better educated. This effect continues as the number of years of education increase so that the number of children a young woman bears diminishes as she stays on in school from ninth grade to finish twelfth grade, then further for finishing a bachelor's degree, and right on through the PhD. The rationale is that education causes women to want smaller families with fewer "higher-quality," better-educated, and healthier children; to have better employment options that makes their time more valuable than spending it all at home in child care; to have better knowledge about use of birth control technology; and to have fewer child-bearing years left as they stay longer in school.

This fertility rate effect from increased female education is extremely important in the poorest developing countries, where family size is often enormous and a major source of poverty. There is rapid population growth, and the gloomy Malthusian predictions of starvation among the poorest groups limiting population growth continue to hold in most of sub-Saharan Africa, not to speak of insufficient attention to child education and health care needs and environmental degradation (King and Hill, 1993; Lam and Duryea, 1999). The advantage of this education-fertility effect is that policies supporting more and better female education are not controversial, whereas family planning programs sometimes are, at least among some religious groups. More female education can accomplish independently the same objective of smaller family size and lower population growth, so in principle neither the heavy-handed family size control measures used in China nor controversial family planning programs are needed if the necessary female education policies are employed. However, where there are also family planning programs the cross-country evidence is that there is significant interaction with the education of females that enhances their effectiveness (McMahon, 2002, p. 87). The disadvantages of increased female education are that when the mother has only primary or junior secondary education the effects it has on improving child health and on lowering infant mortality rates are strong. So population growth rates increase further in this situation, which tends to be in the poor countries or poorest neighborhoods where they are already too high. However, after completing about ninth grade, the effect of increased female education in reducing fertility rates swamps the child-health effects and net population growth rates begin to decline. This can be seen in recent data for Indonesia, and earlier in the data for South Korea, Taiwan, Japan, Singapore, the United States, Canada, and all the European Union countries where female education levels have passed this threshold.

HIV-AIDS is a mechanism limiting population growth; it is the most productive members of the labor force that are lost and ever larger numbers of orphans are left for poverty-stricken villages to care for and educate. The robustness of the female education effects is of enormous significance for the population pressures building in the world (and potentially as well for limiting HIV-AIDS), especially in places like Bangladesh, Nepal, India, and the poorest nations of sub-Saharan Africa where these problems are the most acute. The evidence suggests that the same scenario (and same policy prescription) applies to the urban ghettoes in the United States that contain many poorly educated women.

As more females complete two or four years of college or more, fertility rates and net population growth rates can be expected to decline further. A small amount of this decline is replaced by immigration of skilled, but also mostly of low-wage workers. This population growth rate decline already has happened throughout the European Union, Japan, the rest of the Pacific Rim, Canada, and the United States. Combined with the effect of education as it increases life expectancy, lower fertility rates also contribute to an aging population. One result is that larger social security costs and health care burdens become a drag on economic growth in the United States and the more developed countries of the Organization for Economic Cooperation and Development (OECD) (McMahon and Psacharopoulos, 2008). That is, lower fertility rates help per capita economic growth and the more adequate funding of primary schools in the poor countries, but become a drag on growth in the rich countries.

A major private benefit to individual families from education effects on fertility rates remains, however. Couples are better able to attain their desired family size. The incidence of females with a very large number of children and the poverty that often accompanies this is drastically reduced as more females complete associate and bachelor's degrees. The evidence is clear that contraceptive efficiency is increased by female education (Easterlin, 1968; Ryder and Westoff, 1971; Michael and Willis, 1976; Rosenzweig and Schultz, 1989).

In the history of economics Henry Sidgwick and John Stuart Mill wrote a lot about subjective well-being. In fact, Sidgwick showed that maximizing the total (cardinal) utility in any society requires an income tax with progressive rates. But objective measures of well-being never materialized. Instead, J. R. Hicks in *Value and Capital* replaced the foundations of modern economics with ordinal utility, and the concept of the maximization of welfare morphed into the Pareto criterion, which is sort of a minimal ethical concept that says total social welfare increases if successive changes are made that make at least one person better off and no one worse off. Interpersonal comparisons of utility became anathema, and although a flow of literature about subjective well-being from sociologists and psychologists continued, this was ignored by economists.

Until recently, that is. Remarkable advances in psychology found the part of the brain where happiness is measurable as the intensity of electrical activity in brain waves. This is a cardinal measure that is very highly correlated both for any one individual over time and across individuals with what these individuals report on questionnaires about their level of happiness (Davidson, 2000). Psychologists furthermore have learned a very great deal about what makes us happy, and economists have studied the relation of happiness to income and education. So cardinal utility is back in fashion, and the results of these studies are not only fascinating but the policy implications are substantial (Layard, 2005; Gilbert, 2006; *The Economist*, 2007b).

Although interest here is primarily in the relation of years of college education to happiness, it is helpful to summarize briefly what doesn't matter, and what does. Age, for example, has a negligible effect on happiness, as does gender; in nearly every country men and women are roughly equally happy. Looks, too, make little difference. IQ is also very weakly related to happiness, as are self-rated levels of physical and mental energy (Layard, 2005, p. 62). Life expectancy has increased dramatically in the rich countries, but this has not made people happier. Perhaps the latter, however, is misleading because happiness is measured on a per year basis; if it were measured cumulatively over each person's lifetime, the result probably would be different.

Income does have a positive relationship to happiness, but only up to about $20,000 in per capita income, or $80,000 for a family of four. Beyond this there is a relatively steep falloff in the contribution of income to additional happiness. That is, there is declining marginal utility of income in producing either additional utility or additional happiness. There are policy implications of this, such as reducing the estimate of excess burden from income taxes due to loss of work effort, and revisiting what Sidgwick and Mill had to say about optimum marginal tax rates. Internationally the data shows that people in the poor countries who are earning far below $20,000 a year are not as happy as individuals in the rich countries. This explodes the myth that poor rural farmers are happy with the simple life. As income has risen in the third world it has had a much greater impact on happiness, both at the individual and at the societal level, than has the income growth in Japan, the European Union, or the United States. In these developed countries the evidence is that in spite of substantial income growth since 1945, the level of happiness has not increased at all (Layard, 2005, Chapter 3, pp. 29–38)!

The difference in happiness between rich and poor countries, and between rich and poor individuals, however, is not as large as the absolute income differences might suggest. The evidence is substantial that relative income is very important, and not just the absolute level. That is, we compare our incomes with those of others. If others in our social group and community become richer, this reduces our satisfaction. If a person who is doing relatively well in a middle-income Midwestern city retires and moves to Florida or southern California to live among others who are very rich, he or she becomes far less happy. This applies also to monkeys. When a monkey is moved between groups so that his status falls, he is unhappy, and when he is moved to a group where his status rises, his happiness increases (ibid., pp. 149–50).

With respect to the effect of a college education on happiness, it would be interesting to know whether or not there is a further contribution from education to happiness even after the $20,000 plateau from the contribution of income to happiness has been reached. Beyond this point, we have spent some time on the relation of income to happiness because there must be a control for income (and for relative income?) if the non-market benefit to happiness from education is to be measured in a way that is relevant to education policy. But to get beyond this, a major problem is that of the other things now known to contribute to happiness, at least four depend heavily on education. If there are controls for these things, or if they are in the multiple regression when attempting to estimate the contribution of education, as in Helliwell (2003), they reduce education's explanatory power and can do so to the point that education is insignificant.

The main factors other than income and education that contribute to happiness are the following, with the evidence for each reported in Layard (2005):

1. *Genes.* Some people are born happy, others are not.
2. *Upbringing.* Children growing up in a disturbed home are likely to be disturbed. Major damage occurs to children growing up with a single parent.
3. *Family Relationships.* This is the most important. A stable happy marriage is most conducive to happiness. The birth of children is a source of happiness, but after two years, parents revert to their original level of happiness. Divorce is a major blow. So is widowhood.
4. *Income.* Earning up to $20,000 per capita, or $80,000 for a family of four, annually and some increments relative to peers is crucial, as I discussed above.
5. *Work.* Work often gives purpose to life. Unemployment is a disaster; it reduces self-respect, destroys social relationships, and reduces happiness in an additional amount equal to the reduction in happiness due to loss of income. It hurts after two years of unemployment as much as it does at the beginning. When unemployment rates are higher, those still employed are less happy because of fear of unemployment. Work is vital; low and stable unemployment must be a major objective for any society.
6. *Friendships and Social Capital.* Friendship and the quality of the community, especially whether you feel most people can be trusted and living where they are trustworthy (social capital), does affect happiness. The feeling of trust varies from 5% in Brazil to 64% in Norway. The United States and European Union countries are in between.
7. *Health.* We care greatly about our health, but it does not affect happiness very much, mostly because people adapt to their limitations. Exceptions are chronic pain and mental illness. Own-health is a function of education, as discussed previously.

8. *Personal Freedom and Peace.* The rule of law, stability, the effectiveness of government services, and the lack of violence all contribute a huge amount not just to economic development but also to personal freedoms and to happiness. The benefits of democracy and of functioning civic institutions that ensure human rights depend on education, including that of prior generations as I will explain in the following chapter.

Education's contribution through income aside, college does contribute directly to happiness, according to some of the literature (Di Tella et al., 2003). Helliwell (2003) finds no direct contribution, but this ignores the indirect effects as education contributes to happiness through stable family relationships (3), through increased probability of work (5), through greater trust of others due to lower crime rates (6), through better health (7), and through strengthening civic institutions ensuring freedom and peace (8).

These new developments in the measurement of happiness as well as in the insights into the need to control for income implied by the logic of the household production function brings back to our attention the significance of the large body of research by sociologists, psychologists, and educators on the relation of education to subjective well-being. This research covers life satisfaction, morale, quality of life, and happiness. But with respect to happiness, the latter is no longer subjective but instead objective and cardinally measurable. There are too many of these studies of subjective well-being to review them all here. But a survey of 176 studies by Witter et al. (1984) presents the interesting finding that the correlation between education and well-being is larger for those age sixty-five and older than for those under sixty-five. The problem is, however, that although it is important to control for income for the reasons I have discussed, many of these studies include other explanatory variables in the multiple regression that are highly correlated with and in some cases almost proxies for education. This reduces the explanatory power of education and leads to the tenuous conclusion that the effect of education on well-being is smaller than it really is when the indirect effects of education through employment and health, for example, are taken into account. More study of the net effect of higher education on happiness is needed now that a cardinal measure of happiness exists. But even though higher education's capacity to contribute to happiness after controlling for income should not be overestimated, it is useful to note that college investment decisions by both males and females are influenced significantly by the desire to "find a spouse with college-developed values" (McMahon, 1984b, p. 88). A happy marriage and family life has been noted previously as making the strongest single contribution to happiness.

Apart from these micro-effects at the individual level, the important overall macro-finding is still that happiness has not increased since 1945 in the United States, the United Kingdom, Japan, or other rich Western industrialized nations. This must be because happiness does not increase as incomes exceed $20,000 per capita, but also because happiness depends partly on relative income and not just on its absolute level. Higher education levels have been rapidly increasing in these countries, however, and should have both direct and indirect effects that contribute to greater happiness. The fact that they have not done this is probably because inequality, divorce, and drug use have also been rising in the United States and the European Union. Since happiness is lower among the poor, if as inequality rises there are more who are relatively poor, the adverse effect of relative income on happiness and the fact that the higher end on the income distribution has passed the $20,000 threshold, plus the adverse effects of more divorce and drug use, largely offset the positive overall effects of higher education on nationwide measures of happiness.

IMPROVED EFFICIENCY IN HOUSEHOLD MANAGEMENT

There are a number of ways that those with a college education use their time and knowledge to make better choices. One is in making more efficient consumer choices; another is in better household management and in general making more efficient use of their time spent in the home; and a third is in the more efficient management of household financial assets.

Michael (1982) translates the value of an additional year of education as it makes the individual significantly more efficient as a consumer into dollars of additional income. He estimates that each year of education translates into $290 in additional household income, so that 4 years of college would add $1,160 in 1975 dollars, or $3,150 in 2007 dollars, to the real value of household income. Benham and Benham (1975), analyzing the market for eyeglasses, find that persons with more schooling pay less for eyeglasses than those with less education, or, more specifically, $29 less in 2007 dollars is paid per pair by those with an associate degree than by those with a high school education. Morton et al. (2001) note that those with more education use the Internet to bargain more effectively on the price of a new car. College graduates maintain computational skills over longer periods, an aspect of the contribution of education to lifelong learning that helps to maintain skills (below) but also undoubtedly contributes to the efficiency of consumption and household management (Pascarella and Terenzini, 2007, 1991).

With respect to the contributions of college to the efficiency of household management, Hettich (1972) finds that women with a college education are more efficient in purchasing food and other items in the market for the family. He estimates that this saving alone raises the rate of return to a college education by 1.5 percentage points. In an interesting study, Lemennicier (1978) found that French housewives with a college education shift the use of their time away from time-intensive activities, such as dishwashing, mending, and having large numbers of children, toward more human capital–intensive activities, such as reading, choosing to have fewer children, reading to these children, taking them to the library, maintaining healthier lifestyles for the children, and entering the labor market. This is analogous to a shift in the workplace in the use of time away from more time-intensive tasks such as grocery bagging or time spent on repetitious production lines toward more human capital–intensive managerial service occupations, such as teaching, medicine, the law, and computer programming.

A final aspect of household efficiency is the management of financial assets. Solomon (1975) shows that college graduates get a higher rate of return on their savings. More education is also associated after controlling for income with higher savings rates at each income level (Solomon, 1975). This could be interpreted as part of the tendency of education to make the individual more forward-looking and less myopic. Those with more college education choose better ways to protect their savings against inflation (ibid.) and spend a smaller percent of their income on gambling. The growth of gambling and gambling taxes are very regressive and hence are a mechanism for redistributing income from the poor and less well-educated to the rich and better-educated.

Beyond earnings there is some evidence that education helps to make labor markets function more efficiently and time spent on the job more enjoyable.

The efficiency of labor market searches in particular is enhanced. Beyond earnings, the improved matching of employees to jobs reduces recruiting and training costs (Acemoglu and Angrist, 1999). This is really a social benefit but there is also a private benefit, as the employee spends less time in job search and achieves a happier match. After employment, more schooling is associated with less job turnover for women (Royalty, 1998). Regional mobility is also increased with more schooling, improving job matches (Metcalf, 1973).

On the job, quite apart from earnings, college graduates often have access to the more pleasant white-collar occupations and often explicitly enjoy their work in contrast to the conditions in some of the more physically laborious and dirty jobs such as those in sanitation, mining, production line work, and seasonal farm labor. Duncan (1976) and others have documented these positive non-pecuniary on-the-job satisfactions and the extent to which a college education contributes to them. Beyond this, there are amenities associated with an advantageous location. The value of such amenities associated with location differences for teachers, as well as the non-monetary benefits not included in their salaries due to location on the ocean or on a lake or in other appealing locations, have been estimated by Chambers (1996). These amenities are a private non-monetary benefit, usually available to those with more education who are more mobile.

LIFELONG LEARNING

An extremely important effect of higher education is the extent to which it facilitates lifelong learning. This effect is too often overlooked, or mentioned only in passing. But it is vital in a globalizing economy where visions must shift to the world, and where the living and working environments are changing rapidly due to technology, trade, travel, and better communication. The problem is that all too often human capital is what economists refer to as putty-clay; putty, and malleable, while in school, turning to hard, rigid clay later. After the learning stimulus of the first few years on a job and in a new living environment, most learning often ceases and many individuals become oblivious to scientific, world, and even national events and responsive only to changes within their narrow personal circle. Education tends to change this, and more education changes it even further.

There is a positive relation that exists between the amount of learning that occurs on the job and the amount of prior formal education. Mincer (1962) was among the first to document this extensively. Those with more education are in a position to understand better, to benefit more, and to perceive ways to do things better from their experiences on the job. It is well documented that those who have more education also tend to be the ones that are selected for on-the-job training (McMahon, 2004a). But if a college education is beneficial to more learning on the job, it surely also contributes to lifelong learning from experience at home and in the community. This is not just a direct non-market benefit; lifelong learning also contributes to delayed private and social non-market benefits.

Graduate master's, PhD, and professional education often contributes even more to lifelong learning, in part through access to human capital–intensive occupations that provide organized stimuli to further learning. For example, college faculty have incentives to publish, which keeps them up to date in their fields. The highest-paid physician-specialists are very active in accessing and often in participating in the clinical health research in their fields. All successful scientists and businesspersons must continually come up with new ideas or at a minimum be aware of new developments and adapt to change. Most of the more stimulating social settings involving community, political, and business leaders require up-to-date awareness and understanding of national events and world affairs. Nevertheless, the human capital of many high school and bachelor's graduates morphs from putty to clay soon after leaving school. This is apparent as workers in occupations that are being internationally outsourced with globalization are unable to adapt, as we saw in Chapter 3. Technological change has similar effects. Displaced coal miners, for example, after about age fifty are very difficult to retrain. Established criminals are also difficult to retrain and exhibit high recidivism rates. And so forth. But continuing lifelong learning correlated with more prior education provides greater capacity to adapt, consistent with Mincer's important finding.

So far everything that has been said in this book has been concerned with education's primary role as an investment.

Investment is the expenditure of time or money where there is the prospect of a return in the future. The rate of return, or the benefits in relation to the investment costs, normally can be computed. Although both private and social rates of return to higher education that respectively take private or social costs into account can be calculated, reasonable decisions usually can be made without doing this by merely estimating the returns and relating them to the costs based on approximations without precise calculation.

Consumption refers to the final use of either goods or services for immediate gratification. It includes the enjoyment by the student of new subjects and extracurricular activities at college that exceed the enjoyment of time that could have been spent in the labor force at work. These would include attendance at cultural and athletic events, social fraternity and sorority membership, a comfortable condo, the pleasure of learning, and meaningful extracurricular service and leadership development organizations. However, some activities that are enjoyable such as the latter also yield a particularly high return later in life and hence are an investment. Note that all of a student's time invested in study and at class and hence the resources necessary to support it are an investment in the future, not current consumption.

Some young people from wealthy families are supported at a standard of living while in college by their parents that is higher than they could pay for themselves had they not gone to college and had gone to work instead. To this extent their expenditures exceed their forgone earnings. The difference is a measure of the subsidization of higher consumption benefits while still in school by these parents.

Many kinds of extracurricular activities are enjoyable. But the experience of college changes tastes, and some types of extracurricular activities contribute significantly to the productivity of graduates later in the labor force and in the community. Wise (1975) has shown that those extracurricular activities that include organizing the work of others and responsibility for the joint product of a group develop leadership skills that contribute about 40% to productivity on the job later as measured by earnings and promotions. These experiences occur in part-time jobs while in college but also in some student extracurricular organizations. When the latter stress community service, and national and international concerns, such as the YMCA's "Alternative Spring Break" trips serving disadvantaged groups nationally and abroad and tutoring of K–12 students, or student government and debating society experiences, the skills learned and the transforming experiences that result broaden the students' perspectives and affect the public service they offer later as graduates in their communities.

The effect that college has in changing tastes cannot be counted per se as a non-market private benefit. This is because replacing tastes for one activity like, say, for drag racing with tastes for the symphony results in an unmeasurable net gain or loss in enjoyment. Nevertheless, some tastes may contribute more than others to happiness, which is now more measurable, as is community well-being. The evidence is that college graduates tend to be less addicted to television than those with a high school education or less, more selective in the programs they watch, more inclined to read, more prone to engage in adult education, more likely to attend cultural events and participate in the arts, more likely to take part in community affairs, and more likely to take international vacations (Bowen, 1977, p. 208). The six studies Bowen cites report real patterns, although some of each effect may arise because those who choose to go to college have some of these tastes in the first place. For the purpose of estimating the net contribution of these changed tastes to the value of private or social benefits, these studies do not help because they do not control for income and do not estimate the net effects of these substitutions on private happiness or public well-being. More recent tracer studies in the United Kingdom find several important relations of college attendance to tastes, such as less unquestioning acceptance of authority and greater acceptance of racial diversity, but still there are no controls for income or for tastes upon graduation from high school (Bynner et al., 2003).

UNEMPLOYMENT, DISGUISED UNEMPLOYMENT, AND LABOR FORCE PARTICIPATION RATES

Lower unemployment, lower disguised unemployment, and higher labor force participation rates are all related closely to education levels. They

TABLE 4.1 Unemployed Plus Dropouts from the Labor Force by
Amount of Education

Education level	Unemployment, 2005 (%)	Unemployment plus discouraged workers (%)
Less than high school	8.8	17.6
High school graduate	5.4	10.8
Associate degree	4.2	8.4
Bachelor's or more	2.3	4.6
U.S. average	4.4	8.8

SOURCE: National Center for Education Statistics (2005, Figure 4), from the U.S. Census.

are mostly market benefits of higher education because they affect earnings and are included in the rate of return calculations, as I discussed in Chapter 3. But unemployment and the threat of it contribute to personal happiness beyond earnings, as indicated above, and therefore need to be considered here as also a private non-market benefit beyond earnings. Later, in Chapter 5, we will return to this subject because there are also social benefits from lower unemployment and higher labor force participation rates. These occur because of lower state budget costs for unemployment benefits, welfare costs (Aid to Families with Dependent Children [AFDC], Children and Family Services), and Medicaid costs, and also higher state and federal tax receipts. The level of unemployment rates is largely a function of federal fiscal and monetary policies. But individual states can be at the low end of the national average if they have a highly educated labor force.

Unemployment, a major determinant of happiness, is closely related to higher education, as can be seen in Table 4.1. The data is for the United States, but although the overall level of unemployment is higher in some countries such as France and Germany, the pattern in the European Union (and elsewhere) tends to be similar. The unemployment rate among college graduates was 2.3% in 2005 and therefore the threat of unemployment can be seen to be the very lowest.

Those who remain unemployed after a time lose the incentive to continue seeking work. These are discouraged workers who therefore are leaving the labor force. A standard rule of thumb is that these discouraged workers are roughly equal to the number who are counted as unemployed. So the total in the right-hand column of Table 4.1 that includes these workers is a more accurate estimate of the number of persons affected. This pattern of unemployment and of discouraged workers by education level is the same for all test score proficiency levels, although the overall level is slightly higher for those with lower prose proficiency. Unemployment as a source of unhappiness is in addition to the effects of unemployment on earnings. So the fact that the 4.6% of those with college who are unemployed plus those discouraged individuals who have left the labor force is less than half of the 10 to 17% who have a high school education or less who are unemployed or discouraged can be counted as a significant non-market private benefit of higher education.

It seems wise to remind the reader in this context once again of the fallacies of the over-education argument. Unemployment among college graduates diminishes very sharply after a year or so is allowed for job search. Looking only at unemployment of new graduates is very misleading. Unemployment rates among all college graduates are dramatically lower than unemployment rates among those with a high school education or less at all phases of the business cycle. In South Korea the provision of access to higher education has led to a much larger percentage of the population under age fifty with a college degree than in the United States, slightly lower rates of return, and somewhat longer times that it takes graduates to find jobs. But they eventually do, and the seemingly deliberate policy of making human capital at these levels somewhat cheaper for business firms has apparently harnessed the productivity of more with college-level skills and been supportive of enormously high per capita growth rates in the present and into the future. Persons with college degrees sometimes enter jobs previously manned by persons with less than a college education, apply their creative and adaptive skills, and potentially raise the level of productivity in these production and especially service jobs. So even here the over-education argument is difficult to sustain.

FEMALE LABOR FORCE PARTICIPATION RATES

Although it is well known, the evidence from the Census data reveals that each additional year of college education is associated with higher female labor force participation rates. Within each age group, 10 to 20% more females with bachelor's degrees are employed (see Table 4.2).

TABLE 4.2   Percentage of U.S. Females Employed

Education level	20–24	25–29	30–34	35–39	40–44	45–49	50–54	55–59	60–64
				Age group					
High school graduate	63	65	67	70	74	73	67	59	37
Bachelor's degree	87	84	79	79	86	85	81	70	47

This has positive effects not only on GDP growth, a market return, but also has non-market benefits by reducing poverty and inequality as single women have access to jobs, increasing gender equity and diversity in the workforce. Reduced inequality implies greater happiness, given the diminishing marginal productivity of income in producing happiness I discussed above. Some subtraction from these positive benefits needs to be made for the effects of higher divorce rates for educated women and the costs of caring for children.

The Economic Value of Private Non-Market Benefits

The value of private non-market benefits needs to be estimated more systematically than has been done in the past. This is shown in Table 4.3, with the sources and methods for each item in the table given in Appendix C. The total value of these private non-market benefits then can be added to the value of the market benefits to calculate a true private rate of return to investment in higher education that reflects both the earnings and the non-market benefits. The value of the social benefits is separate from the value of these purely private benefits and is considered in the following chapter.

THE THEORETICAL BASIS FOR VALUING NON-MARKET BENEFITS

The theoretical basis for valuation results in an "income equivalent" value of each non-market benefit from higher education, which is the value of the benefit in monetary terms. The method draws on a standard proposition in economics concerning typical household behavior: individuals tend to substitute among inputs until they find relatively cost-effective

TABLE 4.3 The Value of Private Non-Market Returns to Higher Education

Private non-market benefits beyond income	Value/year following bachelor's	Income coefficient α^a	Education coefficient β^a	Sources (see reference list)
Own health benefits	**$16,800**	This is the mean of the eight studies listed below.		
Self-rated health (United States)		Higher education effects only		Grossman (1975)
Equation 5 (p. 176)	$14,400	0.167***	0.019**	NBER-Thorndike
Equation 6 (p. 176)	$14,967	0.146***	0.012**	Longitudinal Sample, 9,700
Equation 7 (p. 176)	$18,778	0.147***	0.012**	males
Self-rated health (United States)				Grossman (1972)
All whites (p. 71)	$29,977	0.086*	0.018**	Income is divided into four
Insurance control (p. 68)	$25,315	0.111**	0.028***	variables so α' is too small
Self-rated health (Germany)	$6,853	0.059**	0.073**	Erbsland et al. (1995)
Self-rated health (United States)	$19,578	Lee (1982) in 2007 prices		By Wolfe and Haveman (2003, p. 117)
Self-rated health (Sweden) Low health, 1 = low, 0 = other	$4,536	−0.019***	−2.46*	Bolin et al. (2002). Value low due to controls for 1980 and 1996 health
Contributing Factors	**$0**			Below overlap overall health
Smoking cessation (OLS)	$2,160	0.091***	0.178***	DeWalque (2004, p. 24)
Smoking cessation (IV)	$2,808	0.086***	0.219	Cessation in or after college
Longevity/mortality	**$2,179**	1.12 years of life expectancy added per year of college[b]		
Life expectancy	$1,322	0.00021***	0.0483***	Appendix D, Mod ii, Sec only
Life expectancy	$1,672	0.00026***	0.0504**	Appendix D, Mod. I, HE only
Life expectancy (LEXP)	$3,541	Higher educ. effects only		By Grossman (1975)
Lower mortality rate	$0			Deaton and Paxson (2001)[b]

	Amount			Reference
Child health	$4,340		Due to mother's education	
Child health, age 4–8 (Canada)	$1,341	0.182**	0.135**	Currie and Stabile (2003, p. 1819)
Child health, age 4–8 (United States)	$7,339	0.156**	0.322**	Case et al. (2002, p. 1313)
Vaccinations, weight better		Overlaps above		Haverman and Wolfe (2007)
Child education and cog. dev.	$7,892	Mean of Child Education and Cognitive Development averages		
Child education mean	$5,606	Due to mother's higher education		
Child's years of schooling	$6,556	0.187**	0.218**	Ermisch and Francesconi (2000), United Kingdom
Child's years of schooling	$4,657	$835/yr due to grandfather's educ.		By Wolfe and Haveman (2001) from Blau (1999)
Child cognitive dev. mean	$10,178	Quality, rather than quantity of education		
Cognitive development	$1,323	Wolfe and Haveman (2001, p. 117)		Angrist and Levy (1996)
Cognitive development	$5,143	Haveman and Wolfe (1984, p. 395)		Murnane (1981, p. 249)
Cognitive development	$5,256	1.96	11.49**	Murnane (1981, p. 249)
Cog. dev., one-parent family	$2,637	1.31	3.85**	Murname (1981, p. 249)
Cognitive development (IQ)	$22,660	Haveman and Wolfe (1984, p. 396)		Edwards and Grossman (1979)
Cognitive development (IQ)	$16,637	Haveman and Wolfe (1984, p. 396)		Shakotko et al. (1980)
Cognitive development (IQ)	$16,848	0.288**	0.986**	Shakotko et al. (1980, p. 18)
Cognitive dev: reading, math	$18,856	0.271**	0.942**	Shakotko et al. (1980, p. 18)
Cog. dev. parents' valuation	$2,250			Haverman and Wolfe (2007)
Contributing factors	$0	These overlap Child Education and Cognitive Development		
Husband's health	$1,917	0.146***	0.180***	Grossman (1975, Equation 6, p. 176)
Fertility and family size lower	$1,551	75% allocated to secondary		Michael and Willis (1976)
Happiness or well-being				
Contribution to happiness	negative[b]	Many controls related to education[c]		Helliwell (2003, 2005)
Contribution to happiness	positive			Witter et al. (1984)

(continued)

TABLE 4.3 *(continued)*

Private non-market benefits beyond income	Value/year following bachelor's	Income coefficient α[a]	Education coefficient β[a]	Sources (see reference list)
Determinants of happiness				Layard (2005)
Choice of a spouse	positive	Relation to education controlling for income		
Lower divorce rate	positive	Relation to education controlling for income		
Lower unemployment	positive	Relation to education controlling for income		
Social capital, more trust	positive	Relation to education controlling for income		
Better government	positive	Relation to education controlling for income		
Consumption and saving	$3,401	50% allocated to secondary		Average of four studies
Consumption efficiency	$6,358	$290/year in 1972 dollars		Michael (1975)
Consumption efficiency	$1,350			Haveman and Wolfe (2007)
Higher return on assets	$9,954	$895/year in 1980 dollars		Lee (1982)
Higher saving rate	$9,552	0.0793***	0.0955***	Solomon (1975, p. 274)[d]
Job and location amenities				
Better working conditions	positive			Duncan (1976)
Amenities from location	positive			Chambers (1996)
Lifelong learning				
Less obsolescence of HC				Nelson and Phelps (1966)
				Rosen (1975)
Consumption benefits				
Improved tastes	positive			Pascarella and Terezini (2007)
	$0	Overlaps final outcomes since these lead to private and social benefits		

Total value of private non-market benefits	$38,080	Sums items in bold to avoid overlaps
Average earnings increase	$31,428	Mean for males only[c]
Benefits as a percent of earnings increase	122%	This becomes 78% when expressed as a percent of male earnings increments only.

[a]Regression: Non-market benefit, $Z = \alpha Y + \beta S +.+ u$; value of non-market benefit, $P(S) = \beta/\alpha(\Delta Y)$. Standardization of α and β across studies in Appendix C; significance of α and β: *** = 0.01, ** = 0.05, and * = 0.10.

[b]Additional years of life are valued as the average of male and female earnings of college graduates at age sixty-five. This sum of earnings for the additional years of life is then pro-rated over an average sixty-five years of life following graduation in order to compute the benefit per year, since all other benefits are calculated on a per year basis. If the values were discounted back to their present value, the amounts would be smaller, particularly in the earlier years.

[c]Helliwell's negative coefficient for education's effect on happiness can probably be explained by the facts that he includes many control vaiables that are correlated with education, and that his two controls for income do not test for effects from education when per capita income is above $20,000 where the income effect is known to flatten out (see Layard, 2005). Education of course contributes to income and therefore indirectly contributes to happiness. The many studies of subjective well-being that do not control for income do find positive effects from education on subjective well-being (see Pascarella and Terenzini, 2007). More study is needed of the extent to which education contributed to factors determining happiness, and therefore to happiness indirectly, and of the extent to which higher education contributes to happiness at per capita incomes above $20,000.

[d]Solomon does not present any regressions that include both income and a straightforward measure of the education level. However, his regressions in Table 10.5, Panel B, show clearly a much higher propensity to save (saving as a function of income) among those with 4 years of college (0.1748, $t = 11.28$) than among those with a high school education or less (0.079, $t = 3.85$). I have interpreted this increment in the propensity to save that does control for income as the effect of a four-year college education on the saving rate. The income-equivalent value of the college education effect above is $1,204 in 1959 prices, or $9,552 in 2007 prices.

[e]This is the increment of college graduates' earnings over high school earnings averaged from graduation to age sixty-five. Data is from the U.S. Census Current Population Survey adjusted to 2007 prices using the Consumer Price Index.

ways of producing each final satisfaction. In this case the final satisfaction might be better health, for example. The better health might be produced as the result of going to college and learning to use one's time more effectively, or it might be produced by purchasing more health care services, or by some combination of both. As households balance these alternatives, the ratio of the marginal product of education for this purpose to its shadow price will be approximately equal to the ratio of the marginal product of income in producing this same amount of better health.

This method for estimating the value of this and other non-market returns to education was developed by Haveman and Wolfe (1984) and is discussed further by Wolfe and Zuvekas (1997), Wolfe and Haveman (2001, 2003), and Haveman and Wolfe (2007). More specifically, equating of the ratios of marginal products to price for typical households results in the following equation:

$$(\text{Eq. } 4.2) \quad \frac{MP_{\text{education}}}{P_{\text{education}}} = \frac{MP_{X \text{ (market goods purchased with income)}}}{P_{X \text{ (income)}}}$$

The marginal product of education, $MP_{\text{education}}$, in producing, for example, better health, is the education coefficient in a regression equation explaining better health. The marginal product of additional income, MP_X, is the income coefficient in that same regression. If an increment of,, say, \$1,000 in income is used to purchase better health, then MP_X gives the amount of better health this income could purchase.

Rearranging Equation 4.2 gives $P_{\text{education}}$, which is the value of the non-market benefit to better health from education as a function of things largely known from the regression:

$$(\text{Eq. } 4.3) \quad P_{\text{education}} = \frac{MP_{\text{education}}}{MP_X} \cdot P_X$$

This can be simplified if β is the marginal product of education in producing, say, better health from the regression, and α is the marginal product of income in producing health from that same regression, then:

$$(\text{Eq. } 4.4) \quad P_{\text{education}} = \frac{\beta}{\alpha} P_X$$

To implement this approach, based on Wolfe and Haveman (2003, p. 115), and continuing to use the effect of a college education on own-health as an example, if the marginal product of education and the marginal product of the other input are equal, then $\beta = \alpha$ in Equation 4.4, and the price of education per year for the purpose of producing better health is equal to the price of the other input. If the marginal product of education is twice the marginal product of the other input, then the value of one year of education is twice the price of the other input.

The other input in this case, X, is medical services. But what is the "unit" of medical services to which P_X refers? (It is also the marginal cost of the other input in Haveman and Wolfe [1984, Equation 4, p. 394], which they treat as $1/\alpha \, P_X$ in Equation 4.4 above and use for their original imputations.) I will take the "unit" of medical services measured in terms of income to be the amount of medical services necessary to "buy" one unit of own-health, which is a 10% improvement in self health rating (SHR) measured on a scale of 1 to 10 as standardized for the studies in Appendix C, Table C.1A. It is estimated to take about 3 physician visits and related drugs to produce one unit of own-health at a cost of about $1,000, which is the "unit" of medical services purchased by income used to estimate P_X. With this it is possible to use β/α and Equation 4.4 to impute the value of an additional year of college. A bachelor's now takes about 4.5 years to complete, so 4.5 times this value of one year of college gives the $16,800 estimate of the own-health benefits from a bachelor's degree shown in row 1 of Table 4.3. The $16,800 own-health benefit is an average of the estimates based on six independent studies that were first standardized for reasons explained below.

From another perspective this estimate of the $1,000 cost of "buying" one unit of better health can also be inferred from the income coefficients in the regressions. The normalized income coefficient, α, is 0.001 in all three models in Grossman's (1975) study (for example, in Appendix C, Table C.1, column E, rows 1, 3, and 6). His study uses longitudinal data and controls for health status in high school. To produce one unit of better health at the time he did his study would cost in terms of family income, Y:

(Eq. 4.5) $1 = \alpha \, (\Delta Y)$, or $1/\alpha = \Delta Y$, so $1/.001 = \Delta Y$, and $\Delta Y = $1,000$, the estimate of P_X

The estimate would be more if it were in current dollars, or less if the income coefficient, α, were larger as it probably would be if some of the control variables were dropped. But this does give a cross-check on the approximate order of magnitude.

Just because there is poor information among students and parents about outcomes such as better own-health does not mean that the economic value of these health and other non-market outcomes cannot be estimated using the above rationale. The estimate of their value is "as if" there were good knowledge of the health outcomes based on empirical measurements of how further education in fact produces better health. It is true that too little education may have been chosen because there was poor knowledge, and to this extent the estimate of the health benefits may be conservative. But most education decisions are made for reasons unrelated to health, and the point is that they generate health benefits anyway. If families think that the benefits are less than the coefficient β suggests that they in fact are, then the difference becomes an approximate measure of the degree of ignorance and an index of the extent of the market failure.*

THE VALUE OF SPECIFIC NON-MARKET PRIVATE BENEFITS

The estimates of the value of the private non-market benefits of higher education in Table 4.3 are more systematic and comprehensive than those available previously. Key details of the underlying study on which the estimates are based are given in Appendix C. Most studies that do not

---

*This method is based on several assumptions. (1) For the coefficient β to be accurate, all students and their families must not be artificially constrained in their choices. (2) The values in the market input should reflect a competitive market. Most obviously in the case of health care, there are monopoly elements, third-party payers, and in the United States 47 million people with no health insurance and severe budget constraints. So the coefficient α relating to the purchase of health care is not likely to be totally accurate. (3) The method assumes that the composition of other inputs does not change with changes in schooling. Here, with more schooling, there is some increase in efficiency in using the health care inputs in producing the health outcome, which is a source of some inaccuracy. (4) The coefficients must be estimated in a way that they are not biased or inconsistent because of unobserved characteristics. Innate ability is the most frequently mentioned unobserved characteristic. But much bias from this source is unlikely because of the well-known Griliches and Mason (1988) conclusion that ability bias is largely offset by measurement error in the education variable, as discussed in Appendix A. Finally, (5) it must be noted that high degrees of precision are not claimed for Table 4.3 in the text.

control for income are eliminated since this is a necessary requirement for estimating income-equivalent values and also for ensuring that these values are beyond income so that the double counting of market benefits is avoided. Studies are also eliminated from the average and total values if either the income coefficient or the education coefficient is insignificant. Fortunately, most studies using the household production function rationale do include both income and years of education. The many studies that do not include both are largely ignored.

The original income and education coefficients obtained in each study, α and β, are shown in columns 2 and 3 of Table 4.3. These were first standardized and then used to obtain the non-market value per year of one additional year of college education, and from this the value per year of a bachelor's degree taking about 4.5 years, as shown in column 1. Where there is more than one study of a particular outcome, such as own-health effects, the average of the value estimates based on the different studies is shown in bold. The total value of all private non-market benefits of higher education is shown at the bottom of the table. It totals the averages shown in bold to avoid overlap or double counting. It must be emphasized that the total value of the private non-market benefits of a bachelor's totaling $38,080 per year is in 2007 prices, as are all values shown in Table 4.3, because this is not true of prior studies that are in prices for an earlier year.

Where there are several studies of the impact of education on the same outcome, these must be standardized to make them comparable. This has not been done previously. But when it is done it creates much stronger evidence since the average reported is the average of studies done by many independent investigators. Standardization involves:

- Standardizing the units of measurement of the dependent variable, income, and education. Each must be converted to the same units of measurement. For example, income is sometimes measured in logs, sometimes as monthly income, and sometimes as annual income. Education is usually measured as years of schooling, but sometimes by an index of education levels 1, 2, or 3. This means the α and β used to compute the income-equivalent valuations must be rescaled to relate to one standardized unit of measurement, as shown in columns 4, b, and e for the income coefficient and columns 3, a, and d for the education coefficient in Table C.1A in Appendix C.

- Standardizing the income measures and all other values by expressing them in 2007 U.S. dollars. This was done in the last column in Tables C.1A and C.1B using the Consumer Price Index if the original study was done in U.S. dollars. Where the original study was in German Deutsche marks or Swedish kroner, purchasing power parity currency conversion was used to convert these to U.S. dollars.
- Standardizing to correct for strange control variables. For example, an adjustment was made to the income coefficient when family income as well as ln wage or father's education, both of which are proxies for family income, are included in the same regression. The adjustment was made by converting the latter to units of income and then adding their coefficients to the income coefficient.

The family is regarded as the basic decision unit in Table 4.3. This is realistic for undergraduates, which are the focus in Table 4.3, because parents normally cover most of the tuition and fees as well as absorb most of the forgone earnings costs. The implication of this is that child health, child education, and child cognitive development are included in Table 4.3 as private non-market benefits to the family, not as externalities or social benefits. They would be externalities if the individual student were regarded as the sole decision maker. If the reader chooses to focus on the individual student as the decision maker, then these intra-family externalities should be subtracted from the private non-market benefits and added to the social benefits in Chapter 5. I have always preferred treating the family as the decision unit for college investment decisions going back to my 1984b study; it is parallel to regarding the firm as the decision maker in the business sector. Analogously, intra-firm education benefits shared among workers then also would not be regarded as externalities but instead as private benefits to the firm. So just as with intra-family benefits to children and spouses they will not appear as external social benefits to the society in Chapter 5.

There are seven regressions in four independent research studies in Table 4.3 that meet the standards of using both income and education to explain better overall own-health and where both income and education coefficients are significant. These are the studies by Grossman (1972), Grossman (1975), Erbsland et al. (1995), and Bolin et al. (2002), shown at the top of Table 4.3. The mean value to own-health estimated by these studies from 4.5 years of college is $16,800. This does not include the "high" estimate based on Ross and Mirowsky (1999) in Appendix C because its income coefficient is not significant at the 0.05 level. The 1975 Grossman study is the one mentioned earlier as particularly notable since it focuses on the benefits of higher education by controlling for health status in high school. The results based on these seven separate regressions are quite comparable. The average value to own-health of $16,800 per year from finishing a bachelor's degree is 54% of the $31,174 increment to the average earnings over the lifecycle of males and females who are high school graduates. This is quite significant because the $16,800 is almost identical to the average for the Grossman (1975) study that controls for health status on leaving high school, so the health benefit can be interpreted as caused exclusively by higher education. Over the 60 years of the typical graduate's lifetime after college this non-market health benefit has a value of $1,008,000 in future dollars, or about $1 million. This monetary value of better health due to college is an estimate that is not precise but it is just as legitimate a value as the estimates of the additional increment to money earnings due to college.

Some economists have been reluctant to claim a causal link. They suggest that better health and longer life expectancy may be the result of a third factor that causes both more years of attendance and better own-health. However, there is no obvious third factor that has been identified. Innate ability is the most likely candidate, but this claim must contend with the fact that any ability bias is largely offset by measurement error, a near wash that is widely but not unanimously accepted, as I explain in Appendix A. The logic of the process is strongly on the side of causality. Education comes first in the lifecycle, and better health later. This is consistent with the strength of the statistical relationships and the many controls imposed by many different researchers, including instrumental variables to control for feedback effects. It is also consistent with results produced by independent studies in several countries. Given this empirical evidence, causation is then inferred from it based on the logic of the theory. This constitutes what in all fields would be regarded as relatively strong scientific evidence and indicates that education plays an important causal role.

The Bolin et al. (2002) study in Table 4.3 illustrates what happens when theoretically inappropriate controls are used, leading to value estimates that are very low. In this Bolin study the health status for an earlier year (1980–81) and for a later year (1995–96) are both included among the explanatory variables. The latter especially removes a lot of the variation from the dependent 1988–89 health status variable, which is for an in-between year. The result is a smaller increment to health status of $4,536 as would be expected. The reversal of sign is not a problem because the dependent variable is a dummy variable where 1 = low and zero = high health status. But the distorting effect of the control variables suggests that the other studies should carry greater weight, as they do in the $16,800 average.

My more detailed standardized estimate of the value of higher education for improving one's own health of 54% of the average earnings increments can be compared to the 40% estimate by Grossman and Kaestner (1997) earlier. Grossman's (2006) more recent estimate is that health benefits are about 100% of education's effect on earnings. However, in the latter estimate he includes, in addition to own-health, effects on child health, spouse's health, longevity, and fertility rates. If these are included now then my new estimate here is that the total health benefits are not 54% but instead 98% of the average increment to earnings. This reveals that my detailed estimate here of the value of the health benefits at 98% of earnings and Grossman's (2006) independent estimate of about 100% of earnings are remarkably close.

LONGEVITY

The estimate based on the research discussed above of 1.12 years added to longevity by each additional year of college comes to an additional 5.0 years added to the life expectancy of a bachelor's graduate. Although this of course is due partly to better own-health, better health during each year of life is something quite different than the number of years added to the lifespan. The same issue arises with happiness. It is known that greater longevity does not increase happiness, but that again "happiness" is a per year concept. To value this addition to the lifespan, the average of male and female earnings at age 65 (ignoring the value of the non-market time) were multiplied by the additional 5.0 years added to life by a bachelor's degree, and then this total value was pro-rated over the average of 65 years remaining in the lifecycle. This puts the estimate on a per year basis to standardize it with the other per year non-market benefits. The result is that each year of college adds a value due to additional longevity of $484 per year, or $2,179 for those receiving bachelor's degrees. This is a conservative estimate based on the coefficients in the Grossman (1975) study of the National Bureau of Economic Research (NBER)–Thorndike data that controls for health status in high school so the result applies to additional longevity due to only higher education.*

There are a number of other studies of the effect of education on mortality rates. The evidence is reasonably clear that increased education significantly lowers the probability of death at a given age, and lowers the likelihood of specific health problems related to mortality, such as cancer from smoking and coronary heart disease. These studies are surveyed by Pascarella and Terenzini (2007) and by Grossman (2006). But none of these studies could be used in Table 4.3. This is because they did not include income as a control, which is essential for estimating income-equivalent values (the problem with Angus and Paxson, for example) and/or because they relate to a small segment of the population, such as persons at a given age or persons who are ill, which prevents them from being standardized for comparability. They also often overlap the Grossman study, which deals with the overall outcome, longevity. The latter is superior for this reason but also because of good statistical methodology applied to a large longitudinal sample and because his results are specific to higher education.

*This estimate of the value of a bachelor's in increasing life expectancy is a conservative one. The value after retirement is greater than just earnings. Both the quality of life and potential earnings decline for many. But this decline is largely offset by the conservative nature of the estimate that ignores the value of the non-market benefits.

CHILDREN'S HEALTH

There is substantial evidence that children's health benefits substantially from the postsecondary education of the mother. There are fewer children subjected to abusive violence, less risk of childhood death before age two, fewer teenage pregnancies, and so forth when the parents have completed college. But if included, these values would overlap the health status of the child used for valuing the child health benefit. So focusing on the value of the overall benefit to child health, and using the same cost of one unit of better health of $1,000 for this and all imputations to follow, the bachelor's degree of the parent has a value of $4,340 per year in 2007 prices. As shown in Table 4.3, this is the average of two studies.

CHILDREN'S EDUCATION AND COGNITIVE DEVELOPMENT

The benefit to the child's education from the mother's college experience is even greater. The number of years of education the child receives is estimated to be worth $1,246 for each year of the mother's additional education or $5,606 if the mother has a bachelor's. This is the average of calculations based on two studies that produce very similar results.

The value of the better cognitive development of the child is estimated to be $2,262 for each year of the mother's education or $10,178 for a bachelor's, based on averaging nine studies as shown in Table 4.3. Cognitive development can reflect the quality of the school, the choice of which depends on the parents' income and where they can afford to live. So a judgment has been made not to add this to the effect on the length of schooling. Instead, it is averaged with the value of the effect on the number of years of schooling.

With respect to cognitive development especially, this can reflect the mother's willingness to read to the child, as well as how important the parents regard education to be. The three Shakotko et al. (1980, p. 18) regressions all include the father's education as a control variable. This is a proxy for family income and makes the income coefficient small and hence the value of the effect on cognitive development large since the income coefficient appears in the denominator of the valuation formula. Other estimates shown that are high come directly from Haveman and Wolfe (1984) converted to 2007 prices. It is significant, however, that the independent estimate I have made here based on the Murnane (1981) study of the value to the child's cognitive development of $1,168 from each year of the parent's education is essentially identical to the $1,143 obtained independently by Haveman and Wolfe (1984) after conversion to 2007 prices. The range of estimates for the effects of the parents' education on cognitive development is due to the different kinds of test scores used to measure cognitive development and to the different control variables used in the regressions. Nevertheless, it is interesting that the parents' own estimate of the value of their college education to the child's development of $500 per year is considerably below almost all other estimates of its true value. This is consistent with one of the themes of this book that there is poor information about the non-market benefits of higher education, private and social, with the result that there is market failure and need for higher education policy changes. The average value of one year's additional college education of the mother based on nine studies is $1,754 per year, or $10,178 when the mother has a bachelor's, a substantial amount.

SPOUSE'S HEALTH AND EARNINGS

There is a significant benefit to the husband's health from the wife's additional college education. It has an income equivalent value of $426 per additional year of the spouse's education, or $1,917 when the wife has a bachelor's, based on the Grossman study, as shown in Table 4.3. A search was made but apparently it is still true after many years that no one yet has studied the benefits from the husband's college education on his wife's health. The studies that show a beneficial effect of the college education of one spouse on the other spouse's earnings are not in a form that they could be used.

DESIRED FAMILY SIZE

It is again female education that is linked in the research in this case to lower fertility rates. This results in smaller family size and a better capacity to control the size of the family and avoid poverty. Based on the Michael and Willis study, as shown in Table 4.3, there is a substantial monetary value of this non-market benefit of a bachelor's of $1,551. This means that there are fewer but also better-educated and healthier children, in more highly educated families. This may not seem very important until one reflects more broadly on the implications. In Nepal, for example, in the southern rice-growing areas of the Terai women still have twenty-two children on average, about half of which die. The per capita income of these families, even if the parents harvest a substantial amount of rice, is extremely low, often under $1 per day. In the low-income, low-education neighborhoods of U.S. cities the fertility rates also are much higher than the U.S. average. Partly as a result of this the poverty rate is higher in these neighborhoods, and the education and health of the children is lower. Some very large families have a good quality of life but this may be the exception more than the rule.

HAPPINESS

Measures of happiness, or subjective well-being, recently have been found to be quite reliable when subjected to test-retest measures by Krueger and Schkade (2007). This extends work by psychologists that has produced cardinal measures of happiness based on the intensity of brain waves that correlate highly with questionnaire responses about happiness, as I noted earlier. However, in spite of this progress there is still great difficulty in placing any economic value on the value of education in contributing to happiness. Happiness does increase as education increases. But this is largely due to the effect of higher income. When there is a control for income, the relation of further education to happiness is not only insignificant but sometimes negative (Helliwell, 2003, 2005).

One problem is likely to be that the control for income needs to be nonlinear, by including only y^2 in the regression, for example, and specifically to test for the relation of college education to happiness at family-of-four incomes that are over $80,000, or $20,000 per capita. It is known that happiness does not increase above this due to income alone (Layard, 2005). Helliwell (2003) does not use this kind of a control for income, which may result in his negative relation of higher education to happiness (see note 2 in Table 4.3). There is also the possibility that there are controls included in the regression that themselves are a function of higher education, and hence are proxies for education that largely eliminate higher education's effects.

However, on balance the weight of this rather confused and imperfect evidence is that there are some positive effects from higher education on most of the things that contribute to happiness. These are, as identified by Layard (2005) and listed in Table 4.3: (1) greater marital happiness resulting from better choice of a spouse through college; (2) lower probability of divorce; (3) lower probability of unemployment; (4) greater social capital in the community due to greater levels of trust that are related to less inequality and lower crime rates; (5) better government, which therefore becomes a private as well as a social benefit; and (6) better health and longevity even though the relation of health to happiness is not strong.

So although the research on the relation of education to these contributing factors that also controls for income is insufficient to estimate the value of higher education's contribution to happiness, if any, my tentative conclusions are that:

- The relation of higher education to happiness at income levels above $20,000 per capital, or $80,000 for a family of four, is likely positive because of these contributing factors, but probably small. Hence the + signs in these cells in Table 4.3.
- There is a serious need for new research that takes into account key findings such as the nonlinear relationship of income to happiness, and that addresses the relation of higher education to the key determinants of happiness. Also, critical judgment needs to be applied to avoid the introduction of overlapping controls.

BENEFITS TO CONSUMPTION AND SAVING EFFICIENCY

There are considerable benefits from higher education through greater efficiency in consumption and also in the management of savings balances as well as more saving at each income level in the families of graduates over their lifecycles.

The benefits in the form of greater efficiency in consumption average $856 for each year of college and in 2007 dollars after controlling for income based on Michael (1982) and on Haveman and Wolfe (2007). There is some doubt that the Haveman-Wolfe low estimate is in 2007 dollars; if it is in prices for an earlier year, the value of this benefit would be somewhat larger.

Some of the greater efficiency in consumption results in a higher saving rate at each income level. So the value of the latter is not added but instead is averaged with the estimate of the value of the improvement in the efficiency with which saving balances are managed as estimated by Solomon (1975) and Lee (1982).

There are very substantial benefits from higher saving at each income level that is associated with higher education, however. More saving not only provides protection against emergencies and bad health, but it also ensures a comfortable retirement. Apart from the private benefits these are also benefits to the society. This is because those who can finance themselves do not raise public long-term care costs through Medicaid in the United States or other welfare costs. Higher financial saving also helps to finance investment in physical capital. The reason for the higher return on these assets saved by college graduates is analyzed by Solomon (1975, p. 288), who shows that after controlling for income, those with higher education are much more likely to invest in common stocks and mutual funds (t statistic = 6.39), far less likely to hold their savings in low-interest bank savings accounts, CDs, and U.S. savings bonds (t = −5.41), and somewhat less likely to invest in real estate apart from home ownership, at least in earlier years when real estate markets were poor as they were again in 2007–9 (t = −1.70). Higher saving through forgone earnings invested in the college education of children helps to finance economic growth and development.

Averaged together the $3,401 value of a bachelor's degree is a conservative estimate of the benefits from greater efficiency in household management, better consumer choices, a higher fraction of income saved, a higher fraction of income invested in human capital formation, and wiser choices in how savings are invested. These are important benefits of higher education that are often overlooked.

OTHER POSITIVE PRIVATE NON-MARKET BENEFITS

Other private non-market benefits from a college education listed at the bottom of Table 4.3 are benefits for which there is evidence but an inadequate basic research base to be able to estimate their value. These include:

- Better working conditions in higher-skilled jobs (Duncan, 1976).
- Non-cash amenities due to desirable job locations not included in salary (Chambers, 1996).
- More frequent access to on-the-job training and lifelong learning (Mincer, 1962).
- Less obsolescence of human capital due to on-the-job training and lifelong learning (Rosen, 1975; Nelson and Phelps, 1966).
- Greater enjoyment from leisure learning (for example, Elderhostel, Grand Circle Travel, etc.).
- Consumption benefits enjoyed by students while in college (Pascarella and Terenzini, 2007, 1991, Chapter 7; Lazear, 1977). To count, these must be beyond the average forgone earnings costs of room and board. The latter are investment in human capital, but some parents may subsidize comfortable lifestyles for students beyond this.

As more suitably designed research continues, placing a value on these additional non-market private benefits may eventually become possible. In the meantime they also suggest that the total value of the private non-market benefits is quite conservative.

THE TOTAL VALUE OF PRIVATE NON-MARKET BENEFITS

Adding up the values of the private non-market benefits, the total comes to $8,462 for each additional year of college. Assuming the average bachelor's graduate takes 4.5 years to finish in 2007, the value of the non-market benefit per year after graduation for a bachelor's is $38,080, as shown in Table 4.3. This is 78% of the earnings increment the average male can expect, and 122% of the average earnings increment from a bachelor's for males and females on average based on earnings as given by the U.S. Census and expressed in 2007 prices (U.S. Census, 2006). This total is 22% larger than the earlier estimates by Wolfe and Haveman (2001, 2003, 2007), although this 22% difference largely can be explained by the inclusion of a number of non-market private benefits that they do not address. The estimate here is consistent with the estimates by Grossman (1997, 2006) because he focuses primarily on the health benefits and finds them to be about equal to the earnings benefits, as indicated above.

Table 4.3 is unique, however, in standardizing all studies containing the relevant information that deal with the same non-market outcome, averaging these, and showing all of the backup detail, including what variables are included in each regression and how each coefficient was standardized in Appendix C.

For comparison, a very different approach to estimating the total value of the private non-market benefits of education is using the system of "Total Accounts" pioneered by Kendrick (1976) and Eisner (1989). They are based on the National Income and Product Accounts but extend them to include the value of non-market elements of total human welfare. The Total Accounts start from the concept of total final satisfactions, including non-market satisfactions, which are a part of total output and total income. Total final satisfactions and total income in these accounts is roughly consistent with Becker's total final satisfactions and "total income" in his theory of the allocation of time (Becker, 1965). That is, total income includes "total saving," which includes forgone earnings, and "total investment," which includes forgone earnings as part of investment in human capital. Eisner (1989) in his book *The Total Incomes System of Accounts* imputes a value for home production of final satisfactions during leisure hours that is over and above market-based personal consumption expenditures. But his final satisfactions do not include only those produced by human capital, much less those produced by only higher education. Nevertheless, since personal consumption expenditures depend on money income, by subtracting them from total final satisfactions there is available a control for the monetary returns to education. Eisner's measure of these non-market final satisfactions includes the value of child education in the home, the value of health care in the home, and the value of all household work, all of which are included in Table 4.3. He also includes the value of the work of volunteers, which I regard as a social benefit to be considered in the following chapter.

However, Eisner's estimate, as well as those by Kendrick (1976) and by Jorgenson et al. (1987), include the value of the services of females in the home, which includes the value of their primary and secondary education and the value of unimproved labor. So the result is an overestimate of the non-market private returns to higher education alone. Nevertheless, Eisner finds the value of these non-market services produced in the household to be in excess of personal consumption expenditures by $3,252 billion (in 2007 prices). This is approximately equal to personal consumption expenditures. This approach leaves out the effects of higher education on better health, on longevity, on more efficient consumption, on higher savings rates, and on more efficient management of saving. So although this comparison is too rough to be very meaningful, it is a cross-check using totally different methods. The total non-market components of human welfare estimated by this method are consistent with the conclusion that the private non-market benefits of education are as large or larger than the market benefits.

The Policy Implications of Poor Information

If the conclusion is that the scope and the value of the private non-market benefits of education itemized in Table 4.3 are underestimated by students and their families, then higher education markets to this extent do not work efficiently. This in other sectors has always called for policy efforts to try to improve information so markets work better.

Certainly students do not value the non-market benefits very highly, presumably because they do not know what they are. Their view of the future also may still be somewhat short-sighted, or myopic, although this is probably not the basic problem because their view of the earnings benefits seems to be clear. It also seems that they do not know what most of these private non-market benefits are (McMahon, 1984b; Riddell, 2003, 2004). Contributing to market failure is poor information about:

- The *existence* of most of these private non-market benefits. Students do seem very aware of the better opportunities at college of meeting a college-educated spouse (McMahon 1984b)
- The *value* of these non-market benefits to their health, longevity, future children's health and education, family size, and happiness
- Student capacities to repay loans and to provide collateral, leading to *imperfect capital markets* and acute awareness by students of the advantages of government-guaranteed student loans
- *Non-market social benefits* (see Chapter 5)
- *Social benefits* externalities that spill over to benefit others with little private benefit to the student or his family (McMahon, 1984b; see also Chapter 5)

Remedying the problem of poor information requires different higher education policy policies. I address the first two problems briefly below. I consider the last two in the following chapter, which is concerned with the social benefit externalities.

Higher education markets do not function well if there is poor information about the non-market benefits to better health, longevity, child education, child cognitive development, child health, consumption efficiency, saving rates and savings management efficiency, non-market job and location amenities, and personal happiness. If non-market benefits that are about 122% of the earnings benefits are overlooked, then students and their families will not respond to these and there is serious underinvestment. Some of the current skill deficiencies in the U.S. and European Union economies may well be due to this underinvestment by those who most need to invest in their own education.

Consistent with this underestimation of total benefits, economic motives are listed three and a half times more frequently than non-economic motives for attending college by high school seniors in surveys by Leslie et al. (1977) and by Astin et al. (1985). Consistent with but beyond this, the econometric model that controls for parents' income and education, ACT test scores, student financial aid, and other factors has been mentioned earlier (McMahon, 1984b). This study finds that private non-market benefits are of little significance in determining planned investment in a college education, whereas expected increments in earnings are of great significance. The only non-market private benefit of significance was finding a suitable mate, but students could be expected to be more aware of this due to strong inherent mating instincts. Consistent with these studies, focus group interviews sponsored by the American Council on Education (2007) found that parent-respondents seldom mentioned non-market outcomes. But when they were prompted they did not disagree. These all suggest that not many of the non-market benefits other than mating is perceived, and that their value is underestimated.

The classic remedy to this problem of poor information is for the government to provide better information to the participants so that the markets can work. Alternatively, laws are passed that force the sellers to provide accurate and full information to potential buyers if they are to avoid penalties. Examples of this in the United States are numerous:

- The U.S. Department of Agriculture (USDA) provides information directly to farmers about hog prices at local markets, grain and futures market prices, agricultural research, nationwide crop sizes, and weather, and also regulates weighing and grading practices.
- The Securities and Exchange Commission (SEC) requires full and honest disclosure in prospectuses and reports. This is necessary if securities markets are to work. This is very actively enforced, as Enron executives who provided misinformation discovered.
- The Truth in Lending Act requires banks to disclose truthful lending rates and credit card conditions to prospective borrowers.
- The Food and Drug Administration (FDA) requires weights, measures, and contents to be displayed on all food packages.
- The Federal Trade Commission (FTC) Act requires truth in advertising and in labeling.

The U.S. Department of Education and state-level boards of higher education have not been equally active as the USDA, SEC, FDA, or FTC. They collect and provide extensive data increasingly relevant to the merits of different colleges. The accountability movement in higher education is moving in this same direction. But both are largely limited to short-run concepts of higher education outcomes, such as test scores and graduation rates, and are not generally supplemented with information about longer-term outcomes. The accountability movement does not appear to have seriously come to grips with value-added so that standard outcome measures tend to reflect pre-selection of able applicants by selective colleges. The qualifications that have been mentioned include the fact that the Spellings Report (U.S. Department of Education, 2007) does recommend use of value-added measures but does not provide means for implementing them (as I do in Appendix A). The new Rand Corporation tests at graduation do correct the outcome measures for entering test scores for some colleges and universities and thereby take value-added issues into account. Although accountability is important, from a broader human capital formation perspective it is crucial that it not only focuses more on outcomes, corrects for value-added, and includes attention to longer-run outcomes, but also that it does not miss the fundamental point in this chapter, namely that students and parents need to have better information about the non-market benefits and their value to themselves and their families if higher education markets are to work well.

Underinvestment can be corrected by public subsidy. Other things being equal, it stimulates additional investment by families in human capital formation. But when a basic problem is poor information about private benefits, it is better to provide more complete information to students and their families and let them make their own decisions. How this could be done will be considered further in Chapter 6, which is concerned with national, state or provincial, and local campus higher education policies.

POOR INFORMATION IN CAPITAL MARKETS

Imperfect capital markets are a much more familiar problem and one that is very extensively studied and discussed as a source of market failure in higher education markets. Higher education policies designed to deal with this have been implemented extensively in the developed countries, and by fits and starts in the developing world. The main policy response has been to provide government-guaranteed student loans, which makes credit more available to students at lower rates of interest.

The source of the market-failure problem in student loan markets is basically poor information. Banks and other private lenders have little real evidence about the future earning capacity of a given individual student, or his or her willingness to repay, and middle- and lower-income students especially cannot provide collateral. The policy remedy to this type of poor information is different, however, in that it is not to provide better information but instead to guarantee the loan. This can be done best by the government because what is risky for an individual student given his or her unknown prospects is a near certainty for the earning capacity of large numbers of students. It is also because the central government has the capacity to collect student loans anywhere in the country through the tax system if necessary. Therefore, it is practical for the government to stand behind the student, ensuring the repayment of the loan, spreading the risk, and enforcing repayment terms if necessary, all of which makes funds available to the student and his or her family at a lower rate. The government can borrow at a lower rate than is available to students or private banks and re-lend to students. This basic rationale for government intervention to correct the deficiencies of private capital markets applies both to loans by private lenders that are guaranteed by the government and to direct loans to students by higher education institutions that are financed by the government.

Problems have arisen in the United States, however, about the extent to which private banks are to be subsidized for the services they provide in administering these guaranteed loans. For example, the House and Senate acted in 2007 and President Bush signed a law that cuts the interest rate in half on subsidized Stafford Loans from 6.8 percent to 3.4 percent over 5 years. The savings is to be used to aid poorer students. This reduced the subsidy to banks by roughly $19 billion. This provision was bitterly fought, and yet the bill passed the House by 292 to 97 and the Senate by 79 to 12. Only Republicans voted against it. Further illustrating the nature of the political conflict, the Democrats in the House passed several times a measure to extend Medicare health care coverage to 17 million uninsured children. The Republicans and President Bush insisted on going through private health insurance companies even though the Congressional Budget Office estimated that this would be 16% more costly. The bill passed the Senate as well, but President Bush has vetoed this measure twice. This struggle over student loans provided by private banks and over private versus public health insurance for children illustrates another aspect of the struggle over privatization that is a major feature of current higher education policy.

A closely related higher education policy issue relevant to privatization involves the right of colleges and universities to make direct federal loans to students. This cuts private banks out of the process and offers major tax savings. Legislation in fact made this possible originally in order to further reduce the large intermediary payments collected by banks. After an initial surge, banks made efforts to get college and university student aid officers to direct students to them as preferred lenders. The number and amount of direct loans made by higher education institutions flattened out, while loans by banks and other lenders backed by Sallie Mae resumed their growth. This happened even though the costs are higher. It has been charged that some colleges and universities profited from the efforts by banks to obtain preferred status. An investigation is underway into whether unethical incentives have been provided.

Student loans are not designed to be means-tested as are Pell Grants. They are intended as a means of making the capital markets more efficient and to benefit all students as the costs of poor information are reduced, and not as a net subsidy to students from poor families. However, if the interest rates get below what it costs the federal government to borrow, so that the loans are subsidized as are most Stafford Loans, then it becomes important to introduce means-testing as is done with Pell Grants. Otherwise higher-income families who do not need to borrow will be induced to borrow and substitute these lower rates for college support that would otherwise come from their income or assets. This increases the cost to the government, does not increase enrollment rates, and decreases the total public support available for higher education.

In conclusion, the value of the private non-market benefits of higher education is large—approximately 122% or more of the earnings benefits. This does not seem to be commonly realized. If this is the case the poor information possessed by students and their families contributes to market failure and to serious underinvestment in higher education in the United States, the United Kingdom, and European Union countries. Guaranteed student loan policies have been implemented to deal with the poor information leading to imperfect capital markets, although the struggle over the degree of privatization involving bank profits is ongoing. There are higher education policy remedies available to correct poor information about private non-market benefits. But these have not been implemented in any very meaningful way. In the meantime the symptoms of skill deficiencies are widespread in the United States, the United Kingdom, and developed European Union countries. This underinvestment in skills is contributing to slow long-run growth in the United States especially as well as to a protectionist backlash coming mostly from those with a high school education or less who are left out of the growth process.

The failure to articulate the nature and to respond to this economic and social need, as developed in Chapter 3, and the additional failure to move vigorously to improve the information available to students and their parents about the scope and value of the private non-market benefits of higher education constitute two major higher education policy gaps.

CHAPTER FIVE

Social Benefits of Higher Education and Their Policy Implications

It is not the individual, but the society, that creates wealth.

ANDREW CARNEGIE (1889)

S OCIAL BENEFITS of higher education emphasize the benefits of higher education to the society that are externalities, that is, benefits that spill over to others, including future generations, that are beyond the private benefits of higher education to the individual. Social benefits are usually defined as the total benefits of higher education, private plus social including the externalities, although I focus on the externalities in this chapter since these are the main rationale for there being public rather than exclusively private support of higher education. The proportion of the total benefits of education that are externalities is the best guide to how far the trend toward privatization in the financing of higher education should go for achieving optimum efficiency.

The other key basis for public support is equity. This involves the desire to provide for equality of educational opportunity or even something beyond that, such as John Rawls's justice, by providing access to higher education to able students from poor families. This is an important justification for public support as well. It is addressed in higher education policy by funding need-based grants such as Pell Grants in the United States, state need-based grants, state support of higher education institutions, and lower tuition and room and board costs at community colleges. On

purely efficiency grounds, however, students and families who do not receive the benefits from externalities that benefit others have insufficient
incentive to invest in higher education in order to secure them. They,
therefore, will invest less than what is in the best interest of society. Public
subsidy is required to correct this underinvestment source of economic
inefficiency. Taxes can also adversely affect other economic incentives, of
course, and if there is significant government failure this could reduce the
benefits realized from eliminating the market failure that exists because of
externalities. However, the opportunities lost due to taxation are taken
into account by comparing the social rate of return to the return that could
be earned if the taxed funds were used in other ways, as I indicated in
Chapter 3. Accountability measures must also be actively pursued to minimize government failure. If these are both done, the net gain to the society
from public support that permits realizing the social benefits from higher
education can be substantial. In this chapter I will identify and measure
the quantity and monetary value of these social benefit externalities.

Social Benefits and Their Context

The social benefits of higher education can be estimated in three ways.

1. *The Social Rate of Return.* The social rate of return as defined earlier
is calculated by finding that pure internal rate of return that discounts the
stream of future earnings before taxes net of the earnings of high school
graduates back to its present value and equating it to the total public plus
private investment costs of the higher education (the "full method"). This
is the narrow social rate of return based only on money earnings and it
understates the true social rate of return because it leaves out the non-
market social benefits, including the external benefits of higher education
to the society. If it included these, since it does take the full institutional
costs of instruction into account, it would be the best single measure of
the total return to investment in higher education in relation to costs that
is available.

2. *The Contribution of Education to National Income Growth.* The
older method of calculating the overall macro-return from education to
the economy and to the society was to use "growth accounting" based on
the pioneering contributions of Denison (1962) and Schultz (1961). This,

however, was basically an accounting approach that did not explain growth as part of a cause and effect process that also takes the dynamic lags in the process into account. Using basically a Solow (1956) production function augmented with human capital (à la T. W. Schultz) investment in basic education contributes about 17% to growth and higher education contributes another 5% to growth by this method. But there is a very large 20 to 40% unexplained residual left. Undoubtedly included in this unexplained residual is a very large amount due to investment in research creating new knowledge and investment in higher education that is inextricably entwined with the embodiment of this new technology and knowledge and its dissemination. To label this large residual as vaguely due to technology was recognized by Griliches long ago as unsatisfactory and it remains today as a totally unsatisfactory explanation.

So the growth accounting approach has been gradually modified and displaced with a structural explanation. This transformation was pioneered by Griliches in the 1970s and 1980s as described by Heckman (2006). The explanation of growth now relies primarily on endogenous growth theory. This structural explanation most recently has been modified further to incorporate the non-market private and social benefits of education to become a theory of endogenous development. Both endogenous growth and endogenous development theory stress education externalities. Short-term dynamic versions of each are beginning to go still further toward explaining the famous residual (McMahon and Psacharopoulos, 2008; Breton, 2008). Higher education creates human capital that is complementary with university-based research and development in both creating and disseminating new knowledge as well as trains the researchers who create and adapt new technologies in firms as a key part of the structural explanation of the dynamic growth process. I will say more about how this relates to micro-data–based social rates of return later in this chapter.

3. *The Economic Impact of Colleges and Universities.* Economic impact studies are a third way that the spillover benefits of higher education to surrounding communities have been estimated. They are a legitimate way to explain to Chambers of Commerce and other local groups the economic impact of college and student expenditures on the community in which the college is located. But they phase down to zero in impact as

the distance from the campus increases. And the total impact, local plus national, is zero when a larger geographical area that includes the places where the taxes and other resources are collected. For community colleges the impact has been estimated to be about $1.50 to $1.60 in local income created per dollar spent by the college or its students. This is equivalent to 59 local jobs created for every $1 million of the college's operating budget. For 4-year schools these impacts are a bit larger, or $2.20 in local income created per dollar spent and 67 jobs created per $1 million in the campus budget. These estimates are based on the best survey available of many studies by Leslie and Brinkman (1988, pp. 86–103). These are multipliers that are unlikely to change much over time, or even between communities of comparable size throughout the U.S. or Organization for Economic Cooperation and Development (OECD) market economies. They are basically Keynesian multipliers that trace the impact of campus budgets on local demand following methods developed by Caffrey and Isaacs (1971). The multipliers are much larger close to the campus and much smaller farther out. And the short-term dynamic impact multiplier that summarizes the impact over a year will always be smaller than the two- or three-year equilibrium multiplier calculated after successive and diminishing waves of feedback effects have had had a chance to work themselves out.

Beyond this there are some very major problems with this approach. It often gets misapplied and misinterpreted. For one thing, economic impacts are not a measure of the social benefits of higher education because they do not include the non-market social benefits, do not net out the spillover costs, and furthermore are purely local and not statewide or national. An even more serious problem arises when attempts are made to calculate these economic impacts on a statewide or national basis. These impacts are essentially zero and furthermore truly problematical because the resources spent locally by students and by institutions have been withdrawn from other communities where their parents live and by taxes with a roughly equal negative multiplier effect on economic demand for products and services in these other communities. Research universities may draw some federal money from other states. But the net economic impact statewide, or nationwide, of higher education student and institutional expenditures both must be cancelled out against the negative impacts in the places from which the resources are drawn. So the net economic impact as measured by this methodology is due to tunnel vision since for larger geographical areas it is essentially zero.*

The basic idea of economic impact multipliers is that each dollar spent by the campus, such as for salaries, is re-spent in local grocery stores and retail shops, thereby creating jobs for store clerks and revenue for suppliers. This in turn is re-spent by them, but only partly locally, so the local effect of each new round diminishes as it is re-spent multiple times. Allowing a year or two for this repeated re-spending to occur, the impact builds up to the multiplier of 1.6 for the community college and 2.2 or so for the four-year college or research university.† This occurs since a larger proportion of the four-year colleges' and research universities' resources come from outside of the community, and more of the resources spent by community college students and community colleges come from local sources and therefore would have been spent locally anyway. The economic impacts of all colleges and universities measured in this way are smaller as one moves farther out from the campus locality.

Because the results of these impact studies are neither a measure of the private or social benefits of higher education, nor a legitimate measure of the returns from college expenditures, which are really investment in human capital formation, economic impact studies will not be considered further in this book.

Social Rates of Return

Conventional social rates of return are also called narrow social rates of return because they are based only on money earnings, including taxes paid. They therefore underestimate the true social rate of return that

---

*This assumes that balanced-budget multiplier and deadweight tax loss incentive effects are negligible.

†The expenditure multiplier must be applied to local expenditures only (for example, expenditures by research universities on lab equipment produced in other states does not affect the local economy). The sources of the funds spent locally also must be non-local. The assumption made in some studies in calculating the statewide impact of a college or university that the funds obtained elsewhere through taxes, borrowing, or from parents for student support would not have been spent otherwise is totally illegitimate (since it has been many years since there was a deep depression with funds caught in a liquidity trap). For a good discussion of the necessary refinements to economic impact studies and their many pitfalls, see Leslie and Brinkman (1988, pp. 86–103).

should include the value of the non-market spillover benefits of human capital to society generated during the two-thirds of waking hours not earning on the job but spent at home and in the community. Narrow social rates of return therefore exclude most but not all external benefits to society and to future generations. What these externalities are, how they can be measured, their value, and how this helps to reconcile the social rates of return based on micro-earnings data and the net impacts of higher education on growth and development are the main issues I address in this chapter.

With respect to what the data shows, conventional narrow social rates of return for associate degrees were nevertheless a high 16% in real terms for females and also a high 13% for males earning bachelor's degrees in the United States in 2005. These are all well above the benchmark 10% real total return available on alternative investments. They also have been rising for college graduates since about 1980, as I stressed in Chapter 3.

Table 5.1 summarizes these social rates at associate and bachelor's levels, but also at other levels, and also compares all of them to the private rates of return available to students and their families. Typically, the private rates of return are higher than the social rates because for social rates the full costs to society are included. That is, the costs to society such as public subsidies to public institutions and the costs of student financial aid at both private and public institutions are treated as part of the costs, and not just the private costs to students and their families, which are used in computing private rates of return. The estimates by Heckman et al. (2008) are of private rates, for example, as are all estimates by the Mincer method or its revisions since they do not include institutional costs. The "full method" that many have come to prefer is available at my website (McMahon, 2008) together with the data and formulas underlying each cell that provide the backup for the social and private rates of return shown in Table 5.1. For the controls related to "ability bias," see Appendix A.

These narrow rates of return are understated by the omission of non-market benefits but also because true instructional costs are less than educational and general expenditures, which include some non-instructional spending. But even without these adjustments the social rates of return in Table 5.1 reveal that investment in associate and bachelor's degrees are good investments for society. Public support induces additional

TABLE 5.1 Conventional Social and Private Rates of Return in the
United States, 2005

Education level and sex	Social rate	Private rate
High school graduate, male	0.06	0.10
High school graduate, female	0.06	0.12
Associate degree (2), male	0.14	0.18
Associate degree (2), female	0.16	0.24
College 1–3 (average 1.5 yrs), male	0.11	0.16
College 1–3 (average 1.5 yrs), female	0.08	0.13
Bachelor's degree (4), male	0.13	0.20
Bachelor's degree (4), female	0.11	0.21
Master's degree (1.5 past BA), male	0.10	0.17
Master's degree (1.5 past BA), female	0.08	0.17
Doctorate degree, male	0.08	0.22
Doctorate degree, female	0.08	0.28
Professional degree, male	0.13	0.31
Professional degree, female	0.09	0.27

private family and student investment as enrollments increase. Table 5.1
shows that it clearly pays to complete a two-year or a four-year college
degree. The social rate for males that drop out after one to three years is
a lower 11% and for females a still lower 8%. The latter are comparable
to the 8 to 12% private rates obtained by Heckman et al. (2008, Table 3)
for those with two years of college but not necessarily with an associate
degree. This suggests that higher education policy should address improving retention and achieving degree completion more seriously. The private
rates of return in Table 5.1 also show that high private rates of return that
reflect lower private costs because of subsidies to investment by individuals in completing master's of 17% for both males and females, PhDs of
22% for males and 28% for females, and professional degrees of 31% for
males and 27% for females indicate that this is a private investment that
pays off very handsomely.

It is sometimes pointed out that occasionally the calculation of pure
internal rates of return by the full method breaks down because the itera-
tive solution that is involved will not converge and an error message results. This is true, but it is not a serious objection to use of the rate of
return as a criterion. This is because the cause of the breakdown is usually

too many inflection points over the age cycle in the net earnings differential, which is the difference between college earnings and high school earnings at each age. This can easily be corrected by smoothing the age-earnings profile by averaging observations adjacent to the dip since the latter will usually be seen to be due to a smaller sample size at the point where the dip occurs.

This approach is preferable to using the net present value of a college degree because the latter has major drawbacks. First, it normally does not consider the investment costs, and if so is largely irrelevant to policy. Second, to discount future net earnings back to their present value requires choice of a discount rate, which has a big effect on the calculation and yet is somewhat arbitrary. For example, a bachelor's degree for a typical male in the United States is worth $1,398,162 in 2007 prices measured in future values, which is the simple sum of the earnings increments due to college. But its net present value is less than half that, or $584,939, when these earnings increments are discounted back to their present value.* These serious shortcomings do not apply to either social or private rates of return, which do not use a social discount rate since they are pure internal rates of return computed in such a way that the present value of the stream of net future earnings is equal to the investment costs, with the net present value including costs equal to zero.

The rates of return in Table 5.1 computed by the full method are calculated mathematically as a pure internal rate of return as distinguished from Mincer earnings functions, where the education coefficient is referred to as a Mincerian return. Mincer regressions, as indicated in Chapter 3, explain the log of earnings as the dependent variable with years of education, age, age squared, and sometimes additional variables such as test scores as a proxy for ability. A major problem inherent in Mincer regressions for the purpose of our focus on the social benefits in relation to costs in this chapter are the many simplifying assumptions involved. Costs in a Mincer regression are implicitly only forgone earnings costs, which increase with each additional year of education and do not explicitly include institutional costs. Since they include only the private costs to the student, a Mincer return therefore shows only a private return. Age and age-

*This assumes a discount rate of 4%. If the discount rate chosen were 6%, the net present value is $408,532.

squared also ignore the connection of learning on the job to the amount of prior education, a point stressed by Mincer but another major deficiency. They also do not reflect the tuition and fees paid although Heckman et al. (2008) recently correct this. These limitations do not apply to the full method. There are also other problems with Mincer earnings functions that are addressed in a very aggressive recent attack rejecting the approach by Heckman et al. (2005, 2008). Although these authors raise technical issues that are beyond the scope of this book, the main implication that they discuss arises because cross-section age-earnings profiles, which are normally used for the calculations, have been shifting upward over time, especially for college graduates, so that college-level returns are understated. I addressed this issue earlier and found that all rates of return at the college level should be adjusted upward by about 3 percentage points in Arias and McMahon (2001). We found that the upward shifts in cross-section college age-earnings profiles since 1980 raise rates of return by this amount. This is a refinement of the traditional correction for a growth factor. It is upward for college graduates, and flat or downward for those with high school or less, as discussed in Chapter 3.

Given this justification for preferring the full method when considering social benefits, as in this chapter, it should also be noted that control variables sometimes included in Mincer earnings functions are legitimate whereas others are not. It does not make sense to include both education and occupation in the same regression, for example, because entry into most occupations is determined by education. When occupation is included, the explanatory power of education tends to be reduced, with the result that the Mincerian return is understated.

Controls for socioeconomic status also normally are not appropriate. They are short-sighted, as illustrated by the fact that they do not take the intergenerational effects of modern endogenous growth theory into account. Socioeconomic status (SES) is itself a product of the education of earlier generations, especially of the parents. This dependence of human capital formation on the education of earlier generations is explicit in the Lucas (1988, p. 18) model, where the accumulation of human capital depends on its own past levels within the typical family. "Indeed, mother's or father's education generally is considered to be the best proxy for SES" (Leslie and Brinkman, 1988, p. 50). Human capital production also is not subject to diminishing returns over generations. This is an important point that permits increasing education and knowledge to continue to serve as an engine of per capita economic growth perpetually. The short-term dynamic model to be presented later in this chapter includes an explanation of this accumulation of SES over generations within families and hence also within nations quite explicitly. That is, SES is one of the benefits of education in a longer-range rate of return analysis that includes earlier, and later, generations.

Finally, ability as proxied by test scores is sometimes included in Mincer regressions. But there is not a sorting for ability levels in Table 5.1. It is true that ability is an omitted variable that does partly explain some increments to earnings and rates of return. It alone can bias upward the true effects from human capital formed in college and hence private and social rates of return due to its effect on selection of who attends college. But this bias is roughly offset by measurement error, as we will see later in this chapter and in Appendix A. Therefore, avoiding a separate correction for ability as it affects selection bias, as in Table 5.1, is regarded by most professional opinion as leading to the most accurate estimates of rates of return.

To consider this issue briefly, innate ability cannot be measured very well since it is so entwined with the quality of earlier schooling and with parents' education. So it is usually proxied by use of test scores, which themselves are usually called achievement tests and mostly measure prior academic achievement. These in turn are highly correlated with the parents' income and hence their education. So U.S. colleges that select on the basis of ACT or College Board test scores, a practice dominant in poor countries, are largely selecting the sons and daughters of the wealthiest families or bureaucratic elites for admission. Rank in the high school class is well known to be a much better predictor of whether or not the student will graduate than test scores. Both because of its better predictive ability and because it gives a chance to bright students coming from poor districts and poor backgrounds it is often used for admission selection by public universities. A selection index that puts 80% or so weight on rank in the high school class is recommended as the best predictor of success in college, and this weighting is often used in colleges at public research universities.

With this caveat about ability really measuring achievement, nationwide differences in ability among campuses average out and only a small self-selection bias remains that is largely offset by measurement error. But if students at individual campuses are being studied, a correction must be made for differences in ability to measure the value-added. This correction can be done by using entering test scores in regressions to correct test scores at graduation, or to correct average earnings of graduates or average non-market outcomes to get the value-added by the techniques provided in Appendix A. There is a growing trend in the accountability movement supported by work at the National Center for Higher Education Management Systems for use of value-added.

Measures of the non-market social benefits are nationwide averages as is the data on earnings used for Table 5.1. Here again, ability bias is approximately offset by measurement error. This was Griliches and Mason's (1988) conclusion earlier, which has held up very well in recent large sample studies of identical twins. With identical monozygotic twins there is a rigorous control for true innate ability since their innate ability is the same although the amount of education they have may differ. The identical twin studies conclude that (1) there is a net ability bias that is significantly different from zero, and (2) all recent large sample studies converge on a best estimate of the size of this net ability bias as between 6 and 12%. A so-called α coefficient historically used to be used to correct earnings for ability bias. But Griliches and Mason (1988) and now the recent identical twin studies that also consider measurement error conclude that these offsetting biases essentially cancel out (see Appendix A). This measurement error is due to the tendency of individuals and departments of education in many countries to over-report their educational achievement and enrollment rates. The net result of this offset of ability bias by measurement error is that there is no significant net ability bias in estimates that do not correct for ability, whether by Mincer ordinary least-squares regressions or by the full method, as in Table 5.1. It has been important to address this issue again here because this conclusion applies to the many estimates of non-market social benefits of higher education reported later in this chapter. That is, the best modern estimate of the α coefficient is that it is zero.

Education Externalities and the Dynamic Growth Process

The relation of education to economic growth was also introduced previously in Chapter 3. But now it is important to focus on education externalities. These are the social benefits of education that set the stage for each new round of economic growth and for each new round of non-market social benefits. This is an important dynamic process, broadly applicable to the relatively slow process of development over time within families and in the aggregate, within nations.

THE FAMOUS RESIDUAL

The story of the relation of education externalities to economic growth and development can begin with revisiting the famous residual in the economic growth literature. This is the difference between the per capita growth that can be inferred from the national income and product accounts for any country and the portion of this growth that can be explained by increases in capital and labor inputs alone. It can be compared to the dark matter in the universe. This is also a residual and an extremely large one between the mass of what can be calculated from radiation emitted by stars and planets whose signals eventually become too weak, and the overall mass that can be inferred to exist from the gravitational effects on the stars that can be seen. Determining the nature of this missing mass or dark matter is one of the most important problems in modern particle physics. The residual in economic growth is also a measure of our ignorance, and explaining it is one of the most important problems in modern economics (McMahon and Psacharopoulos, 2008).

Although the residual is reduced by about 22% by augmenting increases in raw labor with human capital created by basic and higher education, the troublesome fact is that the lion's share of growth is still in the unexplained residual. When discussing this issue earlier in connection with the limitations of growth accounting approach, I stressed that attributing this residual to "t" for time inserted in growth regressions and calling it "technical change," or "improvements in knowledge," is totally unsatisfactory. This is merely a way of renaming the unexplained residual and implicitly trying to give the result explanatory power, an uncomfortable process of basing conclusions on something that itself is unexplained. However, modern endogenous growth theory and its empirical tests and also the shorter-term dynamic view of the growth and development process are gradually eating away at this residual, enabling the portion that is unexplained to be vastly reduced. The explanation features indirect effects from education that are externalities. They feed back and contribute to growth and development in later periods. The longer this process goes on, the larger the total effects of education and education externalities become. And the more of the residual is explained.

INDIRECT EFFECTS FROM EDUCATION

The indirect effects from education have been defined as those that operate through some other variable. Examples relevant to the empirical measures later in this chapter include the contribution of higher education graduates as they serve civic and governmental agencies by serving on city councils, county boards, library boards, city and county planning agencies, school boards, and mass transit boards. They also contribute to society by donating most of the funds supporting charitable institutions and serve on nonprofit private governing boards of the Urban Leagues, Red Cross, YMCA, family service agencies, public health districts, hospitals, nursing homes, and so forth. They vote more frequently than those with high school education or less and serve on juries and agencies like CASA that assist the criminal justice system. Higher education graduates also are essential to the staffing of R&D laboratories in private firms as well as the research at universities, thereby playing a central role in the creation of new knowledge and technologies.

DEFINITION OF EXTERNALITIES

Higher education externalities, which are the focus in this chapter, have been defined as benefits realized by others in the society that are not realized by those who do the investing in education, whether it be students, families, or researchers. These externalities can be either monetary or non-monetary spillover benefits to others. Education externalities looked at from the reverse side of the coin are merely that portion of the market and non-market benefits realized by the individual that are due to the education of others. This is the way externalities will be measured below.

In the examples cited, these include the benefits from the indirect effects of higher education as it contributes to stable and functioning civic institutions and indirect effects from new knowledge created by others. These are usually benefits that are taken for granted by the individual investing in college.

The indirect effects from education have often been estimated, but their feedback on the growth process generally has been ignored. One result of not ignoring these feedbacks is that a portion of the money earnings of current graduates and a portion of current growth both are the result of education externalities from the education of others.

It is universally recognized by economists that externalities from research are very important since research results are disseminated widely and discoveries can benefit generations still unborn. For example, the value to the economy and the society of the education of just one genius such as John Bardeen, who won two Nobel Prizes in Physics for inventing the transistor that became the foundation for the computer revolution, surely is sufficient to equal the cost of the education of millions worldwide. Marshall (1927, p. 216) said "all that is spent during many years for opening the means of higher education to the masses would be well paid for if it called out just one more Newton, or Darwin, or Shakespeare, or Beethoven."

But although research externalities are not controversial among economists, externalities from the higher education of undergraduates have been quite controversial. The simplistic argument is made by a few, often ignoring the millions of community college graduates, that current graduates earn so much and enjoy such substantial private non-market satisfactions that almost all of the benefits of higher education are enjoyed privately and there are no additional benefits that spill over to the society. The basic problem is that this view involves a superficial identification of the full scope of the social benefits and not much basic thought about the dynamics of the process. It does not take into account the fact that all earnings, however high, are partly due to the prior education of earlier generations and to the dissemination by graduates of the benefits of prior research.

ENDOGENOUS GROWTH AND ENDOGENOUS
DEVELOPMENT DEFINED

The word *endogenous* means that there is an analytic solution for per capita income growth over time that includes a solution for the amount that is invested in human capital. That is, both are solved for endogenously, or within the model. An enormous stimulus was given to the central role of education in endogenous growth theory by Lucas (1988) and Romer (1986, 1990), his student. This same emphasis is present in the human capital–augmented Solow growth model employed by Mankiw et al. (1992) and in empirical tests by Barro (1991, 1997, 2001b) and Kim and Lau (1996). It still largely dominates modern growth theory and empirical tests (Mattana, 2004).

Endogenous growth has been extended to become endogenous development by including household production of non-market private and community benefits by McMahon (2002, 2007b, 2008). There have been new applications to the developed (OECD) countries by Keller (2006), Jamison et al. (2007), and by McMahon and Psacharopoulos (2008). All of the above give human capital formation a central role in the growth and development process. Lucas's model with its emphasis on the average education levels in the community has relevance to developing and developed countries alike, whereas Romer's model with its emphasis on the education of R&D scientists gives an important role to higher education in the creation of new knowledge and the training of researchers, which has greater relevance to the developed countries.

There is no doubt that new technology and knowledge created by R&D is important. But this is treated as having little or no impact unless it is embodied in graduates and disseminated by human capital formation through education. The leading R&D occurs largely in the developed countries that are at or near the technological frontier, and even there it must be disseminated largely by college graduates. This new knowledge has little or no practical effect on growth processes in those poor countries that are without basic education. Education conveys basic capacities to utilize and adapt complicated knowledge and technologies. Higher education trains researchers for R&D departments within firms and government. These all are key major roles of higher education.

The definition of externalities can be made more precise and the foundation laid for understanding the relatively simple dynamic process by considering the Lucas (1998, p. 18) production function. Equation 5.1 basically explains total market output, Y_t, at time t, as produced using physical capital, K_t, and raw labor, N_t. It leaves the residual to be explained by inputs of human capital used inside the firm, h_t, and education externalities as reflected by the average level of education in the community, h_a. Both raise productivity within the firm.

(Eq. 5.1) $Y_t = A \, K_t^{\alpha} \, (u_t h_t N_t)^{1-\beta} \, h_{at}^{\gamma}$

More precisely, the level of economic output usually measured by gross domestic product, Y, is a function of the stock of physical capital, K, and the stock of human capital, $(u_t h_t N_t)$. The latter is the educational attainment of each individual, h_t, times the fraction of time this human capital is used on the job, u_t, times total employment, N_t. Output is also a function of education externalities, h_{at}^{γ}, where the subscript a is the average level of education in the community and the exponent γ is empirically determined, and reflects the strength of the influence of these external factors on the firm's capacity to produce.

Lucas assumes the level of technology level, A, to be a constant once these education externalities are introduced (1988, p. 18). There is a second equation in his model not shown here that determines the production of human capital. Lucas obtains a solution for this endogenous growth model and proves analytically that the optimal per capita growth rate is larger with the education externalities provided than it is with purely private markets. In contrast to the earlier Solow growth theory, which encounters diminishing returns, education externalities make possible endogenous per capita growth without bounds.

Empirical estimates of the Lucas production function find the level of physical and human capital stocks both to be crucial to the level of income per capita (Jamison et al., 2007, Table 5). Jamison et al. find that the residual important to the growth of income is related to education externalities reflected in trade as well as to education quality as measured by test scores. I have tried to relate these test scores to economic growth in the developed OECD countries only but have been totally unsuccessful.

The short-term dynamics of the growth process can be explored by dividing this Lucas production function through by population, which puts everything on a per capita basis, differentiating it with respect to time so that all variables become rates of change over time, and then dividing through by Y_t, which puts things in proportional terms that are more amenable to use with cross-country data because they are independent of exchange rates. Shorter-term five- to twenty-year lags that follow investment in education before their main effects are felt as graduates proceed through their lifecycles then are considered and those lags that are logical are inserted. These lags are what makes the model dynamic, since the size of the outcomes becomes a function of how much time has passed. Then by jumping this difference equation (and the others determining non-market outcomes of education and investment in education) forward through time, the medium-term time path of the growth process within families and within nations is generated and can be studied. The simplified short-term dynamic endogenous development model that this implies is shown in Appendix B.

In the logic of this process, after enrollment rates in higher education increase, the contributions of the additional human capital formed to earnings and non-market outcomes of education come later throughout the lifecycle, peaking about twenty years after graduation. Notice that the technology term, A, in Equation 5.1, which Lucas assumed to be a constant, drops out as his production function is differentiated with respect to time because the differential of a constant is zero. The role of undefined technical change in explaining the residual has been replaced by the effect of education externalities!

EDUCATION EXTERNALITIES IN THE
DEVELOPMENT PROCESS

With the above brief explanation of where everything comes from, it is now possible to provide a very simple but more precise explanation of how education externalities contribute to growth over time within families and within nations. This uses a simplification of the model that defines the short-term dynamics of the process in Appendix B.

Growth of per capita income within a nation or within a typical family, y_t, derived as above is shown in Equation 5.2. It is determined by prior schooling in higher education institutions on average twenty years earlier, s_{t-20}. The direct effect of education is shown by the coefficient α_1, which can be measured by regression methods. The non-market social development outcomes, D_{it} in Equation 5.3, in turn depend on higher education twenty years or so earlier. These also can be and are measured by regression methods. The disturbances ε_2 and ε_3 are other factors determining growth and development that will be ignored here. The determination of the non-market social (and private) benefits of education in Equation 5.3 must include a control for per capita income as discussed in Chapter 4 to prevent double counting the market benefits of education.

$$(\text{Eq. } 5.2) \quad y_t = \alpha_1 \, s_{t-20} + \alpha_{i2} \, D_{it} + \varepsilon_2$$

$$(\text{Eq. } 5.3) \quad D_{it} = \beta_{i1} \, s_{kt-20} + \varepsilon_3$$

The indirect effects from higher education that are education externalities are shown by the arrows to come through the effects of education on civic institutions, that is, from s_{kt-20} in Equation 5.3 to D_{it} after a lag of twenty years, and then from these civic institutions to economic growth, that is, from D_{it} to y_t, as shown by the arrows. Note that there is no constant in the growth equation, Equation 5.2. Lucas treated technology at any given point in time as constant, so it disappeared as the Lucas production function was differentiated with respect to time. The development indicators D_{it}, which include new knowledge dispersed largely by the human capital formation, now substitute for the technology constant. This ratchets the growth equation upward as time passes. So technology is no longer an unexplained, mysterious black box. It is instead identified as measurable features of society that reflect the creation and adaptation of new knowledge through education. These indirect effects are education externalities.

THE DYNAMIC PROCESS: A GRAPHICAL EXPOSITION

How the social benefits of higher education contribute to growth and development, and hence how they can be measured, can best be understood using a graphical exposition of how education externalities unfold over the longer run. Functioning civic institutions, democracy, political stability, and security, which are vital to productivity, for example, do not vary very much among the fifty U.S. states. There is free trade among states, high labor mobility, and relatively homogeneous institutions enhanced by numerous uniform laws enforced by the federal government. There have been a number of studies that attempt to detect education externalities using interstate data for these fifty states. These include studies by Rauch (1993), Acemoglu and Angrist (2000), and Moretti (2002). They have all been criticized by Lange and Topel (2006) on the grounds that high labor mobility among states suggests that there is a spatial equilibrium, which includes the possibility that differences in human capital supplies could be partially demand-determined so that this kind of data does not reveal education externalities very well. Beyond these labor markets the relative homogeneity of political institutions also suggests that all states are operating on a shorter-term flatter relation between increases in education enrollments and increases in growth rates, such as line $D_t BC$ in Figure 5.1. A steeper relation from B to E as these institutions develop and hence a larger medium- to long-run higher education impact can be observed over much longer periods of time as line $D_t BC$ ratchets upward, as suggested by the arrow.

In Figure 5.1 per capita economic growth, y, is on the vertical axis, and higher education enrollment rates lagged twenty years, S_{-20}, are on the horizontal axis. The analysis is in per capita terms, so Figure 5.1 can be interpreted as applying to a nation, or alternatively, to a typical family, and therefore to how development occurs within nations, or within families over generations. Growth is gross domestic product (GDP) per capita averaged over five years because annual changes in GDP can represent recovery from a cyclical recession or transitory fluctuations. There are often misstatements about this by politicians; an annual year-to-year change is not "economic growth" but often recovery from transitory recession dips. The intercepts on the vertical axis are indicators of the level of development, D_i. They vary by large amounts among countries worldwide but only by relatively small amounts among U.S. states. In my illustration, they represent the degree of development of civic institutions, including democracy, human rights, political stability, and security, all of which depend on education in the long run, including higher education,

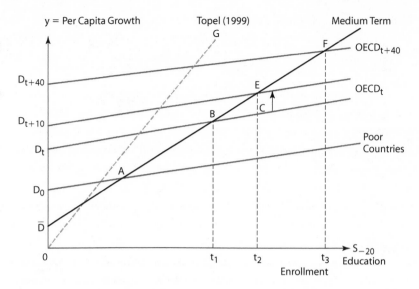

Figure 5.1. Education, externalities, and growth—the dynamic process. *Source:* McMahon (2007a, modestly adapted).

since they change slowly over long periods of time, say, 40 to 150 years. These indicators of the level of development determine the intercept on the vertical axis for the United States or any other OECD country in Figure 5.1. As development increases largely but not exclusively due to education externalities (as shown explicitly in Equation B.2), this ratchets the shorter-term function upward to D_{t+10} ten years hence, and to D_{t+40} forty years later. Sub-Saharan poor countries in Africa (and poor families) remain on a short-run relation below this at D_0.

The dynamic development process, then, works as follows within countries and within families over generations. As education enrollment rates increase from t_1 to t_2, usually encouraged by increased government support, then after a lag averaging twenty years, which allows graduates to learn and earn more in their job, the short-term effects are small, from B to C in Figure 5.1. Over the longer medium term however, the indirect effects of education begin to raise the measures of development from D_t to D_{t+10} in Figure 5.1. This ratchets the whole growth relation upward from B to E. An analytic proof that this medium-term slope from B to E is larger than the short-term slope from B to C is presented in Appendix B. This upward ratcheting can be interpreted as caused by the indirect external effects from education. We have taken some time to explain this dynamic process because the basic point involved has enormous implications both for the continuing research on education externalities and for higher education policy.

What is usually shown in the growth equations in the literature are smaller slopes like BC and not the larger longer-term effects like BE. The former underestimate education's medium- and longer-term impacts. This also explains why education impacts are found to be larger in studies based on micro-data for individuals than in many macro-data–based studies. Since micro-data normally covers age-earnings profiles over forty years after graduation until retirement, it spans a longer term than the five-year growth rates that are normally the dependent variable in growth equations estimated from aggregate data. This largely explains why education effects in micro-data are larger than the smaller effects sometimes found in aggregate data, or even nonexistent in macro-data as in Pritchett (2000, 2006) and Benhabib and Spiegel (1994).

A larger effect over the medium or longer term has been found by Topel (1999, Table 4, p. 2969) for U.S. data, as is illustrated in Figure 5.1. However, Topel does not control for effects other than education that also contribute to growth, a fact that he recognizes. So the slope of the medium-term relation of education to growth identified with Topel, line OG, is steeper in Figure 5.1 than line $\overline{\text{DF}}$ and is biased upward. Line $\overline{\text{DF}}$ assumes that factors other than education that are contributing to growth have been removed, as they have been in Appendix B and on my website (McMahon, 2008), where the large number of controls in the regressions are shown.

After considering what research worldwide has found about the social benefits of higher education, we will return to this dynamic process and what it reveals about higher education externalities within the United States and other of the more typical developed OECD countries.

The Evidence Concerning Specific External Social Benefits

It has long been recognized that the omission of the non-market social benefits of education, and of higher education in particular, is a serious oversight. Schultz (1971) says, "The social rates of return are not in good repair, either theoretically or empirically" (p. 155). This is largely because "so far the non-pecuniary satisfactions that accrue to students have not been reckoned" (ibid., p. 172). And they constitute "a serious omission" (ibid., p. 142). Fundamentally, the recognition and accounting for these major errors of omission is mandatory if economic efficiency is to be seriously discussed or achieved.

There has been prior work on the social benefits of education. It includes important contributions to identifying and valuing the non-market benefits by Haveman and Wolfe (1984, 2007) and Wolfe et al. (1997, 2001, 2003). But their focus is largely limited to the private non-market benefits, although they do mention a few of the social benefits. They also do not attempt to isolate the benefits from higher education from those of basic education. Recently, the social benefits of increasing high school completion rates have been developed very effectively by Levin (2006). Although focused on high school enrollment rates, a portion of the same effects is relevant to community college enrollment rates. Rouse, for example, calculates the tax revenue lost due to high dropout rates by black males (in Levin 2006), and Belefield calculates other social costs when high school enrollment rates are lower (in Levin 2006). Other research on social benefits has been surveyed by Leslie and Brinkman (1988, pp. 78–86) and more recently by McMahon (1997, 1998d, 2001a, 2002, 2004b). But what is needed is a more comprehensive identification of the social benefits specific to higher education and estimation of their value. First, I will review the empirical evidence for each type of social benefit from higher education, and then estimate the economic value of each. I conclude the chapter by returning to the analysis of the dynamic process above by which these social benefits set the stage for each new round of growth and development and cumulate over time.

EDUCATION'S CONTRIBUTION TO DEMOCRACY

Democratization is the term that I will use as shorthand for the development of political institutions at national, state, and local levels. The degrees of democratization are the "political rights" measured by Freedom House (2007) since 1955 and standardized in the 1960s for 191 countries and 14 territories related to these countries. It reflects:

- The right to organize opposition parties and lack of interference in this by the persons in power
- Lack of domination by the military, totalitarian parties, religious oligarchies, economic oligarchies, landlords, or other groups
- Fair election of national and local heads of government. Fairness includes wide extension of the franchise to minorities and other groups
- Fair election of national and state (or provincial) legislative bodies
- Equal campaigning opportunities and honest tabulation
- A realistic opportunity for the opposition to gain power through elections
- A reasonable degree of self-determination by minorities and participation by them in the decision-making process

Freedom House has not extended this index to state and local levels, although a simplified index of this type has been developed and used for studies of states in the U.S. Deep South by McMahon (2007a) and for other states by Besley and Case (2003).

To have the functioning governmental institutions necessary for all of the above conditions requires a considerable number of persons with higher education. The improvement of these institutions, including the criminal justice system essential to human rights, at local and national levels also requires political science and law graduates who specialize in this. Democracy further requires attitudes that are found among college graduates more than among those who have finished high school or less such as less unquestioning acceptance of authority, a desire to participate in public service, and informed participation in the voting process. Originally, higher education institutions in the United Kingdom and the United States had as a primary mission the training of persons for the civil service, criminal justice systems, and public affairs. With the Land Grant Act of 1864 this was dramatically expanded to include the education of persons for industry, business, and agriculture, which changed the primary mission to one of broader economic development that still includes training for the civil service.

Democratization, however, also requires politically a large and growing middle class with significant per capita income that wants a say in governance. This increasingly makes authoritarian regimes unsustainable.

But a large and viable middle class requires widespread primary and secondary education, and not just higher education. This does not exist in Pakistan or in Iraq, for example. In Iraq, literacy, which usually means completion of fifth grade, was only 39% in 2000, and in Pakistan, most of the labor force is illiterate. Lacking a middle class and basic education, authoritarian regimes are likely to persist for many years if the pattern in worldwide data is any guide (see McMahon, 2002, Chapter 7). All of the over one hundred countries with per capita incomes below $600 have authoritarian regimes made possible by illiteracy. The only exception is India, which does have a democracy. But here there is both the unique British heritage of parliamentary democracy and a very influential founder, Pandit Nehru, who was passionately committed to democracy. This democratization process is considered further by Huber et al. (1993). I conclude that the causal flow is from growing per capita income and widespread basic education to democratization, the same conclusion reached by Diamond (1992) in his extensive review of the political science literature. His conclusion is consistent with Glaeser et al.'s (2004). They cite the dramatic transformations from authoritarianism to democracy in South Korea and Taiwan since World War II. In both places rising per capita income and widespread basic education came first, and then democratization came later in 1980, not the other way around. The same thing happened in the twenty-five major Latin American countries and more recently in Indonesia. In Pakistan a military dictatorship has never been interested in reducing illiteracy by giving adequate support for the expansion of basic education, and has done less to provide for growth in other ways. So because these necessary conditions do not exist, the country until recently remained a dictatorship with per capita income of $480, which is barely above what it was fifty-five years ago during the British colonial period. The point is that basic education and a strong middle class are more vital to democratization than is higher education. Pakistan has expanded higher education, but this has contributed to emigration. But once there is a strong secondary education base and rising per capita income, there is need for persons with higher education to operate and improve the political institutions and to establish the rule of law.

The evidence is that democratization worldwide is primarily determined by four things: per capita income growth, which depends on education; widespread secondary education; some higher education; and military expenditure that is low as a fraction of the national budget and not dominant (McMahon, 2002, pp. 97–101; Diamond, 1992; Clague et al., 1996). Other factors are empirically less significant. In Clague et al. (1996) an additional variable for the Muslim religion is negatively related to the degree of democracy, but it becomes insignificant whenever literacy is included, displacing the Muslim religion's role. For the developed OECD nations, secondary education enrollments again are highly significant determinants of democratization; higher education enrollment rates are positive but insignificant; and political stability lagged five years, which also depends on education, is highly significant (McMahon and Psacharopoulos,2008; see also Appendix D). The problem with studying only the relatively rich developed OECD nations is that these nations are relatively homogeneous. The wide variation in the degree of democratization that exists in worldwide data, and where the determinants of democratization therefore can be studied, does not exist. The evolution of democratic institutions is a long, slow process and not enough five-year periods that include the necessary data exist, so there are not sufficient differences among OECD nations. In order to study the relation of income and education levels to democratization it is better to consider a wider range of countries that includes low-income and authoritarian nations, and not just high-income developed nations.

When this is done Keller (2006b), who controls for per capita income and secondary education, finds investment in higher education lagged ten years to be the single most significant determinant of democratization (t = 3.22, R^2 = 0.42). Acemoglu et al. (2005a) contest this conclusion using panel data similar to Keller's (2006b). Acemoglu et al. (2005b) argue that education, democracy, and income are all driven by common long-run factors, with no causal flow from education and income growth to democratization. However, there are many problems with their studies. They are not based on a dynamic model with long lags. They also use schooling achievement, which is a measure of the stock of schooling and includes year-dummies; both operate to eliminate the effects of technology embodied in human capital formed by higher education. As I explained in Chapter 2, achievement is a stock-of-human-capital measure that eliminates the effects from new technology embodied in replacement investment in human capital, and 65% of all graduates replace those who are retiring. Dummy variables for each year further control for and hence remove new technologies disseminated by higher education. Still another problem is that Acemoglu et al. include lagged democracy as an explanatory variable. This eliminates what little variation is left in five-year movements in democratization, a process that is so slow moving that it does not change much over short five- or ten-year periods, even without all of these controls. I am therefore inclined to discount the results of the Acemoglu et al. studies, which are at best very debatable.

BEHAVIORS CONTRIBUTING TO DEMOCRATIZATION

The operation and improvement of civic institutions that are a part of democratization depends upon underlying behaviors, attitudes, and capacities. The latter are studied by means of microeconomic tracer studies that follow up on higher education graduates later in life. A Gallup Poll in the United States finds that those within each income group with higher education give voluntarily of their time to civic, political, and charitable institutions about twice as often (22% give) as those at the same income level with a high school education or less (only 12% give) (National Center for Education Statistics, 1998). Hodgkinson and Weitzman (1988) found a similar pattern earlier in a nationwide survey. With respect to financial contributions, the college-educated give 3% or more of their income to charity about twice as often as do high school graduates at the same income levels.

Table 5.2 reveals that this is true especially in the lower income groups. There 24.7% of the college-educated give generously 3% or more of their income as compared to 12.5% of the high school graduates. In the higher-income groups a smaller 19.1% of the college graduates give generously, whereas only 7.5% of high school graduates do this. Although there is undoubtedly some private satisfaction from these gifts of time and money, there is also clearly a social benefit to others. This giving contributes to strengthening of these civic and charitable institutions, which are important to effective democracy.

Those with higher education also pay more taxes. Taxes give rise to public services that benefit the taxpayer, but these public goods also bene-

TABLE 5.2 Contributions of Time and Money by Those with College, by
Income Group (%)

Annual income	Volunteered time		Charitable contributions	
	High school	Some college	High school	Some college
> $20,000	9.4	16.2	12.5	24.7
$20,000–49,000	16.2	20.9	12.8	14.9
$50,000 and up	10.6	25.6	7.5	19.1

fit others. That is, there are widely shared benefits from public radio and television, primary and secondary education, public health, roads, police protection, the criminal justice system, national defense, the National Science Foundation, the National Cancer Institute, and other public services. But additional taxes paid by those with higher education are included in the narrow social rates of return based on earnings already discussed above. But the non-market social benefits are not included. It is this critical omission I seek to correct.

Dee (2004) finds large and significant effects from higher education on voter participation and on support for free speech. He also finds important effects on the quality of civic participation, as indicated by the frequency of newspaper and newsmagazine readership. In the previous chapter I mentioned how higher education tends to shift tastes away from drag racing and television game shows and toward interests in national and world affairs, as well as toward public radio and public television in-depth news analyses. These shifts in tastes lead to lifelong learning about public affairs that are the foundation of good citizenship and related social benefits. Tracer studies of higher education graduates by Byner et al. (2003) find greater racial tolerance, less cynicism, and less unquestioned support for authority by those with higher education in the United Kingdom than those with only a high school education. They also find greater civic participation, as was found in the United States. This evidence from tracer studies is important because it includes controls for high school graduation, which establishes beyond a reasonable doubt that these kinds of benefits to governance are generated by higher education and not by basic education.

The existence of human rights depends primarily on the degree of democracy after controlling for per capita income and for military expenditure as a percent of the government's budget (McMahon, 2002, p. 103). This means that a significant part of the non-market social benefits from democratization are realized in the form of improved human rights. Human rights are very important to human welfare and a separate social benefit.

Human rights are "civil rights" as defined by Western political scientists and measured by Freedom House (2007) and Human Rights Watch. In the Freedom House index these basic rights depend upon:

- A free, effective, and independent media symbolized by freedom of the press
- Freedom of speech, freedom to assemble and demonstrate, and civil rights
- Legal protections offered by an independent court system, habeas corpus, and trial by jury that must be respected by security forces, the police, army, and intelligence services
- Freedom from intimidation, unjustified seizure and imprisonment, and torture
- Free trade unions and effective collective bargaining
- Free professional organizations, businesses, and cooperatives
- Free religious expression
- Gender equity, property rights, freedom of movement, and free choice in marriage
- Equality of opportunity
- Limited corruption in government and corporations

The evidence is based on worldwide data given the high degree of homogeneity in human rights within the OECD nations. It is that human rights depend positively not only on the level of democratization, but also positively on per capita income and negatively on military expenditure as a percent of the government budget. After controlling for all three of these effects, education independently at both the secondary and higher education levels has highly significant positive relationships to increased human rights (McMahon, 2002, pp. 101–4). There are limitations to human rights and civil liberties in the United States and in some other OECD countries, due to racial discrimination, lack of habeas corpus in some circumstances, the CIA's "extraordinary renditions" and use of water boarding, some corruption due to bribery though political contributions to politicians, some corruption in corporations such as back-dating stock options and the Enron scandals, and the like. But these are so dramatically below the violations of human rights in most authoritarian countries that the variation found in worldwide data is larger.

BEHAVIORS CONTRIBUTING TO HUMAN RIGHTS

There is micro-evidence from Byner et al. (2003) on the contribution of higher education to attitudes that are supportive of human rights. These include higher education graduates that are less prone to unquestioning acceptance of authority and more tolerant of other races. The evidence concerning more contributions of time and money at each income level also is relevant to the support of civic institutions important to human rights, such as time spent on police review boards, in operation of juries and the criminal justice system, and in support of better quality news media (National Center for Education Statistics, 2005; Dee, 2004; Hodgkinson and Weitzman, 1988). This tracer study evidence that higher education contributes to human rights is close to providing evidence of social benefits provided by graduates from colleges of law and criminal justice system programs who contribute directly to the operation and improvement of these same human rights institutions. This is noteworthy because U.S. Department of Education policies that currently define engineering, math, and the certain physical and life sciences as the only ones important to the national interest overlook the contribution of disciplines such as law and political science to human rights, democratization, and the rule of law. The latter have important non-market value in their own right but also set the stage for continuing economic growth.

This is another serious omission and higher education policy gap. It is very interesting, based on the author's experience in a number of developing countries, that authoritarian regimes tend to be quite intent on stressing engineering (which of course is important) while downplaying the contributions of law, political science, and the social sciences that probably have a closer bearing on the development of democracy and human rights.

Secondary education and higher education complement one another, and both in different ways contribute to political stability and security that in turn are basic to sustained economic growth and development (McMahon, 2002, Chapter 7, pp. 105–10).

Occasionally, higher education students in poor authoritarian countries, such as Nepal and Indonesia in the past, have challenged the authorities. But this can be viewed as part of the democratization process. Indonesia has now become a full democracy. Nepal has voted to end the monarchy. But where there is almost no middle class with education and relatively few who remain in the country with higher education there is still chaos and political instability, as in Iraq, Afghanistan, Pakistan, Haiti, and Somalia. This helps to put perspective on the history of the developed countries that are the focus in this book where there now is considerable political and economic stability, but where there was not if one goes far enough back in time. There are still some occasional notable exceptions, where there is education but also chaos, such as earlier in Northern Ireland or Bosnia. Political stability and security are important to economic development and to the level of individual well-being; consider the development problems in countries with continuing chaos, such as the Congo, the Sudan, Palestinian Territories, Somalia, Zimbabwe, and many others. To consider only data from the developed countries is to consider only a relatively homogeneous environment, since these are almost entirely countries with high levels of democracy, human rights, and political stability, and where it is difficult to see in cross-section data the historical effects earlier of education on their political stability.

Political stability is measured by the International Country Risk Guide (2007). The index, which includes political and economic risks that are to some extent interdependent, consists of:

The quality of political leadership	12 points
Not engaged in external conflict	10
Economic expectations realistic	12
Economic planning failures	12
Limited corruption in government and business	6
Military and/or religion not involved in politics	12

Rule of law   6
Limited racial or ethnic tensions and conflict   6
No political terrorism or civil war   12
Developed bureaucracy and political parties   12
                                        Total   100

All have "very high" political stability except Turkey, as seen in Table 5.3. But none of the OECD countries are 100% politically (and economically) stable. The difference between Finland, the most stable, and Turkey, the least, is 25 points.

This measure of political stability has a positive and significant relation to secondary education even within the relatively homogeneous OECD nations (see Appendix D). Secondary education enrollment rates are correlated with higher education enrollments. As a result, when secondary education is dropped as an explanatory variable, higher education's effects remain positive but become significant. So the truth probably is that secondary and higher education complement one another, and both contribute in somewhat different ways to political stability as defined above. This is after controlling for per capita income and democratization, which also independently contribute very significantly to political stability (McMahon and Psacharopoulos, 2008; Barro, 1999; Barro and Sala-I-Martin, 1995, p. 426, and 2007; McMahon, 2002; Olivia and Rivera-Batiz, 2002). Since political stability contributes to earnings and growth, its enhancement is an indirect effect from education and an education externality. But this

TABLE 5.3   Political Stability (Risk) Rating, 2005

Country	Rating	Country	Rating	Country	Rating
Finland	94	Canada	86	Spain	79
Iceland	91	Austria	86	Hungary	79
Luxembourg	93	Netherlands	86	France	78
New Zealand	90	Portugal	85	Greece	78
Sweden	90	Belgium	84	Italy	78
Switzerland	90	United Kingdom	83	Slovak Republic	77
Ireland	90	Japan	83	South Korea	76
Norway	88	United States	82	Poland	74
Australia	88	Germany	81	Mexico	73
Denmark	87	Czech Republic	80	Turkey	69

SOURCE: International Country Risk Guide (2007), C. McKee and T. Sealy, eds.
NOTE: Index numbers above are rounded.

should not obscure the fact that it is a non-market social benefit of higher education in its own right.

When a broader range of countries beyond the OECD is considered, the relation of education to political stability and hence to growth becomes even stronger. For example, all of the countries on the Latin American continent were authoritarian and unstable with frequent coup d'etats twenty-five years ago. But now all are relatively stable albeit fragile democracies enjoying relatively strong growth from 1990 to 2008.

LIFE EXPECTANCY AND NET POPULATION GROWTH RATES

The contribution of higher education to increasing life expectancy is an important private non-market benefit from higher education, as I showed in Chapter 4. These effects increase lifespans, decrease fertility and family size, and lower per capita poverty in ways that are not included in narrow social rates of return. The effect of higher education as it increases the longevity of whole populations, however, reveals some social benefit externalities that are surprising.

The relation of increased life expectancy to economic growth in the developed countries is negative. That is because as lifespans increase and population growth rates slow the result is an aging population with a smaller percentage in the labor force and rising social security and medical costs. This negative effect of greater longevity on growth can be observed in the developed countries, where from 1965 to 2005 higher secondary education enrollment rates increased life expectancy, lowered fertility, lowered population growth rates, and slowed economic growth (see Appendix D). Higher education also has the expected positive effect on life expectancy and negative effect on fertility rates but it only becomes significant when secondary education enrollment rates, with which it is correlated, are dropped.

This negative life expectancy effect is the probable explanation of the negative effects from government subsidies to consumption on growth discussed by Barro and Sala-I-Martin (1995, p. 434). They measure government consumption by removing government expenditure on education and on defense from total government expenditure, so that most of the remainder is government social security and Medicare benefits supporting consumption by the elderly. The result of these negative longevity and/or elderly consumption effects on growth is that this is a negative education externality in developed countries. That is, there are positive non-market benefits from higher education's effects on longer life expectancy and smaller family size, from which must be subtracted the negative effects of increased life expectancy on growth. These will be netted out later when the value of each is calculated. But for now note that to the extent that higher education contributes to a less productive aging population that slows per capita growth, this is a negative social benefit.

ECONOMIC INEQUALITY AND HIGHER EDUCATION

Higher education in the United States and Canada tends to reduce income inequality. Exceptions are in the state of Florida and presumably in other states where the tax system is very regressive. This is because

- In the United States and Canada postsecondary enrollment rates are relatively high (as they are in South Korea).
- There is wide access for high school graduates to low-cost community colleges.
- There are many need-based grants, such as U.S. Pell Grants and state need-based grants, that significantly reduce tuition and living expenses for students from poor families.
- About three-quarters of all students are in public institutions where tuition and fees are relatively low.

Effects on Inequality. The conclusion that increased access to higher education tends to reduce inequality is the outcome of a debate in the literature that began with the now controversial Hansen and Weisbrod (1969) and Hansen (1970) studies of the California system. They suggested that the poor are taxed to provide access to students from higher- and middle-income families. The debate that followed is systematically reviewed by Leslie and Brinkman (1988, pp. 107–21) in the best survey of this literature to date. After standardization they find that all samples except Florida demonstrate that higher education contributes to greater equality in the United States and Canada.

This is not true for most countries in the OECD, however. Higher education perpetuates inequality in those countries that operate a highly selective public higher education system and base college admission on test scores. The latter are highly correlated with the income of the parents. Other features that recent research shows contribute to inequality is the tracking of students into vocational high schools, where they have no possibility of admission to college, and where there is little need-based aid that covers living expenses. On the tax side, unless the value-added taxes cover personal services and exempt food and medicine, they can be quite regressive, so that the conclusion that the studies of Florida (and by Hansen and Weisbrod earlier) are likely to hold. There are other European Union countries where tuition is low or zero, such as in Greece where free tuition is mandated by the Constitution. There again if access is based only on test scores, if enrollment rates are still relatively low, higher education could reasonably be expected to perpetuate inequality. Within the United States, those states that have the highest inequality as measured by the GINI coefficient (Louisiana, Mississippi, and Florida, where it is 0.47 as compared to the 0.43 U.S. average) and have almost no need-based grants, higher education is less likely to reduce inequality (see McMahon, 2007a, p. 479).

The main higher education policy remedies, should the decision be made to reduce the growing inequality, which are discussed further in Chapter 7, are:

- For admission, to use rank in the high school class with at least an 80% weight rather than test scores. Rank in the high school class is known to be a better predictor of success in college than test scores, and it does not have the effect that test scores have of sustaining and increasing inequality
- Incorporate need as one criterion for state student financial aid
- Expand two-year community college access and support more lifelong learning there for older students, many of whom must update their skills to adapt to new technologies and to globalization
- Expand programs that are effective in increasing persistence rates among students from poor families

Trends in Inequality and Higher Education Policy. The trends since 1988 are disturbing for those who may be concerned with social capital and political stability. There has been rather sharply rising inequality both in the distribution of earnings and in the distribution of income as shown by recent studies in the United States and the United Kingdom and in earlier studies in the European Union countries. In spite of this, more states have been choosing to use purely merit-based rather than need-based grants (McMahon, 2005). Purely merit-based aid goes disproportionately to students from middle- and higher-income families who will go to college anyway, as shown by Cornwell et al. (2003). So this trend to purely merit-based aid also has the adverse effect of operating to reduce the total number entering higher education. Ronald Ehrenberg calls on state higher education policy makers to reverse these trends in his chapter in Dicket-Conlin and Rubenstein (2006). The point that merit-based aid retains students in the state whereas need-based aid does not has not been tested, but seems debatable. However, to retain public support for financial aid programs it is essential that students from middle-income families benefit as they do from merit-based aid. So a higher education policy that would attain both objectives is one that continues merit-based aid but adds a need criterion that is broad enough to include middle-income families.

There has also been a disturbing trend in the size of Pell Grants as a percent of total college costs since it has been falling (College Board, 2007a). This means that the widening gap in earnings in the United States between those with a college education and those without and the widening inequality in the United States are addressed less effectively. A similar pattern emerges in France, where the rioting in the Paris suburbs is one symptom. The widening inequality is also a problem in the United Kingdom and some other countries in the European Union, where it creates political tensions and contributes to crime and welfare costs.

Another trend relevant to the relation of higher education to growing inequality is that degree completion rates by students from poor families are falling at the same time that access by these students is diminishing (Dicket-Conlin and Rubenstein, 2006). The result is that fewer and fewer students from these backgrounds have the necessary competitive skills. Low and falling persistence rates and not just diminishing access by these students constitute a serious higher education policy problem that deserves high priority.

So although the Hansen and Weisbrod findings in most of the United States and Canada are passé, higher education policies in a few states, some European Union countries, and many poor countries are still a mechanism of the type that they suggested redistributes income from the poor to the rich. Current trends in the United States are toward weakening the overall effect of higher education as a force that fosters greater equality. A reexamination of higher education policies is needed to consider their role in a context where there is widening inequality in the society. This is another higher education policy gap.

Inequality and Equity Defined. Equity is a normative term that involves a value judgment. Inequality is not; it is simply a description of the facts about the degree of equality in a distribution. The discussion above has assumed, as is common, that at some point too much inequality accompanied by a trend toward still higher inequality is regarded as undesirable by most people. In that limited sense, an overall statewide impact of higher education within each state that slowly reduces inequality in earnings and the distribution of income would be viewed by most within that state as a social benefit.

However, beyond this, distributional issues involve value judgments. These values are rooted in philosophy and in religion, not in the disciplines of economics or education. That is, value judgments lie outside the bounds of a purely positive social scientific analysis. At one polar extreme in an equity continuum some persons believe in commutative equity as the greatest social good. This means let the outcomes in the market prevail, no matter how much inequality this produces. This is the view of libertarians, of those who believe that markets are perfect and should never be disturbed, and of others on the far right. For them, reducing inequality over several generations through higher education policy is not a social benefit but a social evil. At the other philosophical extreme are those who believe in a theory of justice such as Rawls's positivism. Rawls's philosophy favors using policy much more aggressively to redistribute with the goal of righting the wrongs of society. Rawls is not a Marxist. A Marxist/Socialist would go farther to support government ownership of the means of production, perhaps even an authoritarian state, and also nearly complete equality, and not private ownership and the democratic process. But returning to the philosophical dimensions of equity, the two polar extremes mentioned are part of an equity continuum with many in-between positions, as discussed in McMahon and Geske (1982, pp. 20–22). Which end of this continuum is "good" and which is "bad" is a value question, dependent on one's philosophy or religion, and is not a social scientific question.

When the Southern Education Foundation assembled focus groups in

Mississippi, Louisiana, Arkansas, and Alabama, they found very limited support for redistribution through higher education policy. Perhaps reflecting this trend, there is an enormous degree of inequality in expenditure per child in the basic education system in most states, including Illinois, where per pupil spending is eight times as much in some districts as in others. Higher education admission policies are confronted with this inequality in the basic education system in the United States, so analyses of the relation of higher education policy to inequality must take this starting inequality in the backgrounds among entering freshmen into account.

However, Preston and Sarbates (2005) show that reducing inequality through education policies increases social cohesion and hence social capital and lowers crime rates. High per capita economic growth rates also are fully consistent with declining inequality, as demonstrated in all of the fastest-growing countries on the Pacific Rim (World Bank, 1993; McMahon, 2002, p. 120). There is also widespread evidence of popular political support among the American public at least for the goal of achieving equal educational opportunity. This suggests that the views of the public are mostly in the middle of the equity continuum between commutative equity and no redistribution at one extreme and Rawls's positivism with drastic redistribution at the other extreme. Seeking more equal educational opportunity or more equal access does not imply equalizing the outcomes, which is an extreme characteristic of Rawlsian positivism. Equality of educational opportunity is far short of that and a goal that remains to be achieved.

HIGHER EDUCATION'S RELATION TO CRIME RATES

If education reduces crime, then schooling may have large social benefits that are not taken into account by individuals. The substantial evidence concerning these social benefits is in the form of reduced crime rates and criminal justice system costs, but it is especially from increasing secondary education enrollment and high school graduation rates. However, these effects carry over into the next few years of community college and other higher education. The effects are not likely to be as strong as from increasing high school graduation rates, and a judgment call is necessary. Nevertheless, the portion of the social benefits due to improving secondary education is well worth including in the discussion here. This is partly because the squeeze on public higher education budgets and state student financial aid in state legislatures is due to the sharply rising costs of the criminal justice system, Medicaid, and welfare. These in turn are all traceable back in significant measure to inadequacies in the state's basic education system.

In the research, education per se, such as in further education of prison inmates and of high-risk youth, is found to be of limited effectiveness in reducing crime (Witte, 1997). There are claims that education of prison inmates reduces recidivism rates to some extent. But persons who have engaged in a life of crime since an early age seem usually to be set on that path, perhaps with human capital that has morphed into clay. What is most clear is that when secondary education enrollment rates are higher so that more young persons are in school under supervision, and more finish high school, there are fewer out in the streets who get into trouble. So both violent and property crime rates are lower. Witte's evidence does suggest that these supervision and peer group effects continue in the same direction as the years of education increase.

This same productively engaged effect applies to employment. Higher unemployment rates after a lag of about two years are found to be significantly related to higher homicide and property crime rates in the United States after controlling for income (McMahon, 2002, pp. 144, 148). Also broadly consistent with this diversionary effect, studies of social spending during the Great Depression in the United States report that each 10% increment to per capita relief spent during the 1930s lowered property crime rates by close to 1%. This ordinary least-squares estimate was similar to that obtained after controlling for potential endogeneity using an instrumental variables approach, where the same increase lowered crime rates by 5.6 to 10% (Johnson and Kantor, 2007). In the Gaza Strip and Iraq, unemployment rates of 40 to 70% left many out on the streets and undoubtedly contributed heavily to the crime and violence there.

It would appear that many prison inmates and high-risk youth have implicitly chosen a life of crime, often starting at a young age, so that this becomes what they know how to do. It is difficult for further education to divert them from this. The lack of earlier education is highly correlated with incarceration. So early education and productive engagement that involves graduation from high school and at least two years of college divert youth from criminal behaviors. Note, however that white-collar crime, which blends higher education with criminal intent, is a negative social benefit of higher education that must be netted out against the larger positive benefits from education in lowering crime rates.

Lochner and Moretti (2002) estimate the causal effects of education on crime. They find that, on average, one additional year of school lowers the subsequent probability of incarceration for white men by 0.1 percentage point, and for black men by 0.37 percentage point. Declines hold true across all types of crime examined. The authors estimate that a 1% increase in male high school graduation rates would save the nation as much as $1.4 billion. Clive Belefied reports that 54% of all state prison inmates are high school dropouts, and by age 35, 80% of all high school dropouts have a prison record (in Levin, 2006). The costs of crime include victim costs, property losses, criminal justice system costs, and the costs of incarceration. Victim costs reflect an estimate of productivity and wage losses, medical costs, and quality of life reductions based on jury awards in civil suits. Incarceration costs are addressed below.

Hiring more police is a popular approach to lowering crime. Researchers have argued that hiring a single police officer, at a cost of roughly $80,000 per year, would reduce annual costs associated with crime by about $200,000. To generate an equivalent social savings from improving education would require graduating 100 additional high school students for a one-time public expense of around $600,000 in school expenditure. Such a policy would also raise human capital and annual productivity levels of new graduates by more than 40%, or $800,000, based on Lochner and Moretti's (2002) estimates. Therefore, although increasing police forces is a cost-effective policy proposal, increasing high school graduation rates offers far greater benefits in relation to the costs when both crime reduction and the increased productivity of graduates are considered.

New estimates of the very large costs to society from the inadequate education of black males have recently been developed by Levin (2006), who reports work by Rouse, Muennig, and Belfield. Celia Rouse estimates that the additional tax revenue that would be collected if all black males finished high school, with therefore a larger percentage going on to college, compounded over their lifetimes would be $4 billion. Of this, 43% is federal tax revenues due largely to the higher earnings of those who would go on to college (in Levin, 2006). The saving in costs of this policy to the criminal justice system is an additional social benefit. This is more difficult to measure even though the social costs of crime to victims are not included. Nevertheless, the reduction in costs of incarceration at city, county, state, and federal levels; lower parole costs; lower costs for local and state policing; and lower costs of other crime prevention agencies are estimated be Clive Belefield to be $1.3 billion from implementing the high school dropout reduction policy alone (ibid.). Simulations by McMahon (2007a) estimate that a 10% increase in secondary education enrollment rates (t = 2.55) would lower homicide rates in Mississippi and Louisiana by about 20%, or from 11 to 9% in states where they are now twice the U.S. average.*

Higher education policy makers need to take this matter seriously. It is tunnel vision and another higher education policy gap to view the support of basic education as competitive with higher education out of a fixed pool of state or national tax revenues. Basic education and higher education both cause this revenue pool to grow. And inadequate state support for basic education that leaves great inequality in expenditure per child among school districts is a major cause of the budget squeeze on higher education appropriations due to prison and criminal justice system costs. These costs could be reduced by greater attention to the basic and higher education externality benefits to lower crime rates and criminal justice system costs.

LOWER WELFARE, MEDICAL, AND PRISON COSTS
FOR STATES

Each additional year of college also eases the state budget squeeze from public assistance, Medicaid, public health, and other welfare costs. These savings of tax costs to the states are in addition to the non-market benefits to all citizens from lower poverty and crime rates.

With respect to welfare costs to state governments in the United States, only 0.5% of all college graduates ages twenty-five to thirty-four received public assistance or Aid for Dependent Children (AFDC), compared to

*The standard error of the estimate is 1.82 and although a system of equations with explicit interdependencies is involved, the R^2 for the most proximate prediction equation is 0.54.

5.6% of all high school graduates receiving these welfare payments. This is a 5.1 percentage point difference (National Center for Education Statistics, 1992).

When compared to those with less than a high school education, the 0.5% of college graduates on welfare is much lower than the 17.1% of those with nine to eleven years who are on welfare. It is a much higher 35.6% for blacks who do not complete high school. In other words, welfare costs to state governments could be reduced by about two-thirds if both white and black students completed high school, and by another 91% if high school graduates completed a bachelor's degree. This is a workable approach that would supplement recent welfare reform efforts that have sought to move welfare recipients into the workforce. It needs to be drawn to the attention of legislators. It does require a somewhat longer-range perspective that addresses reduction of the number of welfare recipients in the future.

With respect to public health insurance programs, including the public costs of covering uninsured populations in the United States, Muennig (2005) estimates that the lifetime saving in public health care costs from advancing students from 12 to 14 years of education is $6,317, and from 12 to 16 years of education is $11,077 (ibid., Table 4, p. 28). He uses a 3.5% discount rate. When these values are converted to 2007 dollars, the cost saving in public health care costs is $7,770 for each student who completes an associate degree and $13,625 for each student who completes a bachelor's. These values of this social benefit from Muennig are recorded as part of the total value of social benefits of higher education in Table 5.4.

Another social benefit from high school graduation as well as from community college attendance is the saving in incarceration costs and criminal justice system costs. Lochner and Moretti (2002) estimate that the saving in incarceration cost is the incarceration cost per inmate, which is approximately $17,000 multiplied by the incarceration rate for that crime. The authors calculate that a 1% increase in high school graduation rates would have led to nearly 400 fewer murders and 8,000 fewer assaults in 1990. The savings in incarceration costs from murder alone are as high as $1.1 billion, to which must be added $370,000 in savings from fewer assaults. Savings across all eight types of crime, given the predicted decrease in robbery and rape, lead to the estimate of the total cost saving from 1% increase in high school graduation rates as it results in lower crime of $1.4 billion. In 2007 prices, this would save $2.2 billion in incarceration costs. If the savings were only half as much from completing a two-year associate degree, the public saving in incarceration costs in 2007 dollars would be $1.1 billion per year.

HOW HIGHER EDUCATION AFFECTS THE ENVIRONMENT

There now is some direct evidence from worldwide data about the effects of expansion of higher education on the environment. The rationale is that this occurs as education reduces poverty and high population growth rates, and as it increases democratization. Some of the worst deforestation and most rapid destruction of wildlife is occurring in poor, overpopulated countries, and the relatively poor authoritarian states, including the ex-Soviet Union, Africa, and China, tend to be notorious polluters. Education's contribution to less poverty and slower population growth also reduces water pollution. Higher education as well as college environmental courses increase awareness of and contribute to technologies that reduce global warming and air pollution.

Specifically, increased higher education is very significantly related to less water pollution through a robust effect that persists in many alternative specifications (McMahon, 2002, Table 9.3, p. 134). This effect occurs only after about a twenty-year lag for reasons discussed earlier. Higher GNP per capita alone is related to greater water pollution. But lower poverty rates and increased democratization offset this so that education on balance operates to reduce water pollution. Smith (1996) also has studied the indirect effects of education that contribute to better environmental quality.

Air pollution is also reduced by increased higher education in the worldwide data, again after a twenty-year lag (McMahon, 2002, Table 9.4, p. 137). As with water pollution, air pollution increases with higher per capita GNP, presumably due to greater energy use. But slower population growth and again increased levels of democratization tend to offset this (ibid.). No studies could be found on the relation of education to measures of global warming. But to the extent that this is caused by increased air pollution, it is likely to be related to energy use and to deforestation since forests reduce carbon dioxide. Therefore, the relation of education to global warming should respond in a pattern similar to that for air pollution.

Deforestation is a very serious problem occurring in many countries, and still in a few U.S. states. It causes the destruction of wildlife habitats and wildlife, and contributes about 20% of the adverse carbon dioxide effects that are the major source of potential human effects on global warming. The major roles for higher education are through research and through the dissemination of awareness leading to the support for parks and nature preserves. Higher education also reduces female fertility rates, further slowing population growth, which is very destructive to forests (ibid., Table 9.1, p. 129). A large source of deforestation in Latin America is the clearing of forests for agricultural use, which are very highly correlated in Latin American data (ibid., p. 130; t-statistics average 7.0). International agencies such as the World Bank are being asked to compensate poor countries that limit the cutting and burning of forests. Burning generates carbon dioxide and slows oxygen production by trees. To reduce air pollution, carbon emission taxes on energy producers also have been proposed. But in a world where each nation is very protective of its unlimited sovereignty, these measures are difficult to implement. Perhaps to supplement them the role of education should be reexamined.

Finally, much of the research on reducing pollution, improving sanitation systems, improving water quality, renewable energy, preserving forests and wildlife, developing parks, and global warming occurs in research universities. It is disseminated as graduate students involved in this research and undergraduates enter industries concerned with these technologies and government environmental agencies. One index of the impact of higher education on the environment could be the number of graduates in these programs. There are also many activist student groups. The next generation is interested in the environment that is a part of their future.

SOCIAL CAPITAL AND HAPPINESS

Happiness is a private benefit of higher education, as we saw in Chapter 4, but it also is a social benefit that has some externality elements that spill over to benefit others and contribute to social cohesion and hence to social capital. Empirical research on the determinants of happiness and/or well-being finds also a reverse causal flow, namely that social capital has substantial effects on happiness. The latter are effects above and beyond the effect of income on social capital, according to Helliwell (2005).

The connection of higher education to social capital measured as trust and social cohesion comes through factors that are enhanced by education such as lower inequality (Preston and Sabates, 2005), lower crime, democratization, and human rights. Helliwell and Putnam (1999) found that education is correlated with typical measures of social capital, such as trust, social participation in clubs, and community work. In fact, cross-national samples show large effects on happiness from social capital and from the quality of government (ibid.). Both of the latter are causally influenced by education in the United States and Canada as reported by Milligan et al. (2004) and in worldwide data by McMahon (2002).

Happiness is primarily a non-market private benefit and hence I discussed it in much more detail in Chapter 4. But social capital is clearly a social benefit, as the way it is measured by social cohesion, networking, participation in clubs, and participation in community work suggests. Two-way joint causal flows are common. In this case it is likely that social cohesion and trust contribute to happiness, and that the resulting happiness and sense of well-being then also contributes to social cohesion in a reverse causal flow. It has also been found that a climate of workplace trust, which is one aspect of social capital, has a large income-equivalent effect. This effect on productivity is an important finding that department heads and personnel managers must keep in mind since it has a significant economic value.

UTILIZING NEW KNOWLEDGE AND TECHNOLOGY

What is probably the largest and most important social benefit of higher education is the benefit to the broader society from the dissemination of new knowledge. This includes skills in adapting the newly created knowledge and new technologies in all academic fields. New knowledge is created by research at the research universities but also by R&D within firms, government agencies, and universities worldwide. This becomes known to faculty actively engaged in these fields. It is disseminated to graduate students at the research universities, as well as by faculty who are engaged in research and publishing at other colleges, as discussed in Chapter 6. Through these faculty, graduate students who are teaching assistants, and through new textbooks, it is disseminated to undergraduates and embodied in human capital. Beyond this, at other four-year institutions and community colleges faculty are recruited who have been involved in this research, and as they pursue their own research and engage in preparation they pass on the current state of knowledge to their students. The flow of new knowledge in journals cannot be accessed readily by those without a college education. It would remain on library shelves collecting dust unless the capacities to access and use it are continually embodied in each new generation.

The results of most research involve technical knowledge. It cannot be used unless it is understood and this requires formal higher education. In the words of Griliches (2000), who contributed so much to the study of the returns to education and to R&D, says, "knowledge is not a free good. It takes effort to develop it, to transfer it, and to absorb it. Much of the available knowledge is technical and cannot be absorbed without specific and extensive training" (p. 88). Higher education graduates who embody this knowledge become the professionals in the criminal justice system, county planning agencies, architect and construction firms, college and university faculties, primary and secondary school faculties, medical clinics and hospitals, computer systems, and R&D departments in all of the larger firms. This also includes highly skilled personnel working in public agencies such as the National Institutes of Health, National Cancer Center, State Department, Justice Department, Environmental Protection Agency, Defense Department, Energy Department, Federal Reserve Banks, and the World Bank. As globalization proceeds, as it will, the comparative advantage of the United States and other developed nations is in this stock of highly educated human capital, a comparative advantage that is diminishing, as documented in Chapters 3 and 6. This is another higher education policy gap.

Although dissemination and utilization of new knowledge and technology is a major social benefit of higher education, it cannot be cleanly separated from the benefits of R&D (McMahon, 1991). Griliches (2000) recognized and stressed this complementarity early on. He concluded that the "major sources of growth are education, increasing returns to scale, and R&D" and that "educational improvements in the labor force account for about one third" (pp. 24–25) and R&D accounts for another one-third. Physical capital investment, and trade, also contribute to growth of course. But if R&D is effective only to the extent that it is disseminated by higher education, then education including higher education contributes well over one-third of all growth in the industrialized countries.

The regressions for twenty-eight OECD countries for 1969–2005 in Appendix D have real per capita growth as the dependent variable. After controlling for other things, they reveal that higher education investment contributes to per capita growth in a highly significant way (t-statistics at the 1% level; see Model 3). The controls that are significant are for gross capital formation in physical capital as a percent of GDP (GCF), trade openness (TRADE), political stability (PS), and life expectancy (LEXP). Education investment is measured by lagged gross enrollment rates, which include replacement investment in human capital in a way that educational attainment does not. Specifically, a 1% increase in the higher education enrollment rate is estimated to increase the sustainable per capita growth rate by about 0.046 percentage point, or from 2.56 to 2.61 in the United States. South Korea increased its higher education gross enrollment rate not by 1% but by a remarkable 25% from 1995 to 2000. It has sustained a high real per capita growth rate of 4.95% since 2000. The regressions suggest that if the United States had made a similar investment in higher education, its non-inflationary sustainable supply side per capita growth rate would have been 3.68% in 2005, instead of 2.56%. Some of the 0.046 percentage point growth effect from higher education in this estimate is due to secondary education enrollments (see Model 4). But to increase higher education enrollment rates by this much in the United States high school completion rates would also need to be increased. In spite of this, most of the increase in growth would be due to the expansion of higher education since secondary enrollment rates are already moderately high (see Model 2). This conclusion is also based on the fact that higher education social rates of return in the United States are very high as well as high in relation to South Korea.* If higher education enrollments are viewed as a key mechanism for disseminating the new R&D, then this

---

*There is multi-co-linearity between secondary and higher education enrollment rates, which raises the standard errors and reduces the significance of both in Model 2, where both are included. This makes it difficult to sort out the separate effects of each. But the coefficients are not biased because of this, and Model 2 suggests that the effects from increasing higher education (0.0278 to 0.0289) are about twice as large as the effects from increasing secondary education enrollment rates (0.0153 to 0.0183), probably because secondary enrollment rates were already near their upper limit.

contribution to growth is not just the direct effect of higher education skills but is partly due to higher education's effect from the embodiment and dissemination of new knowledge and technology created by research.

Value of the Social Benefits

There are basically five methods for estimating the value of the social benefits of higher education:

- Value each type of social benefit using the Haveman-Wolfe (1984) method for valuing the private non-market benefits discussed in Chapter 4.
- Value the indirect effects of higher education, which are externalities, by means of dynamic simulations. These are discussed earlier in this chapter and in Appendix B and on my website (McMahon, 2008), and are illustrated extensively in McMahon (2002). Since these indirect effects can be expressed as a percentage of the market benefits, this establishes their value.
- Value the aggregate social benefits by estimating a cross-country growth equation and subtracting the private returns to education estimated from micro-data using a Mincer earnings function. This difference has been referred to as the external benefits of education, as in Breton (2008). This method is confined to aggregates, and does not identify specific social benefits.
- Value the aggregate social benefits based on data across U.S. cities or U.S. states using a Lucas production function and examine the significance of the "average level of education in the community" term in raising output (Ciccone and Peri, 2002, p. 6; Rauch, 1993; Acemoglu and Angrist, 2000; Moretti, 2002). The effect of the average level of human capital in the community is said to reflect the aggregate education externality benefit.
- Examine the total social accounts that estimate the total income of the nation (analogous to Becker's "full income") that includes the non-market aspects of social welfare. But the total accounts provide no method for separating social benefits from the private benefits, do not isolate the benefits from education from other effects on the quality of life, and do not isolate the outcomes specific to

higher education. The continuing development of the total accounts was limited by the deaths of John Kendrick and Robert Eisner, who pioneered this approach. Since what exists does not yield a non-market value specific to higher education externalities, this approach will not be pursued further here.

Each of the basic methods for estimating the value of the social benefits have their strengths. But they also have their weaknesses. However, estimation of the monetary value of the social benefits of higher education is possible.

The strength of the first method, developed by Haveman and Wolfe (1984, 2007), is that putting everything in value terms permits adding up the value of all of the very specific kinds of social benefits. It also permits drawing on the large number of independent research studies; often more than one study focuses on a given benefit, adding credibility. Some are based on micro-data, some use aggregate data, and the method permits monetary valuation using either. Its major weakness is that it does not pick up the cumulative dynamic effect as these social benefits repeatedly feed back and cumulate over time, although some authors do attempt to estimate a lifetime benefit. Another weakness is that there is a constant flow of studies of very narrowly defined social benefits. Some are for only one very narrowly defined type of social benefit, or particular age groups, or particular time periods, or particular countries. Many do not control for per capita income and therefore cannot be used. The results therefore are inconsistent with one another and cannot be compared without standardizing the measurements used. This piecemeal approach is not conducive to being comprehensive. There are so many studies of narrowly defined social benefits continuing to emerge that no survey can hope to be perfectly comprehensive.

The strength of the second method, the dynamic simulation approach, is that it reveals the buildup of the impacts of the social benefits over time as each short-term benefit sets the stage for successive phases of development. It also permits attention to an unlimited number of individual social benefits as well as their total effects so it has the potential of being comprehensive. Furthermore, it provides a method for separating the indirect effects from higher education from the direct effects, demonstrating that some of each graduate's earnings are due to the indirect effects from the education of prior generations. The main disadvantage of dynamic simulation is that bias can remain in the estimates of the higher education coefficients due to simultaneity (that is, education causes growth but growth also causes more investment in education). Although there are methods for dealing with this, and extensive efforts are made to prevent bias from simultaneity, it is hard to know precisely how much bias remains. Researchers often include inappropriate controls that overlap and cancel out the indirect effects of higher education, thereby throwing the baby out with the bath water. Another problem is that there is overlap of the returns from higher education with the returns from secondary education because of multi-co-linearity. A third disadvantage is that it is not practical to use data for a single country or a single state partly because of high labor mobility and a spatial equilibrium within countries. It is also because the data for a single entity does not go back far enough on all of the key variables to provide enough degrees of freedom for viable estimates, given the need to use five-year averages to get reasonably independent observations. But none of these disadvantages of the dynamic simulation approach are insuperable. To overcome the lack of capacity to base estimates on a single country, for example, panel data can be used, as is done for the twenty-eight OECD countries from 1960 to 2005 in Appendix D.

The strength of the third method, use of a cross-country growth regression net of the micro-based Mincer return, is that it is simple. Its weaknesses, however, are many. It involves the very strong conceptual assumptions that the Mincer return based on micro-data is a rate of return and that it contains no externalities resulting from indirect effects. The latter implies that private earnings do not add up to the total earnings in the National Income Accounts for some unexplained reason. Furthermore, Heckman et al. (2008) severely criticize this Mincer return as did Arias and McMahon (2001) earlier on the grounds that it does not take shifts in age-earnings profiles over time into account and therefore grossly underestimates rates of return to higher education. Another very major serious weakness is that the aggregate externalities approach looks only at market-measured GDP growth and excludes the additional non-market social benefits of higher education. The latter are substantial in their own right, as I will show. To only count them to the extent that they enhance GDP growth ignores the direct non-market benefits of health, democratization, and happiness, for example.

The strength of the fourth method, use of the average level of education in the community in a regression, is also that it is simple on its face. But it does not permit identification and measurement of individual types of education externalities, only the aggregate. There are technical issues, such as whether workers with different levels of human capital are sub-stitutes in production (Ciccone and Peri, 2002, pp. 8–9). Major concep-tual issues have arisen when this method is applied to interstate data for U.S. states. Lange and Topel (2006) have argued that there is a spatial equilibrium that suggests that geographical differences in human capital intensities can be demand driven, leading them to conclude that "the evidence for positive external returns is weak" based on this method and this kind of data (ibid., p. 479). McMahon (2002, 2007a) has argued that in addition to this, some of the largest education externalities from the indirect effects of education on the degree of democratization and politi-cal stability cannot be expected ever to be observed in U.S. interstate or intercity data, where the degrees of democracy and political stability are relatively homogeneous and the time spans are not sufficiently long. This perceived weakness in the interstate-intercity studies results from a con-ceptual difference about what externalities are, or about how many of them can be omitted and still allow an overall conclusion about education externalities to be drawn.

Because of these weaknesses in the third and fourth approaches, in what follows I develop estimates of the monetary value by the first and second methods. These complement one another in that the Haveman-Wolfe method (1984, 2007) is used to estimate the monetary values of the direct non-market social benefits and the McMahon dynamic simulation method (2002, 2007a) is used to estimate the portion and the monetary value of the benefits that are indirect.

THE VALUE OF SPECIFIC NON-MARKET SOCIAL BENEFITS:
THE INCOME EQUIVALENT APPROACH

Table 5.4 lists and estimates a monetary value for each of the social ben-efits of higher education on the basis of the Haveman-Wolfe method. The method of estimating income equivalent values of each non-market ben-efit was explained in detail in Chapter 4, and for social benefits in Appen-dix E, to which the reader is referred. The main difference is the basis on which the imputations area made for the social benefits. They again are income-equivalent values but for Table 5.4 generally for the income-cost of sustaining the average annual change in the OECD in democratization (0.0017) or the other development variables from 1975 through 2004. Table 5.4 is the first attempt that has been made to comprehensively identify and value the social benefit externalities in a way that does not double count the earnings benefits, that avoids the overlap between education impacts on a final overall outcome with impacts on the behaviors that contribute to that outcome, and that standardize the relevant studies (see Appendix E). For a few outcomes it has been impossible to determine a monetary value because the necessary basic research either does not control for per capita income or does not exist. The total value estimated at the bottom of Table 5.4 therefore is conservative due to these omissions.

Where there is more than one study of a particular outcome, the studies are standardized by putting the dependent variable, education, and income all into the same units, and the value outcomes into 2007 U.S. dollars. Then an average is computed of the values based on each study with the average shown in bold. These steps enable the total value of all of these non-market social benefits to be summed at the bottom of Table 5.4.*

The value of the direct non-market social benefits of higher education totals $27,726 at the bottom of Table 5.4. This is 164% of the average market benefits of $16,832 as given by the growth equation estimates as shown at the bottom of Table 5.4. This $16,832, which is for all levels of education and averages in Pritchett's (2006) debatable estimate of zero, can be compared to the net earnings benefits of a bachelor's degree over high school earnings of $31,174 for U.S. male and female college graduates on average over lifecycles in 2007 dollars. The earnings increment is a smaller $25,664 for females, also based on U.S. Census data. The direct non-market social benefits of a bachelor's valued at $27,726 per year are substantial, and although not precise suggest that it is wrong to conclude that non-market social benefits of higher education cannot be measured or valued.

Democracy. As a part of this total, the income-equivalent value of the contribution of a bachelor's to the operation and improvement of demo-

*Also in some cases secondary education coefficients had to be used and the outcome adjusted downward by the assumption in the footnote to Table 5.4 in light of the pattern of higher and secondary education coefficients observed in Appendix D.

TABLE 5.4   The Direct Social Benefit Externalities of Education

Social benefits, dependent variable	Value of social benefits of bachelor's	Reported coef.[a] of education	Reported coef.[b] of income	Control variables[c]	Source
Democratization and Political Institutions	**1,830**				
Democratization	994	0.018***	0.372*	lnY, M	McMahon (2002)
Democratization	1,726	0.0101*	0.05***	Y	App. D, OECD HE
Democratization	2,771	0.0114***	0.05**	Y	App. D, OECD Sec.
Democratization	59,982	0.00917***	0.032	lnY, P, S	Keller (2006b)[c]
Democratization					Besley and Case (2003)[j]
Human rights, civic institutions	**2,865**				
Human rights	2,865	0.006*	0.194**	Y, M, D	McMahon (2002)
Political stability	**5,813**				
Political stability	8,625	0.0793***	0.00025***	Y, M, D	McMahon (2002, p. 107)
Political stability	4,041	0.0423	4.7E-04***	Y, M, D	App. D, OECD HE
Political stability	3,001	0.0849**	4.1E-04***	Y, M, D	App. D, OECD Sec. Ed.
Life expectancy	**2,308**				
Positive benefits	3,344	0.0504**	2.61E-04***	Y, P	App. D, OECD HE Coef.
Negative growth	590			I, T, PS, Y(70)	App. D, OECD LEXP Coef.
Positive benefits	2,452	0.0483***	2.11E-04***	Y, P	App. D, OECD Sec Coef.
Negative growth	537			lnY, S, G, PS, t	Barro and Sala-I-Martin (1995, p. 425)[j]

Reduced inequality	3,110				
Greater opportunity	+	United States Only		S, T	Leslie and Brinkman (1988)[d]
Reduced inequality	−(OECD)	0.0015**		Y, P, H	App. D, OECD HE[e]
Poverty reduction, Sec	3,110	−1.41***	−5.6*		McMahon (2002, p. 115) Mod2
Lower crime	5,647				
Homicide	719	−15.9***	1447***	lnY, U	McMahon (2002, p. 144)
All other crime	4,928	−974***	22612***	Y, GI, PV	McMahon (2002, p. 148)
Lower public costs	544				
Lower health costs	544				Muennig (2000, p. 28)[d]
Lower prison costs					Lochner and Moretti (2002)[i]
Higher tax receipts					A market social benefit
Environment: indirect	5,609		Effects from less pop. growth and poverty, more democracy		
Cleaner water	136	−3,202**	7.79***	Y, y, P, PV, D	McMahon (2002)
Less air pollution	1,482	−1.32**	−1E+00**	Y, S, D, p, PS	McMahon (2002, p. 137) HE[f]
Less deforestation	3,991	9.9E-05*	6.7E-07**	Y, P, H	McMahon (2002)[f]
Social capital					
Social capital	+	Education effects positive			Helliwell and Putnam (1999)
Happiness	+ (?)	Effect above $20,000	Many		Helliwell (2005) neg. effect[g]
R&D dissemination	++				Non-mkt, apart from growth
Total social benefits	27,726				Direct effect externalities

(continued)

TABLE 5.4 (*continued*)

	Growth equation estimates, macro-data		
	In 2007 dollars	Education coefficient	Source
	28,672	7.20E-03***	Barro (1997)
	18,919	0.05*	Barro and Martin (1995, p. 426)
	13,274	0.005*	Olivia and Rivera-Batiz (2002)
	28,379	0.075***	Keller (2006b, p. 24), globally
	35,568	0.094**	Keller (2006b, p. 30), OECD HE
	9,843	0.047***	McMahon, App. D, OECD HE
	0		Benhabib and Spiegel (1994)
	0		Pritchett (2006)
Average all studies	**16,832**		

[a]Gross enrollment rate includes replacement investment (65% of total).

[b]GDP per capita.

[c]Definitions of control variables (for data sources see article or book cited):

Y = GDP per capita   I = investment in Phys. Cap. as % of GDP

M = military expenditure as % of govt. budget   T = trade openness: exports + imports as %

P = primary gross enrollment rate lag 10 yrs.   PS = political stability, international risk

S = sec. gross enrollment rate lagged 10 yrs.   Y(70) = initial GDP per capita in 1970

H = higher education gross enrollment rate   lnY = log of GNP per capita

D = democratization (Freedom House [2007])   PV = poverty rate

G = government consumption as % of GDP   p = population growth rate

U = unemployment rate lagged two years

GI = GINI coefficient: inequality in the distribution of income

[d]No regression in the survey.

[e]Not included in average because income coefficient is not significant.

[f]Not included in average because education coefficient is not significant.

[g]Helliwell's linear income and other controls contribute to this. See McMahon (2008, Chapter IV).

[h]These feedbacks on the non-market outcomes were also computed in detail in McMahon (2002), chapter 13. For the United Kingdom and the United States, they vary widely. This variation depends on the length of time that is allowed to pass and upon the type of non-market impact in question, with 0% effects at first, then after twenty to forty years building up to higher levels (see Ibid., pp. 238–41). The indirect effects vary also depending upon the type of non-market outcome being considered. They are relatively smaller, for example, in the case of health such as infant mortality and life expectancy than they are for democratization (87%) or homicide, narcotics addiction, and water pollution, where they are 100%. These feedback effects cannot be added up because the outcomes are not comparable; for example, the indirect effects on years of longevity are in different units than the indirect effects on an index measure of water pollution. So the "average" of 70% is crude.

[i]No income variable in the paper.

[j]Government consumption (reflecting social security and aging) as a percent of GDP.

*** = 0.01.

** = 0.05.

* = 0.10.

cratic institutions each year averages $1,830 across three studies, as shown in Table 5.4. The values in the second and third studies are based on data for the developed OECD member countries where there is a degree of homogeneity and the increases in the democratization index tend to be much smaller. The estimate of a larger value based on Keller's (2006b) regression is partly because her democratization uses worldwide data but largely because the income coefficient is not significant. So for this reason this estimate was not included in the average. The value used for the total uses the average of $1,830, which is conservative.

Human Rights. Human rights involve matters important to people's lives, such as civic protections from unlawful searches, seizures, and incarceration. These require a functioning and criminal justice system and civic institutions, but they also depend very heavily on democratization, for which I control and as shown in McMahon (2002, Chapter 7). Although there is considerable research on contributing behaviors, it is impossible to compute income-equivalent values for these social outcomes because it does not control for income (for example, in the United States, Institute for Higher Learning Policy, 2005; and in the United Kingdom, Byner et al., 2003). An income coefficient is necessary to determine income-equivalent values. With no control for income, the non-market outcomes include the market effects, which leads to double counting these when the values of the market and non-market outcomes are added up. However, higher education effects on the overall human rights index yields an estimated value of a typical bachelor's contribution to human rights of $2,865 per year, which is beyond the income benefits and after controlling for democratization.

Political Stability. The estimated value of the contribution of a higher education bachelor's degree to political stability of $5,813 is even larger. A monetary value is estimated in Appendix D, Table D.3, using a regression based on only OECD data. But the education coefficient is not significant, so the value based on it cannot be trusted and is not included in the average. It is the author's opinion, however, that the worldwide data, where there is more variation in things like political stability (assuming that there are controls for other factors that are significant), gives better observations of the longer-run net effects of education externalities.

Life Expectancy. The value of the contribution of higher education to increased life expectancy of $2,308 per year in Table 5.4 is the annual value of increased life expectancy spread out over the 65 years remaining in the lifecycle. That is, it consists of the addition to the typical lifespan by a bachelor's degree (5.4 years) times the value of each year (as in Chapter 4), with this total expressed on a per year basis for each of the 65 years remaining in the typical lifecycle after graduation.

To move from private to social, the negative effect of increasing life expectancy at older age levels on per capita growth must be subtracted. That is, there is a positive value of the non-market contribution of higher education to an increased length of life of $2,898 (averaging the two studies), from which is subtracted the negative effect on economic growth of an aging population in the OECD countries of –$590. As a cross-check on the latter, a very similar estimate is obtained by using the negative coefficient of $587 for "government consumption" from Barro and Sala-I-Martin's (1995) growth equation. That is, Barro-Martin's "government consumption" as a percent of GDP yields an estimate of a negative growth effect (–$537) that is very similar to the negative life expectancy effect (–$590) based on Appendix D. As I mentioned earlier, this is not surprising because most government support of consumption is through social security and health care expenditures that accompany increasing life expectancy.

Reduced Inequality. The best evidence available of the effects of higher education in reducing inequality is the generally positive effect of increasing access in the United States in the research reviewed by Leslie and Brinkman (1988). The probable exceptions are states where the tax systems are especially regressive, such as Florida and Mississippi, and states where there are few or no state-supported need-based grants. Non-need–based grants predominate, for example, in Georgia (98%), Louisiana (99%), Mississippi (93%), Florida (72%), South Carolina (54%), and North Carolina (51%) (McMahon, 2005, p. 3).

For the entire OECD, and not just the above effects within the United States, regressions reveal that investment in higher education increases inequality. This is probably because, as indicated earlier, in European Union countries admission to public institutions remains selective, need-based grants are limited, and students from poor families generally have little access. Regressions with the GINI coefficient as the dependent variable that include the United States and Canada find that the higher education term is insignificant, probably because the positive effect in reducing inequality in the United States and Canada is offset by the negative effects increasing inequality in much of the rest of the European Union. For this reason I estimate that the average effect of higher education on inequality in the OECD on average is zero. The effect depends on the policies each nation pursues.

There are, however, significant positive benefits of higher education from reduced poverty. These are estimated to have a value of $3,110 per year for each bachelor's degree.

Lower Crime Rates. The monetary value of higher education's contribution to lower crime rates is estimated to be $5,647, as shown in Table 5.4. This is composed of the sum of $719 due to less violent crime, essentially murder, and $4,928 for less property and other crime, a much broader category. The latter includes some crimes against persons, such as rape, but also a wide variety of other crimes that are overwhelmingly property crimes. The positive contribution of higher education to white-collar crime rates is more than offset by its contribution to reducing property crime so only the net effect in reducing crime rates is valued. This effect is most likely due largely to the fact that when more young males are enrolled in community college programs, they are productively engaged rather than out on the streets getting into trouble. There are, however, other benefits arising from the training of police officers and others such as probation officers.

Lower Public Health Care Costs. The effect of higher education in keeping people out of the public health care system is estimated to have a discounted present value of $6,813 by Muennig (2005), shown as equivalent to $544 per year in Table 5.4. The Lochner and Moretti study (2002) does not provide the necessary income and education coefficients. This is an instance where state governments are spending huge sums that could be reduced by increasing access to college degree programs that would help offset the current state budget squeeze on higher education support.

Increased Tax Receipts. Increased income, sales, and property tax receipts associated with higher education graduates are important not to overlook. But they are included in the earnings benefits of higher education and therefore are not double counted as non-market social benefits.

Environmental Benefits. There is an estimated positive $136 value from the effects of higher education on less water pollution. The value of the effects in reducing air pollution is $1,482 and deforestation rates is $3,991.

Thus, the total effect of college graduation on the environment, such as through lower population growth rates and through community action to reduce carbon emissions, is estimated to be $5,609.

Social Capital. Education is positively correlated with factors that contribute to social capital such as trust, social participation in clubs, and community work (Helliwell and Putnam, 1999) as well as reduced inequality (Preston and Sabates, 2005). But the existing basic research is inadequate to be able to estimate the monetary value of any contribution of higher education at family-of-four incomes above $80,000 to happiness that also contribute to social capital. There is a large amount of research over many years on the relation of higher education to "subjective well-being," as summarized by Pascarella and Terrenzini (2007), but it normally does not control for income. As a result, the increase of happiness with higher education is largely due to higher incomes. It would be necessary to reanalyze Helliwell's (2005) data to see what the effect of higher education on happiness is for those whose family-of-four incomes are above $80,000, and to see what the indirect effects are through higher education's effects through choice of spouse and lower unemployment and divorce rates. The positive effect of higher education on social capital and the effect through greater happiness needs further research.

Dissemination of R&D Knowledge. The non-market social benefits from the dissemination of new knowledge, much of which is non-rivalrous, are discussed extensively in the following chapter on research and graduate education. As indicated there, these benefits are very hard to separate from the benefits of education per se, and especially graduate education. Momentous innovations, like constitutions providing for the balance of powers by John Adams, the transistor as the basis for modern computers by John Bardeen and William Shockley, the Internet by Tim Berners-Lee, or DNA by James Watson and Francis Crick, clearly have extremely important impacts. But they cannot and do not go very far without large numbers of skilled college graduates able to use them with the concepts, institutional knowledge, technical equipment involved.

To place a value on these it is assumed that some portion is reflected through the impacts of higher education on each of the social benefits discussed above. This begins to value the contribution of master's, PhD, and professional degree programs and not just undergraduate levels.

The Total Value of a Bachelor's Degree. The total social benefits of a bachelor's degree of $27,726 per year must be added to the value of the non-market private benefits (from Chapter 4) and the value of the net earnings benefits from Chapter 3 to obtain the value of the total private and social benefits from higher education. Adding these up, the non-market private benefits had a value of $38,080, the market benefits on average for males and females a value of $31,174, and the non-market social benefits a value of $27,726 for a total of $96,980 in 2007 dollars.

By this income-equivalent method, the social benefits are 29% of the total benefits of higher education. Looking only at the market benefits and ignoring the private non-market benefits, the social benefits are 52% of the total earnings plus social benefits, or about equal to the market benefits as these comparisons are more conventionally stated.

But although this addresses the direct social benefits, it still does not address the full scope of higher education externalities, which include the indirect effects as discussed in Chapter 2.

THE VALUE OF THE SOCIAL BENEFITS BY DYNAMIC SIMULATION

The second method of valuing the social benefits by using dynamic simulations is needed to measure the indirect effects that supplement the direct effects discussed above. These indirect effects are the result of higher education's effects on other variables that then interact with one another as time passes, with more interactions and additional effects as more time passes. These continually feed back, affecting per capita economic growth within families and within nations, as well as the measures on non-market development outcomes such as health or democracy and human rights institutions. Simulated outcomes for each higher education outcome such as growth, health, and democratization are generated by obtaining a recursive solution for each outcome, five years at a time, of the complete model for which the coefficients for each equation have been estimated empirically (McMahon, 2008). (A simplified version of this model appears in Appendix B of this book.) This method has the distinct advantage of taking the interactions over time into account and revealing the buildup over time as the direct social benefits in Table 5.4 set the stage for each new round of growth and development.

It is hard to isolate the effects that are due only to higher education by this method, however. This is because secondary education also contributes to many outcomes and then higher education contributes further, with both of these impacts interacting over time. It is also because higher education's impacts are entwined with the impacts of the new technologies embodied in the human capital of each new cohort of graduates. Nevertheless, new insights on the effects over time of education and knowledge clearly are possible, as shown below in simulations for the United States, the United Kingdom, and twenty other OECD countries. These generate the increasing social benefits of education after twenty, thirty, and forty years. But even more important for the purposes of this chapter, the portion of the private market and private non-market benefits that are indirect benefits is identified, and these are externalities.

The Value of Social Benefits in the Developed Countries. The results of these multiple simulations are summarized for twenty-two of the OECD member countries in Figure 5.2.

Investment in education first is increased by 2% of GDP, an arbitrary but achievable amount. The total effect after each simulation is solved out iteratively for forty years, as shown by the taller bars in Figure 5.2 for each of these countries. There are effects within five years but they build up over time to the total effects shown. This is consistent with the analytic proof given in Appendix B that the short-term five-year effects cumulate to produce a larger benefit from higher education over a longer forty-year period. This buildup occurs not just because the impacts of human capital formation continue throughout the lifecycle, but also because the externalities set the stage in each five-year period for continuing development in the next and successive five-year periods and also interact with one another in the process.

The indirect effects are also social benefit externalities. They are shown by the shorter bars for each country in Figure 5.2, and can be expressed as a fraction of the total benefits shown by the taller bars. The mean for all OECD countries is shown by the two bars farthest to the right in Figure 5.2. This could also be viewed as a typical OECD country.* These are the

---

*To measure the indirect effects, which are externalities, the model at McMahon (2008) was specially programmed to measure the direct effects of education on each social outcome. This was done by suppressing all of the indirect effects from education, which is changed. These net direct effects of education were then subtracted from a second simulation for the same country containing the total effects to obtain the indi-

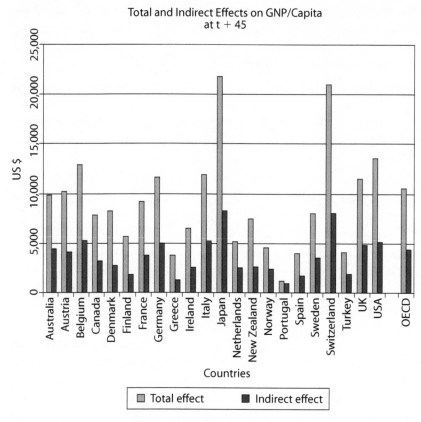

Total and Indirect Effects on GNP/Capita
at t + 45

Figure 5.2. Total effects and social benefits of higher education expansion.

benefits due only to the additional education because all other known effects on growth are contained in a base scenario, which was subtracted. The simulations assume that the additional investment is used largely to finance increased enrollments and provide for access to quality education by more students at the level of quality that has prevailed in the recent past. If there were improvements in quality, that would raise, not lower, the return. On this basis, per capita income would be increased in the typical OECD country by $13,500 within 45 years (the $10,000 shown

rect effects. These are externalities. If one adopts a continental philosophy, as distinguished from the more individualistic social contract, then to these indirect effects should be added the direct effects of education on purely social outcomes such as democratization or political stability, which benefit others but also future generations.

in Figure 5.2 updated to 2007 prices). Of this total effect, the value of the social benefits is $5,650 in 2007 prices, or 42% of the total. This is the percentage of total market plus non-market benefits that are indirect. The indirect benefits as a percent of the market benefits are about equal to the purely market benefits in the developed countries. The latter is not much different from the result obtained by Breton (2008) for the high-income countries by the third method as defined above. For the United States, for example, external benefits are 49% of the total market benefits (ibid., Table A3).

The question remains as to what portion of these education benefits are due to higher education alone. Complete precision is impossible, but a reasonable judgment can be made. The key point is that the simulations automatically channel almost all of the increase in investment in education of 2% of GDP toward increasing higher education enrollments because in most of these developed countries secondary education is already nearly universal. Specifically, in the OECD countries where secondary enrollment rates are 90% or higher virtually all of the additional education investment would be for higher education. These are Canada, the United States, the United Kingdom, Austria, Belgium, Denmark, Finland, France, Germany, Iceland, Ireland, South Korea, Japan, the Netherlands, New Zealand, Norway, Portugal, Sweden, Spain, and Switzerland.

The externalities due to higher education therefore are about 42% of the increments to per capita income in these countries, or stated another way, almost equal to the direct market benefits.* By the dynamic simulation method the value of the externalities that are indirect benefits from higher education is $15,100 per person in 2007 dollars. To this must be added the value of the direct social benefit externalities from Table 5.4 of $16,801 (58% of $27,726). These direct social benefits were represented

---

*These feedbacks on the non-market outcomes were also computed in detail in McMahon, 2002, Chapter 13. For the United Kingdom and the United States they vary widely among outcomes. This variation depends on the length of time that is allowed to pass and upon the type of non-market outcome in question, with 0% effects at first, and then after twenty to forty years building up to higher levels (see ibid., pp. 238–41). They are relatively smaller, for example, in the case of health (such as infant mortality and life expectancy) than they are for democratization (87%) or homicide, narcotics addiction, and water pollution, where they are 100%. These feedback effects cannot be added up because the outcomes are not comparable; for example, the indirect effects on years of longevity are in different units than the indirect effects on an index measure of water pollution.

as Section C-1 of Figure 2.2, where the valuation of these types of benefits by the Haveman-Wolfe method was referred to. By this dynamic simulation method the total value of the social benefits from a bachelor's degree, direct plus indirect, therefore comes to $31,180 in the United States. This is of the same order of magnitude but a bit above their value as the result of each bachelor's degree granted in the United Kingdom, and also somewhat above their value in the other European Union countries, where the market rates of return to higher education are also somewhat lower. It should be kept in mind that this measure overlaps earnings given that 42% of the increments to earnings arise from indirect effects. So this is not in addition to earnings.

A second group of middle-income countries (Australia, Czech Republic, Greece, Italy, Hungary, and Poland) has lower secondary education enrollment rates that are between 80 and 90%, while a third group has the lowest secondary enrollment rates of 57–61%: Mexico 57% (males 57%, females 58%) and Turkey 61% (males 74%, females 48%). So a smaller portion of the effects due to the additional investment in education shown in Figure 5.2 will be due only to higher education in these countries. That is, the benefits from basic education, and the externalities from basic education, would be larger in countries not as far along in their development (as also found by Breton, 2008, pp. 13–14). But the proportion of both the direct returns and the externalities due to higher education as shown by these simulations is smaller.

THE VALUE OF SOCIAL BENEFITS BY AGGREGATE METHODS

In studies of aggregate education externalities by the third and fourth methods I have described it is difficult to isolate the social benefits of higher education from those of basic education. This is because such studies aggregate not only over the specific types of social benefits listed in Table 5.4 but also over all levels of education. Perhaps the study by Moretti (2002) comes the closest to focusing on higher education. He controls for unmeasured ability and using instrumental-variable methods concludes that a percentage point increase in the number of college graduates raises the wages of high school graduates by 1.6%. He attempts to control for the fact that external forces can increase the demand for workers in a locality. But it is still very hard to sort out just how much of the increase in wages is due to the presence of highly educated workers and how much is due to external shocks. There is the further problem of how much must be subtracted to account for the loss of college-educated workers from other parts of the country if one wishes to generalize these results to a nationwide basis. These first two points would suggest that Moretti's (2002) estimates are too high, a view shared by Lange and Topel (2006). But offsetting this to an unknown degree is the fact that it is unlikely that most education externalities related to the effectiveness of democratic institutions can be observed in interstate or intercity U.S. data given the relatively high homogeneity of these institutions within a single country.

Topel (1999) and Heckman and Klenow (1997) estimate education externalities by first estimating the social rate of return to schooling from cross-country GDP per capita regressions and then subtracting the private returns to schooling estimated using Mincer regressions from individual earnings data. Topel's estimate is a 23% total private plus externality social rate of return and Heckman and Klenow's estimate is a 30% social rate of return. After the average private Mincer return of 8.3% is subtracted, this leaves 14.7% and 21.7% respectively for the purely external benefit component of the rate of return. This, as in all these studies, is still a pure market return related to GDP and earnings growth that ignores the non-market private benefits and the non-market direct social benefits such as those estimated in Table 5.4. A second problem is that they do not control for other factors affecting growth as mentioned earlier. So to make a comparison to the new total social rate of return below, non-market benefits would have to be added and controls imposed for other factors such as investment in physical capital and trade that also affect growth. They therefore then introduce life expectancy, which they treat as a proxy for medical technologies and hence for all technology, and also use time dummies. Although a control for life expectancy seems justified, its interpretation as medical technologies rather than as a negative effect on growth due to social security and health care expenditures for an aging population is debatable (see Appendix D). The introduction of time dummies sidesteps a structural explanation of what they are a proxy for and is also a debatable procedure. Enough has been said about the interaction of higher education with technical change that it can be seen that this procedure converts the model to one based on a static interpretation that would wipe out most externalities from higher education. So little is left after these kinds of controls are imposed.

Benhabib and Spiegel (1994) and Pritchett (2000) also use a static interpretation and argue for small or even zero returns to schooling. However, in reviewing these studies, Lange and Topel (2006, p. 479) conclude that there is "little evidence in favor of *negative* external returns to education" and that more recent studies cast doubt on these earlier Benhabib and Spiegel and Pritchett studies. In a later eclectic review of world data Pritchett (2006) does not control for external oil shocks and fiscal-monetary policy shocks, or for increasing life expectancy in the developed countries.

Benhabib and Spiegel (2006) later explore the dynamic process of technology diffusion as education and new knowledge interact. But in their earlier study, which was widely quoted, they remove most human capital formation effects on per capita income growth by using controls for political instability and inequality, and also by using the average years of schooling as a measure of past investment in human capital. They found by these methods essentially no human capital effects and hence no externalities. But this is a function of the controls they use and from using educational attainment, which is a stock as discussed in Chapter 2, in contrast to enrollment rates or investment in education as a percent of GDP that are both flows that contain embodied technology in the 65% of human capital investment that replaces those who retire. Educational attainment nets out this replacement investment. For highly significant effects from increased education enrollments on growth in developed countries, see Appendix D, where there are also controls for life expectancy, but also see Keller (2006a, 2006b), McMahon (2002, pp. 56, 61), and Jamison et al. (2007). Breton (2008) uses cumulative expenditure on education for sixty-one countries to capture quality and finds very significant impacts on national income growth and high social rates of return that justify increased investment. Whenever the effects of higher education on growth are found to be zero, it is usually due to controls that eliminate the role of higher education in technology diffusion by use of time dummies, or by use of educational attainment instead of enrollment or investment expenditure, or both. When education's effects on growth are found to be zero, as in

Benhabib and Spiegel (1994) and Pritchett (2000), then education externalities including higher education externalities are obviously also zero.

To summarize the studies based on U.S. interstate or intercity data discussed earlier, Lange and Topel (2006) conclude in a critique based on a spatial equilibrium analysis that the estimate by Acemoglu and Angrist (2000), who found education externalities to be zero, are too low, and the estimate by Rauch (1993), who found that higher average education levels in a community raise wages by 3 to 5%, is "not-so-implausible." Lange and Topel (2006, p. 479) also suggest that Moretti's (2002) estimate that a 1 percentage point increase in the number of higher education graduates raises average wages in that locale by 1% is "simply huge." However, in this book I have repeatedly suggested that studies looking at only interstate or intercity data within the same country are likely to miss many important education externalities not just because of spatial equilibrium but also because of the homogeneity of civic institutions. Breton (2008) and Table 5.4 avoid these pitfalls.

CONCLUSIONS REGARDING THE VALUE OF EXTERNAL
SOCIAL BENEFITS

Overall, the dynamic simulation method as reported here also is not subject to either the spatial equilibrium or homogeneity objections, mostly because there is limited mobility across borders. It seems to be a good approach for placing a value on the externalities generated by higher education. It has the advantage of including the same list of social benefits valued by the Haveman-Wolfe method (1984, 2007) in Table 5.4, and supplementing this with a measure of the indirect effects on the private market and private non-market benefits. In the most developed countries it comes close to isolating the externalities due to the indirect effects from higher education. These approaches complement one another because they include estimation of the value of the direct and also the indirect effects from democracy, human rights, political stability, aspects of a better environment, and lower crime rates. Effects from higher education's role in spreading capacities to use new information created by research are more implicit.

These benefits are efficiency gains, as distinct from equity gains. The latter involve potential gains to social capital and political stability from reducing the rapidly rising inequality in earnings and income. There has been a remarkable increase in wage inequality in the United States, the United Kingdom, and other OECD countries over the past three decades, as documented by Faggio et al. (2007). Using U.K. panel data they find evidence that increasing inequality in productivity among firms is linked with new technologies and hence significantly with inequality in education, and not other factors. As indicated earlier in this chapter, increased access to higher education does reduce inequality in most U.S. states, and probably also in Canada, given the higher enrollment rates and community college systems. But for most OECD countries with more elite and restrictive public higher education, increased support of higher education probably does not reduce inequality. At least the regressions for the OECD as a whole shown in Appendix D find higher education access to be insignificant as a determinant of the GINI coefficient of inequality. This effect of higher education on the degree of equality is important to consider given the rising inequality in the United States and the European Union. Gottschalk and Smeeding (1997) and Sullivan and Smeeding (1997) stress the trends toward greater inequality since 1980 and the dangers of the gradual elimination of the middle class.

New Social Rates of Return

Using the above estimates of the non-market private and non-market social benefits of higher education, these can be added to the market benefits to obtain a new and more accurate social rate of return. The rates of return can be added because the investment cost base in the denominator of the benefit-cost ratio is the same for both the market and the non-market benefits.

To obtain the new social rates of return, we must start with the standard narrow social rates in column 1 of Table 5.5. These are market rates based on U.S. earnings from Census data computed by the "full method" in rows 1–3. They reflect the increases in institutional costs as well as the increments to earnings at each education level. They are 10.5% for high school graduates, 16% for two-year associate degrees, and 12% for bachelor's graduates.

The non-market private benefits from higher education are 122% of the market benefits (from Chapter 4). The private non-market rate that this implies is shown in column 2, 20% at the associate level and 15% at the bachelor's level. Haveman and Wolfe (1984, 2007) estimated them to be about equal to the market benefits. But in Chapter 4 they come out to be a bit larger because of things that were left out. I have suggested that parents and students have poor knowledge of these non-market benefits. So these results indicating high non-market returns have little influence on investment decisions, implying that higher education markets are not working efficiently, and leading to underinvestment by both private families and government.

Row 5 in Table 5.5 shows an average 8% return to education based on an average from twenty-seven studies computed by Ashenfelter et al. (2000, p. 8). These do not apply to higher education alone, and there are various other problems so they should not be given much weight. I show them for comparison and because they are sometimes cited. The problems are that they cover all levels of education; do not explicitly incorporate institutional costs, and hence are a private Mincer return as distinguished from the social rates of return computed by the "full method" in rows 1, 2, and 3. They also apply to years from 1974 to 1995 averaging in the mid-1980s, and therefore are out of date; and cover nine different countries.

Turning to the social benefits, about 42% of the market and private non market benefits are indirect effects. These overlap the narrow market social rates of return and the non-market private social rates of return just reported. However, the direct social benefits estimated by the Haveman-Wolfe method in Table 5.4 must be added because they are a part of the total social benefits. Referring to Figure 2.2, these direct social benefits are shown as area C-1.

These direct social benefits have now been valued. They are 58% of the total social benefits estimated by using the Haveman-Wolfe method above, or $27,726 less the 42% that are indirect. This leaves $16,081 per year as the value of the direct non-market social benefits resulting from a bachelor's degree that are enjoyed by others in the society or future generations. This component can be converted to a rate of return. It is about 7 percentage points at both the associate and bachelor's levels.

To obtain the new social rates of return in column 4 to replace the narrow rates, the 7 percentage points now can be added to the narrow rate in column 1 plus the private non-market rate in column 2. Column 3,

TABLE 5.5 Total Social Rates of Return for the United States by Education Level, 2005

	Standard market-based social rate of return (%) (1)		Private non-market rate of return (%)[b] (2)	Social benefits[c] only (%) (3)	New social rate of return (%)[d] (4)	External social benefits as % of total (not a RoR)[e] (5)
High school graduates	10.5	+	13	15	28	53
Associate degree (2-yr)	16	+	20	22	43	51
Bachelor's graduates	12	+	15	21	34	51
All levels, nine countries[a]	8	+	10	11	22	50
All levels, United States (Breton, 2008)	22	+	27	10.6	53	48
All levels, United Kingdom (Breton, 2008)	24	+	29	16.2	57	67

NOTE: Row 4 is a Mincer return for nine countries averaged for all levels of education.

[a]Column 1, row 4, from Ashenfelter et al. (2000, p. 8), and column 1, rows 5 and 6 from Breton (2008). Neither of these studies includes non-market private benefits so column 2 is imputed as 122% of the market returns from my Table 4.3.

[b]Column 2 is 122% of the "narrow" market return in column 1. The 122% is from Table 4.3.

[c]Part of these social benefits are indirect effects included in columns 1 and 2, to which must be added the direct social benefits computed by the Haveman-Wolfe method as shown in Table 5.4. Specifically, column 3 is 42% of the earnings benefits in column 1, plus 42% of the private non-market rate in column 2, plus 58% of the social benefits. The latter is 58% of the direct social benefit rate which is 12% at the associate degree level, for example, or 7.1%, which when added to 42% of the other rates gives 22.2% in column 3. (The 12% direct social benefit rate at the associate level is based on the direct social benefits of $27,726 from Table 5.4 by the Haveman-Wolfe method. These are 34% of all benefits, $25,096 private market, plus $38,080 non-market private, plus $27,726 non-market social benefits which equals $80,548 total benefits, which is equivalent to 34% of the private market and non-market rates since the unit cost base for all rates of return is the same. At the bachelor's level the direct social benefit rate is almost 8%, and it is 4.5% at the high school level. Averaged across all education levels and starting from a Mincer return in row 4 above, the direct social rate is 6.6%.

[d]The new social rate of return is column 1 plus column 2 plus the direct social benefit rate of 12%, 8.4%, and 6.6% as in c above.

[e]This is external social benefits as a percent of all benefits, which is the same as column 3 divided by column 4. In the case of rows 5 and 6 it is column 3 divided by column 1 since Breton's (2008) study applies to national income measured market benefits only.

which reports the indirect effects, cannot be added because these indirect effects are already included in columns 1 and 2, as was explained and illustrated in Figure 2.2. After the direct social benefits are included (the 7 percentage points), the result is a new and much improved total social rate of return. It is a high 43% for an associate degree and 34% for a bachelor's degree in the United States—high because they include non-market returns, private and social, that are normally overlooked

Similar corrections can be made for the market-based full method social rates of return found in the United Kingdom and other developed OECD countries that were shown in Chapter 3. That is, for each rate, merely add 122% of that rate for the non-market private returns and 7 percentage points for the direct social benefits. These corrections will not be exactly the same at the high school level, as shown in row 1 of Table 5.5, although the total high school social rate of return that includes private and social non-market benefits of 28% is higher than the current 10.5% narrow rate that is so widely cited. However, if the same procedures are applied to the Ashenfelter et al. (2000) worldwide private rates that averaged all levels of education this would give a 22% social rate of return in row 4, column 4 of Table 5.5, considerably above the lower 8% Mincer return shown in column 1.

In a recent and very thorough study of aggregate externalities, Breton (2008) estimates the market-based social rate of return to be 22% in the United States and 24% in the United Kingdom as shown in column 1 of the last two rows of Table 5.5. His study is based on international cross-section data so since international mobility is restricted his database largely avoids the problem with spatial equilibrium that occurs in studies based only on data for a single country or region as discussed earlier. It also avoids the problem with homogeneity in a single country or region or a short time frame that allows for little variation from the external effects of education through democratization and political stability. He uses instrumental-variable techniques to get away from simultaneous bias by choosing the percent of the population that is Protestant as the instrument for education. He also uses cumulative investment expenditure on education to measure investment in human capital rather than educational attainment, suggesting that this reflects the quality of education as well as quantity and not just the quantity alone that dominates when years of educational attainment is used. On this basis, estimating the social rate using a cross-country growth equation (column 1) and subtracting the private Mincer return based on micro-earnings data he finds the pure external social benefits to be 10.6% in the United States and 16.2% in the United Kingdom as shown in column 3 of Table 5.5. The Breton study, however, is confined to the earnings benefits. So if an imputation is made on the same basis as before for the private non-market benefits as shown in column 2, then Breton's adjusted total social rate of return is even higher as shown in column 4. His external social benefits as a percent of the total in column 5 averages 57% for the United States and the United Kingdom, which is only a little higher and of the same order of magnitude as that found in the other studies in Table 5.5.

Finally, in the last column, total externalities come out to be 52% of the total benefits of higher education. These consist of 42% of the private market and private non-market benefits plus the direct social benefits. *This 52% is not a social rate of return.* It is an estimate of the percent of the total benefits that are social benefit externalities. It is an estimate of the percent of the total investment in higher education that needs to be publicly financed if economic efficiency is to be achieved.

The new total social rates of return are very substantially above the 10% standard benchmark for the opportunity cost of funds. This indicates that investment in higher education is significantly below optimum. This is in contrast to the situation back in the 1980s, when Leslie and Brinkman (1988) concluded that there was not clear evidence that investment in higher education in the 1980s was or was not below optimum. But that was before the sweeps of globalization and new technology contributed to continuing increases in college versus high school graduates' earnings and to substantial increases in inequality.

The Skeptics: High Earnings versus Externalities?

Skeptics sometimes have taken the position that there are no externalities generated by higher education because the increments to earnings are so high. Or because a few studies have not been able to find clear evidence of education externalities.

College graduates are earning 70% more than high school graduates, a number that has increased dramatically since 1970. Graduates of prestigious private universities are earning even more. And there are a few studies reviewed above that conclude that education externalities are low or even zero. But the analysis and the evidence offered in this book suggest some new insights:

- Indirect effects, which are externalities, overlap the market returns. Some of the high earnings represent externalities generated by the education of others and prior generations. The other side of the coin is that some productivity gain due to current graduates is not enjoyed privately but instead benefits others and future generations. Skeptics in prior studies have not addressed this issue.
- Non-market social benefits now have been identified, valued, and counted. Studies by the skeptics have ignored private non-market benefits.
- Externalities from research are made effective as new knowledge is embodied in graduates and disseminated. If skeptics would take a human capital formation perspective that includes embodiment, this is one of the inescapable implications. When the skeptics include time dummies in their regressions, this implies a static perspective that eliminates the role of new technologies and embodiment.
- Skeptics who adhere to the strong form of the screening hypothesis that holds that education itself is not productive will be skeptical. But they must now contend with the new in-depth analysis by Lange and Topel (2006, p. 462) that concludes that there is "little convincing evidence for an important role for job market signaling."
- Recent studies that get away from using average educational attainment and use cumulated expenditures on education to reflect quality (Breton, 2008) or use gross enrollment rates that reflect embodiment of technology (Keller, 2006a, 2006b; McMahon, 2002, Chapters 3 and 4; 1998d) find strong evidence of education impacts on national income growth and of education externalities.

The skeptics are in the minority. The evidence offered in this chapter is not consistent with this minority view. The identification of indirect effects, the demonstration that a dynamic process implies a buildup of education externality effects over time, the rising social rates of return to college based on micro-data since 1980, the concept of embodiment of new technologies as new human capital is formed, the estimates of the value of specific non-market social benefits by the Haveman-Wolfe method—all operate in this direction.

It is likely that many of these externality and social benefit effects, especially those that operate indirectly over time, are neither anticipated nor acted on by families or by public policy makers as they invest in college education. Since social benefit externalities approach 52% of all higher education benefits, there are benefits to society and a social process that is involved. Andrew Carnegie, cited at the outset of this chapter, had it largely right when he said, "It is not the individual but the society that creates wealth."

Conclusion

This chapter has built upon important earlier contributions to the subject of the social benefits of higher education. These include Jefferson (1787), Marshall (1927), Weisbrod (1964), Schultz (1971, 1981), Bowen (1977), Leslie and Brinkman (1988), Lucas (1988), Romer (1990, 2002), Breton (2008), and Haveman and Wolfe (1984, 2001, 2003, 2007). It has identified them more comprehensively through a taxonomy of the specific social benefits, reviewed the research on each, set out a theory of the dynamic development process involving education externalities, defined education's indirect effects, and sought to comprehensively place economic values on the specific higher education external social benefits.

Important social benefits are generated by higher education and not just by research. My best estimate is that the value of the non-market public goods social benefits is about $27,726 per year, almost equal to the average increment to male and female earnings after completing a bachelor's. They include the direct benefits to the quality of life from higher education's contributions to the benefits of living in a democracy, enjoying human rights, political stability, and lower crime rates and criminal justice system costs. But the externalities generated by higher education also include indirect effects that are part of the private market and private non-market benefits. They arise from the higher education of earlier generations, but also going forward, although the former is used as the basis for measurement. This perspective on the accumulation of benefits over time helps to reconcile the discrepancy between the smaller returns found by some in the aggregate data with larger returns to investment in higher education revealed by social rates of return based on the micro-data.

It is the omission of the non-market benefits that causes standard narrow social rate of return estimates to be most seriously understated. The human capital used in the community includes social benefits as time is spent serving on juries, serving on community boards and commissions, serving and contributing to charitable organizations, and assisting community college contributions to lower crime and criminal justice system costs. College graduates are more likely to vote, and to vote for elected officials who are less authoritarian, and are less likely to violate the rights of others. College students are often actively engaged in efforts to protect the environment. And graduates spread new knowledge as they bring new technologies and skills to their work environment and their community. Higher education policies also can be designed to improve educational opportunity and lower inequality. These social benefit efficiency gains and potential equity effects on opportunity and reduced inequality give more specific meaning to "higher education and the public good."

But since these social benefits and their value are poorly understood by the public, steps need to be taken to reduce this source of market failure in higher education markets. Externalities are likely to be another source of the current underinvestment and another higher education policy gap. The estimate that social benefit externalities constitute about 52% of the total benefits of higher education is an approximate guide to how far the privatization of higher education should proceed before public investment falls below the level conducive to optimum efficiency. How close or how far higher education is currently from this approximate criteria and some possible policy options will be considered in Chapter 7. But for now this would appear to be roughly the balance between the private benefits of higher education and higher education's contribution to the public good.

CHAPTER SIX

University Research
Social Benefits and Policy

All that is spent during many years in opening the means of higher education to the masses would be well paid for if it called out one more Newton or Darwin, Shakespeare or Beethoven.

ALFRED MARSHALL (1927, P. 216)

"THOSE WHO LOOK mainly to universities as a source of human capital often tend to be critical of the lack of obvious dividends from university research" (Sims, 1989). This statement highlights the often underestimated but extremely important benefit that universities provide to research by the creation, dissemination, and adaptation of new knowledge. Research conducted at universities impacts national economic productivity and the gross national product (GDP) as well as improving the quality of leisure time and community life throughout the world. But equally important, research keeps the faculty in touch with new technologies and knowledge developed worldwide, which then is embodied in master's, PhD, and professional students at the research universities and elsewhere who then teach undergraduates, and leave to teach at other colleges or to fill research and administrative positions in firms, in government, and abroad. Research is an integral part of the higher education process that has at its heart the creation and dissemination of new as well as existing knowledge.

The benefits from basic research are largely externalities, which means they are social and not private benefits. This is not in dispute. Nevertheless, it is the main theme of this chapter given the problems with measurement of the social benefit outcomes and in light of the trends. The benefits from most research performed at universities are social benefits since there is distribution of the results required through publication and also since master's and PhD graduates spread the methods and results of basic and applied research to others throughout the society. These others include the benefits to research departments in firms to which they go, government and international agencies where they take jobs and also consult, students at other colleges and universities, and future generations.

Some of the benefits of university-based research, however, are privatized by patenting. The research benefits can be captured through patents by the private business firms that finance the research and/or hire the PhDs and sometimes by the universities themselves. The types of research most amenable to patenting are the results of applied research, as distinguished from basic research, and also the results of research in engineering and the life sciences including agriculture. Very few ideas and results from research in the social sciences, humanities, mathematics, business, agricultural economics, or other fields result in objects that can be patented and manufactured, although they can sometimes have sweeping effects on the economy, the rule of law, or other aspects of the quality of life. This chapter's emphasis on the fact that there are social benefits from research relates to a basic theme of this book because it is patenting that has been the basis for most of the measurement and valuation of the literature of the outcomes of research. Since patenting is also basic to the later privatization of the benefits, this means that most of these studies are of those benefits that can later be privatized and the social benefits of research are largely overlooked. This is a very serious gap in the literature.

This measurement gap has implications for higher education policy in that the capacity to privatize the benefits of applied research by patenting often leads to a distortion of research priorities. Private for-profit funding by firms will tend to be mostly for applied research in engineering and life science fields, and not for basic research in any field or research in the social sciences, humanities, or mathematics, for example. Public funding of research has also gravitated somewhat in this same direction, as will be shown This trend will only be accentuated as the degree of privatization in financing university research proceeds.

The second theme of the chapter is that the new knowledge created by research is embodied in master's and PhD students as new human capital is formed. It has been argued that the results of modern research and hence of new technologies would not have much impact on either the economy or on the quality of life if they were not disseminated by graduates who have the capacities to utilize them. This knowledge capital involves not just new technologies in engineering but new knowledge in all fields and includes the capacities to evaluate evidence that modern research methods convey. To be sure, this knowledge capital is not just that produced by higher education but includes basic education and skills transferred from parents; early immigrants to the United States, for example, brought many skills and a great deal of knowledge capital with them. But modern technologies are more complex. All major firms now have research departments and conduct their own R&D, as do all major government departments. They build on the basic and applied research conducted at universities and must have researchers who have been extensively trained at universities if they are to conduct meaningful R&D.

Today few would question the centrality of the creation of new knowledge as a vital component of the university's mission. And few will challenge the importance of research in a knowledge-based economy of the future. New knowledge and technologies are an engine of growth because they allow per capita GDP to increase without increasing the stock of physical capital or the amount of raw labor. The new knowledge and technologies make existing labor and capital more productive. The new endogenous growth models, such as those of Lucas (1988) and Romer (1990), depend on basic and higher education for the dissemination and utilization of this technology and are the rationale for the modern knowledge economy. This was addressed in Chapter 3, and broadened to become endogenous development in Chapters 4 and 5 as non-market benefits and indirect effects were introduced.

The point is that the creation of new knowledge and its embodiment and dissemination through higher education cannot be cleanly disentangled. Research creating new technologies and human capital are jointly produced primarily by higher education institutions in a process developed further by De Groot and McMahon (1991) and by Cohn et al. (1989). The benefits of research and the benefits of human capital formation are also joint outcomes, as implied by Griliches (2000) and Romer (1990), outcomes that deeply involve graduates at the master's, PhD, and professional degree levels. It is this point of joint production and joint outcomes at the postgraduate level that I will develop further in this chapter.

The Conceptual Framework: Embodiment of New Knowledge

Basic to the conceptual framework of this chapter is the embodiment of new knowledge and skills through higher education. New vintages of human capital are created with each graduating class. These concepts were introduced in Chapter 2 and used in a general way heretofore in this book. But now they help to explain how education and research outcomes are inextricably entwined, and how higher education contributes to growth in ways that are somewhat different from basic education. Their definitions therefore need to be repeated, as well as extended and discussed.

- *Embodiment* of new knowledge, including new technologies, occurs as the cumulative results of existing knowledge, new research results, and skills are transferred to graduate students through formal instruction and apprenticeship roles. These skills include the capacities to reason, critically evaluate evidence, and create new knowledge. They also include the embodiment of new technology in engineering graduates but also embodiment of knowledge and skills in other fields. Some fields such as English and mathematics, for example, are basic to other fields but also are vital to almost all jobs. Other applied fields can be very technical and the creation of new knowledge and methods can move very rapidly. New knowledge created by recent worldwide research is embodied in master's, PhD, and professional students at graduate degree–granting institutions, but this can include the education of undergraduates at other institutions when their faculty stays up to date.
- *Obsolescence* of human capital occurs as the knowledge within each field changes over time. The knowledge and skills available to be learned systematically change as research and innovation

push out the frontiers of each subject and change the tools available for retrieving knowledge. A constant flow of new journal articles in each field published every day is the main vehicle for this transmission and makes it very hard for both faculty and especially for practitioners to keep up with worldwide developments; they must have a strong incentive to do so. Sometimes new knowledge reveals that the received knowledge is incorrect (for example, the earth is flat). But much more often it augments previously available knowledge or reveals that received knowledge was less general than was supposed earlier. Similarly, changes in technology, trade, and immigration patterns render useless and obsolete human capital skills associated with prior methods. A great deal was said about the higher education policy implications of this in Chapter 3. The innovation attributable to research extends to all fields. Even innovation in teaching methods and better knowledge of what contributes to effective learning can reduce the cost of education systems and improve learning outcomes. The latter helps to offset diminishing returns in the production of human capital and new knowledge. But this said, it is nevertheless true that obsolescence occurs more rapidly in some fields than in others, and more rapidly in those individuals who do not engage in lifelong learning.

• *New vintages* of human capital are created as each year's graduates enter the labor market, carrying with them the latest knowledge and technologies. These can be valued because the skills are traded in labor markets and rental values contain the same information as capital values. The earnings premium that new college graduates are able to command from employers who recognize the higher value of newer vintages of human capital has been stressed in Chapter 3 (Bartel and Lichtenberg, 1987, and later work were cited there). The older vintages of human capital gradually fall in value when they are not updated, with real earnings peaking at age forty-eight for college graduates and then falling up to retirement and death. Some individuals with older vintages engage in lifelong learning, retool, and learn new techniques, but this involves replacement investment in human capital, which is costly. So human capital that has been "putty" during the college years and early years of learning on the job usually hardens into "clay" and older vintages become more and more obsolete. But just as this does not hold for some individuals it also does not hold in some professions. College faculty, for example, have incentives to continue to engage in research and publication, which forces them to stay up to date. Those medical doctors who locate in larger clinics where there is peer group stimulation and incentives to be on top of new developments are known to have better effectiveness in using new technologies than those in solo practice.

The significance of this is that the creation of new knowledge through research and the creation of new human capital are so deeply entwined that the returns to investment in research and to investment in graduate education are inextricably linked. The output of master's, PhD, and professional degrees in each field is an index of the embodiment of the new knowledge created by research at universities, in firms, and worldwide in that field with which faculties at the research universities are in touch. New knowledge is, of course, also embodied in machinery as it is manufactured (Phelps, 1962). But this limited concept of embodiment is largely confined to engineering fields, and misses almost all of the social benefits from research.

A second reason that the embodiment of new knowledge is so significant is that if one looks at the entire population of each country as embodying a stock of human capital of various vintages, each year some retire and die, and each year the higher education system replaces these with new graduates. This replacement investment consists of newer vintages possessing newer knowledge and technologies. Tracing the impact of that on economic growth and development one would expect that if the new knowledge (as compared to the existing knowledge) has any impact at all, it would be much larger when measured by gross investment or by gross enrollment rates in higher education than it would using the average educational attainment rate of the entire human capital stock, which changes very, very slowly. This in fact does appear to be the case, as we see in Chapter 3 and Appendix D.

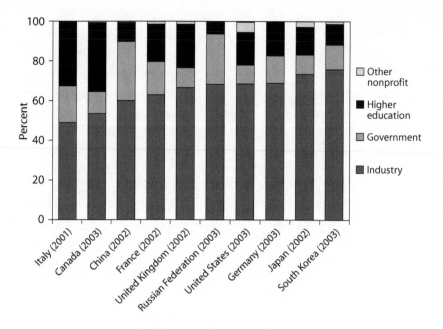

R & D expenditures for selected countries,
by performing sector (2001–03)

Figure 6.1. Percent of research performed by higher education, government, and firms. *Source*: National Science Foundation (2006).

TABLE 6.1 Percent of Research Performed by Higher Education, Government, and Industry

	Higher Education	Government	Industry
Italy (2001)	32.6	18.4	49.1
Canada (2003)	34.9	11.2	53.7
China (2002)	9.8	29.7	60.4
France (2002)	18.9	16.5	63.2
United Kingdom (2002)	21.8	9.9	66.8
Russian Federation (2003)	6.1	25.3	68.4
United States (2003)	16.8	9.1	68.9
Germany (2003)	17.1	13.7	69.2
Japan (2002)	14.5	9.5	73.7
South Korea (2003)	10.1	12.6	76.1

Investment in Research and Graduate Education

Research results and methods embodied through graduate degree programs give a preliminary idea of the scope and nature of the potential impacts of the research on society.

ACADEMIC RESEARCH

Research and development expenditures in 10 major countries as collected by the National Science Foundation are shown in Figure 6.1 and Table 6.1. These show that 16.8% of the research in the United States is performed at universities. Larger percentages than this are performed at universities in the United Kingdom (21.8%), Canada (34.9%), Italy (32.6%), France (18.9%), and Germany (17.1%) and smaller percentages in Japan (14.5%) and South Korea (10.1%). In China and Russia, less is performed at the universities and more in the government research institutes. This probably reflects the fact that they are or have been more centralized planned economies. The nonprofit sector is more important in the United States (5.4%) than elsewhere.

Academic institutions perform 55% of the basic research and 10% of the more highly applied development in the United States, whereas industry does almost all of the remaining 90% of the development. This is important to the trend toward privatization because basic research generates almost purely social benefit externalities, whereas more applied development expenditures that often lead to patents generate benefits that can be captured privately by firms or for the public by governmental agencies. Few firms will fund basic research, although there are exceptions, such as Bell Labs. The U.S. federal government accounts for 60% of the funding of research at academic institutions, and institutional sources are the second largest share. But although there has recently been a minor up tick, the federal share has been slowly declining from 68% in 1972.

Most but not all of the federal research funding is in the life and physical science fields and in engineering. Between 1973 and 2003, there was a substantial relative shift in the share of academic R&D funds received. However, all gained substantially in terms of absolute dollars, even after adjusting for inflation.

TABLE 6.2 Master's and Ph.D. Degrees Conferred by Field

Field of study (to two-digit CIP levels)	Master's degrees		Ph.D. degrees	
	Total	Percent	Total	Percent
Total, all fields	430,164	100.0	46,010	100.0
Agricultural business and production	627	0.1	224	0.5
Agricultrual sciences	1,475	0.3	700	1.5
Architecture and related programs	4,347	1.0	131	0.3
Area, ethnic, and cultural studies	1,617	0.4	181	0.4
Biological sciences/life sciences	6,261	1.5	4,961	10.8
Business management and admin. services	101,609	23.6	1,288	2.8
Communications	5,611	1.3	354	0.8
Communications technologies	564	0.1	5	0.0
Computer and information sciences	11,246	2.6	858	1.9
Conservation and renew. natural resources	2,373	0.6	378	0.8
Construction trades	16	0.0	0	0.0
Education	114,691	26.7	6,729	14.6
Engineering	25,936	6.0	5,980	13.0
Engineering-related technologies	1,136	0.3	14	0.0
English language and literature/letters	7,795	1.8	1,639	3.6
Foreign languages and literatures	2,927	0.7	959	2.1
Health professions and related sciences	39,260	9.1	2,484	5.4
Home economics	2,888	0.7	424	0.9
Law and legal studies	3,228	0.8	66	0.1
Liberal/general studies and humanities	2,801	0.7	87	0.2
Library science	4,871	1.1	48	0.1
Marketing opers./market. and distribution	562	0.1	2	0.0
Mathematics	3,643	0.8	1,259	2.7
Mechanics and repairers	0	0.0	0	0.0
Military technologies	0	0.0	0	0.0
Multi/interdisiplinary studies	2,677	0.6	508	1.1
Parks, recreation, leisure, and fitness	2,024	0.5	129	0.3
Personal and miscellaneous services	0	0.0	0	0.0
Philosophy and religion	1,307	0.3	585	1.3
Physical sciences	5,332	1.2	4,569	9.9
Precision production trades	15	0.0	0	0.0
Protective services	2,000	0.5	39	0.1
Psychology	13,747	3.2	4,073	8.9
Public administration and services	25,144	5.8	499	1.1
Science technologies	29	0.0	2	0.0
Social sciences and history	14,938	3.5	4,127	9.0
Theological studies/religious vocations	4,692	1.1	1,460	3.2
Transportation and material moving workers	736	0.2	0	0.0
Visual and performing arts	11,145	2.6	1,163	2.5
Vocational home economics	26	0.0	0	0.0
Undesignated fields (non-respondents)	868	0.2	85	0.2
Totals (for 2005–6 academic year)	574,618		52,631	

SOURCE: U.S. Department of Education, National Center for Education Statistics, Integrated Postsecondary Education Data System Surveys, 1997–98.

*Number and percent by field, U.S. Institutions, 1998. Title IV institutions are those available to Pell Grant and Stafford Loan students, which is nearly all.

- The life sciences (59% share in 2003), computer sciences (3% share), and engineering (15% share) experienced share increases. However, more recently, between 1993 and 2003, the engineering share declined.
- The physical sciences (8% share in 2003); earth, atmospheric, and ocean sciences (6% share); social sciences and psychology (6% combined shares) had share losses.

GRADUATE EDUCATION

The number of master's and PhD degrees completed in each academic field in the United States appears in Table 6.2 for the 6,463 Title IV institutions. These are the institutions that are accredited and approved by the U.S. Department of Education to accept Pell Grant and Stafford Loan students. The data is for 1998 because although the data on degrees completed in all fields has been collected by the U.S. Department of Education (Integrated Postsecondary Education Data System [IPEDS]) up through 2006 it has not been published by the Bush administration except for fields that they have defined as "areas of national need," which are 65% of the total degrees awarded. "Areas of national need" are defined to exclude architecture, business, communications, natural resources, English and foreign languages, home economics, law, library science, the humanities, philosophy, psychology, public administration, the social sciences (including political science and economics), history, and the performing arts.

The points to consider here are that there are non-market benefits from graduate education that embodies new knowledge created by research that contribute to human welfare and the quality of life apart from earnings and the growth of GDP. But putting this important contribution to true social rates of return and the public good to the side, if a dynamic view of the process is taken, some fields make unique additional contributions to GDP growth albeit indirectly. For example:

- The rule of law is known from work by Barro and Sala-I-Martin (1995, 2007), for example, to be clearly related to democratization and to sustaining a functioning court system. Education in law and legal studies, which has been so greatly disparaged by some as unrelated to economic growth and the national interest (3,228 graduates in Table 6.2), is essential to a functioning court system. Political science and history (4,127 doctorates above in social sciences and history) lay the groundwork for continuing democratization.

- Economics has contributed improved knowledge about managing the economy. There have been no deep recessions since 1929–36 or runaway inflations partly because of basic and applied research resulting in strengthening the institutions, policies, and techniques helpful to stability. Economic development in the developed and developing world have also benefited, although often vested interests dominate. The 2009 recession will eventually turn around because of this knowledge of what to do.
- Better hybrids and agricultural technology have contributed massively to improved productivity in agriculture, as will be discussed below (924 PhD graduates per year).
- Improved business management undoubtedly contributes significantly to improved productivity in the business sector (101,609 master's and 1,288 PhD graduates).
- Language training is important to business competitiveness in the world economy with continuing globalization, not to speak of the serious language needs of American forces and diplomats abroad (2,927 master's and 959 PhDs).
- Fields where patents can be secured that privatize the profits from the results are already widely recognized to contribute to growth. Beyond this, they contribute to the university's operation when the university holds the patent. A common formula is for one-third of the profits from the patent to be given to the principal investigator, one-third to the faculty member's department, and one-third to the research park or administrative agency for support of its overhead and reinvestment in other patenting activity. Sometimes there is a cap on the amount for the investigator or department, and sometimes the surplus can go to the campus for support of university-wide research or support of the university library. However, the seed money initially drew, and could continue to draw, on campus resources.

The non-market quality of life also has linkages to specific research and graduate education fields when a modern human capital approach to higher education policy is considered. For example:

- Research and graduate education in the humanities contribute a flow of new books and the English teachers needed for teaching the reading and writing required for a functioning society. In cross-country studies basic literacy shows up as critically important for economic growth. Advanced literacy is highly prized in business and government employments (about 9,000 master's and PhDs in English and 2,900 in humanities).
- Compositions, works of art, and the performing arts (music, theater, opera, dance) all contribute to the quality of life, as well as the development of tastes such as the classical music appreciation of undergraduates (11,145 master's and 1,163 doctorates in the visual and performing arts).

Although stretching the economic model a bit, these and other links can be made. Nothing has been said about the cost of the research or the cost of the graduate education in relation to the value of the benefits. In research there are failed experiments and investments in faculty that sometimes do not produce creative new research, or worse, let their human capital become obsolete. The true cost to the sponsor of the research is not just the costs of particular highly successful projects, the ones that are often publicized, but also includes the costs of these "failed experiments." In graduate education, although producing some master's and some PhD graduates in fields like English, math, athletics, or the performing arts may be vital to GDP growth and the national welfare, producing too many can incur high costs in relation to the potential return. Sometimes too many degree candidates are admitted to serve at low cost in teaching basic courses, provide athletic entertainment, or seek access to the performing arts with the result that the job markets cannot absorb such large numbers. The higher education policy remedies may be obvious, with the result that the private and narrow social rates of return would be raised. But a true calculation of the social rates of return to research and graduate education must consider the full costs.

Returns to Research Relative to the Costs

Most studies of the social rates of return to research are confined to those fields where it is possible to capture the benefits through patents, or in some cases, measure the outcomes of process innovation by the savings in costs. It is difficult to measure the benefits because often there is a very long time lag between the publishing of research in academic journals and its transmission into productivity gains within firms and economy-wide. The average time before commercial introduction is seven years, and before its effects on industrial productivity is about twenty years (Adams, 1990).

Edwin Mansfield has done some of the most extensive studies of the social rates of return to investment in research. They are reported in Table 6.3 and do include the cost of failed experiments. However, Table 6.3 also illustrates how if the area of research is sufficiently narrowly defined, as in the case of the 700% return to research on field corn hybrids, this excludes the costs of most research and experiments that either failed or did not result in such enormous returns. Mansfield (1995b) analyzes the social rates of return attributable to academic research in a number of selected disciplines, including engineering and life science disciplines (Mansfield, 1995a), finding that the social rates of return to investment in all research in manufacturing and agriculture averages 30 to 50% (see rows 1 and 2 in Table 6.3).

Mansfield also finds the connection to academic research to be highest in the drug industry and medical areas. These are heavily dependent on biology, microbiology, and physiology. Academic rates of return are lowest in the petroleum industry, which is more heavily dependent on applied development but which in turn depends on basic academic research in chemical engineering, chemistry, and geology.

Mansfield's estimates of the value of new products in 1985 alone in seven industries based on academic research is $24 billion, and on new processes is $7 billion. The portion of this attributable to research at individual universities can be approximately inferred from the percentage of academic researchers nationwide cited by sixty-six major firms in these same seven industries as contributing most importantly to their new products and processes introduced in the 1980s (Mansfield, 1995a, Table 2, p. 58). For electronics, information processing, and chemicals industries,

TABLE 6.3   Returns to Investment in Research, by Field

Field	Social rate (%) of return
Manufacturing	30
Agriculture	40–50
Seed corn research[a]	700
All agricultural research[a]	31 to 171
Industrial R&D[a]	
1959–63	10
1964–68	20
1969–73	35
Industrial R&D[b]	
Transportation	20
Chemical	30
Machinery	40
Electrical	30
Life Sciences[c]	
Polio vaccine	12
Mansfield's (1995b) survey of sixty-six firms	
Academic research	20–30
Percent of new products based on academic research done in last fifteen years	11
Percent of new processes based on academic research done in last fifteen years	9

[a]Griliches (1984).
[b]Nadiri (1993).
[c]Weisbrod (1971).

high percentages of the key research totaling 58 to 68% is attributed in Mansfield's data to specific academic departments.

Other industries reported 5% or less of their key research was done by local universities. For Mansfield the overall average contribution to new products and processes was 4% while specific university-based research concentrated at a few universities has accounted for a rough estimate of $1 billion in new products and $280 million in new processes per year in these seven industries alone. This $280 million alone is significantly higher than most public investment in organized research in all fields. In the case of the University of Illinois at Urbana Champaign, for example, the investment return is fifteen times higher than the annual $85 million in state investment.

With respect to fields other than the life sciences and engineering, there are no comparable social rates of return because of the difficulty in measuring the benefits. The next step must be to identify the direct and indirect impacts of research in each academic field, as Mansfield has done for engineering and certain life sciences. There are five possibilities:

1. Identify the outcome created by the research and estimate the cost of producing that outcome by other means. This is the Haveman and Wolfe (1984, 2007) approach.
2. Measure the costs saved through process innovation (the Griliches approach). This misses the value of the products created through research, and also only is workable in a few fields.
3. Estimate a growth equation containing aggregate R&D and then compute this impact as a percent of GDP. This is very difficult, yields nothing by field, and ignores non-market benefits not included in GDP.
4. Use the numbers of master's and PhDs completed in each field as a proxy for the production and dissemination of new knowledge. This assumes that new knowledge is ineffective unless it is embodied. This assumption is less of a problem than the fact that numbers of graduates does not place a value on the new knowledge per graduate.
5. Count the number of journal articles produced by faculty in each field, weighting the publications by use of the journal impact factors or by numbers of citations of the article. The cost of producing these publications within each academic department can be calculated from internal institution data, and a cost-effectiveness measure can be calculated.

The fifth approach, or at least the part that goes so far as counting the publications and then weighting them based on the reputation of the journal, and sometimes the number of citations related to these, is the standard measure of research productivity by individuals and by departments within academia. It is the most comprehensive, apart from the judgmental qualitative weightings applied to numbers of master's and PhD completions based on the potential contribution of each field to economic growth and development, which is also done implicitly by vice chancellors for academic affairs as they allocate research support and graduate instructional budgets.

The Cost-Effectiveness of Investment in Research by Academic Field

Before turning to the cost-effectiveness of academic publications, we need to note that most campuses describe successful research outcomes to the public and to those who financially support research as a means of sustaining support for research and for the university. For example, the invention of the transistor (basic to the computer) by John Bardeen, who won two Nobel Prizes in Physics, was followed by sweeping impacts of the computer on the economy. This is an impressive example of the impacts of research.

Although this is useful, this descriptive approach of successful outcomes does not produce a systematic measure across all disciplines of the ultimate impacts on growth and well-being. It is not objective because it does not take into account the cost of the failed experiments. It is suggestive and informative, but it is also casual empiricism that highlights a few interesting cases. As such, it is not objective social scientific research. Furthermore, these descriptions often are confined to engineering and life science fields, ignoring impacts of research in the social sciences, education, or law, for example, although they would not need to be skewed in this way.

There have been some national attempts to initiate comprehensive assessment systems to measure research-based outcomes and departmental and university-wide research productivity. For example, in Great Britain the Research Assessment Exercises (RAE) have changed the research environment and the manner in which university and academic departments receive government funding (Alexander, 2000a). They rank institutions and departments nationwide quite extensively. In the United States some state governments have attempted to annually assess the research productivity of faculty and institutions. In most of these assessment systems the number and quality of articles and books published, and the amount of grant support received, are used to attempt to measure research-based productivity. These sometimes controversial systems have the merits of providing some quality control through peer review, and also of not being narrowly confined to only those fields where patenting is possible.

Publications that resulted from the investment in research in each department are shown for the University of Illinois in Urbana Champaign in Table 6.4. This university was chosen because the necessary internal access to data was available and also because it is a reasonably typical public research university. Column 1 shows the output of quality-weighted publications. Column 2 estimates the cost-effectiveness of the investment in research. The latter is expressed as the cost per refereed article, which is used as the basic unit of measurement. Column 3 shows the number of master's and PhD student instructional years produced by each department, the related measure of the output of research-embodied knowledge discussed earlier. These measures are incomplete because although they show the cost-effectiveness of dollars invested by department, they do not trace the ultimate outcomes from the research or graduate students. Sometimes there could be a very high cost, for example, for one pioneering article that may actually become a very low cost to society of the benefit from the new knowledge reported. Therefore, columns 3–16 attempt to trace these more ultimate outcomes (which I will discuss later).

The table uses one article in a refereed academic journal in the field as the standard unit of measurement for each department in column 1. This is the common approach used by Alan Carter and other authors in this field. Each department head was asked to name the five top academic journals in his or her discipline. Articles in these more significant and usually more general journals were then given a larger value of 2 in the index. One article in a specialized journal in the subfield, which must have passed critical review by two or more referees to be accepted by the journal editor, therefore has the base value of 1. Non-refereed articles and shorter communications and textbooks summarizing prior contributions were given a value of 0.25, with academic books reporting original contributions given a value of 2. The peer group review process for journal articles and books and therefore the index is not perfect. Extremely important contributions can appear in specialized journals not ranked in the top five, and articles about narrow, unimportant matters do appear in the top five journals. But there is no better process than peer review for imposing quality control on research outcomes.

Given that there is a twenty- to twenty-five-year lag before there are normally measurable impacts of academic research, the relevant time period for measuring article outputs whose impacts are to be traced is for the period 1971–76. These are exactly the years for which measures of the output for each department at the university were reported by McMahon in the report for the university Senate Budget Committee (1979). These are shown in columns 1 and 2 of Table 6.4.

Research output is high and the costs per research unit are very low in quite a number of fields. In chemistry, for example, thought to be an internationally leading and relatively high-cost department, the cost per article was not particularly high ($40,956) in relation to biochemistry ($107,644) or many of the fields in engineering and agriculture. This is because the article output in chemistry (127) is relatively high. The same is true in law, a high-salary field but low in research costs ($2,868) because the article output is high. Articles in law, however, although involving serious legal research, may not involve the very extensive data collection and analysis necessary for publication in the physical, life, and social sciences. The cost per article in the physical sciences, social sciences, business, education, and the humanities is also well below the average. As in chemistry, this sometimes reflects larger article outputs, lower research support available through grants and from the campus, lower salaries in these fields, and sometimes combinations of these.

The cost per article, or of one research unit (RU), is extremely high in a few fields. These include the Center for Advanced Computation ($748,792) and the Materials Research Lab ($2,685,200). But this is misleading because the engineering faculty work in the places where the research costs are reported but give details about published articles through their home academic departments. In a few departments as distinguished from these separate labs the three-year average cost per article is very high. This is the case for food sciences ($190,200) and architecture ($512,400), for example. This kind of oversight should alert a campus administration to investigate further to determine whether such costs are or are not justified.

This may help to put in perspective Mansfield's overall estimates of the social rate of return from investment in academic research, including both that which is cost-effective and that which is less so, to be 20 to 30%. His framework, however, is confined to the federal-, state-, and foundation-supported expenditures on research in engineering, the life sciences, and agriculture fields. A more comprehensive appraisal of the contribution of

TABLE 6.4 Cost-Effectiveness of Research by Academic Field and Types of Long-Term Effects

Academic discipline	Immediate output			Medium and long-term effects													
				Direct effects on economic growth and development							Indirect effects through other variables					
	Total articles per year, each dept. (1)	Cost per article in 2001$ (cost effectiveness ratio) (2)	M.A. and Ph.D. students/yr (3)	Economic growth (4)	Health (5)	Democracy, HR (6)	Political stability (7)	Poverty and GINI (8)	Environment (9)	Crime (10)	Economic growth (11)	Health (12)	Democracy, HR (13)	Political stability (14)	Poverty and GNI (15)	Environment (16)
Humanities																
Philosophy	17	1,425	109			X	X	X			X	X	X	X	X	
English, lit, ESL	120	557	774			X	X	X			X	X	X	X	X	
Foreign languages	159	3,515	603				X				X	X	X	X	X	
History	59	1,600	349			X	X	X	X		X	X	X	X	X	
Journalism, radio, TV, comm. res.	31	28,068	152	X	X	X		X	X		X	X	X	X	X	
Advertising	5	5,828	113		X	X						X	X			
Classics	49	573	101			X	X				X	X	X	X	X	
Social science																
Political science	54	2,373	244	X		X	X	X			X	X	X	X	X	
Economics	60	8,400	597	X	X	X	X	X	X	X	X	X	X	X	X	
Psychology	85	34,300	694		X							X				
Sociology, criminology	31	13,400	256		X	X		X		X	X	X	X	X	X	
Anthropology	38	10,400	227			X		X				X				
Asian, LAC studies	5	14,656	71			X	X				X	X	X	X	X	

(continued)

Linguistics	38	3,032	22			X				X		X
Speech and comm.	14	384	68		X	X				X		
Physical science												
Astronomy	58	21,072	107	X	X	X	X	X		X	X	X
Mathematics, stat.	117	12,580	975	X	X	X		X	X	X	X	X
Physics	184	41,600	1242	X	X	X		X		X		X
Chemistry	127	40,956	1260	X	X	X	X	X		X		X
Geography	21	6,484	130	X	X	X		X	X	X		X
Geology	37	3,948	201	X	X	X	X	X		X	X	X
Life sciences												
Physiology	46	37,720	356	X	X	X	X	X		X		X
Botany	35	13,420	175	X	X	X		X		X		X
Biology	2	460	220	X	X	X		X		X		X
Zoology	55	18,678	178	X	X	X	X	X		X	X	X
Biochemistry	27	107,644	449	X	X	X		X		X		X
Microbiology	26	79,489	237	X	X	X		X		X		X
Entomology	29	20,132	168	X	X	X	X	X		X		X
Speech and hearing	3	664	315	X	X	X				X		X
Business administration												
Accounting	29	3,912	407		X	X				X		X
Finance	25	6,204	253		X	X				X		X
Business administration (personnel, management, info. systems, marketing)	54	6,844	1557		X	X				X		X
Bur. bus. research	Incl	Above	F+B		X	X						
Engineering												
Computer science	27	72,332	707		X	X				X		X

TABLE 6.4 (continued)

Academic discipline	Immediate output			Medium and long-term effects												
				Direct effects on economic growth and development							Indirect effects through other variables					
	(1) Total articles per year, each dept.	(2) Cost per article in 2001$ (cost effectiveness ratio)	(3) M.A. and Ph.D. students/yr	(4) Economic growth	(5) Health	(6) Democracy, HR	(7) Political stability	(8) Poverty and GINI	(9) Environment	(10) Crime	(11) Economic growth	(12) Health	(13) Democracy, HR	(14) Political stability	(15) Poverty and GINI	(16) Environment
Electrical engr.	95	54,000	1350	X							X	X			X	X
Mechanical	27	55,424	450	X							X	X			X	X
Nuclear	32	36,600	406	X							X	X				X
Civil engineering	96	60,188	963	X					X		X				X	X
Aero and astro	9	112,272	134	X					X		X				X	X
Ceramic engr.	6	65,972	118	X							X					
Metallurgical, mng.	32	45,172	356	X							X					X
Materials res. lab	69	2,685	na	X							X					X
Coor. sci. lab	8	113,740	na	X							X					X
Ctr. adv. computation		748,792	na	X							X	X			X	X
Chemical engr.	14	51,768	220	X							X	X				X
General engr.	4	16,612	6	X							X	X			X	X
T and A mechanics	29	46,072	265	X							X					X
Education																
Educational psych.	32	31,200	1,245	X	X	X	X		X		X	X	X		X	X
Educ. org. and lshp.	19	664	463	X	X	X	X				X	X	X		X	X

Field				1	2	3	4	5	6	7	8	9	10	11	12	13
Educ. policy studies	23	672	467	X					X	X	X	X	X	X	X	X
Elementary educ.	23	564	508	X					X	X	X	X	X	X	X	X
Secondary and cont. educ.	7	4,216	423	X			X	X	X	X	X			X	X	X
Special education	0	0	349	X					X	X			X	X	X	X
Student teaching	0	0	85	X					X	X	X	X			X	X
Voc. and tech. educ.	12	41,912	295	X			X	X	X	X	X			X		X
Agriculture																
Agronomy	72	96,476	380	X				X	X	X	X			X	X	X
Agricultural economy	54	52,800	246	X				X	X	X	X			X	X	X
Agriculutral engr.	34	44,836	35	X					X	X	X	X		X	X	X
Animal sciences	35	86,128	266	X			X		X	X	X	X		X	X	X
Agr. entomology	16	39,640	Na	X					X	X	X	X		X	X	X
Food sciences	18	190,200	193	X	X				X	X	X	X	X	X	X	X
Forestry	20	51,724	26	X	X			X	X	X	X			X	X	X
Human res. and fam.	6	63,404	152	X		X			X	X				X	X	X
Dairy science	30	95,400	128	X	X				X	X	X			X	X	X
Horticulture	67	34,000	58	X					X	X	X	X		X	X	X
Plant pathology	43	40,100	138	X					X	X	X	X		X	X	X
Law	56	2,868	2573			X	X	X	X	X	X	X	X	X	X	X
Fine and app. arts																
Art and design	10	4,260	371	X					X	X	X	X		X	X	X
Architecture	9	512,400	676						X	X		X				X
Music and bands	31	6,852	985													X
Dance	2	0	53													
Theater	1	2,800	96													
Urban and regional planning	6	3,574	238	X			X	X	X	X	X	X		X	X	X

(continued)

TABLE 6.4 (continued)

Academic discipline	Immediate output			Medium and long-term effects															
				Direct effects on economic growth and development							Indirect effects through other variables					
	Total articles per year, each dept. (1)	Cost per article in 2001$ (cost effectiveness ratio) (2)	M.A. and Ph.D. students/yr (3)	Economic growth (4)	Health (5)	Democracy, HR (6)	Political stability (7)	Poverty and GINI (8)	Environment (9)	Crime (10)	Economic growth (11)	Health (12)	Democracy, HR (13)	Political stability (14)	Poverty and GNI (15)	Environment (16)
Landscape arch.	7	14,296	76						X	X					X	
Small homes co. and housing research	8	236,000	na													
Veterinary med.																
Clinial vet. med.	31	1,920	663	X							X	X				
Vet. pathology	51	17,600	367	X	X				X		X	X				
Vet. physiology	6	223,477	230	X	X						X	X				
Medicine																
Basic med. science	2	382,344	476		X						X	X			X	
Clinical medicine	na	na	na		X						X	X				
Nursing	na	na	na		X						X					
Pharmacy	na	na	na		X						X					
Applied life std.																
Public health	15	8,242	120		X						X	X			X	X

Discipline	Col. 1	Col. 2	Col. 3	Cols. 4–10 (direct effects)							Cols. 11–15 (indirect effects)				
Physical education	29	3,798	415			X					X	X			
Leisure studies	8	11,686	169			X					X	X			
Center for adv. study	2	1,206	na				X								
Labor and indus. relations	18	121,200	150			X	X	X			X	X	X	X	
Library science	27	12,964	809			X	X				X	X			
Social work	24	3,193	803	X		X	X	X			X	X	X	X	

NOTE: Col. 1: Refereed articles by discipline, lagged twenty-five years to allow for impacts.
Col. 2: Cost per article, based on research grant support plus time allocation of salary.
Col. 3: Master's and PhD students per year as transmitters of embodied knowledge.
Cols. 4–10: Direct effects inferred from education coefficients from worldwide data.
Cols. 11–15: Indirect effects of research inferred from indirect education impacts.

research would have to include estimates of the contributions to productivity of, say, newly devised management techniques, new information technologies, contributions to economic stability and development, new environmental technologies, new insights into sources of effective learning in education, criminology research into the sources of crime, contributions such as the discovery of penicillin to better public health, and so forth. Tracer studies are needed on the impacts of research these fields, apart from just the number of master's and PhD graduates, which keep track of the costs of the research support as above as well as the costs of the graduate programs. This method recognizes the embodiment of new knowledge created by research in graduates that results in a strong complementarity between postgraduate education and research within the research universities.

A few insights, however, are possible. The indirect effects of higher education, assuming these include graduate education and research, were estimated to be 42% of the direct effects in Chapter 5. If each fields is labeled in Table 6.4 with X's identifying its direct and indirect contributions to the private and social benefits, such as to better health (the life sciences, medicine, nursing), to the rule of law (democratization, human rights, political stability as studied in political science, law, and history), to advancing trade (foreign languages and business), and to social capital (journalism, criminology), then these fields also contribute to economic growth, albeit indirectly. Fields like engineering and business administration make fewer of these indirect contributions; most of their contributions to growth are direct. In contrast, most of the indirect benefits to economic growth come from research and graduate programs in liberal arts (including the social sciences, history, and the humanities), as well as from law, social work, education, and labor relations. Their indirect contributions to growth would come to about 42% of the total contribution of higher education and research to growth.

The non-market direct contributions to the quality of life, apart from these indirect benefits, were valued in Chapter 4, and we saw that they are more than equal to the earnings and growth benefits. These also deeply involve still additional academic fields. For example, better health is surely especially dependent on research and graduate training in the life sciences, medicine, nursing, pharmacy, and applied life studies. There are also non-market benefits to the quality of community life from research and graduate education in urban planning, parks and recreation, criminology, political science, history, education, and social work (Table 6.4). And finally, although Beethovens are rare, surely the quality of life is improved by master's and PhD graduates in the performing arts, such as music, dance, and theater, as well as architecture, art, and design.

Many years ago I estimated narrow social rates of return by field and by degree level based on the degree costs and on both expected and actual earnings of graduates. These clearly confirm that using only the earnings of master's and PhD graduates is misleading and seriously underestimates the non-market returns in many fields. For example, the expected social rate of return based on earnings for clergy was −2.8%, and the realized actual rate of return was −17.5% (McMahon and Wagner, 1982, p. 172). PhDs in education expected +3.1% and realized −2.8%. Social rates of return for graduate programs in fine and applied arts were often negative, whereas master's, PhD, and professional degree graduates in medicine (12.2%), law (15.5%), and engineering (7.4–10%) were among the highest. Social rates of return at all degree levels have gone up for master's and PhD graduates since 1982, as was documented in Chapter 3.

But there are obviously non-market benefits, both private and most especially social, from the services of the clergy, teachers and school administrators, and postgraduates in fine and applied arts that are not included in these narrow social rate of return calculations for these fields. The point from Table 6.4 is that these non-market returns are higher in some fields than in others, and that narrow social rates of return based only on the earnings of master's, PhD, and professional graduates later are a very poor basis for allocations of graduate student support and research dollars among departments.

A reasonable guess might be that the social rates of return to graduate education (and perhaps to research) in these other fields where the non-market benefits and the indirect effects are both larger is the average market rate of return to graduate education, since these fields have lower earnings but contribute heavily to the 42% indirect effects from higher education to earnings in all fields (based on the narrow social rates of return in Chapter 5): master's (9%), PhD (8%), and professional (11%). The non-market private benefits are roughly equal to the market benefits that occur across all fields, for a total social rate of return of: master's (18%), PhD (16%), and professional (22%). The private total rates of return are of course much higher because of the subsidies in the form of fellowships and teaching and research assistantships that graduate students receive.

These are a bit lower but not drastically different from the 30% narrower social rates of return to patenting in engineering that Mansfield finds. When the contributions of research to increased effectiveness in the public sector (from computer science to public administration), the indirect contributions to growth (from literacy to the rule of law), and the non-market private benefits to the quality of life (from health to happiness) are considered, the benefits of research that go beyond patents that allow privatization loom very important. This suggests that there is market failure in research markets as well because information about broader and longer-run research outcomes important to the public good is so poor. The implications are that going too far with privatization in the funding of research, which has implications for graduate student funding, can lead to a serious distortion of priorities.

Policy Strategies for States: Support for Research and Graduate Education

For each state the social rates of return and the growth equations when interpreted with a dynamic perspective that includes indirect effects show that public investment in higher education by states within the United States, as well as within most OECD countries, is growth enhancing. But recent research strongly suggests that the weighting of this investment as between two-year community college levels and graduate master's and PhD levels embodying new research depends on how close that state or country is to the technological frontier.

It finds, not surprisingly, that these most highly educated graduates at the master's and PhD levels are motivated to move to the higher-income areas where their skills are in demand and higher salaries are available. Within the United States this tends to be the larger cities and higher-income regions, such as parts of California and the Eastern Seaboard where the highest salaries are paid. It is not surprising, therefore, that this new research finds that investment in academic R&D and in advanced master's and PhD graduate education has the highest payoff in higher-income states such as California, the Eastern Seaboard, including New

England, and Michigan and Illinois. It is in the larger cities, firms, and academic institutions where the higher salaries are paid that attract and retain these graduates (Aghion et al., 2005; Vandenbussce et al., 2006).

Their analysis covers nineteen OECD countries as well as U.S. states. It is based on the proposition that innovation is a relatively more skill-intensive activity than imitation, and hence requires the most highly educated graduates. Farther from the technological frontier, imitation and application of technologies is the main engine of productivity growth and economic growth in general. They find that the growth-enhancing margin in OECD countries is that from skilled human capital rather than total human capital, and that this highly skilled human capital has the strongest growth-enhancing effects in economies that are closest to the technological frontier.

The implications of this at the state level are not that the lower-income states, such as those within the Deep South in the United States or those in Eastern and Southern Europe, should not invest in master's and PhD programs. These have a positive return, especially if these locations develop strategies to retain their graduates (as has Indonesia by promising them promotions and raises when they return). But the largest returns to growth in other than the highest-income regions are from investment in undergraduate two- and four-year degree programs. Community college graduates are very unlikely to leave the state, and most four-year graduates will also remain. Those who leave tend to be largely offset by other college graduates who come in from other states.

The comparative advantage to U.S. states from increasing investment in advanced master's and PhD graduates as well as supporting academic research support lies in those states where there are employment opportunities with higher salaries within the state for those graduates. If each state increases its investment judiciously in line with its comparative advantage, then each state grows the fastest. It is true that it is hard for the followers to catch up in this race between technology and human capital formation. But it is not impossible, given the right policies.

Conclusions

Research in higher education institutions enables faculty to stay up to date on new knowledge within their field worldwide. The education of master's, PhD, and professional students embodies this new knowledge and technologies in graduates who disseminate it as they take employment in firms, in government, or at other universities. Because of this embodiment it is hard to separate the outcomes from graduate education and research. But it is possible to gain some insights into the returns to research and graduate education by field in relation to the investment costs. There are higher education policy implications of this embodiment of new knowledge and technologies in human capital. They relate to policies among fields within universities, but also to state-level policies involving the best kind of investments to make in higher education.

The best estimates available of the social rates of return to investment in research are 30% in engineering fields and 20 to 30% campus-wide. Isolated cases can be found that are far above as well as below this. As cited by Mansfield above, Griliches estimated the return to investing in the development of seed corn varieties at land grant universities at 700%, for example, and the rate of return to research by John Bardeen who invented the transistor could well approach infinity if one considers the transformations brought about by the computer worldwide. The problem is that almost all of the studies of the returns to research are confined to fields where it is possible to obtain patents, whereas major sources of economic growth and development arise from social benefits from fields that contribute to the rule of law, good government, political stability, trade (for example, foreign languages), and efficient management of market economies where patents are irrelevant.

One way to get at this contribution coming from all fields is to recognize that the new knowledge created by research (which accesses new knowledge worldwide) is embodied in master's and PhD graduates, who then disseminate it to undergraduate students, firms, other colleges, and government as they graduate. The number and quality of these advanced graduates is an index of the impact of each field on development in the society. One must look at the valuations placed on the various social outcomes of higher education in Chapter 5, and then relate each outcome to specific fields to the extent that that is possible. Then the values of these outcomes can be related to the costs of the academic research and graduate programs in each field. The research supports the quality of the graduate programs, but the instructional costs per student in each master's and PhD program must also be taken into account.

This approach is not perfect. And increasing degrees of specificity will require continuing research. But it is better than looking only at patents, which as a basis for internal departmental allocations distorts university priorities and can also lead to distortions as research funding is related to patents and to profitability and further privatized. Patents allow the benefits of the research to be captured privately by firms, an advantage available only in a few fields. The approach used by most universities, however, is to count and weight publications of the faculty. This has the strong advantage of not being limited to just a few fields. But it also has the strong disadvantage that it is not a cost-effectiveness measure unless these publications are related to their costs. This step is possible, as I showed in this chapter, and it is very revealing. But even when publications are augmented with the number of citations, it still does not lead to an estimate of the economic value of the research outcome.

There is one final implication of this embodiment of new knowledge for higher education policy as it relates to investment in research and advanced postgraduate degree programs. Each state will, and should, invest at both graduate research and undergraduate levels. The issue, however, is in what proportion? Recent research suggests that those states that are at or closest to the technological frontier have the greatest advantage when investing in university-based research and graduate degrees. This is for the simple reason that the master's and PhD graduates have the best job opportunities in the larger urban centers and academic communities there. States farther from the technological frontier have higher social rates of return on investments in two- and four-year degree programs, and their greatest comparative advantage lies there. Not only are these undergraduates more likely to settle locally. But also the costs at these degree levels are lower, and there is not the need to spend on so many costly failed experiments, a major cost in the richer regions of remaining at the frontier.

Advances in knowledge through research and its embodiment through graduate education contributes broadly to society's needs, the quality of life, and jobs in service industries, and not just to short-term industrial growth. However, the embodied knowledge also contributes to pure economic growth and development. But most of this occurs indirectly and over longer periods of time.

CHAPTER SEVEN

New Higher Education Policies

I think by far the most important bill in our whole code, is that for the diffusion of knowledge among the people.

THOMAS JEFFERSON (1786, P. 396)

FAMILIAR HIGHER EDUCATION policy issues involve access, affordability, accountability, and the trend toward privatization. Dramatically changed conditions in the economy with enormous skill deficits due to globalization, a human capital perspective that has established the critical role of education in the knowledge economy, new research on the nature and value of private and social benefits of higher education, and implications of all of these for the degree of market failure in higher education markets and for privatization trends require revisiting these traditional policy themes. These new perspectives will indicate that some major new departures are needed in higher education policy.

After summarizing the evidence concerning the need for new policies, the main higher education policy options and conclusions relating to them that draw on analyses in Chapters 1–6 in this book will be considered. This chapter will not seek to address all higher education policy debates. Some relate to internal personnel management and not to issues that are closely related to the theme of this book. A good source for updates on the details of these debates is the *Inside Higher Education* website at http://insidehighered.com/news/. Background for still other policies is covered in Paulsen and Smart (2001) and Monk (1990). This chapter focuses on policies and policy options that are consistent with a human capital formation perspective and implied by the analysis presented. Policy implications will be considered first at the national, then at the state (or provincial), and then at local campus levels. The emphasis is on U.S. higher education policies, but most options are also relevant to the United Kingdom and the European Union, except where noted.

The Need for New Higher Education Policy

Higher education policy is often very introspective. This is necessarily true for many faculty and department heads, who are primarily concerned with their own disciplines, as well as for deans, chancellors, and even some university presidents. It is also true for some state boards of higher education that take a narrow internal management view of their role, and for some legislators and governors. This myopic and introspective view persists in spite of the ongoing debate at the national and state levels about access and about reductions of state funding creating pressures for higher tuition and privatization and in spite of the debates about the future of higher education. For example, presidents and representatives from all levels of higher education at a TIAA-CREF Leadership Conference dealing with "Trends and Issues" explored the implications and need for "transformational change in higher education." In the summary by Lord (2007), very few even mentioned the needs of the society that their institutions serve. Many focused on devices for attracting students to their school, most focused on internal management issues, and most were preoccupied with competition with other types of institutions. This internal conflict and competition within the higher education community, although it is not all bad, clouds recognition that institutions have diverse and complementary missions and that cooperation in developing strategies to meet society's needs is vital.

There were, however, exceptions. President Bacrow (Tufts) stressed that "one of the biggest transformational changes that we could make is to, as a group, commit ourselves to need-based financial aid" (ibid., p. 11). This does suggest broader cooperation among institutions and recognizes the trend in many states toward purely merit-based aid where it would be possible without excluding the middle class from benefits to add a need criterion. Another president, King Alexander (California State University,

Long Beach), commented on the need to be accountable for student outcomes. He went on to highlight the enormous pent-up demand for enrollment in California when tuition is affordable, and to stress the need for a national policy to deal with helping states to help institutions provide for access. This is a theme this chapter will return to. And Chancellor Kirwan (University System of Maryland) described a unique deal negotiated with their legislature whereby a range of efficiency measures were implemented by the university, and the state legislature followed through to fund a 21% increase in appropriations over two years to cover a ten thousand-student enrollment growth as negotiated. There is some question about the quality of the education provided as the result of this "deal" in Baltimore and elsewhere, but it is a unique new development. Many public universities including the state flagship campuses are capping their enrollments because they are short of funds to serve the needs of society, and others, including Maryland, are hiring many adjunct faculty for extremely low salaries who are teaching huge teaching loads.

There is, however, creative thinking. But there is also political conflict. Some academic leaders are trying hard to respond to the broader societal issues.*

EVIDENCE OF THE NEED FOR NEW INITIATIVES

In the 1980s it was not clear whether higher education was above, at, or below its optimum level, as indicated by Leslie and Brinkman (1988, p. 183). There had been an increase in the number of college graduates in the 1970s due to the baby boomers. The new community college expansion beginning in the 1960s was producing graduates. And the Education Amendments of 1972 had expanded student financial aid. This was coupled with a temporary economic recession in 1975. Freeman (1976) did not recognize this demographic bulge or the recession effects on the demand for graduates as transitory. He also ignored the non-market private and social benefits of higher education. This bears mention since his erroneous conclusions are still sometimes quoted in the higher education lit-

*Quotes and citations are from the summary of the TIAA-CREF Leadership Conference focused on "Trends and Issues" and the need for transformational change in higher education offered by Lord (2007).

erature. The conclusion in this book based on evidence presented in Chapters 3 and 5 is that since 1980 there has been mounting evidence that forms a consistent pattern indicating that investment in human capital through higher education has been for some time and is now even farther below optimum.

A balanced appraisal must discount narrow exceptions, such as the PhD surplus in Silicon Valley after the temporary dot com technology bubble. Instead, there are strong underlying forces of technical change, globalization, freer trade, and immigration that have all contributed to large skill deficiencies in the United States. As we also noted in Chapter 3, large middle- and lower-income groups are socially and economically excluded from the benefits of growth. They are rapidly joining a growing protectionist backlash against free trade, globalization, and immigration. This pattern in the United States is repeated in the United Kingdom, France, Germany, the Netherlands, and some other OECD nations.

A summary of the evidence of the serious need for major new higher education policy initiatives from the new human capital perspective in earlier chapters indicates that:

- Real earnings of college graduates have risen since 1980 by 57% in the United States, whereas the real earnings of those with a high school education or less have remained flat or have fallen. The latter group constitutes 64% of the population. This earnings divergence is a major source of growing inequality, creating disenchantment and backlash.
- The difference between the earnings of high school and college graduates was 20% in 1980; it is now 70%.
- Considering the increase in college costs, narrow social rates of return for two- and four-year college degrees have risen since 1980 from 10 to 16% for an associate degree and 15% for a bachelor's in 2007. Considering that these rates are in real terms and include no non-market benefits, this is a very high return. Estimates by some based on Mincer earnings functions are lower. But they also all show increases since 1980 although they do not take the rising institutional costs into account. If the dynamic upward shifts in age-earnings profiles are considered, a point that Heckman et al. (2008) have also stressed, this adds about 3 percentage points

(Arias and McMahon, 2001). The corrected narrow social rates of return in the United States are then closer to 18% for a bachelor's degree. If institutional costs per student were limited to instruction costs, the rate of return would even be higher. These estimates for associate degrees are now based on a longer span of data since community colleges were expanded in the 1960s so that it is possible to have confidence in them. High school social rates of return have remained flat at 10% since 1980. The narrow social rates of return alone provide strong evidence that higher education is below its optimum. The evidence, however, does not reveal how far below.*

- The largest percentage and absolute increases in current and projected jobs are in occupations requiring two, four, or more years of college. The largest percentage decreases are in those occupations requiring a high school education or less. The only significant exception is home health care, due to the aging population in the United States and the European Union.

- In the United Kingdom, there are 7 million without basic literacy skills. Business persons say they should not be expected to provide these skills for sixteen-year-old dropouts because there are plenty of immigrants from Eastern Europe who have the skills and the work ethic.

    Seeking immigrants rather than domestic workers who have skills is very hard on the poorer developing countries, however, as they lose their skilled human capital. In the United States a similar policy gives preference to those who have advanced degrees, MDs, and nursing credentials. This undercuts medical care in the poor countries and weakens support by businesses for domestic efforts to finance higher education when they can get skilled workers elsewhere.

---

*It is never possible to say how far it is necessary to go to reach "optimum," only that with this comparison in rates that more investment is needed to move toward optimum. If demand for graduates does not grow more rapidly, then larger investment will eventually lower these social rates of return. But this is a very long, slow process, taking decades. In any event, to check whether or not optimum has been achieved, it is necessary to collect new earnings data and re-compute. In principle, a true social rate of return should be used for all comparisons, not the narrow rate based only on money earnings.

- The real costs of higher education have gone up only about half as much as the increase in institutional costs. Congressionally mandated studies of college costs have incorrectly focused on only institutional costs. The lower true rate of increase is because forgone earnings costs that are roughly equal to institutional costs at public institutions have remained flat. Another distortion in public perceptions is based on publicity that stresses costs that have gone past $50,000 in 2007. But this is only at some elite private institutions and generally does not apply to public institutions. The absolute increases in tuition and costs have been largest at private institutions, although percentage increases in the past few years have been larger at public institutions as state support has diminished since the base for the percentage is smaller. Focusing only on percentage increases, therefore, provides a somewhat distorted picture. This is done in proposed legislation that threatens to punish the lowest-cost institutions. The point is that accountability is very desirable, but it is important to measure true costs, and true outcomes, if economic efficiency is to be improved.
- The contribution of higher education to economic growth can be demonstrated for developed OECD nations. But this is possible only after controlling for an aging population (by using life expectancy, for example) and by using a dynamic approach that pays attention to the embodiment of new technologies in replacement investment (see Appendix D). A few studies use time dummy variables that eliminate the effects of new technologies embodied in the human capital of new graduates. Others eliminate the indirect effects from higher education with controls for the rule of law and political stability, wiping out some of the more important externalities. Others use educational achievement stocks of human capital rather than investment or enrollment rate gross additions to these stocks, which has much of the same effect.

  The above does not address the contribution of higher education to growth in poor countries. The conditions are different there, partly because many of the graduates often migrate to the richer countries and partly because very limited basic education contributes to skill shortages at that level.
- The evidence for non-market private benefits from higher educa-

tion beyond income is extensive. The annual value of these benefits for bachelor's graduates is estimated to be $38,080 in 2007
dollars. This is 122% of the earnings-based returns. This suggests
that:

1. There is greater underinvestment in higher education than commonly believed.
2. Poor information about these non-market private benefits is
   contributing to poor performance in higher education markets.
3. Higher education policies to develop and disseminate better
   information about these non-market private benefits is
   warranted.

• The evidence for social benefits on balance, weighing the limitations of some studies to the contrary, is substantial. A major effort
  has been made to identify what they are, to analyze the dynamic
  process over time by which indirect effects feed back to contribute
  to growth, and to estimate their monetary value.

  The value of these social benefits is estimated to be about 52%
  of the total benefits, both market and non-market. This consists of
  42% of the market and non-market benefits that are indirect effects,
  plus about 10% (or 7 percentage points in the social rate of return)
  that are direct public good social benefits.

  Using the Haveman-Wolfe method, the monetary value of the
  public good social benefits alone (direct and indirect) is estimated
  to be $27,726 per year for each bachelor's graduate. Both of these
  perspectives suggest that:

1. Public good benefits and additional externalities due to indirect
   effects constitute another major source of market failure in
   higher education markets. These benefits that will not be provided privately are the main rationale for public support of
   higher education. The existence of externalities has been challenged by some economists. But there has been much additional
   work, and new perspectives have emerged since that have been
   addressed and weighed in Chapters 3, 5, and 6.
2. Although externalities per se are a source of market failure,
   quite apart from this poor information about social benefits is
   potentially an additional reason higher education markets are
   working poorly when it comes to society's needs. When infor-

mation about externalities is poor, they are poorly understood and often overlooked.

- Although the estimate that 52% of higher education benefits are externalities is tentative, it is the best available that is based on their individual value and estimates of the indirect effects. Its implication is that about 52% of total investment (consisting of institutional costs plus forgone earnings) needs to be supported by governments and endowment funds, and 48% covered privately through tuition, fees, and forgone earnings (roughly room and board) if economic efficiency is to be achieved.

By this 52% criteria, colleges and universities whose funding is 100% private (assuming small or no endowment) are not efficient since this must include providing for the external benefits that include charity and the public good. Examples perhaps include for-profit Internet offerings such as the University of Phoenix, which is currently in some trouble, or DeVry, a private for-profit vocational college in Chicago. Some other universities are moving in this direction as privatization proceeds.

But inefficiency also occurs in universities where most all of the funds are public. This occurs in some universities like the Sorbonne in France, the University of Moscow, and other universities in the European Union. There tuition is close to zero and resource recovery from parents is low. This does not tap available private resources so either admission is highly restricted or else expenditure per student is low and quality suffers This latter pattern can be observed in Greece, where the Constitution mandates zero tuition, and in Pakistan. If the higher education policy seeks to maintain expenditure per student, and quality, by using highly selective admissions as in Russia, the Netherlands, and elsewhere, then there is inefficiency because the total needs of the middle class for higher education are less well served and also inequality is perpetuated.

It is apparent that major higher education policy implications depend on the size of the social benefits. The 52% of the total benefits that are indirect or social suggest that it is desirable from an efficiency point of view that privatization proceed to cover about 48% of higher education undergraduate plus graduate costs, since about 48% of the benefits are purely private. But if privatization should proceed much beyond 48 to 50% of total investment costs, questions can be raised about higher education's service to the public good and about whether overall economic efficiency can be achieved.*

National Higher Education Policy Implications

There are some major higher education policy gaps. Some of these are at the national level. It is a national problem that over 64% of the population are being excluded from enjoying the fruits of economic growth. This is largely because of skill deficits due to the automation and new skill needs attributable to new technologies, and by international job outsourcing associated with globalization. I have suggested that the mainstream of higher education policy has largely been asleep to these needs, and that there is a serious need for a major new departure.

A balanced evaluation of all the evidence points in this direction. It includes the high and rising narrow social rates of return, largely overlooked non-market private benefits, new evidence that indicates substantial direct social public goods benefits, and valuable indirect benefits that are externalities. The new total social rates of return to higher education when the overlooked non-market benefits are taken into account are even higher, and much higher than the opportunity cost of funds, Other evidence includes the enormous skill deficits. There is some evidence to the contrary that must be weighed. It includes the rising demand for low-skilled home health care aides, but also growing desires for greater professionalism. There are some growth equation regressions that have been unable to find higher education effects on growth or higher education externalities, and the temporary declines in the demand for college grads

*Economic efficiency includes production efficiency and exchange efficiency. In the education literature the former is usually referred to as internal efficiency, and the latter as external efficiency. DeVry might be internally efficient, for example, but not exhibit external efficiency (since the latter includes externalities). Some heavily subsidized public universities in Europe may or may not be efficient, in that resources are likely to be so limited that quality is low (which raises questions about efficiency), or where policies involving extensive use of test scores and high selectivity are followed, questions can be raised about whether or not too few graduates are being supplied (and about equity).

during recessions.* But this latter evidence to the contrary is often flawed and sometimes transitory. On balance, the evidence that higher education is now considerably below its optimum is substantial.

Different aspects of this problem need to be addressed with different kinds of policies, national, state, and local. All are needed to contribute to the solution.

PROVIDING BETTER INFORMATION TO ENABLE HIGHER EDUCATION MARKETS TO WORK

The first type of major new national higher education policy initiative needed involves a larger commitment than in the past by the U.S. Department of Education and by the American Council on Education to develop and provide more extensive and specific information identifying and placing an economic value on the non-market private and social benefits of higher education. This information needs to be provided to colleges and universities as well as directly to prospective students, parents, state legislators, and the media. But also better information needs to be provided by the leaders of higher education institutions to those who finance what they do. Similar efforts are needed in the United Kingdom, Germany, France, the Netherlands, and the more developed OECD member countries.

Most parents typically make enormous sacrifices for their children when they have information they trust. Their support for their children in school is part of total personal and national saving and investment as they refrain from their own consumption (the definition of saving) and invest in human capital formation. Such saving and investment are vital to economic growth and to the national interest. Parents' forgone consumption is not part of private financial saving but is over and above that. In the United States especially, where domestic financial saving has fallen to almost zero, it is a little recognized but vital margin of total saving and investment contributing to sustainable growth (see Appendix D).

But this private saving and private investment only occurs when par-

---

*Transitory declines in the demand for workers due to recessions, including the typical declines in the demands for college graduates, should not be the basis for policies relating to very long-term investment in human capital formation. The investment is one that yields returns for at least sixty-five years after graduation, as long or longer than the very longest-term types of investment in the private sector.

ents and students have full and accurate information. The estimated $38,080 value of private non-market benefits for a bachelor's, 122% of the market value, combined with the lack of awareness of such benefits, indicate that this is a major source of market failure that is not being addressed.

Information made available by the U.S. Department of Education provides data annually on the overall health status at each income level as a function of the amount of education (National Center for Education Statistics, 2000–2007). But the information provided is essentially limited to that, with no analysis of the additional private non-market benefits and no estimates of the value. Among the special analyses conducted each year by the U.S. Department of Education there have been none on the non-market benefits of higher education. The Office of Research of the U.S. Department of Education did commission a series of papers on the social benefits of education some time ago. But apart from good surveys of the research on health benefits by Grossman and Kaestner (1997) and crime benefits by Witte (1997), the volume and summary articles that were the result focused on abstractions, static models, debatable controls, and overlapping contributing behaviors and outcomes. It contained no reference to the valuation of outcomes and did not result in a systematic identification of credible outcomes. It also confined attention to only a very few social benefits and ignored evidence based on aggregate worldwide data. The latter is probably the only context in which it is possible to observe slowly changing civic institutions and their effects on democratization and political stability. On this latter point, Thomas Jefferson's (1786) observations in France on the importance of education just before the French Revolution were better. So these papers seriously need to be updated.

In comparison, the U.S. Department of Education has done far less in providing comprehensive information than has, for example, the Security and Exchange Commission about securities, the U.S. Department of Agriculture about agricultural markets, the U.S. Department of Justice enforcing the Robinson-Patman Act that requires truthful advertising, the Food and Drug Administration that provides for accurate food and drug labeling, or even the Federal Reserve System that requires truth in lending. As I write this, there is an issue about the Federal Reserve's responsibility in supervising lenders who made sub-prime loans. That is, it is very well established in national policy that national agencies assist in providing and/or ensuring that full and accurate information is provided so that markets can work. It is a higher education policy gap that the higher education market is for the most part an exception when it comes to information about substantial non-market returns and indirect benefits.

The American Council on Education sponsors a commission with an advisory group chaired by Stanley Ikenberry that is making a commendable effort to publicize some of these non-market benefits of higher education. It has a website called *Solutions for Our Future* that lists its publications. A number of national higher education organizations have joined in and are supporting this effort, including the Educational Testing Service, the College Board, the NCAA, TIAA-CREF, Campus Compact, and hundreds of individual colleges and universities around the country. They are urging more universities and state boards of higher education to register and join. This can be done at http://survey.acenet.edu/Scripts/rws3 .pl?FORM=Solutions_Project_2 . But more substantial funding is needed from the American Council on Education and others, and this effort needs to be coupled with a commitment within the U.S. Department of Education to provide more complete and better information so that higher education markets can work better.

The return could potentially be a significant increase in private saving and investment in human capital formation with major national benefits to sustainable growth. The United States and the European Union are far behind South Korea, for example, where 47% of the population ages twenty-five to thirty-five has completed college compared to only 39% of this same age group in the United States. South Korea's per capita growth rate is much higher than that of the United States, as we observed in Chapter 3. Much of this in South Korea is through private saving and investment by families. Canada and Japan marginally exceed South Korea's 47%, but the United States, the United Kingdom, Germany, and other OECD countries are falling far behind (OECD, 2006).

NEED-BASED FINANCIAL AID: THE PELL GRANT APPROACH

A second policy option is to increase Pell Grant support much more rapidly. The fraction of total college costs covered by Pell Grants has fallen, and although the number of Pell Grants supported has increased, it has not increased fast enough to sustain the needed increase in enrollment rates.

The fact that students from middle- and lower-income families are increasingly being excluded is another evidence that need-based financial aid such as that provided by Pell Grants in the United States and Council Grants in the United Kingdom that include maintenance are not increasing nearly fast enough. This is in spite of the fact that Pell Grants allocated over $14 billion in aid to one-fourth of all U.S. undergraduates in 2008. Need-based aid benefits both private and public higher education institutions. In contrast to purely merit-based aid, the evidence is that it is more effective in inducing additional enrollment since those receiving purely merit-based aid would normally attend anyway (McMahon, 2005, and others cited there). Merit-based aid is often defended on the grounds that it keeps students in the state. But need-based aid offered by states also does this. The total enrollment effect, which is greater for need-based aid, means that additional private investment is induced as students and families cover the remaining tuition, maintenance, and forgone earnings costs. A 10% increase in the maximum Pell award also is associated with a 15% increase in the revenues received by the average institution (Curs et al., 2007, p. 258). So although about 40% of Pell disbursements go to students who attend two-year institutions, the revenues received by private institutions is not much disturbed by an increase in public support of Pell Grants.

In defense of merit-based aid, students from middle- and higher-income families benefit, so this retains public support for these financial aid programs. They also feel that their good performance in high school is rewarded. However, it is quite possible to add a need criterion to merit-based aid that is sufficiently broadly defined that these programs continue to benefit the middle class and thereby retain their support.

FEDERAL SUPPORT FOR STATE AND LOCAL HIGHER
EDUCATION INSTITUTIONS

A third policy option designed to keep tuition affordable and support the social benefits, while also enabling community colleges and four-year public universities to absorb the kind of additional increases in enrollments and lifelong learning that is needed, is to provide federal matching grants for higher education institutions through the states. Parents, students, and firms have no incentive to invest in support of the social benefit externalities from higher education and research. So they will not do so. Although endowment funds are increasing, only about 10% of all graduates contribute and these alone are insufficient. To reduce the large skill deficits that exist, enrollment increases and more lifelong learners are essential, and yet these incur additional institutional costs that local property taxes and state revenue systems are unlikely to be able to bear. The external social benefits received through indirect effects from the education of others and from prior generations are taken for granted and these costs are unlikely to be borne privately. There is need for some national public subsidy that does not interfere with the independence and freedom from political interference in the public universities and community colleges, which is a major source of their strength. This means that supplemental federal institutional support (except for peer group–reviewed research support) needs to be channeled through the states and made conditional on the states sustaining and increasing their support.

Almost no institutional support for instruction in higher education currently comes from the national government in the United States. This pattern is very different in the United Kingdom and the rest of Europe. In the United States national support, however, does come indirectly for institutions through tuition and fees paid by students who have Pell Grants or Stafford Loans, and from National Science Foundation and National Institutes of Health support of graduate students in engineering and the physical and life sciences.

Federal support for university-based research is substantial. $30.7 billion of federally supported grants and contracts were received by universities in 2006, the latest year for which data is available (National Center for Education Statistics, 2007). This is 7% of total $410.6 billion total expenditure on both education and research by both public and private institutions, which in turn is 3.3% of gross domestic product (GDP). Federal research support is much more important for the research universities, public and private, and is often over half of their budgets. It is important that this research support is on a peer group review basis, which avoids most political interference, and is much better integrated with the training of PhD students in the United States. Research assistants learn through apprenticeships and transmit their skills to students in other universities, firms, and governments. PhD research assistantships are not the pattern in the United Kingdom, the European Union, Russia, Pakistan, and elsewhere where there are separate research institutes that are more isolated from graduate education in the universities. These institutes hire mostly permanent full-time aging research assistants who do not graduate and hence do not transmit the technology in a system that is relatively inefficient. This is slowly beginning to change in the United Kingdom, France, Sweden, and Germany especially.

The public institutional support for instruction at U.S. community colleges comes primarily from local property taxes. These have climbed to remarkably high levels as the financing of public services has been pushed increasingly down to local levels. Support for public four-year colleges and universities comes from state governments that depend largely on sales tax revenues and are under extreme pressures from rising prison and criminal justice system costs, sharply rising Medicaid and health care costs, and other welfare costs that all are partly the result of earlier underinvestment in basic education. Partly as a result of this shortsighted planning and these budget pressures, state appropriations as a percent of revenues of all public higher education institutions have fallen from 44.8% in 1980 to 30% currently. This falling state support and the rising demand for skills have been the main sources of the average increase of 8% a year in tuition and fees, a rate that is often noted to exceed the rate of inflation.

Public institutions and state government budgets probably cannot absorb significant additional increases in enrollment without some additional federal support. California State at Long Beach, for example, turned 52,500, or two-thirds, of their applicants away in the 2006–7 academic year. This strained capacity of the higher education institutions is limiting the growth of access to higher education. President King Alexander at California State suggests that the federal government create incentives for states to maintain certain levels of tax support for higher education (in Lord, 2007, p. 4). Matching grant formulas are currently widely used with Title I funds in K–12 education, Medicaid, and highway construction and maintenance. As the formula for matching changes, from, say, 20% federal–80% state to 50–50 (Medicaid) to 90–10 (interstate highways), the power of the incentive provided to the state increases as does the actual amount of outside help provided. Matching grants through the states to public colleges and universities that accept additional students would help hold tuition down, prevent further cuts in state support, and help most those two- and four-year public institutions that must be prepared to serve the largest increase in the numbers of students. Only the federal government is in a position to help significantly with this financing problem. It is also the responsibility of the federal government to address the nation's skill deficit and help to ensure the nation's future. It can be concluded that a program of federal matching grants to the states, with matching that ensures that states will not reduce but instead are encouraged to increase their support, is a viable option.

ACHIEVING A 20% INCREASE IN ENROLLMENT RATES

A fourth and related policy option is to choose a specific goal of seeking to achieve a 20% increase in two- and four-year college enrollment rates above the current level. Some federal institutional support would be necessary to keep tuition sufficiently low and to retain middle-class support. Supplementing this with the Pell Grant approach, this would require an increase of about $2,472 (in current 2007 dollars) in the average Pell Grant. This would approximately double the average $2,500 Pell Grant per student. These grants would also need to be made available to the larger number of students who would choose to attend. This estimate is based on the coefficients computed from time series data by McPherson and Shapiro (1994, p. 201).* It would constitute a reduction in the net tuition cost for these students at both public and private colleges. Since the percentage reduction would be larger at lower-cost two-year institutions, the larger percentage enrollment increases could be expected there. McPherson and Shapiro settle the question in their article about the effect of student financial aids on enrollment, obtaining coefficients under controlled conditions from time series data that are equivalent to those obtained from cross-section data. Enrollment from lower-income groups has not increased significantly since earlier in the history of the Pell Grants, but this is understandable in that Pell Grants currently cover a lower percentage of college costs than earlier, and the remaining costs are a larger

---

*Their coefficient indicates that a $100 change in net cost (in 1982–83 prices) leads to a 1.6% change in enrollment. It is extremely close to the 1.8% enrollment effect following the same change in cost reported by Leslie and Brinkman (1987) based on cross-section data. The amount reported above is based on converting the 1982–83 prices to 2005 prices using the consumer price index, and the amount needed to attain a 20% as opposed to a 1.6% enrollment effect.

percentage of the household income of students from lower-income house-holds. Studies since such as Curs et al. (2007) find the same positive effects on enrollments under controlled conditions as McPherson and Shapiro. They find revenues and enrollments at two-year institutions most sensitive to increases in the number of eligible Pell recipients and least sensitive to increases in the maximum Pell award. Pell awards also are known to have a positive effect on persistence (see Leslie and Brinkman, 1988).

An increase of $2,387 per student compares to the current actual maximum of $4,310 or average $2,421 Pell Grant per full-time equivalent student. The latter maximum has just been raised by $1,100 to $5,400 per student but it will not reach that until 2012. This average current Pell Grant fell specifically from 52% of the tuition, room, and board costs at 4-year public institutions in 1986–87 to 30% of these costs in 2007 (College Board, 2007a, p. 18). So approximately doubling the average Pell Grant award, twice what has just been done, would cover about half of the average tuition room and board costs at public 4-year institutions, and restore the Pell Grant in purchasing power terms to a little more than it was in 1977.

In 2007, 5,165,000 were receiving Pell Grants (College Board, 2007a, p. 10). If total full-time college enrollments of 10,800,000 were increased by 20%, this would require an increase in enrollments of 2,160,000 (College Board, 2007b, p. 22). The total additional cost of attaining this goal would be about $28,403,180,000. Since $12,881,510,000 is currently being spent for Pell Grant financial aid, the cost of attaining this goal will be slightly over a doubling of the amount currently invested in human capital formation through Pell Grants. Of the additional $28.4 billion, if the average (but not the maximum) Pell Grant were doubled, or increased from $2,494 by $2,472, about $16.2 billion could be expected to go to students at public institutions (many of which are 2-year community colleges) and about $4.6 billion to students at private institutions (calculations based on College Board 2007a, p. 10, and 2007b, p. 22). Increasing the maximum grant, as has just been done to $5,400 a year by 2012, ensures that private institutions will benefit substantially as well. But the number receiving grants must also be increased, or the effects are modest.

Since the new average level of the Pell Grant covers about 50% of total tuition, room, and board costs at 4-year institutions, the additional private saving and investment by families that this public initiative induces is $20.8 billion. Since tuition and fees cover only about 33% of institutional unit costs at public institutions, to support a 20% enrollment increase, or 2.5 million new students, will require additional state-level support of about $10 billion at 4-year institutions and $10 billion at 2-year institutions (based on National Center for Education Statistics, 1996, middle projections, pp. 93, 95, and McPherson-Shapiro coefficients by income group, discussed below). Together, this adds up to about $40.8 billion public and $40.5 billion private saving and investment in new human capital formation. This would yield at a minimum a real social rate of return of 15% in increased earnings alone, which includes a substantial increase in tax revenue. When the private and social non-market benefits are added, the total real social rate of return is closer to 41%.

To put the U.S. federal budget requirement in perspective, this $20.8 billion for additional Pell Grants is about 8% of the amount that has been spent annually in Iraq, with many veterans coming home to face flat real earnings. The GI Bill was enacted originally to prevent World War II veterans from coming home to either no jobs or a life of low-paying unskilled labor, and it was dramatically successful in preventing both. President George W. Bush's earlier fiscal 2007 budget had proposed increasing the Pell Grant by $500, or $100 a year over 5 years. The budget had also proposed reducing by 90,000 (2.25%) the number receiving these grants. But this budget was not passed by Congress. The new Congress with Democrats in control of both chambers has now passed legislation that increases the Pell Grant by $1,100 by 2012, $260 in the first year, or the maximum grant from $4,310 a year eventually to $5,400 as mentioned. The vote was 292–97 in the House and 79–12 in the Senate and President Bush signed this legislation into law.*

In the United Kingdom and other European Union countries, the cost of attaining a 20% increase in college enrollments also can be estimated

---

*Senator Barack Obama of Illinois had proposed an increase of $1,050 per year in the maximum Pell Grant, expected to cost about $2 billion, very close to what was passed. He proposed to cover this cost by eliminating the subsidies paid to banks that participate in the federal student loan program. Senator Obama said he chose the $1,050 to correspond to the amount President George W. Bush promised during his presidential campaign.

based on the McPherson-Shapiro-Curs coefficients. Assuming that the price response of middle- and lower-income families is similar for reductions in maintenance and tuition costs, a comparable doubling of maintenance grants could be expected to lead to a 59% increase in enrollments of students from low-income families, an increase of 12% in students from middle-income families, and a 3% increase in students from upper-income families. Enrollment rates among high-income students are already much higher in all countries; 85% in the high-income quartile in the United States compared to far below that for students from the low-income quartile (College Board, 2004b, p. 17). The increase can be expected to be concentrated at two-year colleges, perhaps leading to a much needed expansion of access to these types of institutions in Europe. Nevertheless, 20% of all undergraduates at a typical public research university in the United States receive Pell Grants, and larger percentages at other four-year institutions.

Some of this enrollment rate increase has been occurring in the European Union, as evidenced by the fact that enrollment rates in European Union countries have been rising since 1991. This has not been occurring in the United States during this period. But there is generally less resource recovery in the European Union from parents than from those in the United States. There is also lower institutional expenditure per student, which raises some questions about whether quality can be maintained without increasing both tuition and need-based maintenance grants.

Finally, with respect to a 20% increase in higher education enrollment rates, 51% of the high school graduates from large metropolitan schools in the United States are not going on to college; 36% of high school graduates nationwide are not going beyond high school. To reduce this, tuition, fees, and campus living costs will have to be lower in relation to middle-class family incomes. Where this is true there is a large pent-up demand, as was illustrated by the Long Beach campus in California that accepted 8,500 new students out of 61,000 applicants (Lord, 2007). President Alexander points out that the state of California allows for tuition to be maintained at a low level of $1,400 per semester, "yet we turned away two-thirds of the applicants at an institution that is not supposed to turn anybody away" (ibid., p. 6). The percentage dropping out after high school is even larger in the United Kingdom and in some other OECD countries. It is much lower in Canada and South Korea, which offers evidence that higher enrollment rates can be successfully sustained.

A UNIVERSAL ENTITLEMENT APPROACH

A fifth and more dramatic higher education policy option for bringing total investment in higher education closer to its optimum would be a college entitlement available to all high school graduates. This would be closer to the approach used by the GI Bill, which entitled all U.S. World War II veterans to college if they were high school graduates. The disadvantage is that this approach is much more expensive. It is not similar to the free tuition in Greece and some other European countries because the latter do not include maintenance grants. In some places such as Russia higher education is very selective based on test scores that tend to be highly correlated with the parents' income. A universal entitlement would go farther than free tuition to include a partial maintenance grant and would cover all high school graduates. The advantage is that a universal entitlement is more likely to secure the widest parental support since upper-income groups would also benefit substantially. Its disadvantage is its higher cost, which would incur greater opposition from taxpayers, especially those with no children nearing college age.

A COMPROMISE SOLUTION

A sixth policy option is an in-between compromise solution. It would use means-tested Pell Grants that limit costs but increase the threshold for availability while at the same time provide federal matching grants to states for higher education institutions to help them serve additional students. That is, the student financial aid would continue to use the standard Family Financial Statement means test. Students from families in the top income quartile over $89,000 in the United States in 2007 dollars would be eligible for only a token grant whereas the size of the grant would be larger for students from middle-income families and still larger for students from low-income families. As is characteristic of entitlement programs, once the per capita amount and the formula is set, the appropriations to the program are driven by the number eligible. This combination of federal matching grants through the states and student financial aid entitlements would ensure higher education institutions a much greater degree of financial stability. There would be some buffer protecting them against transitory federal budget cuts and state budget pressures due to unreformed health care and criminal justice system cost increases.

This and all preceding options do not mean that all high school graduates would be eligible for admission to the more highly selective private and public colleges and universities. A significant part of the new enrollees would be older and would attend community colleges, which often already accept all high school graduates, irrespective of their high school performance. They offer remedial programs and lifelong learning programs, and provide the skills necessary for entry into productive occupations. This offers another excellent example of the complementary roles of the more selective higher education institutions, the comprehensives, and the community colleges. This complementarity is an important basis for cooperation among them in place of the tendency for each to regard the others as competing for funds and students in order to achieve greater fiscal stability while better serving society's needs.

A major advantage of providing for more universal college access by high school graduates is that these options would strengthen the incentives to complete high school. Some now drop out of high school in part because they do not feel that attending college is a likely possibility. It would also operate to increase the incentive for older persons to complete the GED, assuming Pell Grant-type aids would be equally available to older persons who do so. Many of the benefits to society discussed above also derive from lower high school and college dropout rates, as well as from lifelong learning by older persons with skill deficiencies.

NEW NATIONAL SUPPORT OPTIONS

A seventh higher education policy option is for college and university leaders to join together in education finance reform policies conducive to more adequate, stable, and income-elastic levels of support for higher education by the states. Currently state budgets are dominated by rising criminal justice system costs, Medicaid costs, and welfare costs. The result is that higher education not only gets squeezed but all too often has to take the leavings. The states could do more on their own if they would be more courageous in enacting standard school finance reform measures. And higher education leaders would actively support this. This needs to be recognized more widely as also in the interest of higher education. The standard school finance reform formula (1) reduces over-reliance on the property tax, which helps community colleges too; (2) provides more adequate foundation levels per primary and secondary pupil that eventually reduces state health, prison, and welfare costs, which are squeezing higher education budgets; and (3) increases revenue from state income taxes that tends to generate more state revenue above the costs of the tax swap and support of basic education, which also helps higher education.

But state capacities have their limits. Individual states cannot raise their sales tax rates more than a percent or two above nearby states or they begin to lose their tax base. As more students go to college in response to the above national initiatives, the capacities of public higher education institutions to accommodate them and to hold tuition and fees at reasonable levels will be severely strained. Some help from the national government through the states to the higher education institutions needs to be seriously considered.

How Can These Policy Changes Be Paid For?

Public opinion polls tend to show strong support for public spending on just about anything.* The real questions are: (1) What options provide the highest benefits in relation to the costs? (2) What are the costs of the various options? (3) Are Americans willing to pay taxes for things even if the benefits in relation to the costs are overwhelming?

- First, improving the amount of information about private non-market benefits and non-market social benefits costs very little in public resources, relatively speaking, almost nothing.

  To the extent that this increases enrollment rates, a high proportion of the additional investment would be investment by students and their families. Investment in attaining a college degree is

---

*These include a national Gallup Poll in the United States in 2007, and other U.S. national opinion polls refereed to by The Economist (2007a).

already a partnership between families and government. At least half of the total costs at public institutions are borne privately by parents in the form of forgone earnings, roughly room and board costs, plus a little, and more is borne privately as they pay tuition. In some countries in the European Union resource recovery from parents is more limited; there probably increased tuition accompanied by increasing need-based maintenance grants would increase the resources per student and help with the financing.

- Second, higher education is an investment. The increased investment can be expected to more than pay for itself over time. A 20% higher education enrollment rate in South Korea is associated with a per capita growth rate there that is almost twice that of the United States (5% compared to 2.6%, from McMahon 2006b, Figure 8). But with respect to the public resources required, an increase of 20% in the higher education enrollment rate would within a few years result in an estimated $2.5 billion to $3 billion in additional state and federal income and sales tax receipts each year.* This and the saving in state health, public assistance, and criminal justice system costs would go a long way toward covering the costs of the increase in Pell Grants, for example, that would be needed to achieve this enrollment increase. If the financial aid also increases persistence, the entire public costs might be covered by the increased tax receipts alone.

- Third, the additional private saving and investment is a critically important component of sustainable growth. This is especially important in the United States, where domestic financial saving rates have fallen essentially to zero. The high social rates of return that include the non-market private and social benefits indicate that the investment would be more advantageous than most other alternative uses of the same private and public funds in advancing development, including social capital, health, and happiness.

Focusing on the costs without referring to the benefits is not reasonable.

---

*This assumes that there are about 400,000 additional associate and bachelor's graduates, 20% of the approximately 2,000,000 in 2007 (National Center for Education Statistics, 2007, Tables 27 and 28). If these on average earn $25,000 more than the average high school graduate, and pay 25% of their additional income in federal and state income and state sales taxes, the additional tax revenue is $2.5 billion.

Implications for State Higher Education Policies

At the state level, where most public higher education policy that relates to public institutions is made, there are a number of implications of the analysis for new policy options.

ACCOUNTABILITY

With respect to accountability, the first policy option is that how the campus provides for the efficient use of the student's time needs to be considered just as important as institutional costs per student. Graduation rates and time to degree reflect these costs better than institutional costs, although institutional costs per graduate also increase as time to degree increases. Some students work part-time and take lighter course loads, which needs to be set aside and attention focused on full-time equivalents. But as full-time students increasingly take 4.5 and often 5 or 6 years to finish a bachelor's, this represents a significant increase in costs.

The second policy option with respect to accountability is to supplement outcome measures such as the persistence and graduation rates with estimates of the private and social benefits from higher education. The latter are the reason higher education institutions exist, and this should be explained to legislators. When these are explained in relation to specific institutions, they should be in terms of value-added (see Appendix A). Most important, these outcome measures must be related to the costs. Discussions of the institutional costs in isolation always need to be brought back to the benefits, and vice versa.

HIGHER EDUCATION DEPENDS ON SCHOOL
FINANCE REFORM

The third policy option at the state level is for college and university presidents and state boards of higher education to recognize that their interests depend in part upon school finance reform, as mentioned earlier, and that in turn their leadership is vital to its success. That is, it is important that higher education leaders join together with the leaders of the K–12 system in supporting state school finance reform efforts. Most are currently sitting on the sidelines, and some are considering K–12 to be competitors for the state's resources. But, as discussed above, the standard tax swap, income tax revenues for property tax revenues with more state-wide support for basic education, plus a little extra revenue for other state needs helps higher education. It reduces the drain on state revenue for public assistance, health, and prisons (Levin, 2006), and graduates of the basic education system that are better prepared and increased state income tax revenue both help higher education. This policy only has a chance if the traditional coalition that has proven effective many times in the past is unified (see McMahon and Geske, 1982, Chapter 10). The coalition consists of:

1. Local taxpayer associations that want property taxes reduced (or more realistically, want them not to continue to increase as the pressure for use of them is released)
2. Farmers who also want the pressure on the property tax reduced and are generally more supportive of income taxes as well as of education
3. Primary and secondary education teachers, administrators, and parents—a very large group
4. Higher education faculty, administrators, and parents of college students
5. Businesses that are well aware of the skill deficits in the society

These education finance reform efforts also are more likely to succeed if the private and social benefits of education are more widely understood. They are normally defeated by some newspapers and legislators from wealthy districts who emphasize the tax costs and ignore the benefits in relation to the costs. The higher-income residents of suburbs, for example, do pay income taxes but they also receive very substantial benefits from public universities for their children, as well as from the lower state tax support needed for public assistance, health, and criminal justice system costs as reduced inequality in the basic education system generates indirect benefits (Levin, 2006).

ACCESS

A fourth policy option is that for increased access increased state support per student in real terms for public universities and community colleges helps maintain quality while keeping tuition low. This service to the middle class is the traditional role of public higher education. With a middle class that is not sharing in the benefits of growth, is diminishing, and is severely stressed, this support by state governments is needed more than before.

NEED AS ONE CRITERION FOR STUDENT FINANCIAL AID

A fifth state policy option is to add a need criterion to merit-based financial aid. The research indicates that need-based student financial aid increases enrollments and access. This contributes to economic development in the state, whereas purely merit-based aid with no need criterion does not increase statewide enrollments, and hence does not contribute to state economic development. There is no evidence that it retains students within the state better than or as well as merit-based aid with a need criterion. Apart from positive incentive effects within the high schools it does not use tax dollars to the best advantage (Cornwell et al., 2003). It is widely supported by the middle class and higher-income families because they benefit. But this advantage of broad public support could be retained by adding a need criterion to the merit criterion that is not so restrictive that it excludes the middle class from benefits. A number of states, however, remain heavily committed to merit-based aid without a need criterion—Florida, Louisiana, Mississippi, and Georgia, for example. This is a situation where with no additional tax cost a significant additional benefit to state economic development and to expanding educational opportunity could be realized.

STATE HIGHER EDUCATION FINANCING STRATEGY

A sixth state policy option is that states need to consider new research as it applies to the levels of higher education that are most advantageous for them to finance. States at or close to the technological frontier are known to benefit the most from investment in master's, PhD, and high-quality four-year undergraduate programs. These are generally the states along the Eastern and Western Seaboards and Midwestern states where there are large cities that can offer the highest-paying jobs to attract the most highly educated graduates. These states also benefit positively from investing in two- and four-year degree programs since these social rates of return are known to be significant and positive. But states and regions below the technological frontier, generally the lower per capita income states, benefit the most from additional investment in these standard two- and four-year degree programs. For them, the studies show that the social rates of return to investment in master's and PhD programs are not as high, in part because more of the advanced graduate student graduates later leave the state for higher-paying jobs elsewhere (Vandenbussche et al., 2006).

IN SUMMARY, the analysis of the total private and social benefits of education in relation to the costs shows that the total social rates of return to investing more in higher education are very high in relation to the opportunity costs of the funds. This is evidence that public and private investment in higher education is below optimum, and that states need to take the lead by investing more. This then induces additional private investment by families.

With respect to the continuing trends toward privatization, higher education leaders need to consider that if the external social benefits of higher education are about 52% of the total benefits, the balance between public (plus endowment) financing and private financing is currently about right. This suggests that privatization should not go much farther if higher education is to remain economically efficient, which includes serving the public good.

Implications for Campus-Level Policies

Most of the above options for higher education policy at the state level also are relevant to campus-level policies. This includes fostering a better understanding of the importance of state school finance reform efforts to the well-being of each local higher education campus and being judicious about how far further privatization as a source of easy money is carried. There are however some additional policy implications at the campus level.

- Market and social returns differ by discipline.
- Campus-level missions differ widely but are complementary statewide.

- There is need to consider the value-added by each campus that is independent of the ability of entering students.
- Rates of return can be developed that are specific to each institution.

MARKET RETURNS AND SOCIAL BENEFITS THAT DIFFER BY DISCIPLINE

One of the more important insights offered in this book is that there are indirect benefits from higher education to economic growth by disciplines that are not often thought of as having significant connections to growth and development. For example, disciplines that contribute to better health, to the rule of law, to civic institutions, to democracy, to political stability, and to lower criminal justice system costs are seen to contribute indirectly to economic growth and development. Even foreign languages can be thought of as important to trade and thereby indirectly important to growth. Much of the discussion affecting campus budgeting decisions, including faculty salaries, office support, research support, and teaching loads among academic disciplines, is driven by considerations relating to the external economy, potentials for grant support and patents, and direct contributions to economic growth. Recognizing the indirect contributions of other disciplines to growth dramatically changes the terms of the discussion. Even those fields funded by the National Science Foundation, for example, are heavily in the engineering, mathematics, and the life sciences because these fields are seen to contribute more directly to economic growth in ways that can be measured by the number of patents and links to product and process innovation.

Yet fields that contribute to the rule of law, such as political science, law, and criminology, and to more efficient economic and business management, may contribute as much or more to growth if the indirect contributions are considered. This is relatively a dramatically new perspective. It is certainly not accepted by dictators who are not interested in democratization and often do not support human rights. For example, military dictatorships (like those in Pakistan and earlier in Brazil) limit most of their higher education funding to engineering and physical science fields and tend to be very intolerant of political scientists and lawyers.

Other examples include the English language and ability to read and write that are very basic to almost every job and to economic growth, although English faculty seldom articulate this. Colleges of education train teachers who are vital to the human capital formation that is central to knowledge-based economies. And so forth.

This emphasis on the direct and indirect contributions of higher education to growth will probably seem strange to those in the fine arts and humanities. But, practically speaking, much of higher education funding is driven by this. But beyond this, Chapter 4 has developed how non-market private benefits of higher education to which these fields contribute are part of valuable outcomes of higher education that contribute to the quality of life and happiness and are worthy of support.

The contribution of master's and PhD graduates based on the embodiment of new knowledge created by research in all fields also offers a preliminary way to think about and measure the contributions of graduate programs and research. The cost of the graduate degree programs on a per student basis is known, as is the investment in research in each department. This investment can be related to the articles published and the number of graduate degrees completed, as was shown in Chapter 6. The salaries these graduates earn is a very imperfect measure of the value of the output. But if the number of graduates in each field could be related to non-market outcomes in that field by regression methods, such as medical, nursing, and life sciences graduates to health outcomes, or social work graduates to social work outcomes. Perhaps a way of valuing these research and graduate program outcomes by the income equivalent method could eventually be developed. Certainly, there are many tracer studies of undergraduates to which relevant questions could be added. Tracer studies could also be conducted to provide better measures of the contributions of master's and PhD graduates over their lifecycles that are interdependent with research outcomes.

DIFFERING CAMPUS MISSIONS

Meaningful accountability requires the recognition that different campuses have different missions. These missions range from community college missions that serve local and regional needs for skilled nurses, medical technicians, and computer technicians as well as for lifelong learning to the mission of research universities that involves serving the national and international need for new knowledge through research and its dissemination by graduates.

With this wide range of missions, the ability level of those students who are selected for admission also differs. Subject matter fields and programs also differ widely. The important point is to recognize that these roles are complementary, and all are needed as part of a statewide higher education system. Rather than so much emphasis on competing for funds, and for students, there needs to be broader recognition of this complementarity as the basis for a common joint effort of all types of higher education institutions, as well as the basic education system are to cooperate in better addressing the national skill deficits and in securing the financing necessary to meet this challenge, perhaps along the lines of the financing strategy outlined above.

VALUE-ADDED BY THE CAMPUS

When estimating the extent to which a campus-level degree contributes to earnings increments or non-market private and social benefits later, it is necessary to measure the value-added by the local educational programs, and not just the prior education and innate ability of those who are admitted. Ability bias is important in making comparisons among campuses because the selectivity of admissions varies widely among campuses in line with their missions. Nationwide this ability bias averages out for graduates from many institutions. Any that remains is largely offset by measurement error, and thereby eliminated, as seen in recent studies of large samples of identical twins as discussed in Appendix A. But for evaluating the productivity of individual campuses ability bias must be removed or the results are rather meaningless. Ability affects both increments to earnings and increments to non-market private and social benefits, so it must be removed from both to obtain a truer value-added by each campus that does not merely reflect admission policies.

If a campus is at the national average with respect to its ACT or SAT test scores for entering freshmen, and tracer studies are done that follow up its graduates' earnings and contributions to the community, there is no ability bias (which is largely measured as prior achievement) to be removed. The situation is the same there as for the national averages. Recent monozygotic identical twin studies that apply to large samples conclude that nationwide average ability bias is about 6%. After correction for measurement error, it can even be a bit smaller than this. But the twins in the sample who attend the national conventions of identical twins in Twinsburg, Ohio, are likely to have earnings and ability levels a bit above the average. This results in a modest overstatement of true ability bias because the samples are not weighted to be typical of all college graduates nationwide. Until such time as these samples are properly weighted to be representative, it can be concluded that the ability bias is very small, and since it would be reduced further by proper weighting, it is reasonable to make no correction to the earnings or non-market returns data. This assumes that ability bias, and measurement error including the self-selection of twins who attend, offset each other and cancel each other out.

For individual campuses, however, this does not apply. The ability levels and family backgrounds of entering freshmen classes as measured by the mean ACT or SAT scores vary widely above or below the mean. Most campuses now collect data on the earnings and other contributions of their graduates 5, 10, 20, and 30 or more years after graduation. To use these and adjust them to obtain the campus value-added, percentage adjustments are given in Table 7.1, which is based on Appendix A, Table A.3, column 8. They can be applied to the raw data on earnings and on private and social non-market benefits collected in tracer studies that are specific to each campus.

As already indicated above, those campuses at or near the national mean in ACT or SAT test scores need apply no adjustment, since they are at the 0.50 percentile level in Table 7.1. The prior discussion of national average rates of return and non-market private and social benefits applies directly. However, selective campuses with freshmen in the 0.95 percentile of ACT/SAT test scores, for example, will generate outcomes that are in part the result of prior ability, and this ability bias must be removed. The table shows that both the earnings after graduation and private and social non-market benefits should be reduced by about 6.76 percent to remove the upward bias in the returns. The remainder is the value-added as the result of additional learning due to programs on campus. Comparable reductions need to be made at other campuses whose freshmen are above average in ability but at other percentiles as shown in Table 7.1.

For campuses whose entering freshmen are below the national mean, upward adjustments need to be made in the outcomes revealed by tracer

TABLE 7.1   Adjustments to Remove Ability Bias to Get Value-Added

Campus percentile among nationwide ACT/SAT scores	Correction to earnings and to non-market benefits to remove bias (%)
0.95 (high-ability freshmen)	−6.76
0.85	−9.08
0.75	−4.2
0.65	−3.02
0.55	−4.98
0.50 (nationwide median)	0
0.45	+2.48
035	+5.25
0.25	+5.02
015	+7.65
0.05 (low-ability freshmen)	+5.43

studies for that campus in order to normalize them to the national mean where there is no ability bias. The reason for this is that if their earnings, for example, are below average, a portion of this is due to the fact that the ability of the entering freshmen was below average, an adverse effect on earnings that should not penalize estimates of the value-added by that campus. The 2.48 to 5.43% upward adjustments in the earnings and non-market benefits revealed by tracer studies specific to that campus are shown in column 2 of Table 7.1 for campuses whose freshmen have average test scores below the national average.

In summary, the value-added at the more prestigious elite campuses where the raw unadjusted returns are higher is a bit lower than the raw data indicates, and the value-added at those community colleges and other institutions where freshmen are below average is a bit higher than the raw data indicates.

RATES OF RETURN SPECIFIC TO EACH INSTITUTION

A useful policy option is that social rates of return can be calculated that are specific to individual campuses. The programs referred to earlier in Chapters 3 and 4 as professional backup for the nationwide private and social rates of return discussed there can also be used to compute earnings-based private and social rates of return specific to each campus, using also the value-added adjustments in Table 7.1 (McMahon, 2008). But this requires a policy decision by the chancellor to conduct tracer studies that collect information about earnings of graduates and about non-market benefits to health, children, and civic organizations in the graduates' communities. These outcomes need to question graduates who are 10, 15, and 25 years beyond their graduation in order to measure the pattern over each lifecycle. It also requires that the institution assemble its internal data on institutional costs per student.

Most colleges and universities already conduct tracer studies to collect data on the earnings of their graduates. This is now required in some states by state boards of education for all public universities and community colleges. This tracer study data also can be used to compare salaries of graduates in various career fields to nationwide Census Bureau salary data for college graduates. But the above corrections for ability bias must be applied to obtain value-added by the campus. For example, tracer studies of the University of Illinois at Urbana-Champaign's graduates report earnings 1, 5, 10, and 15 years beyond graduation. These earnings then have been used to estimate earnings over the remaining lifecycle of these graduates The latter is done by assuming that the shape of the age-earnings profile in the later years (but not its level) follows the shape of age-earnings profiles nationwide for persons of the same gender and same degree level (McMahon, 1998b, 1998c).

Starting salaries after graduation are very misleading, and should not be used for anything beyond a very highly qualified and skeptical judgment. For one thing, many students do not find a job immediately, especially those in liberal arts. Starting salaries reflect this. But six months later the latter are normally employed, and twenty years later because of their grater adaptability they are often earning more than engineers. Starting salaries are also a distortion because it takes time for employers to evaluate the productivity of new employees. The "sheepskin effect" (if any) wears off as employers correct their mistakes. Finally, starting salaries reflect the ability of entering freshmen, and hence contain an ability bias when compared across campuses that does not measure the true value-added by the campus degree. However, after graduates have been in the workforce for five or ten years beyond graduation they have had time to find jobs and employers have had time to recognize employees' true productivity and potential. The individual is more settled into his or her life-

time career pattern. The shape of this more permanent age-earnings profile is very similar for similar degree programs at other institutions. So
using tracer study data on earnings ten, fifteen, or more years after
graduation, the remaining earnings path can be mapped because it will be
typical of the age-earnings profile in the national Census data. A single individual can deviate from this pattern, but the average for graduates
campus-wide when corrected for ability bias defines the returns and value-
added at any one institution.

With respect to costs, there are two components, the institutional costs
per student and the forgone earnings costs. Institutional costs are the instructional costs per student, from the institution's internal cost data.
Forgone earnings costs are the earnings of high school graduates for the
4 or 4.5 years in college. The increment to earnings attributable to college
is the net earnings differential above high school graduates' earnings at
each age. A standard social rate of return can then be computed by means
of the program given for the individual campus that is that rate that discounts the stream of net earnings differentials over the lifecycle back to
the present and sets it equal to the total investment costs associated with
each student.

Earnings data for master's, PhD, and professional graduates from
tracer studies can also be used to compute private and social rates of return at these levels, as well as to compare the earnings of former graduate
students to those given by the Census Bureau for graduates at these levels
nationwide. If Graduate Record Examination scores are available for
entering graduate students, they can be related to nationwide data and a
percentile rank for entering students on the campus obtained so that ability bias adjustments for undergraduates from Table 7.1 can be applied to
obtain an approximate value-added at the graduate level.

CAMPUS-LEVEL POLICIES NEEDED TO IMPROVE
TRACER-STUDIES

Unfortunately, analyses of tracer study data on the earnings of graduates
at 5, 10, or 15 years after graduation along the lines above are rarely done.
This is a higher education policy gap at the level of the chancellor's office.
But worse, little is asked in these tracer studies about the private non-

market benefits of the education received by graduates, or about their service to society. This is another higher education policy gap. Enough research is now available to suggest which questions need to be asked.

Instead, institutions survey their graduates to ascertain levels of educational satisfaction with their collegiate experiences These usually have public relations and fundraising objectives rather than objective analysis of accountability outcomes on a value-added basis. As mentioned, in some states surveys of graduates are externally mandated, leaving public institutions little choice but to repeatedly survey their graduates. If properly constructed to relate to the current research on what is known about private and social benefits, these surveys could easily be improved and would become much more meaningful and valuable. They would allow each campus to compare the earnings increments received by their graduates to national averages, and provide a whole new accountability tool that relates costs to the more ultimate outcomes of degree programs. This could become a whole new frontier for the often rather limited discussions of accountability using short-term measures such as instructional units (IUs) and research units (RUs). Instead, faculty motivation is normally based on the more ultimate outcomes from what they do, as well as on what individual campuses do (all in relation to costs). This is also a much more meaningful kind of accountability.

CHAPTER EIGHT

New Strategies for
Financing Higher Education

There are long lags, sometimes very long lags. But in the end education determines the future.

W. MCMAHON (2007A)

A modern human capital approach to higher education policy reveals a number of higher education policy gaps. But it also offers criteria suggestive of solutions that were considered in Chapters 3–7. These both permit some overall conclusions relevant to a new financing strategy to be drawn.

Higher Education Policy Gaps

There are major current higher education policy gaps that this book has sought to address:

- What is higher education's mission regarding the race in the advancement of technology and diffusion of new knowledge versus the large and growing skill deficits in globalizing economies?
- What are the private non-market benefits and the social benefits of higher education? How are they measured, and what is their value?
- What are the additional sources of market failure in higher education markets that these measurements reveal?

321

- What is the appropriate total investment in higher education—financed by both public and private sources—for economic efficiency? That is, is higher education investment above, or below, optimum?
- What is the true meaning of *economic efficiency,* a term that is thrown about with wild abandon?
- What is the appropriate degree of privatization of higher education and research programs for economic or social efficiency?
- What are appropriate policy options at national, state, and campus levels for addressing the major higher education policy gaps that have been identified, including issues of access, affordability, accountability, efficiency, and equity?
- What are the implications of all of the above for new strategies for financing higher education?

The answers to each question have been addressed in detail in Chapters 3–7, and will not be repeated here, although some arise as part of the discussion of conclusions and their implications below.

Equally important, this book has sought to consider these issues within a cohesive conceptual framework for analyzing contemporary higher education policy and devising solutions for the policy gaps that it reveals. Introducing a symposium on the "Economics of Higher Education," Clotfelter (1999, p. 3) once referred to "The Familiar but Curious Economics of Higher Education." And so it has continued to be, familiar but curious, a scatter of studies of isolated economic aspects of higher education, many quite sophisticated, but with no comprehensive framework to draw them together. This book has sought to fill this gap, as suggested by an anonymous referee by "developing a coherent and cohesive modern human capital conceptual framework that is conceptually and substantively accessible to higher education policy makers and a general audience. This is a formidable task." But the terms used have been defined in Chapter 2 and the explanations as these terms are used were phased in so by now they should be familiar. A modern human capital conceptual framework using the terms that are vital to higher education policy involves:

- The theory of the allocation of time, attributable to Becker. This is the basis for defining household production of non-market satisfactions. This is extended here for measuring not only the private but also the social non-market benefits of higher education that are over and above the earnings benefits.

- New endogenous growth theory, attributable to Lucas and Romer, which puts education externalities in a central role in achieving economic efficiency and is the conceptual basis for the knowledge-based economy.

- Endogenous development theory and empirical tests. This extends endogenous growth models to include private and social non-market benefits beyond income or growth. The shorter-term dynamic framework distinguishes short-term, long-term, and indirect effects. The short-term and indirect effects repeatedly set the stage for the next round of growth within families, and in per capita terms within nations.

- Embodiment of new knowledge in human capital, the sources of its obsolescence, and continually new vintages. These are central to the interpretation of the impacts of research at the research universities and the complementarity of these research impacts with graduate education. Human capital that is malleable putty during the college years but turns intro harder clay several years after graduation in environments where there is not sufficient stimulus to lifelong learning is a serious individual and social problem. The concept has implications for evaluating national skill deficits as well as the quality of higher education programs and external accountability.

- Valuation of the non-market social benefits. This has been based on the Haveman-Wolfe method supplemented by dynamic simulations of the endogenous development process for valuing the indirect effects from higher education.

- A modern human capital approach. This also involves the theory and evidence of market failure in higher education markets. There is poor information about the true private and social non-market benefits of education, and not just market failure due to imperfect capital markets. The conclusion is that private higher education markets do not work very well because of this poor information, and this has major implications for financing higher education.

- Modern human capital concepts, including endogenous growth and endogenous development theory. These also help define the nature, extent, and value of positive externalities from higher education. These are not just in the analytic proofs related to long-run steady states. There are also analytic proofs presented relating to the short-term dynamics of the process. The empirical tests of the latter offer evidence consistent with the hypotheses, and also define the indirect effects from higher education as they compound over time and benefit others in the society and future generations.

With this brief summary of where we have been, all that is left is a few comments relevant to new financing strategies.

The Spellings Report

The Spellings Report on the "Future of Higher Education" issued in 2007 by a commission appointed by Margaret Spellings, U.S. secretary of education, calls for restructuring student aid, simplifying the application for federal aid, and curbing college costs. To this end:

- It calls for using a value-added approach. But no specifics are provided on how this should be done and no support for research is recommended on how to better do this.
- It stresses improving accountability and reducing costs. But accountability for what? It does not recommend financial support for obtaining better value-added measures, or for measuring and valuing private and social non-market outcomes beyond income, or for measuring forgone earnings costs, or for relating the total benefits to the costs as a criterion for economic efficiency.
- With respect to college costs, in addition to ignoring forgone earnings costs borne privately, it also ignores the fact that the costs passed on to parents through higher tuition at public institutions have largely been the result of the decline in state support per student in real terms at public institutions. With less competition from low tuition at public institutions, private colleges and universities have been free to raise their tuition and fees even more dramatically in absolute terms.

Lawrence Bacrow, president of Tufts University, says, "I don't think that the report acknowledges the reality that the public sector has disinvested in higher education in recent years" (in Burd, 2007, p. 4). Douglas Bennett, president of Earlham College, says, "This is a commission report that wants to improve higher education on the cheap" (Bennett, 2007, p. 2).

With respect to student aid, Charles Miller, the commission's chairman, repeatedly said at public meetings and in news reports that he wanted to "nuke" the federal student aid system (in Burd, 2007, p. 4). The initial draft called the government's financial aid programs "counterproductive." It did mention the Pell Grant program, which is the largest federal program benefiting higher education. Burd (2007) also indicates that North Carolina Governor James B. Hunt pressed Miller to include a proposal calling for increased funding for the Pell Grant program, which is in the final report. But the final report continues to call for paying for this in large part by consolidating other federal aid programs. This makes the Perkins Loan program and SEOP grant programs vulnerable, which are targeted respectively to increase affordability for students from middle-class families that just miss the cutoff for Pell Grants and to supplement Pell Grants for the lowest-income students. David Warren, president of the National Association of Colleges and Universities, says, "The problem is not with the design of the aid programs. The problem is that we have not had an increase in the funding of these programs in the last five years" (in Burd, 2007, p. 5).

It can be concluded that the commission has missed the main problems of massive skill deficits in the United States, and the need for financing solutions, and missed the rising social rates of return to investment in higher education since 1980. It also misses the important point that underfunding by the states is contributing to rising tuitions at the public universities. These have implications for the main policy issues it addresses in the "Future of Higher Education." Richard Vedder of the American Enterprise Institute and Ohio State University also says it is "too vague. A lot of statements could be read as platitudes" (in Burd, 2007, p. 2). This is a commission report that is likely to have a short shelf life. It also illustrates the need for new policy.

Privatization

Some privatization in the financing of higher education makes additional resources per student available from parents who are able to pay, reducing the stress on public funds and contributing to the quality of the education provided. About twice as much is spent per student by colleges and universities in the United States, where there is more privatization than in the European Union, for example. Countries where the degree of privatization in the financing is very low, such as Austria, Switzerland, Iceland, France, Germany, Greece, Sweden, Denmark, Norway, the Netherlands, Portugal, and Turkey, might study further the methods of resource recovery through higher tuition coupled with need-based grants means tested using very successful Family Financial Statement methods employed in the United States, Canada, and the United Kingdom. In these countries out-of-pocket private financing accounts for 40 to 53% of all expenditures per student (McMahon, 2006b, Table A-5).

But although some privatization can be helpful, and needs to be a part of a new and efficient financing strategy, too much privatization is like more water for a drowning man. The estimates in this book indicate that about 52% of the benefits of higher education are social. Most of these are the result of indirect benefits from higher education that are not anticipated and poorly understood. The latter, which have been extensively discussed, include better health, effects of freer trade on growth, political institutions, and stability. These are supplemented by direct non-market benefits to the quality of life through higher education's contributions to civic institutions, democracy, human rights, and other community effects. By this estimate, 48% of the costs should be borne privately and 52% publicly. With currently 53% of the direct costs in the United States borne by families (which includes 100% of the direct costs at the private for profit universities), and 48% publicly, the United States is close to but already a little beyond the efficient balance between privatization and public funding. If the roughly 50% of total investment costs in higher education that are forgone earnings at most public institutions are included in total costs, as they should be, then 76% of the total costs currently are being borne privately and 24% publicly. The latter measure suggests even more than the former that privatization may already have gone somewhat too far in the United States for true economic and social efficiency.

An example of privatization of research funding and its potential effects is the Academy on Capitalism and Limited Government that has just been established at a public Midwestern research university. It is similar to the twenty-five colleges receiving grants from the banking giant's BB&T

Charitable Foundation for the Advancement of American Capitalism. These all have a political mission as indicated by their titles. They do not predetermine research conclusions directly, but pre-select the faculty, adjuncts, courses, and PhD dissertations that are to be funded. The Academy is governed by an independent board, independent of the standard peer group review and faculty shared-governance of academic programs. Political economy, which is the mission of these grants, studies private markets, the efficiency of the public sector in supplying public goods, and the efficient balance. It remains to be seen how balanced and objective the studies that they publish will be.

This brings us back to where the book started, the meaning of economic efficiency and equity. Economic efficiency includes internal efficiency within the higher education system, known by economists as production efficiency. But it also includes external efficiency, or how well higher education relates to the needs of the society, known by economists as exchange efficiency. In the latter case, to the extent that there is market failure due either to poor information about non-market private and social benefits or to externality-type benefits to the society and future generations that are not served, privatization per se can result in overall economic inefficiency. The conclusion is that higher education policy is approaching the latter in the United States. The emphasis on further privatization in the Spellings Report, the faster growth of private profit making colleges and universities, the new growth of private funding of research devoted to special interests, and the rapid growth of vocationalization are all symptoms of this trend. Again, considerable privatization is helpful to efficiency, but the financing strategy also needs to be balanced. This trend is another instance of the need for new higher education financing policy concerning the appropriate balance of privatization and its limits in securing economic efficiency.

Higher Education and the Public Good

The importance of measuring and valuing the earnings, private non-market, and social benefits of higher education and relating their total to the costs of higher education cannot be overstated. More than anything else, it reveals the need for new policy. It is also helpful in suggesting new financing policy options.

There are, however, many incorrect or distorted ideas afloat:

- Human capital outcomes refer only to money benefits.
- The non-market private and social benefits of higher education are unmeasurable and cannot be valued.
- Free or extremely low college tuition is the best means of providing for adequate funding per student, quality, and access.
- High tuition and fees that cover or nearly cover full costs campus-wide (endowment funds to the side) are conducive to economic efficiency.
- Rising institutional costs provide an accurate view of the true costs of higher education.
- Since opportunity costs as well as per year costs of education rise over the lifecycle, there are diminishing returns to investing in advanced education and investment in preschool and lower primary levels is the most advantageous (Heckman). Without denying that investment in the early years is desirable, this conclusion does not take into account the rising demand and higher rates of return for college graduates.
- Studying rising costs without studying what has happened to benefits is meaningful.
- Decentralization that pushes funding from federal to state levels, and from state to local levels, is an equitable and efficient way to raise revenue and continues to be acceptable to local property tax payers.
- Accountability per se is good without considering how to measure the more ultimate outcomes or to measure value-added. The issue is "accountability for what?"
- Only science, engineering, and mathematics contribute to economic growth.
- Investment in higher education is at or above its optimum, as Vedder (2007) has suggested.
- Privatization beyond the current 48 to 52% of total funding of degree and research programs will bring about greater economic efficiency.

Slaughter and Leslie (1997) present statistics and analyses of policy that strongly suggest that higher education is supportive of the public good to a decreasing degree. Lyall and Sell (2006) in another good analysis conclude the same thing. This book, focusing on the measurement and valuation of the social benefits in relation to costs, as well as market failure, concludes essentially the same thing from a different perspective. The evidence mounts that higher education's service to the public good is seriously at risk.

Although a large majority of the population is being excluded economically and socially from the benefits of growth in the United States, the United Kingdom, and European Union nations, so far the response of higher education policy is inadequate.

To help to correct this, there are new financing strategies that are implied by the human capital approach developed in this book. They include the following:

- With the provision of better knowledge of the private non-market benefits of higher education and their value, increased *private* investment by students and their families would help to reduce the national skill deficits that exist. This could occur through a cooperative effort involving colleges and universities, public and private, the U.S. Department of Education, and state boards of higher education to increase the information available to local campuses, parents, students, and legislators about these non-market private benefits. This requires very little public resources, but the commitment would help higher education markets work better.
- A second strategy implied is the need to increase accurate information about specific social benefits of higher education, which is also needed to achieve overall economic efficiency. Partly because of poor information, states are cutting their support for higher education. State budgets are squeezed by public assistance, prison costs, Medicaid costs, and lagging tax revenues, but legislators and the public fail to realize that these pressures are largely due to state underinvestment in education earlier. Poor information about how graduates contribute to broader measures of economic development also may contribute to misdirection of state economic development efforts.
- A third strategy follows from the high total social rates of return

to higher education reported in this book as well as from the analysis of the major skill deficits due to technical change and globalization. Both imply the need for larger public investment in human capital through higher education. Options include increased federal support of Pell Grants and Stafford loans, matching federal grants to states in support of state higher education institutions, cooperation to achieve state education finance reform in more states, and better state support of public institutions and of merit-based aid with a need criterion. As enrollments increase, private family saving and investment (of forgone earnings and tuition) is automatically induced, both vital to development. So the balance of public versus private investment is not significantly affected even though public investment takes the lead.

• Fourth, financing strategies involving privatization of education and research costs need to consider the current estimates of social benefits as about 52% of total benefits. This offers a preliminary guideline to the degree of privatization that is appropriate if overall economic efficiency is to be achieved. It allows for the external benefits to others and to future generations that are part of the greater good.

The goal of new higher education policy needs to be to contribute efficiently to graduates' and society's longer-term private and social benefits in ways that include but are not limited to earnings. It also needs to relate these benefits to the costs of higher education to continually evaluate cost-effectiveness, efficiency, and accountability. When this is done, the conclusion is that higher education investment, public and private, is below its optimum. Sustained underinvestment has its price. Human capital formation through education, including higher education, over time does determine the future. And yet higher education and with it the greater good are at risk. This also puts the nation at risk.

Correcting for Ability Bias
in Returns to Higher Education

In estimating both the market and the non-market returns to investment in higher education, some of the returns are due to innate ability and related family factors. These largely average out for large numbers of families or in nationwide data with exceptions to be discussed. But they are not part of the value-added by a particular campus or part of the pure return to higher education for certain individuals or curricula. These are biased due to ability differences and need to be removed from the increments to earnings and to non-market private and social benefits to remove the bias that would overstate both types of returns to education.

In addition to this ability bias, there is also measurement error, especially as schooling levels are self-reported or reported by departments of education, particularly in developing countries. This measurement error due to overstating education quality or enrollment levels operates to increase the estimated return to education and therefore is normally in an offsetting direction from ability bias. The downward correction to the effect of education on earnings or on non-market outcomes for ability must therefore be reduced by an upward correction for measurement error especially to get the net ability bias needed to obtain the true value-added by education. For nationwide or statewide data, these two biases largely cancel out.

However, some campuses and some curricula are above the median in the ability of their entering students, and others are below. There is some self-selection by individuals of higher ability in choosing further education, even at the median campus, which is reinforced by some institutions that are very selective in admitting students. The result is that some campuses are above and others below the median ACT or SAT test scores. Some individual students also learn more at college than others. So the size of the correction for net ability bias needs to be related to whether a particular campus, or curricula, or student, is above or below this median. In what follows the issue is addressed of how much the correction for net ability bias must be for those situations that are at, above, or below the median achievement test scores of entering students.

Ability Bias for Individuals, Curricula, or Campuses at the Median

All estimates of net ability bias at, above, or below the median ability level are best made using large samples of identical twins. This provides rigorous experimental laboratory-like controls for ability and for other family factors as between genetically identical twins who have grown up in the same household, given that the innate intelligence and family background for within twin pair comparisons is identical. It permits isolation of differences in market and non-market returns to education that are due to differences in their formal education and not to differences in their ability or family background.

A significant advance was made recently in studies of identical twins using reports by others to control for measurement error in self-reported schooling to estimate the net ability bias in the returns to schooling. For clarity, we will refer to net ability bias as any (normally upward) bias in earnings due to innate ability as distinguished from earnings after any offsetting measurement error has been netted out. These types of computations were introduced into the literature by Ashenfelter and Krueger (1994) and Behrman et al. (1994). There is wide agreement that identical twins studies offer probably the best basis for estimating the pure returns to education since they provide highly controlled conditions for the identical abilities and family backgrounds between monozygotic twins. This recent evidence to be discussed indicates that ability bias is significant (Behrman and Rosenzweig, 1999, pp. 165–67), but there is also wide agreement that measurement error in an offsetting direction is significant.

In practice, it is the net ability bias obtained from identical twins studies in relation to ordinary least-squares applied to raw data without controls for either ability or measurement error that is most important and useful. That is because it is seldom possible to fully control for ability. Even where test scores, such as the widely used SAT and ACT scores, are available, they measure achievement and not innate ability. Other such micro-studies often are not replicated annually or are not representative of the education system. Furthermore, most existing national-, state-, or community-wide data that is representative is based on self-reporting by education institutions and national education departments of their own records and therefore is subject to the same type of reporting and measurement error. This is true of the Current Population Survey (CPS) data used in this appendix, of worldwide labor force surveys of households collecting earnings data now conducted by almost all governments, and of data on enrollment rates at each education level collected by the National Center for Education Statistics or by UNESCO worldwide since the latter involve self-reporting by governmental units, which have an incentive to overestimate and therefore look better in national and worldwide circles.

The estimates since 1994 of net ability bias based on samples of identical twins are summarized briefly in Table A.1. The estimates of Mincerian rates of return to education net of ability bias and corrected for measurement error in column 2 as well as of the net ability bias in column 3 vary widely among studies.* But, with some judgment, it is possible to get reasonable estimates of the upper and lower bounds of net ability bias after netting out the partially offsetting measurement error.

There are reasons for giving the more recent studies in 1998 and 1999 heavier weight, which narrows the range of the estimates considerably. They all involve larger samples with smaller sampling variation, and use actual earnings as distinguished from earnings imputed from Census occupational classifications. Larger samples seem warranted since it has recently been shown by Rouse (1999) that sampling variation led to the large estimate of measurement error in the Ashenfelter and Krueger study (1994), which then contributed both to their high (corrected) return to schooling and the anomaly in the direction of the net ability bias. In the Behrman et al. (1994) study (rows 2 and 3), the sample size is about the same and it seems possible that similar sampling variation could explain the extraordinarily large net ability biases there as well. Furthermore, rows 2 and 3 are based on white males alone who have experienced lower increases in their earnings than females since about 1980 (as will be shown later in this appendix).

This may explain their lower returns to education after correction for ability and measurement error ("Instrumental Variable (IV) Within MZ") than the other studies. It also contributes to a larger difference for the numerator when computing the net ability bias in column 3. Also, the correction for the measurement error in schooling in this study is based on reports of the monozygotic twins' schooling by their eldest children, who are likely to reflect what their parents have told them. So it is possible that a child's report on his or her father's schooling is both biased and less accurate than reports by the father's twin, whose development was parallel to the father's. Finally, the 80% estimate of ability bias appears to be based on a parameter that varies widely across samples (ibid., col. 5, p. 1153). So although there does appear to be some positive reinforcement of endowments in the home, it seems wise to place less emphasis on this 80%, at least until the effect is replicated.

*The estimates also vary somewhat within studies, depending on the sample and on the precise specification, but in general each author's preferred estimate is presented here.

Finally, the Miller et al. (1995) study is based on a larger sample of Australian identical twins. It also has lower net returns to education after correction for measurement error. This is probably because it is based on earnings that were imputed from Census occupational categories, which ignore earnings variability within occupations (as does the earlier Minnesota study included in row 3 before the twins were re-interviewed) and because of the more equal distribution of income in Australia.* After correction for measurement error, their return to education in Australia rises by 2.5 to 5.5 percentage points.

Again, in contrast, the results obtained in the 1998 and 1999 studies, which implement rather rigorous controls for innate ability, family background, and measurement error, appear to be converging toward a narrower range. Ashenfelter and Rouse (1998, Table III, cols. 6, 9–10) find that innate ability and family background account for about 31% of the net returns, which is partially offset by the necessary correction for measurement error. The measurement error correction is somewhat less than in Miller et al. (1995, p. 597) but somewhat more than in Behrman and Rosenzweig (1999, p. 166). This results in a net ability bias of 12 to 13.7% in Ashenfelter and Rouse (1998), or about a 13% overstatement when the returns to education are based directly on the raw data. Behrman and Rosenzweig (1999) estimate this net ability bias with a different sample of twins and totally independently at 11.8%, which is very close. Rouse's (1999, p. 152) best estimate is 6 to 9.5% and a bit smaller, but close, whereas the 0.9% in her second computation may be affected by the presence of additional covariates (for example, covered by a union, which is highly significant) and depending on what these covariates do could be a bit on the low side.

Although I am mindful that there are earlier estimates that are both larger and smaller, I conclude that the current best estimates of net ability bias results in the net earnings differential overstating the returns to education by somewhere between 6 and 13.7%, with a mean that rounds to 10%, very close to the 11.8% obtained most recently by Behrman and Rosenzweig (1999). In his survey of the literature, Card (1998) reaches very similar conclusions, which are consistent with earlier conclusions reached by many others in the field such as Griliches (1977, 2000), Griliches and Mason (1988), Butcher and Case (1992), Ashenfelter and Zimmerman (1997), Kane and Rouse (1993), Card (1993), and Becker (1993), among others.

However, the effect of this 10 to 12% upward bias on my computation of the return to education by the "full method" is another matter. Since institutional

*As the authors indicate, "rates of return to schooling in Australia are lower than in the United States because of (lower) dispersion of the distribution of income" (p. 597).

Authors	OLS	IV Within MZ	Net Ability Bias (%)
1. Ashenfelter and Krueger (1994) n = 147 MZ twins pairs	0.084	0.129	−53.6
2. Behrman et al. (1994) n = 141 MZ white male twins pairs	0.094[a]	0.050[b]	46.8
3. Behrman et al. (1994) n = 141 MZ white male twins pairs	n.a.	0.039[c]	80.0[d]
4. Miller et al. (1995) n = 602 MZ twins pairs	0.064	0.045	29.6
5. Ashenfelter and Rouse (1998) n = 333 MZ twins pairs	0.102	0.088	13.7
6. Rouse (1999), A&K sample increased n = 453 MZ twins pairs	0.105	0.095	6.0[d]
7. Rouse (1999) n = 445 MZ twins pairs	0.111	0.110	0.9[e]
8. Behrman and Rosenzweig (1999, p. 167) n = 720 MZ twins pairs	0.118	0.104	11.8[f]
9. Arias et al. (1999, pp. 28, 30) n = 858 MZ twins pairs	0.131	0.123	6.12[g]

NOTE: OLS = ordinary least-squares; MZ = monozygotic; IV = instrumental variable.

[a]Generalized least-squares controlling for correlation in the error terms, but close to OLS, from Table 5.4A, column 1.

[b]Instrumental variables estimate from Table 5.4A, column 4.

[c]This is the return uncorrected for measurement error used in the Behrman et al. (1994, p. 1156) calculation of the 80% net ability bias. It also includes the Minnesota subsample, which imputes earnings based on occupation and thereby ignores the returns to earnings within occupations, as the authors recognize (p. 1154).

[d]Rouse (1999, Table 5.2A, p. 152).

[e]Rouse (1999, Table 5.4A, columns 1 [generalized least squares] and 3). This controls for marital status and tenure, unlike the preceding line.

[f]This controls for full-time work experience, but not marital status, so is probably the most comparable to row 6.

[g]Calculated at the median.

costs average about 50% of total investment costs that appear in the denominator of the internal rate of return calculation, then my return to education based on the raw data is upward biased by less than 10 to 12%. There is little evidence that any net ability bias that remains in my rate of return estimates taking also the offsetting measurement error into account changes *markedly* over time.*

---

*Behrman and Rosenzweig (1999) suggest that ability bias may vary somewhat over time. To gain some insight on how large this variation might be, Cawley et al. (1998, p. 1) applied nonparametric methods to National Longitudinal Survey of Youth

In summary, the recent studies based on large samples of identical twins using these techniques conclude that (1) there is a net ability bias that is significantly different from zero, and (2) all recent large sample studies converge on a best estimate of the size of this net ability bias as lying between 6 and 12%.

This 6 to 12% net ability bias can be interpreted as applying to groups of individuals, or to entering freshmen at campuses, who are approximately at median ability, and who at a campus of average quality would also presumably have approximately median increments to earnings. That is, there is some self-selection by those who choose more over less education and therefore choose to go to college in the first place, including going to those campuses that are exactly at the median. So for these individuals on average, and these campuses, a 6 to 12% reduction in the net increments to earnings after graduation takes care of that.

It might be said that this net ability bias best applies to campuses that are slightly above the median since the regression methods that are used for these estimates minimize the sum of the squares of the deviations about the regression line, which gives greater weight to the outliers, and these outliers would tend to be toward the upper end of both the earnings and ability distributions. However, a few of the individuals in the identical twins sample did not go to college, creating a slight offset in the other direction. The net effect of these deviations from the median is very likely to be negligible.

Net Ability Bias for Freshmen above and below Median Ability

Some campuses admit freshmen who are on average at the median ability level of all college freshmen, whereas some campuses are above and others below. So next I seek to estimate the net ability bias in the returns to graduates at those campuses that are in the deciles above and below the median. This will permit me to correct my estimates of market rates of return and non-market returns by campus for elements due to innate intelligence and family factors, elements that are extraneous to the value of the instruction received, and hence must be removed to get at the net value-added by the college or university.

———

(NLYS) panel data to investigate the possible effect of a rising return to ability in the rising return to education. They conclude that "we find little evidence that the rise in the return to education is centered among the most able." Also, the continuing expansion of the higher education system to children from poorer families suggests that the net ability bias may be declining, if anything, at that level. These points offer some support for my assumption. Additional corrections for (nonlinear) ability are needed when studying the returns to education at a particular school or college, given much wider variation in ability among schools.

For this purpose, there is an unusual and insightful recent paper using a large sample of 858 monozygotic twins by Arias et al. (2001) that provides a basis for calculating the net ability bias by deciles of groups above and below the median. However, since these estimates of bias are based on outcomes after graduation, when grouped by deciles they include the effects of the quality of instruction at the college chosen. So their gross ability plus quality bias must be further refined to remove the portion due to quality differences. The result should be the cleanest possible estimate of ability bias due to innate intelligence and family factors useful for correcting the estimates of market and non-market value-added by each campus. Fortunately, for this latter purpose there is an excellent article by Behrman et al. (1996) that also is based on a sample of monozygotic twins. They estimate the effect of differences in college quality on the earnings later, which I will use to estimate and show the return to college quality by deciles. These in turn are used to correct the Arias et al. (2001) estimates so that the latter can be applied to get at the true value-added.

ABILITY DECILES

Column 1 in Table A.2 shows the gross ability deciles from Arias et al. (2001) arrayed about the median, where the deciles (actually quintiles in their article, simplified here) apply to the log of earnings. The last column in Table A.2 shows ability deciles for U.S. campuses based on SAT test scores from *US News and World Report* (1999), a widely available source that is updated annually. The latter is better for classifying campuses because earnings are an output measure and we want a measure of the ability of the inputs before they experience college, as well as a measure that is available to the reader.

The reason for using SAT scores to classify campuses for purposes of relating to the studies of identical twins must be briefly explained, given the controversy that rages in the education community about test scores. It is well known that neither SAT nor ACT test scores taken alone are the best predictor of success in college, partly because they do not fully reflect motivation. A much better predictor of the probability of graduation uses rank in the high school class as a major component of a selection index, with a weight of 75% or more together with these test scores. Such a selection index is a far superior basis for use in admissions decisions since it reflects not only students' innate ability and past subject matter achievement but also their motivation to apply themselves to the task at hand in relation to their peers. A large number of public universities use such a selection index because of its better predictive capacity. It has the further merit of relating to the high schools and the public since it offers the strong probability of admis-

TABLE A.2   Net Ability Bias and Corrections by Ability Deciles

Ability level	Deciles (bold) and quantiles (1)	Mincer return to education by OLS (2)	Return by IV, MZ twins, no measurement error (3)	Ability bias plus quality (cols. 3–2) (4)	Net ability bias plus quality (as % of OLS) (5)	Ability bias plus quality by deciles (%) (6)	SAT score deciles, nation (math) (7)
Low	**0.05**	0.0924	0.0987	-0.0063	-6.81	-9.40	0–325
	0.1	0.0904	0.1013	-0.0109	-12.06	-13.30	325–379
	0.15	0.0848	0.0975	-0.0127	-14.98		
	0.2	0.0811	0.0905	-0.0094	-11.59	-8.60	380–436
	0.25	0.0944	0.0981	-0.0037	-3.92		
	0.3	0.1034	0.1171	-0.0137	-13.25	-8.70	437–457
	0.35	0.1121	0.1266	-0.0145	-12.93		
	0.4	0.1185	0.1237	-0.0052	-4.38	-4.49	458–467
	0.45	0.1251	0.1195	0.0056	4.49		
Median	**0.5**	**0.1306**	**0.1226**	**0.0080**	**6.12**	**6.12**	**492**
	0.55	0.1332	0.1226	0.0106	7.96		
	0.6	**0.1314**	**0.1226**	**0.0088**	**6.70**	7.96	468–526
	0.65	0.1305	0.1264	0.0041	3.20		
	0.7	0.1255	0.1288	-0.0033	-2.63	5.00	527–585
	0.75	0.1326	0.1310	0.0016	1.21		
	0.8	0.1270	0.1137	0.0133	10.47	-0.70	586–634
	0.85	0.1323	0.1051	0.0272	20.55		
	0.9	0.1398	0.1070	0.0328	23.47	15.50	635–677
High	**0.95**	**0.1313**	**0.1316**	**-0.0003**	**-0.22**	**11.60**	**678–800**

sion to high school valedictorians and salutatorians, as well as to others who rank very high in their class, even though the applicant may be from a smaller high school that does not offer some of the subjects covered in the tests.

The reader can easily look up the SAT scores for the 50th percentile (5th decile) of the entering freshmen at his or her campus in the June 1 issue of *US News and World Report* (1999 and later issues) for purposes of relating his or her campus to Tables A.1, A.2, or A.3. It is given for more than three thousand U.S. campuses in this source, and similar nationwide test score data is given by percentiles or deciles for campuses in many other countries worldwide. (Data on rank in the high school class is also given, but it is in the form of the percent ranking in the top tenth, top quarter, and top half, which cannot be converted to a median rank.) The SAT test score data furthermore is given for the 25th, 50th, and 75th percentiles in this same source from which other percentiles can be interpolated for more detailed relation of specific campuses to the tables that follow if the user wishes. But the median ability level of the entering freshmen as measured by the SAT test scores is best for correcting the net ability bias in the market and non-market returns to a college education not only because it relates to the ability of the student inputs but also because the weight for rank in the high school class used in the selection index by different campuses will vary, and because it is closest to the concept of (unmeasured) ability and family factors isolated by the identical twins studies.

For those campuses that are at the ability median, as indicated in columns 6 and 7 of Table A.2, a reduction of 6.12% in the Mincerian (1974) returns to education can be applied to remove the average net ability bias. This 6.12% is computed from Arias et al. (2001) at the median of the earnings increments for their large sample of 858 identical twins, and is within the 6 to 12% range of estimates of net ability bias obtained by all of the most recent large sample identical twins studies discussed earlier. Their identical twins data is the same as that used by the Ashenfelter and Rouse (1998) and the Rouse (1997, 1999) studies. The result means, for example, that if the Mincerarian (1974) return to education for this median group as estimated from the raw data by ordinary least-squares in column 2 of Table A.2 is 13.08%, then it should be reduced by 6.12% of 13.08% to 12.27% to remove the effects of ability and family factors to get the return to higher education net of ability bias, which is then the value-added by a campus that is at the median.

This group of median campuses in terms of earnings increments (column 1) will be assumed to also be of median quality and have entering freshmen who on average have median SAT scores.

For those groups at higher ability deciles (and quantiles), the rates of return to education are higher than for those at the lower deciles. This can be seen whether estimated by ordinary least-squares (in column 2) or estimated using only the net differences between two individuals of the same identical twins pair (as in column 3, showing the family effects model, which eliminates measurement error by use of instrumental variables techniques). In the lowest decile (0.1) the ordinary least-squares estimate of the Mincer return is 9.04%, whereas in the highest decile (0.9) it is 13.98%. These higher ordinary least-squares returns reflect both higher quality of the college attended and also higher ability of the entering student. It is the latter we seek eventually to eliminate.

The estimates based only on differences within monozygotic twin pairs using instrumental variable techniques in column 3 indicate that fully controlling for ability bias and for measurement error, the Mincer-type rates of return are higher for those twin pairs in the higher ability deciles. That is, the more highly educated twin from those twin pairs that have higher innate ability and better family background than other twin pairs in the lower deciles has higher earnings. The return to education in column 3 of Table A.1 varies from 9.87% in the lowest ability quantile to 13.16% in the highest ability quantile, for example, with the rate of return moving steadily upward from the 0.05th through the 0.75th quantile (although there is a dip at 0.8, 0.85, and 0.9 quantiles). These monozygotic twins estimates do not reflect hardly any differences in college quality since it can reasonably be assumed that identical twins went to much the same quality schools given their identical family backgrounds and given that it is only the differences in earnings within twin pairs that are being measured.*

To obtain the net ability bias by decile, the monozygotic difference instrumental variables estimates that are free of this bias (column 3) are subtracted from the ordinary least-squares levels estimates in column 2 that are not. The result is shown in column 4, which therefore is the net effect of ability, measurement error, and college quality on earnings by decile. This in turn is then expressed as a percent of the ordinary least-squares rate of return in column 2, with the result shown in column 5 by quantiles and in column 6 by deciles.

The result shows that the net ability plus quality bias is positive above the median (which is the lower half of the table), and negative at the lower ability deciles (top half of the table). That is, the bias for the Mincer return is higher in those groups, and at those campuses, where the students are of higher ability. But part of this is not a true bias because it is partly due to higher college quality, which I next seek to separate out.

*To the extent that the twin who gets the larger amount of education goes to a better-quality school, however, the return and the quartile rank will reflect the quality of the education associated with his or her higher earnings. At the present stage of research this cannot be known, however, since there is not data on which school each respondent attended.

Returns to the Quality of Education at Institutions above or below the Mean

The return to college quality by deciles above or below the mean quality is computed and shown in Table A.3. It is based on the regression estimates by Behrman et al. (1996, Table 5.3A, column 3) using differences within 403 monozygotic twin pairs.

Most studies of the impacts of school and college quality on earnings outcomes use measures of the quality of the inputs. These normally include teachers' salaries, as a measure of whether or not the school is able to attract and hold the most able faculty in competition with the private sector, expenditures per pupil, total students per faculty member, and a composite index of school quality that contains all of the above plus measures of books per pupil, teacher educational background, and so forth. A recent example at the secondary school level using a fixed effects model focused on differences between siblings with instrumental variables to control for city size is the study by Altonji and Dunn (1996), which finds strong effects from the expenditure variables, much stronger than some studies that do not control for family fixed effects.

At the college level, the Behrman et al. (1996) study also focuses on increments to earnings later, uses a similar approach (monozygotic twin fixed effects instrumental variables), and reaches similar conclusions. As indicated in their Table 2, they find professors' salaries, expenditures per student, PhD-granting institution, and private institution to all be significant determinants of the increments to students' earnings later in the within-monozygotic twin and even larger sample within monozygotic and dizygotic twin instrumental variables fixed effects estimates. In this study it is remarkable that both members of all twin pairs went to the same primary and secondary schools, and not only have identical intelligence (monozygotic twins) but also the same family background and same primary and secondary school quality. But there is considerable within-pair variance in the colleges attended. So this study is well suited to our purposes.

To compute the percent of difference in the returns later due to differences in college quality, the standard deviation of each explanatory variable about its mean was used to interpolate the deviations in each variable at the ten decile levels about the mean. These are shown for all variables in the regression in Table A.3, columns 2–9. Total students per teacher is not statistically significant, probably because this number merely reflects expenditure per student, which is already included. Nevertheless, it may have some predictive capacity and is highly significant, with a coefficient of about the same size when it is used with the larger sample of both monozygotic and dizygotic twins.

The regression coefficients for the within monozygotic twin regression then

TABLE A.3   Percent of Differences in Log Earnings Due to Differences in College Quality[a]

Log earnings, by deciles[b] (1)	Indices of quality of the college						Controls for		Percent earnings increment due to quality (10)[c]
	Professor salary (1975 $) (2)	Ph.D. granting institution (3)	Private institution (4)	Exp. per student (5)	Students per teacher (6)	Enrollment (7)	College Years (8)	Work experience (9)	
5	-2.95	-0.32	-0.47	-1.28	-12	-0.24	-1.51	-10.5	-0.42
15	-1.5	-0.16	-0.23	-0.64	-6	-0.12	-0.75	-5.25	-0.42
25	-1.07	-0.11	-0.17	-0.45	-4.28	-0.08	-0.53	-3.75	-0.42
35	-0.43	-0.07	-0.10	-0.27	-2.56	-0.05	-0.32	-2.25	-0.39
45	-0.215	-0.02	-0.03	-0.09	-0.86	-0.02	-0.11	-0.75	-0.45
Deviation from mean	0	0	0	0	0	0	0	0	0
55	0.215	0.02	0.03	0.09	0.86	0.02	0.11	0.75	0.37
65	0.43	0.07	0.10	0.27	2.56	0.05	0.32	2.25	0.40
75	1.07	0.11	0.17	0.45	4.28	0.08	0.53	3.75	0.40
85	1.5	0.16	0.23	0.64	6	0.12	0.75	5.25	0.41
95	2.95	0.32	0.47	1.28	12	0.24	1.51	10.5	0.42
Difference within MZ twins log earnings									
Mean	1.90	0.01	0	121	0.94	296	-0.10	0.46	2.51[c]
Std. deviation	2.95	0.32	0.47	1.28	12	24059	1.51	10.51	0.62[c]
Went to other college	53%	53%	53%	53%	53%	53%	53%	53%	
No. of colleges	90	90	90	90	90	90	90	90	
N[b] (MZ pairs)	403	403	403	403	403	403	403	403	429[b]

SOURCE: Calculations based on Behrman et al. (1996, Table 1, column 4, and Table 3, column 3).

[a] Deviations from the means, by decile, for differences between identical twins.

[b] 156 (or 39%) of these MZ twin pairs contribute to the identification of school quality effects since one or both in the other twin pairs did not attend college.

[c] Md of log earnings = 2.508 and the standard deviation = 0.618 from Arias et al. (2001, Table 1).

were applied to these deviations from the mean value of each variable at the decile break points, as well as to analogous deviations in the control variables (that is, size of the institution, years of college, and years of full-time work experience, all of which are significant) to obtain the log of the earnings increment attributable to quality. This was then expressed as a percent of the log of the earnings increment above or below the mean, again at these decile break points to obtain the percent of each earnings increment that is due to college quality. The results shown in column 10 of Table A.3 suggest that from 37 to 45% of the increments to earnings are due to college quality, whereas the remainder is due to ability differences among pairs of identical twins.*

Controlling for the Ability of Entering Freshmen

It is now possible to get at the value-added by a campus to the market and non-market returns and externalities generated by its graduates. The net ability bias due to the ability and family factors of entering students, net of measurement error, must be removed from any measures of these returns, but the effects of the differences in the quality of education among campuses must not be removed in the process.

To do this, the estimates of net ability bias obtained in Table A.2 are corrected to remove the element due to the quality of the college or university obtained in Table A.3. Table A.4 summarizes this correction, and the final result.

Column 2 shows the ACT scores and columns 3 and 4 show the SAT scores nationwide, a close approximation to the freshmen at all campuses in the United States arrayed by decile. As indicated earlier, any U.S. campus can be located in this array, as can any campus in other countries given nationwide test score data by decile for that country. Column 5 shows the earnings increments, or decrements, about the median in the United States (the analog of the log earnings in the large Arias et al., 2001 sample). Column 6 merely repeats the gross net ability plus quality bias from Table A.2, and column 7 repeats the percentages of this due to college quality as estimated in Table A.3.

The final results give the percent of the rates of return due to quality in each ability decile (column 8) and the percent due to net ability bias (column 9). The former is obtained by multiplying the gross ability and quality effects in column

---

*This procedure assumes that the values of the quality indices and of the log of earnings in this equation are approximately normally distributed about the mean. This makes possible interpolation of the decile break points about the mean. If they are not exactly normally distributed, the deciles will be a little off, but the percent of earnings increments due to college quality (which hover around 40% anyway) would be largely unaffected.

TABLE A.4   Correction to Campus Rates of Return for Net Ability Bias[a]

Campus mean percentile (1)	ACT scores nationwide[b] (2)	SAT math scores,[c] national (3)	SAT verbal scores, national (4)	Earnings above or below median ($) (5)	Ability and quality bias in returns[d] (%) (6)	Earnings increments due to quality[e] (%) (7)	Ability and quality bias due to quality[f] (%) (8)	Bias in returns due to ability[g] (%) (9)
Low 0				−310				
0.05	14.8	0–325	0–311	−303	−9.4	−0.42	−4.0	−5.4
0.15	16.1	325–79	311–62	−252	−13.3	−0.42	−5.6	−7.6
0.25	17.5	380–436	363–74	−180	−8.6	−0.42	−3.6	−5.0
0.35	18.9	437–457	375–99	−108	−8.7	−0.40	−3.4	−5.2
0.45	20.2	458–67	400–57	−36	−4.5	−0.45	−2.0	−2.5
Med. 0.5	20.9	492	442		6.1			6.1
0.55	21.6	468–526	458–84	36	8.0	0.37	3.0	5.0
0.65	22.9	527–85	485–507	108	5.0	0.40	2.0	3.0
0.75	24.3	586–634	508–14	180	−0.7	0.40	−0.3	−0.4
0.85	25.7	635–77	515–59	252	15.5	0.41	6.4	9.1
0.95	27.0	678–800	560–800	302	11.6	0.42	4.8	6.8
High 1.0				310				

[a]Differences due to variation in college quality are retained. Column 5 is in 1993 dollars.
[b]From *ACT High School Profile Report*, National, 1999, American College Testing, Iowa City, IA.
[c]From http://nces.ed.gov/pubs/ce/c9622do3.html.
[d]From Table A.2.
[e]From Table A.2, column 10.
[f]Column 6 times column 7.
[g]Column 6 less column 8.

6 by the percent due to quality, and by then subtracting this result from the gross effects to get the percent correction that should be applied to campus-level rates of return to arrive at the value-added by the institution.

The final result in column 9 of Table A.4 needs to be applied as a correction factor to campus-level rates of return obtained either by use of Mincer earnings functions or by the full method used in Chapter 3, which computes pure internal rates of return and takes institutional costs into account. At campuses where the entering students have high ability, as measured by their entering ACT or SAT test scores, as well as at the median campus, the results indicate that rates of return will be overstated from 3 to 9%, as indicated in Table A.4. The understatement of −0.42% in the 75th percentile appears to be an anomaly probably due to sampling variation, and it is best smoothed out by averaging it in with the adjacent cells (9.28% + 3.02%/2 = 6.15% in this case). Conversely, rates of return at the campuses where students have lower entering ability tend to be understated from 2 to 7.65%.

Conclusions

It still would appear to be true that the rates of return to investment in higher education, counting only the market returns, are higher at the high-ability campuses, as was suggested in Table A.1. This is consistent with an independent study by Dale and Krueger (1999, p. ii) that finds a "substantial rate of return from attending a more costly college." But the main conclusion here is that the true returns to education at campuses serving students with less ability on average are about 5 to 7% higher than the raw earnings data would suggest, and at those serving students with high ability are about 6% lower than the either the ordinary least-squares Mincer earnings functions or full method pure internal rates of return estimates based on the raw data would indicate.

Somewhat as a byproduct, it is estimated that about 40% of the increments in earnings after college are attributable to differences in the quality of colleges and universities, the latter as measured by differences in expenditure per pupil and in faculty salaries, as well as to student choice among institutions choosing PhD-granting and private status.

It is true that most of these estimates (but not all) are based on twins attending a nationwide convention of twins, and that there may be some self-selection among those who choose to attend that introduces self-selection bias into the estimates. But it is reasonable to assume that those who attend are above the average of all identical twins in earnings and in ability levels. If this is the case, then the direction of the ability bias would be upward, and the size of the correction needed for ability would be overstated, not understated. In this case the 6.12%

correction (at the mean) for the effect of ability on average earnings, net of measurement error, is most likely to be too large, and not too small.

In conclusion, some campuses, some curricula, and some individual students may be either above or below the median nationwide. In these situations it is appropriate to apply a correction for ability bias from Table A.4, column 9, to obtain the net value-added by the higher education to earnings or to non-market outcomes. Some campuses or some curricula also may be above or below median quality and in this case this is estimated and can be drawn from Table A.4, Column 8.

However, most estimates of the private and social rates of return to higher education in this book, both market and non-market, apply to nationwide or statewide averages. This means that 6.12% (not percentage points) of the private and social rates of return and of the non-market returns as well can be attributed to ability bias and hence not to education. However, the measurement error bias operates in the opposite direction and largely cancels out this ability bias, leaving the modern best estimate of the alpha coefficient to be zero.

A Simplified Dynamic Model with Higher Education Externalities

It is possible to clarify and be more specific about indirect effects and externalities and how they cumulate over time within families and within nations by setting out the equations of a simplified short-term dynamic model of endogenous development, exploring the short-term dynamics of the augmented Lucas (1988) model. My website (McMahon, 2008) presents the empirical estimates, which are the basis for estimating the indirect effects.

For endogenous development, as distinguished from endogenous growth, the Lucas production function is supplemented with a separate household production function (and thereby becomes a three-sector growth model). The latter allows households to use their human capital during their non-labor-market hours at home and in the community (roughly seventy-two hours each week) to produce non-market outcomes, or final satisfactions. It is reasonable to view household production based on Becker (1965, 1981) as potentially also influenced by externalities analogous to those in Lucas (1988).

Lucas (1988, p. 11) expresses economic output as a function of human capital used on the job, physical capital, and externalities, the latter represented by the "average level of education in the community." Totally differentiating this production function shown as Equation 4.1 expressed in per capita terms with respect to time, dividing through by per capita income, and inserting lags that are significant in the short term as will be discussed gives Equation B.1. Now per capita economic growth depends on the rate of investment in human capital, s_{-20} and the rate of investment in physical capital, D_i, both relative to per capita income, but also on externality effects generated by the education of others in the community, the other D_js. This derivation implies that the rate of investment in human capital is measured by investment in education, a flow (relative to per capita income), or by enrollment rates, s_{-20}, which is also a flow of additions to the human capital stock (and relative not to per capita income but to the number of persons in the age bracket). This result is the new Equation B.1.

THE SIMPLIFIED DYNAMIC MODEL

Per Capita Economic Growth

(Eq. B.1) $y = \alpha_1 s_{-20} + \alpha_{i2} D_i + \varepsilon_1$

Development Goals

(Eq. B.2) $D_i = \beta_{i1} s_{-20} + \beta_{i2} y_{-20} + \beta_{i3} D_{j-20} + \varepsilon_2, i \neq j$

Investment in Schooling

(Eq. B.3) $s = \gamma_1 s_{-20} + \gamma_2 y_{-10} + \varepsilon_3$

y = Economic growth of real income (or GDP) per capita

s_{-20} = Education enrollment rates lagged twenty years. Gross enrollment rates include replacement investment in human capital, a major means of diffusing new technologies. Lags allow time to graduation as well as time for graduates to learn on the job.

D_i = Development outcomes, i = 1,...14, some lagged. In Equation B.1, D_1 is the rate of investment in physical capital as a percent of income derived from the Lucas (1988) production function. Other development outcomes (D_is) are education externalities (specifically $\alpha_{i2}\beta_{i1} s_{-20}$) that frequently appear in growth equations as indirect effects. They are contributions by the education of others to institutions such as the rule of law (Barro, 2001a) or better health that also aids productivity. The D_is in Equation B.2 include additional development goals.

y_{-10} = growth of per capita GDP lagged ten or so years, a reverse causal flow in (2) and (3).

$\varepsilon_1, \varepsilon_2, \varepsilon_3$ = Disturbances that are less significant in determining growth and development outcomes

Household production of non-market outcomes of education, D_i, is in Equation B.2. Each individual uses the same human capital but during the seventy-two or so non-labor-market hours each week spent at home and in the community. This equation is obtained again by totally differentiating with respect to time the household production function given in Chapter 4 but expressed in per capita terms as it relates to production of the main development outcomes. Interpreting this model as relating to a single household, this is what generates endogenous development over time within the family, covering several generations. For many similar families, as their human capital and income grows, development occurs within states and within nations. The effect of schooling on each non-market final satisfaction, $(\beta_{i1} s_{-20})$, is augmented by the effect of income representing market-produced goods $(\beta_{i2} y_{-20})$ since market-produced goods and not just human capital

348   APPENDIX B

are also in household production functions. Controlling for these by including per capita income in every equation dealing with non-market development outcomes ensures that the market effects from education contained in $(\beta_{i2}y_{-20})$ are not double counted. There are also feedbacks from other development outcomes, the D_js in Equation B.2. The latter also contain indirect effects due to the education of others that raise household productivity, as in the growth equation.

Finally, Equation B.3 deals with the third type of production, the production of human capital through schooling. This is also a part of the Lucas (1988, p. 12) endogenous growth model. Here additional schooling as measured by enrollment rates is a function of the prior schooling of the parents (s_{-20}). Interpreting the model as applied to a collection of typical households, this becomes earlier schooling within the community. But schooling is also a function of the parents' per capita income needed to pay the teachers. Since education has contributed to this income in Equation B.1 it is part of the reverse causal flow.

If this short-term difference equation version of the model is solved and its roots are shown to converge, then the solution of the lag-free long-run version, such as in Lucas (1988), is not misleading. If it does not converge, and in simulations run for forty-five years there is no evidence of explosive behavior, then the long-run solution would not hold up. But whatever happens in the long run, politicians probably seldom look beyond forty-five years, and usually far less than that. So the medium term is probably more relevant to higher education policy

To show that the medium-term slopes that incorporate the indirect effects of education are larger, the simplified model is solved recursively for y by substituting Equations B.2 and B.3 into B.1. After further substitutions, collecting terms, and simplifying, y becomes a function of declining distributed lags on enrollments representing schooling, s, and on the indirect effects, D. If their coefficients are assumed to decline geometrically:

(Eq. B.4) $y = \delta\lambda^0 s_{-40} + \delta\lambda^1 s_{-50} + \delta\lambda^2 s_{-60} + ... + \theta\lambda^0 D_{j-30} + \theta\lambda^1 D_{j-40} + \theta\lambda^2 D_{j-50} ... + \varepsilon_4$

Multiplying both sides at time t–10 by λ:

(Eq. B.5) $\lambda y_{-10} = \delta\lambda^1 s_{-50} + \delta\lambda^2 s_{-60} + ... + \theta\lambda^1 D_{j-40} + \theta\lambda^2 D_{j-50} ... + \varepsilon_5$

Subtracting Equation B.5 from Equation B.4:

(Eq. B.6) $y = \delta s_{-40} + \lambda y_{-10} + \theta D_{j-30} + \varepsilon_6$

This is the reduced form version of the short-term relation of education to growth shown in the graph in the text as D_2 BE or D_3C. To compare this short-term education coefficient, δ, to the coefficient reflecting education's net effect over 40 years or more, the terms in Equation B.4 can be summed up:

$$\text{(Eq. B.7)} \quad y = \sum_{t=0}^{\infty} \delta\lambda^t s_{40-t} + \sum_{t=0}^{\infty} \theta\lambda^t D_{j-30-t} + \varepsilon_7 = k\hat{s} + \bar{D}$$

Here k is the relation to per capita economic growth of the accumulation of education over generations, $\hat{s}$. $\bar{D}$ stands for other development factors that also contribute to growth. This is the intercept in the graph in the text that ratchets upward. It is very important to notice that $\theta\,D_j$ controls for all other factors affecting growth that appear in Equations B.1–B.3, so the parameter k and the slope of the longer-term net education effect shown on the graph are not biased upward. The other important point is that this is a proof that the medium-term permanent education effect, k, is larger than the short-term reduced form effect, δ (since $0 < \lambda < 1$), which in turn is larger than the short-term structural effect, α_1, the coefficient normally estimated in growth equations.

As mentioned, something closer to this larger medium-term effect has been estimated using U.S. data by Topel (1999, Table 4, p. 2969). But Topel does not control for things other than education, $\bar{D}$, that also affect growth and development. His medium-term relation of education to growth, including these other things, is shown in the graph as the even steeper line OG. These medium-term effects of education, k, that exclude non-education effects like $\bar{D}$, are reflected in simulations by first simulating the effects that include a change in education policy and then subtracting a simulation with no policy change.

The reason for stronger effects over the longer term is that education affects socioeconomic status (SES) factors that change slowly, such as the health and education of the parents, community factors such as political stability, the rule of law, and the rate of investment in physical capital. These are often treated as fixed effects in Mincer regressions and growth equations even though they do in fact change over longer periods. It is known, nevertheless, that education affects the rule of law and political stability, investment in physical capital, and hence growth (Barro, 2001a, p. 24; McMahon, 2002, pp. 45–47, 63, 74, 161). The dynamic process can be thought of starting with the poorest countries (or poorest families) at D_1 in the graph with the short-term function ratcheting upward over time. The true effects of education, therefore, are not just the short-term immediate impacts but instead the medium- to longer-term effects incorporating education externalities as they set the stage for each new round of growth and development within families, within communities, within states, and within nations.

Valuing the Effects of Higher Education on Private Non-Market Outcomes

Methods and Sources

This appendix provides the basis for the estimates of each of the values of the private non-market benefits of higher education in Table 4.3. Columns 1 and 2 of Tables C.1A and C.1B are the education and income coefficients exactly as they appear in the regressions in the original articles, with the asterisks indicating their level of significance. The successive columns adjust the education and income coefficients (β and α in the text) to standardize the studies so that they are comparable and can be averaged, as well as to convert them all to 2007 dollars. For the formulas underlying each cell, as well as the other sheets that these formulas reference, the EXCEL spreadsheet for HE Chapter IV App C can be downloaded from my website (McMahon, 2008).

The computed marginal effects of education and of income in columns 3 and 4 are these same original education and income coefficients after they have been standardized to make the units comparable. In columns 5 and 6 they are corrected for standardization of the dependent variable (for example, Self-Health Rating, SHR, is placed on a scale of 1 to 10 for all studies). Columns 7 and 8 (also labeled d and e) are these same education and income coefficients converted to an annual basis (for example, income is sometimes expressed as the weekly wage). Column 9 then is the ratio of these corrected education and income coefficients, the β/α called for by Equation 4.4 in the text, but also allowing for conversion at this stage to 2007 prices. The last column in Tables C.1A and C.1B is the income equivalent value of each of the non-market private benefits from a bachelor's degree that connect to the values reported in Table 4.3 in the text. All regressions have been controlled for per capita income, so these estimates of the non-market values are all over and above any income or earnings benefits from the bachelor's degree.

Table C.2 provides the details on the units in which each of the key variables is measured. This faces up to a very major problem in trying to make the many different studies comparable. The last column in Table C.2 indicates all other control variables that appear in each regression. With the information in Tables C.1A, C.1B, and C.2, and in the Excel spreadsheets on the website (McMahon, 2008) the reader can reconstruct all of the private non-market benefit valuations that appear in Table 4.3 in the text.

TABLE C.1A Basis for Valuating the Non-Market Private Benefits of Higher Education

Explanation of computations for table 4.3	Reported education coefficient	Reported income coefficient	Computed education effect (antilog)	Computed income effect (antilog)	Normalized education coef., SHR[a] (a)	Normalized income coef., SHR[a] (b)	Normalized educ. coef. (per year) (d)	Normalized income coef. (annualized) (e)	Ratio of educ. (β') to inc. (α') (d)/(e)	Value of NM private benefits of bachelor's
Self Health: Grossman (1975, p. 176)										
Equation 5	0.019**	0.167**	0.075	0.092	0.187	0.231	0.187	0.001	0.64	$14,400
		−0.001		−0.004		−0.010		−0.010		
		0.004		0.016		0.039		0.302		
Equation 6	0.012**	0.146***	0.047	0.081	0.118	0.202	0.118	0.001	0.66	$14,968
		−0.005		−0.020		−0.049		−0.049		
		0.003		0.012		0.030		0.227		
Equation 7	0.012**	0.147***	0.047	0.081	0.118	0.203	0.118	0.001	0.83	$18,780
		−0.001		−0.004		−0.010		−0.010		
		0.002		0.008		0.020		0.151		
Self Health: Grossman (1972, p. 68)										
All whites	0.018**	0.086*	0.056	0.001	0.140	0.004	0.140	0.03738	3.73	$29,988
		0.053		0.000		0.000		0.00005		
Males with sick time	0.022***	0.060**	0.068	0.001	0.171	0.003	0.171	0.03720	4.58	$36,858
Model with dummy for insurance	0.028**	0.111**	0.087	0.00189	0.217	0.005	0.217	0.06882	3.15	$25,355
		0.041		0.00001		0.000		0.00003		

(continued)

TABLE C.1A   (continued)

Explanation of computations for table 4.3	Reported education coefficient	Reported income coefficient	Computed education effect (antilog)	Computed income effect (antilog)	Normalized education coef., SHR[a] (a)	Normalized income coef., SHR[a] (b)	Normalized educ. coef. (per year) (d)	Normalized income coef. (annualized) (e)	Ratio of educ. (β') to inc. (α') (d)/(e)	Value of NM private benefits of bachelor's
Self Health: Erbsland et al. (1995)										
Health capital model	0.073**	0.059**	0.532	0.00061	0.484	0.001	0.082	0.078	1.06	$6,854
Self Health: Lee (1982)										
Estimate is by Wolfe and Haveman (2003, p. 117) converted to 2007b prices.										$19,578
Self Health: Bolin et al. (2002, p. 103)										
Low category	-0.019***	-2.464*	-0.019	-2.464	-0.095	-12.320	-0.024	-0.041	0.59	$4,535
Medium category	-0.164*	-21.726	-0.164	-21.726	-0.820	-108.630	-0.206	-0.358	-0.57	$4,439
High category	0.183***	24.190*	0.183	24.190	0.915	120.950	0.230	0.399	0.58	$4,449
Self Health: Leigh (1983)										
1973 (p. 231)	0.005*	0.000010	0.0047	0.000010	0.0068	0.00001	0.00677	0.000014	474	$2,168,230
1977 (p. 232)	0.000	0.000001	0.0004	0.000001	0.0006	0.00000	0.00056	0.000002	279	$933,628
Self Health: Ross and Mirowsky (1999, p. 112)										
Work and well-being	0.053***	0.00001	0.0530	0.00001	0.1060	0.00002	0.10600	0.00002	5,096	$7,919,119
Health practices	0.108***	0.00800*	0.1080	0.00800	0.2160	0.01600	0.21600	0.01600	14	$37,767

[a]Education and income effects on self-health rating (SHR) are normalized across studies, re-scaling SHR when necessary to a scale of 1–10.
*, **, *** significance at 10%, 5%, and 1%, respectively.

TABLE C.1B   Basis for Valuating the Non-Market Private Benefits of Higher Education

	Reported education coefficient	Reported income coefficient	Computed education coefficient	Computed income coefficient	Ratio of educ. coef. to inc. coef.	Value of NM private benefits of bachelor's
Smoking: De Walque (2004, p. 24)						
Smoking cessation college graduates	0.178***	0.091***	0.089	0.091	0.978	$2,158
Smoking cessation risking induction	0.219	0.086***	0.1095	0.086	1.273	$2,810
Child Health: Currie and Stabile (2003, p. 1819)						
Ages 4–8, mother's ed. 12+	−0.135**	−0.182**	−0.0675	−0.182	0.371	$1,339
Child Health: Case et al. (2002, p. 1313)						
Ages 4–8, mother's ed. 12+	−0.322**	−0.156**	−0.322	−0.156	2.064	$7,340
Cognitive Development: Murnane (1981, p. 249)						
Full sample	3.85**	1.31	3.85	1.31	2.939	$2,637
Child in two-parent family	11.49**	1.96	11.49	1.96	5.862	$5,260
Cognitive Development: Shakotko et al. (1980, p. 18)						
Children's IQ	0.986**	0.288**	0.986	0.288	3.424	$2,943
Reading, math scores	0.942**	0.271**	0.942	0.271	3.476	$2,988

*, **, *** significance at 10%, 5%, and 1%, respectively.

TABLE C.2 Explanatory Variables and Units of Measurement

| | | Explanatory variables used in regressions | | |
Study and model	Dependent variable	Income	Education	Other control variables
Bolin et al. (2002)				
Low category (p. 103)		Hourly wage rate (SEK/h) 54.27	Used a discrete variable index that was developed by Statistics Sweden to reflect education level. Mean: 3.01	For the year 1996–97, age
High category (p. 103)				Same as above
Erbsland et al. (1995)				
Econometric study, German micro health capital model (p. 178)	High self-health rating (index of 1–11). Mean: 1.9903 (in logs)	Log of net monthly income (Deutschemark/month). Mean: 7.4279	Education Index (scale of 1–3). Mean: 2.0422	Sex, age, nationality, doing sports, private insurance, community size, accessibility of resident physician
Grossman (1972)				
All whites in labor force (p. 71)	Log of health stock rating (1—poor, 2—fair, 3—good, 4—excellent, all whites. Mean 3.1 (not log)	1) Log of weekly wage rate adjusted for earnings lost per work-loss week. Mean: Not available. 2) Log of annual family income adjusted for lost earnings.	Schooling completed. Mean: Not available	Dv for sex, log of family size

Males with positive sick time (p. 72)	Log of health stock rating (1—poor, 2—fair, 3—good, 4—excellent) of males with sick time. Mean: Not available	1) Log of weekly wage rate adjusted for variations in net earnings lost per work-loss week. Mean: Not available. 2) Log of annual family income adjusted to lost earnings.	Years of formal schooling completed. Mean: not available	Dv for sex, log of family size
Model with dummy for disability insurance (p. 68)	Log of health stock rating (1—poor, 2—fair, 3—good, 4—excellent), all whites. Mean: 3.1 (not log)	Wage rate adjusted for variations in net earnings lost per work-loss week. Mean: Not available. 2) Log of annual family income adjusted to lost earnings. Mean: not available	Years of formal schooling completed. Mean: not available	Dv for sex, log of family size, dummy for disability insurance, gorss earnings lost
Grossman (1975)				
Equation 5 (p. 176)	Log of health stock rating (1—poor, 2—fair, 3—good, 4—excellent), all whites. Mean: 3.9 (not log)	1) Log of hourly wage rate in current job. Mean: 1.963 (in log). 2) Other income. Mean: 1,508	Years of formal schooling completed. Mean: 15.054	Age, education of father, education of mother, visual perception, log of health stock while in high school

(continued)

TABLE C.2 (continued)

| Study and model | | Explanatory variables used in regressions | | |
	Dependent variable	Income	Education	Other control variables
Equation 6 (p. 176)	Stock rating (1—poor, 2—fair, 3—good, 4—excellent), all whites. Mean: 3.9 (not log)	Wage rate in current job. Mean: 1.963 (in log). 2) Other income. Mean: 1,508	Years of formal schooling completed. Mean: 15.054	Age, education of father, education of mother, visual perception, log of health stock while in high school, wife's education, job satisfaction, weight difference
Equation 7 (p. 176)	Stock rating (1—poor, 2—fair, 3—good, 4—excellent), all whites. Mean: 3.9 (not log)	Wage rate in current job. Mean: 1.963 (in log). 2) Other income. Mean: 1.508	Years of formal schooling completed. Mean: 15.054	Education of mother, visual perception, psychomotor control, mechanical ability, intelligence, numerical ability, log of health stock while in hgh school, wife's education, job satisfaction
Leigh (1983)				
(p. 231)	Self-health evaluation (rating of 1–7). Mean: 6.011	Annual earnings of respondent (US$/ year). Mean 9.930.79	Years of schooling completed. Mean: 12.608	Dv for hazardous job, dv for smoking, education, dv for sex, dv for white, age, annual earnings. number of kids, dv for skinny, dv for fat, dv for married, dv for union membership, other family income, dv if job pays sick leave

1977 (p. 232)	Self-health evaluation (rating of 1–7). Mean 5.230	Annual earnings of respondent (US$/year). Mean: 12.510	Years of schooling completed. Mean: 12.502	Dv for hazardous job, dv for smoking, probability of exercising, education, dv for sex, dv for white, age, annual earnings, number of kids, dv for skinny, dv for fat, dv for married, dv for union, organization size, membership, other family income, dv if job pays sick leave, work experience, spouse schooling, urbanization
Ross and Wu (1995)				
Work, family, and well-being survey, 1989 (p. 112)	Self-reported health (1—poor, 2—fair, 3—don't know, 4–5—good)	Total household income for 1989. Mean: not available	Years of formal education completed. Mean: not available	Dv for married, dv for white, dv for sex, age, age-by-household income, age-by-education
Health practices survey, 1979 (p. 113)	Health rating (1—very poor, 2—poor, 3—satisfactory, 4—good, 5—very good)	Total household income scored as an ordinal variable with five categories: from less than $2,500 to more than $30,000.	Years of formal education completed coded as follows: 0 for none; 2.5 for 1–4 years; 5.5 for 5–6 years; 7.5 for 7–8 years; 10 for	Dv for married, dv for white, dv for sex, age, age-by-household income, age-by-education

(continued)

TABLE C.2 (continued)

Study and model	Dependent variable	Income	Education	Other control variables
			Explanatory variables used in regressions	
		Mean: Not available	9–11 years; 12 for 12 years; 14 for 13–15 years; 16 for college.	
DeWalque (2004)				
OLS (Model 8, p. 24)	Smoking cessation	Log family income in 1983. Mean: $12,352	Years of education college and above	Male, Vietnam veteran, black, other race, years of education above high school
IV (Model 8, p. 25)	Smoking cessation	Log family income in 1983. Mean: $12,352	Years of higher education college and above. Mean years after high school: 2	Male, Vietnam veteran, black, other race, years of education above high school
Deaton and Paxson (2001)				
Mean ages 25–59 (regression 1, p. 43)	Mortality	Log income per adult equivalent. Mean: $12,339 in 1985	Years of education	Age dummies
Men ages 60–85 (regression 1, p. 43)	Mortality	Log income per adult equivalent. Mean: $12,339 in 1985	Years of education	Age dummies
Men, all ages (regression 1, p. 43)	Mortality	Log income per adult equivalent. Mean: $12,339 in 1985	Years of education	Age dummies

Currie and Stabile (2003)				
Ages 4–8 (health-ordered probits, mother's education > 12): p. 1819	Health status (1—excellent; 5—poor) of children ages 4–8	Log of family income in 1998 (CAN $50,000/year)	Dummy variable for mother's education (1 if more than high school, 0 otherwise) (58% of sample)	None
Case et al. (2002)				
Ages 4–8 (health-ordered probits, mother's education > 12); p. 1313	Health status (1—excellent; 5—poor) of children ages 4–8	Log of family income in 1997. Mean: $48,343	Mom's education > 12. Mean: 12.69	Mom's education = 12; dad's education = 12; dad's education > 12
Murnae (1981)				
Full sample (p. 249)	Children's cognitive skill level (scores on Iowa test of vocabulary skills)	Household income in 1971. Mean: $5,000	Years of schooling of mother. Mean: 10.37	Hours per week mother in labor force, child's skill level prior to observation period, dv if child is female, number of children in the family, dv if two-parent family, years of schooling of father
Family with two parents (p. 249)	Children's cognitive skill level (scores on Iowa test of vocabulary skills)	Household income in 1971. Mean: $5,000	Years of schooling of mother. Mean: 10.37	Hours per week mother in labor force, child's skill level prior to observation period, dv if child is female, number of children in the family, dv if two-parent family, years of schooling of father

(continued)

TABLE C.2 (continued)

| | | Explanatory variables used in regressions | | |
Study and model	Dependent variable	Income	Education	Other control variables
Shakoto et al. (1980)				
Dynamic model (p. 18)	Reading and arthimetic scores	Family income in 1967–69. Mean: $8,060	Years of schooling of mother. Mean: 11.216	Years of schooling of father, number in household less than 20 years of age, dv if mother is working full-time or part-time, dv if youth is living in state in Northeast, Midwest, or South; dv for youth's birth weight; dv if youth is living in an urban area with population of more than 3 million, or 1 to 3 million, or less than 1 million; parental assessment of child's health; dv if child is breastfed; dv if age of mother at youth's birth is less than 20, or more than 35; dv if not living with the father, dv if youth is firstborn; dv if twins; dv if youth is male; cognitive and health scores at first survey

Higher Education and Growth, U.S. and OECD Countries, 1960–2005

The direct effects of higher education on economic growth in OECD countries are shown in Table D.1. This growth equation contains the direct effects from education as gross enrollment rates increase, but also shows the significance of various indirect effects that are also a function of education. The latter are explored in Tables D.2 through D.6.

The variables in Tables D.1 through D.6 are as follows:

GNPPC5 = the real economic growth rate, the dependent variable in Table D.1. It is measured as the percent increase in real Gross National Product Per Capita over five-year periods from 1960 to 2005.

GER1T.20, GER2T.20, & GER3.20 = Primary, Secondary, and Higher Education Gross Enrollment Rates, respectively, each lagged twenty years.

GCF = Gross Capital Formation, measured as Gross Private Domestic Investment as a percent of Gross National Product, also for five-year averages.

TRADE = Trade Openness, measured as total exports plus imports as a percent of Gross National Product.

PS = Political Stability, measured on a scale of 1 to 100, from the International Country Risk Guide (2007, and earlier issues).

LEXP = Life Expectancy

GDPPC70 = Gross Domestic Product per capita in 1970. This is a test for conditional convergence, and a control for differences in the production function intercept among countries. Practically, it reflects all of the same determinants of growth that are in the growth equation that have been operating in all years prior to 1970.

NEWDEM = Democratization, measured on a scale of 1 to 8 by the index for political rights from Freedom House (2007, and earlier issues).

MILX = Military Expenditure as a percent of each government's budget.

The data was collected for each of these variables for the twenty-eight developed OECD countries for 1960 to 2005, and the growth equation including indi-

TABLE D.1   Economic Growth in the OECD Countries: Growth Equation, 1960–2005

	Model 1		Model 2		Model 3		Model 4	
	(i)	(ii)	(i)	(ii)	(i)	(ii)	(i)	(ii)
(Intercept)	3.56	—	3.67	—	1.51	—	3.23	—
	(0.86)		(0.88)		(0.38)		(0.77)	
GER1T.20	0.0212	0.0214	—	—	—	—	—	—
	(1.4)	(1.4)						
GER2T.20	0.0221*	0.0192*	0.0183*	0.0153	—	—	0.0282***	0.0252***
	(2)	(1.8)	(1.7)	(1.5)			(3.1)	(3.1)
GER3T.20	0.0287	0.0276	0.0289	0.0278	0.0468***	0.045***	—	—
	(1.6)	(1.5)	(1.6)	(1.5)	(3.1)	(3.1)		
GCF	0.227***	0.227***	0.221***	0.221***	0.214***	0.215***	0.2***	0.201***
	(5.8)	(5.8)	(5.7)	(5.7)	(5.5)	(5.5)	(5.4)	(5.4)
TRADE	0.0133***	0.0132***	0.0131***	0.013***	0.0143***	0.0142***	0.0114**	0.0113**
	(2.9)	(2.9)	(2.9)	(2.9)	(3.1)	(3.1)	(2.5)	(2.6)
PS	0.0447	0.0445	0.0472	0.047	0.0553*	0.0547*	0.0446	0.0446
	(1.6)	(1.6)	(1.6)	(1.6)	(1.9)	(1.9)	(1.5)	(1.5)
LEXP	-0.186***	-0.135***	-0.154**	-0.101***	-0.121*	-0.0999***	-0.139**	-0.0932***
	(-2.7)	(-3.8)	(-2.4)	(-3.8)	(-1.9)	(-3.7)	(-2.1)	(-3.5)
GDPPC70	-9.56E-05**	-0.000103***	-0.000109***	-0.000117***	-0.000109***	-0.000113***	-0.000106***	-0.000113***
	(-2.4)	(-2.7)	(-2.8)	(-3.1)	(-2.8)	(-3)	(-2.7)	(-3)
df	96	97	97	98	98	99	98	99
R^2	0.385	0.803	0.371	0.799	0.353	0.794	0.355	0.794
Adj. R^2	0.333	0.787	0.326	0.785	0.314	0.782	0.316	0.782

NOTE: t-statistics are in parentheses.
Significance levels are: * = 10%, ** = 5%, and *** = 1%.

rect effects from education was estimated to support the analysis of growth effects from both higher and secondary education in developed countries as revealed by the macro-data. Table D.1 reveals that in Model 3, investment in higher education that supports increased gross enrollment rates is a highly significant determinant of real per capita economic growth. This controls for life expectancy, and is in sharp contrast to the discussion of this matter by Pritchett (2006) but consistent with the findings by Keller (2006b) and my earlier work on this issue. Secondary gross enrollment rates with which higher education enrollments are correlated are also highly significant (Model 4). But the coefficients for secondary are only about half the higher education coefficients. This pattern reappears in Model 2. Model 3 is shown in bold for emphasis, since it will receive most of the attention in the discussion that follows concerning the indirect effects of education on growth.

Economic growth is also affected by trade openness, political stability, and life expectancy as shown in Table D.1. The first two effects are positive, and the third is negative, as discussed in Chapter 5.

Table D.2 suggests that political stability (PS) is highly significant in the OECD countries as a determinant of larger exports and larger imports as a percent of each nation's GDP. Education is not a significant factor, and initial GDP per capita

TABLE D.2   Trade Openness as a Function of Political Stability

	(i)	(ii)
(Intercept)	−77.7	−16.3
	(−0.87)	(−0.17)
GNPC5	3.19	3
	(1.6)	(1.5)
GER2T.20	—	0.129
		(0.69)
GER3T.20	−0.259	—
	(−0.88)	
PS	2.43***	2.44***
	(4.0)	(4.0)
LEXP	−0.322	−1.29
	(−0.23)	(−0.88)
GDPPC70	−0.00272***	−0.00288***
	(−3.1)	(−3.4)
d.f.	99	99
R^2	0.238	0.236
Adj-R^2	0.199	0.197

NOTE: t–statistics in parentheses.
* = 10%.
** = 5%.
*** = 1%.

Political Stability as a Function of Education and Democracy

	(i)	(ii)
(Intercept)	47.6***	47.3***
	(7.3)	(7.6)
GDPPC.10	0.00047***	0.000412***
	(5.4)	(4.8)
GER2T.20	—	0.0849**
	(2)	
GER3T.20	0.0423	—
	(0.7)	
NEWDEM	4.27***	3.59***
	(4.5)	(3.7)
MILX	−1.97***	−1.84***
	(−3.9)	(−3.8)
LEXP	—	—
d.f.	61	61
R^2	0.737	0.751
Adj-R^2	0.719	0.735

NOTE: t-statistics in parentheses
* = 10%.
** = 5%.
*** = 1%.

in 1970 is negative, suggesting a convergence, with older countries slowing down and lower-income countries catching up (if they are politically stable) in trade.

Political stability (PS), which is important to growth (above), is positively affected by the degree of democracy as shown in Table D.3, which in turn is a function of education as shown in Table D.4. It is apparent that secondary education particularly is associated with greater political stability. Both secondary and higher education enrollments lagged twenty years contribute significantly to democratization, however. Education also contributes indirectly to both political stability and democracy through its contribution to higher per capita income.

The positive contributions of both higher and secondary education to life expectancy are clear in Table D.5. But note that rising life expectancy in the mature developed nations acts to slow economic growth.

Higher education is found to be associated with higher inequality as measured by the GINI coefficient in the OECD member nations in Table D.6. This is discussed further in Chapter 5.

TABLE D.4   Democracy as a Function of Education and Per Capita Income

	(i)	(ii)
(Intercept)	6.07***	5.69***
	(41)	(30)
GDPPC.10	3.59E-05***	2.27E-05**
	(3.5)	(2.1)
GER2T.20	—	0.0114***
		(3.3)
GER3T.20	0.0101*	—
	(1.7)	
PS.5	—	—
LEXP	—	—
d.f.	105	105
R^2	0.226	0.282
Adj-R^2	0.212	0.268

NOTE: *t*-statistics in parentheses.
* = 10%.
** = 5%.
*** = 1%.

TABLE D.5   Life Expectancy and Education's Indirect Negative Growth Effect

	(i)	(ii)
(Intercept)	64.5***	63.4***
	(29)	(30)
GDPPC.10	0.000261***	0.000211***
	(7.3)	(5.8)
GER1T.20	0.0641***	0.0599***
	(3.2)	(3.2)
GER2T.20	—	0.0483***
		(4.2)
GER3T.20	0.0504**	—
	(2.4)	
d.f.	105	105
R^2	0.518	0.565
Adj-R^2	0.504	0.553

NOTE: *t*-statistics in parentheses.
* = 10%.
** = 5%.
*** = 1%.

TABLE D.6   Higher Education and Inequality in the OECD

	(i)	(ii)	(iii)
(Intercept)	0.315***	0.291***	0.304***
	(14)	(18)	(13)
TRADE	3.61E-05	−4.55E-05	−8.41E-05
	(0.24)	(−0.32)	(−0.56)
LEXP	—	—	—
GER2T.20	−0.00062	—	9.97E-05
	(−1.5)		(0.34)
GER3T.20	0.00154**	0.000832*	—
	(2.4)	(1.9)	
d.f.	48	49	49
R^2	0.113	0.071	0.008
Adj-R^2	0.058	0.033	−0.033

NOTE: t-statistics in parentheses.
* = 10%.
** = 5%.
*** = 1%.

Valuing the External Social Benefits of Higher Education
Methods and Sources

This appendix explains the basis for the estimate of the economic value of each of the direct external social benefits in Table 5.5. The rationale and the pattern are the same as that for the valuation of the direct non-market private benefits in Table 4.3 that was discussed in Appendix C, so the reader should also refer to that. Both are based on the Haveman-Wolfe method (1984, pp. 394–97), which is also discussed in Wolfe-Haveman (2001, pp. 115–18; 2003, pp. 242–45).

The education and income coefficients in each original article that appears in Table 5.5 are repeated in Table E.1, followed by the step-by-step adjustments to these coefficients that are necessary to standardize the studies so that they are on a comparable basis. This is followed by an explanation of the basis on which each imputation is made to arrive at income-equivalent valuations. Table E.2 shows the units in which each of the key variables are measured and the units for other control variables that appear in each regression used for the valuations. The explanation in this appendix follows the pattern of the formulas underlying each cell as these education and income coefficients are standardized. To more easily reproduce each estimate the reader is referred to the Excel version of Tables E.1 and E.2 at my website (McMahon, 2008).

Standardizing the Studies

In order to make the results of the various studies of specific external social benefits comparable, the studies in Table 5.5 must be standardized. For example, some measure per capita income in logs and others do not; in some the coefficients reflect 1985 prices and some 1995 prices, some measure education in years and others in enrollment rates as a percent of the school-age group, and so forth. So the units in which education, income, and the dependent variable (the latter only in cases where there is more than one study to be averaged) must be corrected to make them more comparable. This is done in Table E.1 by standardizing the two key regression coefficients.

The studies used for valuation of the benefits are only those studies that contain both education and income, and studies in which both of these coefficients are significant. All that could be found that meet these criteria are included.

With respect to the units of measurement of the dependent variable, all studies that are averaged within each category in Table E.1 use the same measure of benefits. For valuing the private non-market benefits in Appendix C this was not true.

Education. For specific social benefit externalities, the education variable is usually measured as the gross enrollment rate. The unit of measurement is as in 50% = 50, that is, not 0.50. Further details are shown for this variable in each study in Table E.2.

However, enrollment rates are always expressed as a percentage of the persons in the relevant school-age age group, not as the number enrolled as a percent of the population. So these enrollment rates are converted to per capita terms, which is enrollment as a percent of the population in column 3. To do this the enrollment rate in column 1 is multiplied by the ratio of the number in the relevant school-age group to the number in the population. This conversion is applied by adjusting the education coefficient rather than the enrollment rate by use of this ratio in the formula underlying column 3 in the spreadsheet cited. The result is then called the Computed Education Effect in Table E.1. One percentage point of the per capita enrollment rate is interpreted as enrollment by one person for a college degree.

Income. When measured in logs, the analog is obtained in column 4 by multiplying the income coefficient by one over the mean of income using the mean GDP per capita worldwide. The result is called the computed income effect. In column 5 this income effect is converted to 2007 prices by reducing the size of the income coefficient in column 4 to reflect the increase of per capita income from the base year to 2007 prices.

Imputing the Income-Equivalent Valuations

The ratio of the corrected education coefficient to the corrected income coefficient, β/α, has now been obtained and is shown in column 8 of Table E.1. It is this that is required to obtain income-equivalent valuations, since the basis for the imputations is the per capita income that is a variable in all of the regression equations. That is, as in Chapter 5 (as well as Chapter 4), the monetary value of one additional college degree, P_E, is:

(Eq. E.1) $P_E = (MPP_E/MPP_X)P_X = (\delta D/\delta E)/(\delta D/\delta Y) = (\beta/\alpha)P_X$

The ratio of the marginal products, the MPPs, is given by the ratio of the standardized education coefficient, β, and the standardized income coefficient, α, for each specific social benefit as computed in column 8 of Table E.1. These came originally from each regression equation in each study listed in Table E.1. The regression equations are all of the form:

(Eq. E.2) $D = \alpha Y + \beta E + \text{(control variables)}$, where:

D = the dependent variable, which is democratization in row 1, for example
E = the enrollment rate
Y = per capita income
α = the marginal physical product of income in producing D
β = the marginal physical product of education in producing D
Control variables as indicated in Table E.2

The imputation is made on the basis of the amount of income it would take to achieve the average annual change in democratization (or other dependent variable) that has been typical on average in the twenty-eight OECD countries from 1975 through 2004. These bases for each imputation are shown in column 6 of Table E.1. The change was 0.0017 in the democratization index, for example, at the top of the table. To achieve this ΔD the amount of income required, using the income coefficient, was 41.3 as shown in column 7. So:

(Eq. E.3) $\beta/\alpha\ (P_g) = 24.08\ (41.3) = \$994$,

which is my estimate based on the first study in column 9 of Table E.1 of the value in 2007 dollars of a bachelor's degree per year for its contribution to improvements in democracy. Each of the other external social benefits follow the same pattern, but the basis for the imputations varies a little due to data availability or to the nature of the social benefit involved.

For the other outcomes, the imputation is based on the income-cost of attaining for:

Human Rights. The average improvement per year in the human rights index as measured by Freedom House (2007), which was 0.0020 for the OECD countries from 1975 through 2004.

Political Stability. The average improvement per year in the political stability index as measured by the International Country Risk Guide (2007), which was 0.13 for the OECD countries from 1975 through 2004.

Poverty Reduction. The average annual rate of poverty reduction in the United States, which was 0.0570 from 1985 to 2000.

Life Expectancy. The average annual rate of increase in life expectancy which was 0.2205 years in the OECD countries for 1960 to 2004.

Homicides. The average annual reduction in homicide rates in the OECD countries, which was thirty-nine from 1995 to 2004.

Other Crime. The average annual cost in the United States of federal, state, and local expenditure on the police and justice system, which was $660 for holding crime rates at the current levels of 5,375 per 100,000 in the population as given by the U.S. Department of Justice (2007).

Deforestation. The estimated cost per capita of $500 for a 0.142 annual increase in forest land. The 0.142 is the amount of average annual decrease in forestland in the OECD, 1985–1995.

Water Pollution. The estimated cost per capita of $100 per year to eliminate the 0.40 increase in river pollution which has been the average for 1980–2004 for the OECD countries.

Air Pollution. Estimated average annual cost per capita of $64 to reduce U.S. greenhouse gas emissions by 1.1% per year. This cost is based on the

TABLE E.1   Methods Used in Estimating the Values of the External Social Benefits of Education

Category	Source/year	Reported education coefficient β' (1)	Reported income coefficient α' (2)	Computed education effect β (3)
Democracy (D)	McMahon (2002)			
	Model 1, p. 98 (SE)	0.02***	0.372*	9.72E-04***
	Keller (2006b)			
	Political, p. 31 (HE)	0.01***	0.032[1]	8.71E-04***
	McMahon, Appendix D			
	Model I, OECD (HE)	0.01*	0.00004***	9.60E-04*
	Model ii, OECD (SE)	0.01***	0.00002**	6.16E-04***
Average for democratization				

0.7% per year of GDP spent on pollution abatement in the United States. The 1.1% is the average percent of increase from 1990 through 2005, so this level of expenditure is the amount estimated that would keep emissions flat.

Where there is more than one study of a specific social benefit, the estimates based on the different studies are averaged, and these averages are shown in column 9. They correspond to those in the last column of Table 5.5, as does the $27,726 total value of the external social benefits that sums these averages that is shown at the bottom of Table E.1.

Description of Key Elements in Underlying Studies

Table E.2 explains the units in which the key variables in each study are measured. Reviewing it makes clear why the studies have to be standardized to be able to get any meaningful result, as they have been in this book for the first time. Table E.2 also lists the other explanatory variables in each of the models used in Tables 5.5 and E.1.

Computed income effect $\delta(lnY) = \alpha'/Y$ (4)	Income effect in 2007$ α (5)	Basis for imputation av. annual change in dependent variable OECD 1975–2004[7] (6)	$P_X = \Delta Y$ for 1 yr. Δ in D Col 6/5 ($) (7)	Ratio col. 3/ col. 6 β/α (8)	Social benefit value $P_E = (\beta/\alpha)P_X$ (9)
		Av.OECD ΔD/Yr.'75-04			
7.6E-05*					
	0.000040	0.0017	41	24.1	994
		Av.OECD ΔD/Yr.'75-04			
6.6E-06[1]					
	0.000005	0.0017	339	177.1	59,982
		Av.OECD ΔD/Yr.'75-04			
0.00004***	0.000030	0.0017	55	31.5	1,726
0.00002**					
	0.000019	0.0017	87	32.0	2,771
					1,830

(continued)

Category	Source/year	Reported education coefficient β' (1)	Reported income coefficient α' (2)	Computed education effect β (3)
Human rights (HR)	McMahon (2002)			
	Model 1, p. 103 (SE)	0.02***	0.194***	1.20E-03[8]**
Political stability (PS)	McMahon (2002)			
	Model 3, p. 107 (SE)[6]	0.08***	0.00025***	0.002***
	McMahon, Appendix D			
	Model I, OECD (HE)	0.04	4.7E-04***	0.004
	Model ii, OECD (SE)[6]	0.08**	4.1E-04***	0.002**
Average for political stability				
Poverty reduction	McMahon (2002)			
	Model 2, p. 115 (SE)[6]	−1.41***	−5.6[1]	−0.038***
Life expectancy	McMahon (Appendix D)			
	Model I, OECD (HE)[2]	0.05**	2.61E-04***	0.050***
(LEXP)	Model ii, OECD (SE)[2]	0.05***	2.11E-04***	0.024***
	Less effect on growth	−0.12*		
Average for net life expectancy				
Lower crime	McMahon (2002)			
	Homicide,			
	p. 144[3] (SE)[6]	−15.90***	−1447***	−0.859***
	Other, p. 148[3] (SE)[1]	−974.00***	22612***	52.6***
Lower public health costs	Muennig (2000, p. 28)	Muennig:		
	Lower public costs	$11,007		
Forestation	McMahon (2002)			
	Reforestation,			
	p. 129 (SE)	0.001	6.7E-07**	5.3E-06
Clean water	McMahon (2002)			
	Water Pol., p. 134 (SE)[3]	−196.00	7.79***	10.588
Clean air	McMahon (2002)			
	Air pollution, p. 137 (SE)[3]	−0.58*	5E-04[1]	0.031*
	Air pollution, p. 137 (HE)[3]	−1.32**	5E-03**	0.125**
Total external social benefits				

Computed income effect $\delta(InY) = \alpha'/Y$ (4)	Income effect in 2007\$ α (5)	Basis for imputation av. annual change in dependent variable OECD 1975–2004[7] (6)	$P_X = \Delta Y$ for 1 yr. Δ in D $\overline{\text{Col } 6/5\ (\$)}$ (7)	Ratio col. 3/ col. 6 β/α (8)	Social benefit value $P_E = (\beta/\alpha)P_X$ (9)
		Av.OECD ΔHR '75-04			
4.0E-05***	0.000021	0.0020	95	30.2	2,865
		Av.OECD ΔPS/Yr'75-04			
2.5E-04***	0.000132	0.13	1,007	8.6	8,625
4.7E-04***	0.000353	0.17	473	8.6	4,041
4.1E-04***	0.000309	0.17	539	5.6	3,001
					5,813
−0.001[1]	−0.000608	0.0570	94	33.2	3,111
		Av.ΔLEXP,OECD 1960–2004[7]			
2.61E-04***	0.000196	0.2205	1,126	3.0	3,344
2.11E-04***	0.000158	0.2205	1,392	1.8	2,452
					590
					2,308
		Av.ΔH,OECD,'95–'04[9]			
−0.297***	−0.157091	−39	248	2.9	719
13.3***	7.0	\$660/cap. for Police[11]	660	7.5	4,928
		\$11,007, annual basis			544
		OECD Av.Δland '85–95			
6.7E-07**	0.0000004	−0.142	500	8.0	3,991
		AV.Δ Pol.OECD '80–'04			
7.79***	5.85	0.40	100 Cost[12]	1.4	136
		%Δ Gas Emits90–05[10]			
5E-04	0.000375	1.1	64	62.3	3,977
5E-03**	0.004052	1.1	64	23.2	1,482
					27,726

(continued)

[1]Income coefficient is not significant, which casts doubt on the reliability of the estimated value, so it was not included in the average or total.

[2]To convert to a per year basis to be comparable with other outcomes, value was divided by sixty-five years of life after graduation.

[3]The dependent variables of crime rates, water pollution, and air pollution are "bads" so the negative education coefficient was changed to positive since it is a positive benefit.

[4]In economic growth models in Table 5.5 the education coefficient was multiplied by per capita income to get the social benefit.

[5]The effect of life expectancy on growth was subtracted from the final value of social benefits.

[6]In these models there was no control for higher education. So the coefficient for secondary education must be reduced, and was divided by 2.

[7]All data for OECD and the United States is in a spreadsheet file (OECD Psach-McMahon-Dunnick 7-19-06.xls) available on request. LEXP data is from the OECD Factbook, 2007, crime data is from the UN Survey of Crime Trends, 1995–2004.

[8]Includes indirect effect through democratization shown in cell C18.

[9]Homicides per year per 100 million in the population.

[10]Source, OECD Environmental Data, Compendium 2006–7.

[11]Average per capita expenditure on police, criminal justice, and prisons: from U.S. Department of Justice (2007), Criminal Justice Statistics.

[12]The United States spends 0.7% per year on pollution abatement. This is 0.007(45,594), or $319 per capita. It is assumed that one-fourth of this is for the reduction of greenhouse gasses, and that doubling this would achieve sustainability.

*, **, *** = significance at 10%, 5%, and 1%; HE = higher education; SE = secondary education.

TABLE E.2 Explanatory Variables in Each Study

Category	Study and models	Dependent variable	Income	Education	Other control variables
Democratization	McMahon (2002)				
	Model 1 (p. 98)	Democratization (scale of 1–8, 8 is the highest)	ln GNP per capita (units: 1000 = $1,000)	Gross enrollment rate for secondary education	Military expenditure
Democratization	Keller (2006b)				
	Political rights (p. 31)	Political rights (0–1 scale with 1 as most favorable)	ln GDP per capita (units: 1000 = $1,000)	Higher education enrollment (units: 1 = 100%)	Primary and secondary enrollment
Democratization	Appendix D				
	Model (i)	Democratization (scale of 1–8, 8 is the highest)	GNP per capita (units: 1000 = $1,000)	Gross enrollment rate for higher education (units: 100 = 100%)	
	Model (ii)	Democratization (scale of 1–8, 8 is the highest)	GNP per capita (units: 1000 = $1,000)	Gross enrollment rate for secondary education (units: 100 = 100%)	
Human rights	McMahon (2002)				
	Model 1 (secondary enrollment; p. 103)	Human rights (scale of 1–8, 8 is the highest)	ln GNP per capita	Secondary enrollment (units: 100 = 100%)	Military expenditure, democratization

(continued)

TABLE E.2 (continued)

Category	Study and models	Dependent variable	Income	Education	Other control variables
Political stability	**McMahon (2002)**				
	Model 1 (p. 107)	Political stability (scale of 1–100, 100 is the highest)	ln GNP per capita (units: 1000 = $1,000)	Gross enrollment rate for primary education (units: 100 = 100%)	Military expenditure, communications, democratization, social security expenditure, urbanization
Political stability	**Appendix D**				
	Model (i)	Political stability (scale of 1–100, 100 is the highest)	GDP per capita (units: 1000 = $1,000)	Gross enrollment rate for higher education (units: 100 = 100%)	Democratization, military expenditure
	Model (ii)	Political stability (scale of 1–100, 100 is the highest)	GDP per capita (units: 1000 = $1,000)	Gross enrollment rate for secondary education (units: 100 = 100%)	Democratization, military expenditure
Poverty reduction	**McMahon (2002)**				
	Model 2 (p. 115)	Rural poverty (% of rural households with incomes below poverty threshold)	ln GNP per capita (units: 1000 = $1,000)	Gross enrollment rate for secondary education (units: 100 = 100%)	Primary and higher education gross enrollment rate, military expenditure, human capital stock, physical capital, democratization

Life expectancy	Appendix D				
	Positive social benefit from life expectancy, Model (i)	Life expectancy (in years)	GDP per capita (units: 1000 = $1,000)	Gross enrollment rate for higher education (units: 100 = 100%)	Gross enrollment rate for primary education
	Positive social benefit from life expectancy, Model (ii)	Life expectancy (in years)	GDP per capita (units: 1000 = $1,000)	Gross enrollment rate for secondary education (units: 100 = 100%)	Gross enrollment rate for primary education
	Negative effects on growth	GDP per capita			Appendix D, HE
	Negative effects on growth		−0.121 LEXP		Barro and Sala-I-Martin (1995)
Lower crime rates	McMahon (2002)				
	Violent crime rate (model 6; p. 144)	Homicides per 1,000 population	In personal income per capita in 1982$	Secondary completion	Unemployment, narcotics addiction
	Property crime rate (model 1; p. 148)	Property crime per 1,000 population	In GNP per capita units: 1000 = $1,000	Gross enrollment rate for secondary education (units: 100 = 100%)	GINI coefficient, poverty incidence, labor force with secondary education
Forestation	McMahon (2002)				
	Reforestation	Reforestation (% increase in forest land) (units: 100 = 100%)	GNP per capita (units: 1000 = $1,000)	Gross enrollment rate for secondary education (units: 100 = 100%)	Primary and higher education gross enrollment rates, rural poverty, change in agriculture

(continued)

TABLE E.2 (continued)

Category	Study and models	Dependent variable	Income	Education	Other control variables
Clean water	McMahon (2002)				
	Water pollution (model 1; p. 134)	Water pollution sewage in rivers near urban areas	GNP per capita (units: 1000 = $1,000)	Gross enrollment rate for secondary education (units: 100 = 100%)	Primary and higher education gross enrollment rates, urban poverty, democratization, population growth
Clean air	McMahon (2002)				
	Air pollution (model 2; p. 137)	Air pollution (mean concentration of sulfur dioxide in air)	GNP per capita (units: 1000 = $1,000)	Gross enrollment rate for secondary education (units: 100 = 100%)	Primary and higher education gross enrollment rates, democratization
Economic growth	Barro (1997)				
	GDP growth rate	Real GDP per capita growth rate (in decimals)		Years of secondary schooling of male	ln GDP per capita, ln GDP per capita (squared), gov't consumption, rule of law, democracy index
Economic growth	Barro and Sala-I-Martin (1995)				
		Real GDP per capita growth rate (in decimals)		Years of higher education of male	Male secondary education, female secondary education, female higher education, in

Economic growth			GDP, in life expectancy, public education expenditure/GDP ratio
Economic growth	Olivia and Rivera-Batiz (2002)		
	Model 1 (p. 253)	Real GDP per capita growth rate (in decimals)	Average years of secondary schooling of the male population ages twenty-five years and above	Government consumption, foreign direct investment, capital flows, Latin America dummies for: Africa, East Asia 1975–79, 1980–84, 1985–89, 1990–94
Economic growth	Keller (2006b)		
	GDP per capita growth (p. 24)	Real GDP per capita growth rate (in decimals); ten-year average	Higher education enrollment rate (units: 100 = 100%)	Primary and secondary enrollment rates, physical capital investment/GDP raio, in fertility, trade/GDP ratio, inflation, democratization
Economic growth	Appendix D		
	GDP per capita growth	Real GDP per capita growth rate (in decimals); five-year average	Higher education enrollment rate (units: 100 = 100%)	Gross physical capital formation, trade openness, political stability, life expectancy. GDP per capita in 1970

Acemoglu, Daron, and J. Angrist (2000). How large are the social returns to education? Evidence from compulsory schooling laws. *NBER Macroannual* 9–59. New York: National Bureau of Economic Research.

Acemoglu, Daron, S. Johnson, J. Robinson, and P. Yared (2005a). From education to democracy? NBER Working Paper 11204. Cambridge, MA: National Bureau of Economic Research.

Acemoglu, Daron, S. Johnson, J. Robinson, and P. Yared (2005b). Income and democracy. NBER Working Paper 11205. Cambridge, MA: National Bureau of Economic Research.

Adams, James D. (1990). Fundamental stocks of knowledge and productivity growth. *Journal of Political Economy* 98(4): 673–703.

Aghion, Philippe, L. Boustan, C. Hoxby, and J. Vandenbussche (2005). Exploiting states' mistakes to identify the causal impact of higher education on growth. UCLA Online Papers No 386, http://ideas.repec.org/p/cla/uclaol/386.html.

Alexander, F. K. (2000a). The changing face of accountability: Monitoring and assessing institutional performance in higher education. *Journal of Higher Education* 71(4): 412–31.

Alexander, F. K. (2000b). Student tuition and the higher education marketplace. *Journal of Staff, Program, and Organization Development* 17(2): 79–93.

Alexander, F. K. (2000c). The silent crisis: The fiscal capacity of public universities to compete for faculty. *Review of Higher Education* 24(2): 113–29.

Altonji, Joseph G., and T. A. Dunn (1996). Using siblings to estimate the effect of school quality on wages. *Review of Economics and Statistics* 78 (November): 665–71.

American Council on Education (2007). *Solutions for our future*. Washington, DC: American Council on Education. http://www.acenet.edu/Content/NavigationMenu/GovernmentRelationsPublicPolicy/Solutions/Solutions1.htm, and solutions@ace.nche.edu.

American Council on Education (2006). ACE national survey aggregates. Washington, DC: The Winston Group (see also focus group interviews they conducted for ACE).

Angrist, Joshua A., and Victor Levy (1996). The effect of teen childbearing and single parenthood on childhood disabilities and progress in school. NBER Working Paper 5807. New York: National Bureau of Economic Research.

Arias, Omar, Kevin Hallock, and Walter Sosa (2001). Individual heterogeneity in the returns to schooling: Instrumental variables quantile regression using twins data. *Empirical Economics.*

Arias, Omar, and W. McMahon (2001). Dynamic rates of return to education in the US. *Economics of Education Review* 20(2): 121–38.

Ashburn, Elyse (2007). The Spellings Report: Commission calls colleges "self-satisfied" and "risk-averse." *The Chronicle of Higher Education, Government and Politics* 53(2): A4.

Ashenfelter, Orley, C. Harmon, and H. Oosterbeek (2000). A review of estimates of the schooling/earnings relationship with tests for publication bias. NBER Working Paper 7457. Cambridge, MA: National Bureau of Economic Research.

Ashenfelter, Orley, and Alan Krueger (1994). Estimates of the economic return to schooling from a new sample of twins. *American Economic Review* 84(5): 1157–73.

Ashenfelter, Orley, and Cecilia Rouse (1998). Income, schooling, and ability: Evidence from a new sample of identical twins. *Quarterly Journal of Economics* 113(1): 253–84.

Ashenfelter, Orley, and David Zimmerman (1997). Estimates of the returns to schooling from sibling data: Fathers, sons, and brothers. *Review of Economics and Statistics* 79(1): 1–9.

Astin, A. W., K. C. Green, W. S. Korn, and M. Schalit (1985). The American freshman: National norms for fall 1985. Los Angeles: Higher Education Research Institute, University of California at Los Angeles.

Barnett, R. (1992). *Improving Higher Education: Total Quality Care.* The Society for Research into Higher Education. London: Open University Press.

Barro, Robert J. (2001a). Economic growth in east Asia before and after the crisis. NBER Working Paper 8330. Cambridge, MA: National Bureau of Economic Research.

Barro, Robert (2001b). Education and economic growth. Chapter 3 in John Halliwell, ed., *The Contribution of Human and Social Capital to Sustained Economic Growth and Well Being.* Paris and Ottawa: OECD and Canadian Government.

Barro, Robert J. (1999). The determinants of democracy. *Journal of Political Economy* 107: S158–S183.

Barro, Robert (1997). *The Determinants of Economic Growth: A Cross Country Empirical Study.* Cambridge, MA: MIT Press.

Barro, Robert J. (1991). Economic growth in a cross section of countries. *Quarterly Journal of Economics* 106(2): 407–44.

Barro, Robert J., and Xavier Sala-I-Martin (2007, 1995). *Economic Growth*. New York: McGraw Hill.

Bartel, A. P., and F. R. Lichtenberg (1987). The comparative advantage of educated workers in implementing the new technology. *Review of Economics and Statistics* 69: 1–11.

Becker, Gary (1993). *Human Capital*. 3rd ed. Chicago: University of Chicago Press.

Becker, Gary (1981). *A Treatise on the Family*. Cambridge, MA, and London: Harvard University Press.

Becker, Gary S. (1976). *The Economic Approach to Human Behavior*. Chicago: University of Chicago Press.

Becker, Gary S. (1965). A theory of the allocation of time. *Economic Journal* 75(299): 493–517. Reprinted in G. Becker, ed.,(1976), *The Economic Approach to Human Behavior*. Chicago: University of Chicago Press, pp. 89–130.

Becker, Gary S., and C. B. Mulligan (1997). The endogenous determination of time preference. *Quarterly Journal of Economics* 112: 729–58.

Becker, William E., and Darrell R. Lewis, eds. (1992). *The Economics of Higher Education*. Dordrecht, The Netherlands: Kluwer Academic Publishers.

Behrman, Jere R., and Mark R. Rosenzweig (1999). "Ability" bias in schooling returns and twins: A test and new estimates. *Economics of Education Review* 18(2): 159–67.

Behrman, Jere, M. R. Rosenzweig, and P. Taubman (1994). Endowments and the allocation of schooling in the family and marriage market: The twins experiment. *Journal of Political Economy* 102(6): 1131–74.

Behrman, Jere R., M. Rosenzweig, and P. Taubman (1996). College choice and wages: Estimates using data on female twins. *Review of Economics and Statistics* 73(4): 672–85.

Behrman, Jere R., and N. Stacey, eds. (1997). *The Social Benefits of Education*. Ann Arbor: University of Michigan Press.

Benhabib, Jess, and Mark Spiegel (2006). Human capital and technology diffusion. Chapter 13 in Philippe Aghion and S. N. Durlauf, eds., *Handbook of Economic Growth*. Oxford: Elsevier, pp. 935–66.

Benhabib, Jess, and M. Spiegel (1994). The role of human capital in economic development: Evidence from cross country data. *Journal of Monetary Economics* 34: 143–73.

Benham, Lee, and A. Benham (1975). Regulating through the professions: A perspective on information control. *Journal of Law and Economics* 18(2): 421–47.

Bennett, Douglas C. (2007). Underinvesting in the future. *The Chronicle of Higher Education* 53(2): B7.

Besley, T., and A. Case (2003). Political institutions and policy choices: Evidence from the US. *Journal of Economic Literature* 41(March): 7–73.

Bhatta, Saurav D., and J. Lobo (2000). Human capital and per capita product: A comparison of US states. *Papers in Regional Science* 79: 393–411.

Blau, David (1999). Effect of income on child development. *Review of Economics and Statistics* 81(2): 261–76.

Blau, Francine, and Lawrence Kahn (2002). *At Home and Abroad: US Labor Market Performance in International Perspective*. New York: Russell Sage Foundation.

Bok, Derek (2003). *Universities in the Marketplace: The Commercialization of Higher Education*. Princeton: Princeton University Press.

Bolin, K., L. Jacobson, and B. Lindgren (2002). The demand for health and health investments in Sweden. In B. Lindgren, ed., *Individual Decisions for Health*. London: Routledge, pp. 93–112.

Bourdieu, Pierre (1986). Forms of capital. In J. G. Richardson, ed., *Handbook of Theory and Research for the Sociology of Education*. Westport, CT: Greenwood Press, pp. 241–60.

Bowen, Howard R. (1977). *Investment in Learning: The Individual and Social Values of Higher Education*. San Francisco: Jossey-Bass.

Breton, Theodore R. (2008). Schooling and national income: How large are the externalities? *Education Economics*: 1–26.

Burd, Stephen (2007). Plenty of ideas about student aid but no road maps. *The Chronicle of Higher Education* 53(2) (September 1, 2006), at http://chronicle.com/weekly/v53/i02/02a04001.htm.

Burke, J., and A. Serban (1998). *Performance Funding and Budgeting for Public Higher Education: Current Status and Future Prospects*. New York: Rockefeller Institute of Government Affairs.

Butcher, Kristin, and Anne Case (1992). The effect of sibling sex composition on women's educational attainment. *Quarterly Journal of Economics* 109: 531–63.

Bynner, John, P. Dolton, L. Feinstein, G. Makepeace, L. Malmberg, and L. Woods (2003). *Revisiting the Benefits of Higher Education*. Bedford Group for Lifecourse Statistical Studies, Institute of Education. London: University of London.

Caffrey, J., and H. Isaacs (1971). *Estimating the Impact of a College or University on the Local Economy*. Washington, DC: American Council of Education.

Card, David (1998). The causal effect of education on earnings. In Orley Ashenfelter and David Card, eds., *Handbook of Labor Economics*, vol. 3. Working Paper 2, Center for Labor Economics, University of California at Berkeley.

Card, David (1993). Using geographic variation in college proximity to estimate the return to schooling. NBER Working Paper 4483. New York: National Bureau of Economic Research.

Card, David, and Alan B. Krueger (1992). Does schooling quality matter? Returns to education and the characteristics of public schools in the United States. *Journal of Political Economy* 100(1): 1–40.

Carnegie, Andrew (1889). Wealth. *North American Review* 148(June): 653–64, as quoted by David Nasaw, *Leherer NewsHour*, PBS, December 19, 2006.

Carneiro, Pedro, and James J. Heckman (2003). Human capital policy. OZA Discussion Paper. Bonn, Germany: Institute for the Study of Labor (IZA), available at http://ssrn.com/abstract=434544.

Case, A., D. Lubotsky, and C. Paxson (2002). Economic status and health in childhood: The origins of the gradient. *American Economic Review* 92: 1308–34.

Cawley, J., J. Heckman, and E. Vytlacil (1998). Cognitive ability and the rising return to education. NBER Working Paper W6388. New York: National Bureau of Economic Research.

Chambers, Jay (1996). Public school teacher cost differences across the United States: Introduction to a teacher cost index (TCI). In William J. Fowler, ed., *Developments in School Finance 1995*, NCES 96–344r. Washington, DC: U.S. Department of Education, pp. 21–32.

Ciccone, Antonio, and G. Peri (2002). Identifying human capital externalities: Theory with an application to US cities. IZA Discussion Paper 488. Bonn: IZA.

Clague, Christopher, S. Gleason, and S. Krack (1996). Determinants of lasting democracy in poor countries. Mimeo. San Diego: Department of Economics, University of California.

Clotfelter, Charles (1999). The familiar but curious economics of higher education: Introduction to a symposium. *Journal of Economic Perspectives* 13 (Winter): 3–12.

Cobern, M., C. Salem, and S. Mushkin (1973). Indicators of educational outcome Fall 1973. Publication OE 73–11110, U.S. Department of Health, Education, and Welfare. Washington, DC: U.S. Government Printing Office.

Cohen, Daniel, and Michael Soto (2007). Growth and human capital: Good data, good results. *Journal of Economic Growth* 12(1) (March): 51–76.

Cohn, E., S. L. Rhine, and M. C. Santos (1989). Institutions of higher education as multi-product firms: Economies of scale and scope. *Review of Economics and Statistics* 71: 284–90.

Coleman, James S. (1988). Social capital in the creation of human capital. *American Journal of Sociology* 94: S95–S120. Reprinted in Partha Dasgupta and

Ismail Serageldin, eds.(1990). *Foundations of Social Theory*. Cambridge, MA: Harvard University Press, pp. 13–39.

College Board (2007). Education pays: The benefits of higher education for individuals and society. Report by the College Board. Washington, DC: The College Board.

College Board (2007a, 2004a). Trends in student aid. Washington, DC: The College Board. www.collegeboard.com.

College Board (2007b, 2004b). Trends in college pricing. Washington, DC: The College Board. www.collegeboard.com.

Cornwell, Christopher, D. B. Mustard, and D. J. Sridhar (2003). The enrollment effects of merit-based financial aid: Evidence from Georgia's HOPE Scholarship. Department of Economics. Athens: University of Georgia.

Cowen, R. (1996). *The Evaluation of Higher Education Systems*. London: Kogan Page.

Currie, J., and M. Stabile (2003). Socioeconomic status and health: Why is the relationship stronger for older children? *American Economic Review* 93: 1813–23.

Curs, Bradley, L. D. Singell, and G. R. Waddell (2007). Money for nothing? The impact of the Pell Grant Program on institutional revenues and the placement of needy students. *Education Finance and Policy* 2 (Summer): 228–62.

Dale, Stacy Berg, and A. B. Krueger (1999). Estimating the payoff to attending a more selective college: An application of selection on observables and unobservables. Working Paper 409, Industrial Relations Section. Princeton: Princeton University.

Davidson, Richard (2000). Affective style, psychopathology, and resilience: Brain mechanisms and plasticity. *American Psychologist* 55: 1196–1214.

Deaton, A., and C. Paxson (2001). Mortality, education, income, and inequality among American cohorts. In D. A. Wise, ed., *Themes in the Economics of Aging*. Chicago: University of Chicago Press, pp. 129–65.

De Groot, Hans, and W. W. McMahon (1991). The cost structure of American research universities. *Review of Economics and Statistics* (August): 424–31.

De Walque, D. (2004). Education, information, and smoking decisions: Evidence from smoking histories, 1940–2000. Working Paper 3362. Washington, DC: The World Bank.

Dee, Thomas (2004). Are there civic returns to education? *Journal of Public Economics* 88: 1697–1720.

Denison, E. F. (1962). *The Sources of Economic Growth in the United States*. New York: Committee for Economic Development.

Diamond, Larry (1992). Economic development and democracy. *American Behavioral Scientist* 35: 450–99.

Dickert-Conlin, Stacy, and Ross Rubenstein, eds. (2006). *Economic Inequality and Higher Education*. New York: Russell Sage Publishers.

Di Tella, R., R. MacCulloch, and A. Oswald (2003). Preferences over inflation and unemployment: Evidence from surveys of happiness. *American Economic Review* 91: 335–41.

DuBois, W. E. B. (1973). The field and function of the Negro college. In Herbert Aptheker, ed., *The Education of Black People: Ten Critiques, 1906–1960*. New York, Monthly Review Press.

Duncan, Greg J. (1976). Earnings functions and non-pecuniary benefits. *Journal of Human Resources* 11(3): 464–83.

Easterlin, Richard A. (1968). *Population, Labor Force, and Long Swings in Economic Growth: The American Experience*. New York: National Bureau of Economic Research.

The Economist (2007a). A bridge too far gone. August 11: 23–24.

The Economist (2007b). Happiness. (January).

Edwards, Linda N., and M. Grossman (1979). The relationship between children's health and intellectual development. In S. Mushkin, ed., *Health: What is It Worth?* Elmsford, NY: Pergamon Press.

Eisner, Robert (1989). *The Total Incomes System of Accounts*. Chicago: University of Chicago Press.

Erbsland, M., W. Reid, and V. Ulrich (1995). Health, health care, and the environment: Econometric evidence from German micro data. *Health Economics* 4: 169–82.

Ermisch, John, and M. Francesconi (2000). Educational choice: Families and young people's earnings. *Journal of Human Resources* 35(1): 143–76.

European Commission (2006). Efficiency and equity in European education and training systems. Communication from the Commission to the Council and to the European Parliament, SEC (2006) 1096. Brussels: European Union Commission Staff.

Faggio, Giulia,, K. G. Salvanas, and J. Nan Reenen (2007). The evolution of inequality in productivity and wages: Panel data evidence. NBER Working Paper 13351. New York: National Bureau of Economic Research.

Frank, John W., and J. F. Mustard (1994). The determinants of health from a historical perspective. *Daedalus* 123(4): 675–82.

Freedom House (2007, and earlier issues). *Freedom in the World*. New York: Freedom House.

Freeman, Richard B. (1976). *The Overeducated American*. New York: Academic Press.

Friedman, Thomas L. (2007). *The World is Flat*. New York: Macmillan.

Fuchs, Victor R. (1982). Time preference and health: An exploratory study. In

V. R. Fuchs, ed., *Economic Aspects of Health*. Chicago: University of Chicago Press, pp. 93–120.

Gilbert, Daniel (2006). *Stumbling on Happiness*. New York: Knopf.

Gilbert, F. (1999). The response in North America to government expectations for greater accountability in the university sector—examples from three jurisdictions. Oxford: International Round Table on University Leadership.

Glaeser, Edward L., Rafael La Porta, Florencio Lopez-de-Silanes, and Andrei Shleifer (2004). Do institutions cause growth? *Journal of Economic Growth* (June): 1–53.

Gottschalk, Peter, and Timothy Smeeding (1997). Cross national comparisons of earnings and income inequality. *Journal of Economic Literature* 35(2): 633–87.

Green, Andy, and A. W. Little (2007). *Education and Development in a Global Era: Strategies for "Successful Globalisation."* London: Department for International Development.

Griliches, Zvi (2000). *R&D, Education and Productivity: A Retrospective*. Cambridge, MA: Harvard University Press.

Griliches, Zvi (1984). *R&D, Patents, and Productivity*. Chicago: University of Chicago Press.

Griliches, Zvi (1977). Estimating the returns to schooling: Some econometric problems. *Econometrica* 45: 1–22.

Griliches, Zvi, and W. M. Mason (1988). Education, income and ability. In Zvi Griliches, ed., *Technology, Education and Productivity*. New York: Basil Blackwell, pp. 182–212.

Grossman, Michael (2006). Education and non-market outcomes. Chapter 10 in E. Hanushek and F. Welch, eds., *Handbook of the Economics of Education*. Amsterdam: North Holland, pp. 576–33.

Grossman, Michael (2000). The human capital model. In A. J. Culyer and J. P. Newhouse, eds., *Handbook of Health Economics*. Vol. 1A. Amsterdam: Elsevier, pp. 347–408.

Grossman, Michael (1975). The correlation between health and schooling. In N. E Terleckyj, ed., *Household Production and Consumption*. New York: Columbia University Press, pp. 147–311.

Grossman, Michael (1972). *The Demand for Health: A Theoretical and Empirical Investigation*. New York: Columbia University Press.

Grossman, Michael, and R. Kaestner (1997). Effects of education on health. In J. R. Behrman and N. Stacey, eds., *The Social Benefits of Education*. Ann Arbor: University of Michigan Press, pp. 69–123.

Grubb, W. Norton, and Marvin Lazerson (2004). *The Education Gospel: The Economic Power of Schooling*. Cambridge, MA: Harvard University Press.

Gurin, Patricia (1999). The compelling need for diversity in higher education. Ann Arbor: University of Michigan. www.umich.edu/newsinfo/Admission/Expert.

Hansen, W. L. (1970). The income distribution effects of higher education. *American Economic Review* 60: 335–40.

Hansen, W. L, and B. Weisbrod (1969). The distribution of costs and direct benefits of public higher education: The case of California. *Journal of Human Resources* 4: 176–91.

Hanushek, Eric, and L. Wobmann (2007). The role of education quality in economic growth. World Bank Policy Research Working Paper 4122. Washington, DC: The World Bank.

Haveman, Robert, and Barbara Wolfe (2007). Valuing the non-market and social benefits of higher education. Wider Benefits of Learning Center, Institute of Education, University of London, www.learningbenefits.net.

Haveman, Robert, and Barbara Wolfe (1984). Schooling and economic well being: The role of non-market effects. *Journal of Human Resources* 19(3): 377–407.

Healy, Tom D., and David Istance (1998). *Human Capital Investment: An International Comparison*. Centre for Educational Research and Innovation. Paris: Organization for International Cooperation and Development.

Heckman, James (2006). Contributions of Zvi Griliches. NBER Working Paper 12318. Cambridge, MA: National Bureau of Economic Research.

Heckman, James, and P. Klenow (1997). Human capital policy. Working Paper. Chicago: Economics Department, University of Chicago.

Heckman, James, L. Lochner, and P. Todd (2008). Earnings functions and rates of return. Working Paper 13780. Cambridge, MA: National Bureau of Economic Research.

Heckman, James, L. Lochner, and P. Todd (2005). Earnings functions, rates of return, and treatment effects: The Mincer equation and beyond. Chapter 7 in E. Hanushek and F. Welch, eds., *Handbook of the Economics of Education*. Amsterdam: North Holland, pp. 307–458.

Heckman, James, and D. V. Masterov (2007). The productivity argument for investing in young children. *Review of Agricultural Economics* 29(3): 446–93.

Heller, Donald E., ed. (2001). *The States and Higher Education Policy: Affordability, Access, and Accountability*. Baltimore: Johns Hopkins University Press.

Helliwell, John (2005). Well being, social capital, and public policy: What's new? NBER Working Paper 11807. New York: National Bureau of Economic Research.

Helliwell, J. (2003). How's life? Combining individual and national variables to explain subjective well-being. *Economic Modeling* 20: 331–60.

Helliwell, John F., and Robert D. Putnam (1999). Education and social capital. NBER Working Paper 7121. New York: National Bureau of Economic Research.

Hettick, Walter (1972). Consumption benefits of education. In Sylvia Ostry, ed., *Canadian Higher Education in the Seventies*. Ottawa: Economic Council of Canada.

Hodginkson, V., and M. Weitzman (1988). *Giving and Volunteering in the United States: Findings from a National Survey, 1988 Edition*. Washington, DC: Independent Sector.

Huber, Evelyne, D. Rueschemeyer, and J. D. Stephens (1993). The impact of economic development on democracy. *Journal of Economic Perspectives* 7(3): 71–85.

Hyman, Herbert, Charles R. Wright, and J. S. Reed (1975). *The Enduring Effects of Education*. Chicago: University of Chicago Press.

Inside Higher Education (2007). The non monetary value of a college degree, by Elia Powers, at www.insidehighered.com.

Institute for Higher Education Policy (2005). *The Investment Payoff: A 50-State Analysis of the Public and Private Benefits of Higher Education*. Washington, DC.: Institute for Higher Education Policy.

International Country Risk Guide (2007, and earlier issues). *A Business Guide to Political Risk for International Decisions*, C. McKee and T. Sealy, eds. Syracuse, NY: Political Risk Services.

Jaffe, A. (1989). Real effects of academic research. *American Economic Review* 79: 957–70.

Jefferson, Thomas (1786). Letter from Paris to Mr. Wythe of Virginia. In B. L. Rayner (1834), *Life of Thomas Jefferson*. Boston: Lilly Wait, Colman, and Holden. Page citation is from *Memorial Edition of the Writings*, Andrew Lipscomb and Albert Bergh, Thomas Jefferson Memorial Association, 1904.

Jamison, Eliot, Dean Jamison, and Eric Hanushek (2007). The effects of education quality on mortality decline and income growth. Paper for the Dijon Economics of Education Conference, June 2006, and an NBER Working Paper.

Johnson, Ryan, and Shawn Kantor (2007). Striking at the roots of crime: The impact of social welfare spending on crime during the great depression. NBER Working Paper 12825. New York: National Bureau of Economic Research, http://ssrn.com/author=140516.

Johnstone, Bruce (2004). The economics and politics of cost sharing in higher education: Comparative perspectives. *Economics of Education Review* 23(4): 403–10.

Joint Economic Committee (2000). Investment in education: Private and public returns. Vice Chairman Jim Saxton (R-NJ). Washington, DC: U.S. Congress.

Jorgenson, Dale W., F. M. Gollop, and B. M. Fraumeni (1987). *Productivity and U.S. Economic Growth*. Cambridge, MA: Harvard University Press.

Kane, Thomas J., and Cecilia E. Rouse (1993). Labor market returns to two- and four-year colleges: Is a credit a credit and do degrees matter? NBER Working Paper 4268. New York: National Bureau of Economic Research.

Keller, Katrina (2006a). Education expansion, expenditures per student and the effects on growth in Asia. *Global Economic Review* 35(1): 21–42.

Keller, Katrina (2006b). Investment in primary, secondary, and higher education and economic growth. *Contemporary Economic Policy* 24(1): 18–34.

Kendrick, John (1976). *The Formation and Stocks of Total Capital*. New York: Columbia University Press.

Kenkel, D. S. (1991). Health behavior, health knowledge, and schooling. *Journal of Political Economy* 99:287–305.

Kim, Jong, II, and Lawrence J. Lau (1996). The sources of economic growth of east Asian newly industrialized countries: Some further evidence. AEA Papers and Proceedings, May.

King, Elizabeth, and M. A. Hill, eds. (1993). *Women's Education in Developing Countries*. Baltimore: Johns Hopkins University Press.

Kinkel, D. S. (1991). Health behavior, health knowledge, and schooling. *Journal of Political Economy* 99: 287–305.

Kirk, David L. (2003). *Shakespeare, Einstein, and the Bottom Line: The Marketing of Higher Education*. Cambridge, MA: Harvard University Press.

Klein, Michael, Scott Schuh, and Robert Triest (2003). *Job Creation, Job Destruction, and International Competition*. Kalamazoo, MI: W.E. Upjohn Institute for Employment Research.

Krueger, Alan B., and M. Lindahl (2001). Education for growth. Why and for whom? *Journal of Economic Literature* 39(4): 1101–36.

Krueger, Alan, and David Schkade (2007). The reliability of subjective well-being measures. National Bureau of Economic Research (NBER) and Institute for the Study of Labor (IZA) Working Paper, available at http://ssrn.com/abstract =979932.

Lange, Fabian, and R. Topel (2006). The social value of education and human capital. Chapter 8 in E. Hanushek and F. Welch, eds., *The Handbook of the Economics of Education*. Oxford: Elsevier, North Holland, pp. 459–510.

Lam, David, and S. Duryea (1999). Effects of schooling on fertility, labor supply, and investments in children, with evidence from Brazil. *Journal of Human Resources* 34(1): 160–92.

Layard, Richard (2006). Happiness and public policy: A challenge to the profession. *Economic Journal* 116(March): C24–C33.

Layard, Richard (2005). *Happiness: Lessons from a New Science*. London and New York: Penguin Press.

Lazear, E. P. (1977). Education: Consumption or production? *Journal of Political Economics* 85: 569–97.

Lee, Lung Fei (1982). Health and wage: A simultaneous equation model with multiple discreet indicators. *International Economic Review* 23(1): 199–222.

Leigh, J. Paul. (1983). Direct and indirect effects of education on health. *Social Science and Medicine* 4: 227–34.

Lemennicier, B. (1978). *Education et technologie de consummation: Incidences de l'education sur la consummation*. Paris: Centre de Recherche pour l'Etude et l'Observation des Conditions de Vie (CREDOC).

Leslie, L., and P. Brinkman (1988). *The Economic Value of Higher Education*. New York and London: Collier Macmillan Publishers.

Leslie, Larry L., and Paul T. Brinkman (1987). Student price response in higher education: The student demand studies. *Journal of Higher Education* 58: 181–204.

Leslie, L., G. P. Johnson, and J. Carlson (1977). The impact of need-based student aid on the college attendance decision. *Journal of Education Finance* 2: 269–85.

Leslie, L. L., G. Rhoades, and R. Oaxaca (1999). Effects of changing revenue patterns on public research universities. A report to the National Science Foundation, Grant No. 9628325.

Levin, Henry (2006). The social costs of an inadequate education. Symposium Summary, October 24–26, 2005. New York: Teachers College, Columbia University, http://www.tc.columbia.edu/i/a/3082_socialcostsofinadequateEducation.pdf.

Little, Angela, and Jasbir Singh (1992). Learning and working: Elements of the diploma disease thesis examined in England and Malaysia. *Comparative Education* 28(2).

Lleras-Muney, A. (2005). The relationship between education and adult mortality in the United States. *Review of Economic Studies* 72:189–221.

Lochner, Lance, and Enrico Moretti (2002). The effect of education on crime: Evidence from prison inmates, arrests, and self-reports. Working Paper 287. Joint Center for Poverty Research. Chicago: Northwestern University and University of Chicago.

Lord, Mimi (2007). Trends and issues; transformational change in higher education: Positioning your institution for future success. TIAA-CREF National Higher Education Leadership Conference, TIAA-CREF, www.tiaa-crefinstitute.org.

Lucas, Robert E. (1988). On the mechanics of economic development. *Journal of Monetary Economics* 22(1): 3–42.

Lyall, Katherine C., and K. R. Sell (2006). *The True Genius of America at Risk: Are We Losing Our Public Universities to De Facto Privatization?* Westport, CT: ACE/Praeger Series on Higher Education.

Mankiw, N. Gregory, David Romer, and David N. Weil (1992). A contribution to the empirics of economic growth. *Quarterly Journal of Economics* 107(2): 407–37.

Mansfield, Edwin (1995a). Academic research underlying industrial innovations: Sources, characteristics, and financing. *Review of Economics and Statistics* 77(1): 55–65.

Mansfield, Edwin (1995b). Economic returns from investments in research and training. Working Paper. Washington, DC: The World Bank.

Marshall, Alfred (1927). *Principles of Economics*. 8th ed. London: Macmillan.

Marshall, R. (1995). The global jobs crisis. *Foreign Policy: The U.N. in Crisis* 100(3). Washington, DC: The Carnegie Endowment for International Peace.

Mattana, Paolo (2004). *The Uzawa-Lucas Endogenous Growth Model*. Aldershot, England: Ashgate Publishing.

McMahon, Walter W. (2008). Website at http://netfiles.uiuc.edu/wmcmahon/www/.

McMahon, Walter W. (2007a). An analysis of education externalities with applications to development in the deep south. *Contemporary Economic Policy* 23(3): 459–82.

McMahon, Walter W. (2007b). Endogenous development. Working Paper, Department of Economics, April.

McMahon, Walter W. (2006a). Education finance policy: Financing the non-market and social benefits. *Journal of Education Finance* 32(2): 264–84.

McMahon, Walter W. (2006b). International economic forces driving higher education policy: The race involving technology, globalization, and needs for higher education. Global Human Resources Forum, Seoul, South Korea, November 9.

McMahon, Walter W. (2005). *Higher Education Financial Aid Policies: Multiplying Their Impact on State Economic Development*. Atlanta: Southern Education Foundation.

McMahon, Walter W. (2004a). *Lifelong Learning in Developing Countries: An Analysis with Estimates of Private Returns and Externalities*. The World Bank Policy Research Series, Washington, DC: The World Bank, www.worldbank.org/education/lifelong_learning/.

McMahon, Walter W. (2004b). The social and externality benefits of education. In Geraint and Jill Johnes, eds., *The International Handbook of the Economics of Education*. London: Edward Elgar Publishers.

McMahon, Walter W. (2002). *Education and Development: Measuring the Social Benefits*. New York and Oxford: Oxford University Press.

McMahon, Walter W. (2001a). The impacts of human capital on non-market outcomes and feedbacks on development. In John Helliwell, ed., *The Contribu-*

tion of Human and Social Capital to Sustained Economic Growth and Well Being. Paris: Organization for Economic Cooperation and Development.

McMahon, Walter W. (2001b). The measurement of externalities, non-market effects, and trends in the returns to education. In The Appraisal of Investments in Educational Facilities. Paris: European Investment Bank/OECD.

McMahon, Walter W. (1998a). Conceptual framework for the analysis of the social benefits of lifelong learning. Education Economics 6(3): 307–43.

McMahon, Walter W. (1998b). Education for great cities: Measuring the contribution of investment in higher education at the University of Illinois at Chicago. Urbana: Office of the Vice President for Academic Affairs.

McMahon, Walter W. (1998c). Knowledge for the future: Measuring the returns to investment in education and research at the University of Illinois at Urbana-Champaign. Urbana: Office of the Vice President for Academic Affairs.

McMahon, Walter W. (1998d). Education and growth in East Asia. Economics of Education Review 17(2): 159–72.

McMahon, Walter W. (1997). Recent advances in measuring the social and individual benefits of education. Special issue, International Journal of Education Research 27(6): 449–531.

McMahon, Walter W. (1991). Relative returns to human and physical capital in the US and efficient investment strategies. Economics of Education Review 10(4): 283–96.

McMahon, Walter W. (1984a). Sources of the slowdown in productivity growth: A structural interpretation. In John W. Kendrick, ed., International Comparisons of Productivity and Causes of the Slowdown. Cambridge, MA: Ballinger, pp. 93–108.

McMahon, Walter W. (1984b). Why families invest in higher education. In Seymour Sudman and Mary A. Spaeth, eds., The Collection and Analysis of Economic and Consumer Behavior Data: In Memory of Robert Ferber. Urbana-Champaign: Bureau of Economic and Business Research, University of Illinois, pp. 75–91.

McMahon, Walter W. (1976). Influences on investment by blacks in higher education. American Economic Review 66(2): 320–24.

McMahon, Walter W., and George Psacharopoulos (2008). Revisiting the residual: Education, externalities, and growth. Working Paper, Department of Economics, University of Illinois at Urbana Champaign.

McMahon, Walter W., and Alan Wagner (1982). The monetary returns to education as partial social efficiency criteria. In W. McMahon and T. Geske, eds., Financing Education: Overcoming Inefficiency and Inequity. Urbana, and London: University of Illinois Press, pp. 150–87.

McPherson, Michael (2004). President's comments. The Spencer Foundation Annual Report. Chicago: The Spencer Foundation.

McPherson, Michael, and Morton Shapiro (1994). Does student aid affect college enrollment? New evidence on a persistent controversy. In Elchanan Cohn and Geraint Johnes, eds., *Recent Developments in the Economics of Education.* Aldershot, England: Edward Elgar Publishing, pp. 184–95.

Metcalf, David (1973). Pay dispersion, information, and returns to search in a professional labor market. *Review of Economic Studies* 40(4): 491–505.

Michael, Robert (1982). Measuring non-monetary benefits of education. In W. W. McMahon and T. Geske, eds., *Financing Education: Overcoming Inefficiency and Inequity.* Urbana: University of Illinois Press.

Michael, Robert (1975). Education and consumption. In F. Thomas Juster, ed., *Education, Income, and Human Behavior.* New York: McGraw Hill.

Michael, Robert T., and R. J. Willis (1976). Conception and fertility: Household production under uncertainty. In N. E. Terleckyi, ed., *Household Production and Consumption.* Studies in Income and Wealth, 40. New York: National Bureau of Economic Research.

Miller, P., C. Mulvey, and N. Martin (1995). What do twins studies tell us about the economic returns to education? A comparison of US and Australian findings. *American Economic Review* 85(3): 586–99.

Milligan, Kevin, E. Moretti, and P. Oreopoulos (2004). Does education improve citizenship? Evidence from longitudinal and repeated cross sectional data. *Journal of Public Economics* 88 (August): 1667–95.

Mincer, Jacob (1974). *Schooling, Experience and Earnings.* New York: National Bureau of Economic Research.

Mincer, Jacob (1962). On the job training: Costs, returns, and some implications. *Journal of Political Economy*, Supplement, 70(October): 50–79.

Mishel, Lawrence, J. Bernstein, and S. Allegretto (2005). *The State of Working America.* Ithaca: Cornell University Press.

Monk, David H. (1990). *Education Finance: An Economic Approach.* New York: McGraw Hill.

Moomaw, Ronald L., J. K. Mullen, and Martin Williams (2002). Human and knowledge capital: A contribution to the empirics of state economic growth. *American Economics Journal* 30(1): 48–60.

Moore, Mark, and P. Ranjan (2005). Globalization vs skill-based technological change: Implications for unemployment and wage inequality. *Economic Journal* 115: 391–422.

Moretti, Enrico (2004). Estimating the social returns to higher education: Evidence from longitudinal and repeated cross section data. *Journal of Econometrics* 121: 175–212.

Morton, Fiona S., F. Zettelmeyer, and J. Silva-Risso (2001). Consumer information and price discrimination: Does the internet affect the pricing of new cars to women and minorities? NBER Working Paper 8668. New York: National Bureau of Economic Research.

Muennig, Peter (2005). The health returns to education interventions. New York: Teachers College, Columbia University, http://www.tc.columbia.edu/centers/ EquitySymposium/symposium/resourceDetails.asp?PresId=5.

Murnae, Richard J. (1981). New evidence on the relationship between mother's education and children's cognitive skills. *Economics of Education Review* 1(2): 245–52.

Nadiri, M. Ishaq (1993). Innovations and technological spillovers. NBER Working Paper 4423. New York: National Bureau of Economic Research.

National Center for Public Policy and Higher Education (2004). Measuring up 2004: The state by state report card for higher education. San Jose, CA, and Washington, DC: National Center for Public Policy and Higher Education.

National Committee of Inquiry into Higher Education (1997). Higher education in the learning society. Report of the Deering Commission. Norwich, England: HMSO.

National Center for Education Statistics (2007). Digest of education statistics. Chapter 4, Federal programs for education and related activities, Table 362, and enrollment, Tables 184–90. Washington, DC: U.S. Department of Education.

National Center for Education Statistics (2005). Education pays. Washington, DC: U.S. Department of Education, http://www.collegeboard.com/prod_down loads/press/cost06/education_pays_06.pdf.

National Center for Education Statistics (1996, 2000, 2007). Projection of education statistics. Office of Educational Research and Improvement, U.S. Department of Education. Washington, DC: National Center for Education Statistics.

National Science Foundation (2006). *Science and Engineering Indicators*. Washington, DC: National Science Foundation.

Nelson, R., and E. Phelps (1966). Investment in humans, technological diffusion, and economic growth. *American Economic Review* 56: 69–75.

Olivia, Maria-Angels, and Luis A. Rivera-Batiz (2002). Political institutions, capital flows, and developing country growth: An empirical investigation. *Review of Development Economics* 6: 248–62.

Olsen, M. E. (1968). Multivariate analysis of national political development. *American Sociological Review* 35: 699–712.

Organization for Economic Cooperation and Development (2003). First results, PISA 2003, Andreas Schleicher, Head of Research Team. Paris: Organization for Economic Cooperation and Development.

Organization for Economic Cooperation and Development (1998). Human capital investment, an international comparison. Centre for Educational Research and Innovation. Paris: Organization for Economic Cooperation and Development.

Pascarella, Ernest T., and P. T. Terenzini (2007, 1991). *How College Affects Students*. San Francisco: Jossey Bass.

Paulsen, Michael B., and John C. Smart (2001). *The Finance of Higher Education: Theory, Research, Policy, and Practice*. New York: Agathon Press.

Phelps, Edmund (1962). The new view of investment: A neoclassical analysis. *Quarterly Journal of Economics* 78(4): 548–67.

Pierce J. P., M. C. Fiore, T. E. Novotny, E. J. Hatziandreu, and R. M. Davis (1989). Trends in cigarette smoking in the United States: Projections to the year 2000. *Journal of the American Medical Association* 261(1): 61–65.

Powers, Elizabeth, and Emilie Bagby (2008). Poverty and inequality in Illinois. *The Illinois Report, 2008,* Institute of Government and Public Affairs, University of Illinois, Urbana, pp. 49–60.

Preston, John, and Ricardo Sabates (2005). The relation of inequality to social cohesion and social capital. Wider Benefits of Learning Research Report. Institute of Education. London: University of London.

Pritchett, Lant (2006). Does learning to add up add up? Returns to schooling in aggregate data. Chapter 11 in E. Hanushek and F. Welch, eds., *Handbook of the Economics of Education*. Amsterdam: Elsevier-North Holland, pp. 635–96.

Pritchett, Lant (2000). Where has all the education gone? *World Bank Economic Review* 15(3): 367–91.

Psacharopoulos, George (2005). Why some university systems are collapsing: Realities from Europe, Vienna, December 2, 2005, available at gpsach@rcn.com.

Psacharopoulos, George, and Harry Patrinos (2004). Returns to investment in education: A further update. *Education Economics* 12(2): 111–35.

PURE (2001). Final report, Public Funding and the Private Returns to Education (PURE), Helsinki: Publications, www.etla.fi/PURE.

Rauch, J. (1993). Productivity gains from geographic concentration in cities. *Journal of Urban Economics* 34: 380–400.

Riddell, W. Craig (2004). The social benefits of education: New evidence on an old question. Paper presented at conference at University of Toronto, December 3, 2004. Working Paper, University of British Columbia, Department of Economics.

Riddell, W. Craig (2003). The role of government in post secondary education in Ontario. Panel on the Role of Government in Ontario, August 2003. Working Paper, University of British Columbia, Department of Economics.

Robbins, Lionel (1945; first edition 1932). *An Essay on the Nature and Significance of Economic Science*. London: Macmillan and Co.

Roenker, Jonathan M., and Eric Thompson (2003). Education's role in explaining the per capita income gap. Working Paper. Atlanta: Southern Education Foundation.

Romer, Paul (2002). Redistributional consequences of educational reform. In Edward Lazear, ed., *Education in the Twenty First Century*. Stanford: Hoover Institution Press.

Romer, Paul (1990). Endogenous technical change. *Journal of Political Economy* 98(5): S71–S98.

Romer, Paul (1986). Increasing returns and long run growth. *Journal of Political Economy* 94(5): 1002–37.

Rosen, Sherwin (1975). Measuring the obsolescence of knowledge. Chapter 8 in F. Thomas Juster, ed., *Education, Income, and Human Behavior*. Carnegie Commission on Higher Education and NBER. New York and London: McGraw Hill, pp. 199–234.

Rosenzweig, Mark R., and T. Paul Schultz (1989). Schooling, information, and non-market activity. *International Economic Review* 30(1989): 457–77.

Ross, C. E., and J. Mirowsky (1999). Refining the association between education and health: The effects of quantity, credential, and selectivity. *Demography* 36:445–60.

Ross, Catherine E., and Chia-Ling Wu (1995). The links between education and health. *American Sociological Review* 60(5): 719–45.

Rothstein, Richard (2002). Out of balance: Our understanding of how schools affect society and how society affects schools. 30th Anniversary Essay. Chicago: The Spencer Foundation.

Rouse, Cecilia E. (1999). Further estimates of the economic return to schooling from a new sample of identical twins. *Economics of Education Review* 18(2): 149–57.

Royalty, Anne B. (1998). Job-to-job and job-to-non-employment turnover by gender and educational level. *Journal of Labor Economics* 16(2): 392–443.

Ryder, Norman B., and C. F. Westoff (1971). *Reproduction in the United States, 1965*. Princeton: Princeton University Press.

Ryoo, J-K, Y-S Nam, and M. Carnoy (1993). Changing rates of return to education over time: A Korean case study. *Economics of Education Review* 12(1): 71–80.

Schultz, T. W. (1981). *Investing in People: The Economics of Population Quality*. Berkeley: University of California Press.

Schultz, T. W. (1971). *Investment in Human Capital: The Role of Education and of Research*. New York: Macmillan/The Free Press.

Schultz, T. W. (1961). Education and economic growth. In N. B. Henry, ed., *Social*

Forces Influencing American Education. Chicago: University of Chicago Press, pp. 46–88.

Sims, Geoffrey (1989). The universities. In Michael D. Stephens, ed., *Universities, Education, and the National Economy.* London: Routledge.

Shakoto, R. A., L. Edwards, and M. Grossman (1980). An exploration of the dynamic relationship between health and cognitive development in adolescence. NBER Working Paper 454. Cambridge, MA: National Bureau of Economic Research.

Slater, Brian, and T. Topper (1992). *The State and Higher Education.* London: Woburn Press.

Slaughter, Sheila A., and Larry L. Leslie (1997). *Academic Capitalism: Politics, Policies, and the Entrepreneurial University.* Baltimore: Johns Hopkins University Press.

Smith, V. Kerry (1996). Social benefits of education: Feedback effects and environmental resource. Chapter 6 in Jere R. Behrman and N. Stacey, eds., The *Social Benefits of Education.* Ann Arbor: University of Michigan Press.

Solomon, L. C. (1975). The relation between schooling and savings behavior. In F. T. Juster, ed., *Education, Income, and Human Behavior.* New York: McGraw-Hill.

Solomon, Lewis C., and Paul J. Taubman, eds. (1972). *Does College Matter?* New York: Academic Press.

Solow, Robert (1956). A contribution to the theory of economic growth. *Quarterly Journal of Economics* 70(1): 65–94.

Spence, M. (1973). Job market signaling. *Quarterly Journal of Economics* 87: 355–79.

Stacey, Nevzer (1998). Social benefits of education. *Annals of the American Academy* 559(September): 54–63.

St. John, Edward P., and M. Parsons, eds. (2004). *Public Funding of Higher Education: Changing Contexts and New Rationales.* Baltimore: Johns Hopkins University Press,.

St. John, Edward, and Michael B. Paulsen (2001). The finance of higher education: Implications for theory, research, policy, and practice. Chapter 15 in M. B. Paulsen and J. C. Smart, eds., *The Finance of Higher Education: Theory, Research, Policy, and Practice.* New York: Agathon Press.

Strauss, John, P. J. Gertler, O. Rahman, and K. Fox (1993). Gender and life cycle differentials in the patterns and determinants of adult health. *Journal of Human Resources* 28(4): 791–837.

Sullivan, Dennis, and Timothy Smeeding (1997). Educational attainment and earnings inequality in eight nations. *International Journal of Education Research* 27(6): 513–25.

Topel, Robert (1999). Labor markets and economic growth. In O. Ashenfelter and D. Card, eds., *Handbook of Labor Economics*, vol. 3. Amsterdam: Elsevier, pp. 2942–84.

UNESCO (2005). *World Education Report*. Paris: UNESCO.

University of Illinois at Urbana Champaign, Senate Budget Committee (1979). Report on instructional units and research units in relation to cost, by department. Working Paper, Department of Economics, University of Illinois at Urbana-Champaign, available from wmcmahon@uiuc.edu.

U.S. Bureau of Labor Statistics (2007). Economic and employment projections. Washington, DC: U.S. Bureau of Labor Statistics, Table 6 at http://www.bls.gov/news.release/ecopro.to6.htm.

U.S. Bureau of Labor Statistics (2005). *Occupational Outlook Handbook, 2004–5 Edition*, Tomorrow's jobs by occupation, charts 7–9. Washington, DC: U.S. Bureau of Labor Statistics, U.S. Department of Labor, www.bls.gov/oco/oco2003.

U.S. Census (2007, 1980). Current Population Survey. Educational attainment, people 18 years old and older by total money earnings in 2006, both sexes, at www.census.gov.

U.S. Census (2006). Current Population Survey. Educational Attainment, people 18 years old and older, by total mean earnings in 2005, at www.census.gov.

U.S. Department of Education (2007). A test of leadership: Charting the future of U.S. higher education. Report of the Secretary's Commission on the Future of Higher Education (the Spellings Report): http://www.ed.gov/about/bdscomm/list/hiedfuture/reports.html.

U.S. Department of Education (1998). Report of the National Commission on the Cost of Higher Education. Washington, DC: U.S. Department of Education.

U.S. National Commission on the Cost of Higher Education (1998). *Straight Talk About College Costs*. Phoenix, AZ: The Oryx Press.

US News and World Report (1999, 2007). The best colleges in 2008.

Vandenbussche, Jerome, P. Aghion, and C. Meghir (2006). Growth, distance to the frontier, and composition of human capital. *Journal of Economic Growth* 11: 97–127.

Varga, Attila (1998). *University Research and Regional Innovation*. Boston: Kluwer Academic Publishers.

Vedder, Richard (2007). Over invested and over priced: American higher education today. Policy paper for the Center for College Affordability and Productivity. Washington, DC: Center for College Affordability and Productivity.

Vorhees, Richard A. (2001). Financing community colleges for a new century. In Michael Paulsen and John Smart, eds., *The Finance of Higher Education: Theory, Research, Policy, and Practice*. New York: Agathon Press.

Wagstaff, A. (1986). The demand for health: Some new empirical evidence. *Journal of Health Economics* 5: 195–233.

Weisbrod, B. A. (1971). Benefits and costs of medical research: The case of poliomyelitis. *Journal of Political Economy* 79(3): 527–44.

Weisbrod, B. A. (1964). *External Benefits of Public Education*. Princeton: Princeton University.

Winston Group (2006). ACE national survey aggregates. Report to ACE. Washington, DC: American Council on Education.

Wise, David (1975). Academic achievement and job performance. *American Economic Review* 65: 350–66.

Witte, Ann Dryden (1997). The social benefits of education: Crime. In Jere R. Behrman and N. Stacey, eds., *The Social Benefits of Education*. Ann Arbor: University of Michigan Press, pp. 219–46.

Witter, Robert A., Morris A. Okun, William A. Stock, and Marilyn J. Haring (1984). Health and subjective well-being: A meta-analysis. *International Journal of Aging and Human Development* 19(2): 111–32.

Wolfe, Barbara L., and R. H. Haveman (2003). Social and non-market benefits from education in an advanced economy. In Yolanda Kodrzycki, ed., *Education in the 21st Century: Meeting the Challenges of a Changing World*. Boston: Federal Reserve Bank.

Wolfe, Barbara L., and R. H. Haveman (2001). Accounting for the social and non-market benefits of education. In John Helliwell, ed., *The Contribution of Human and Social Capital to Sustained Economic Growth and Well Being*. Paris: Organization for Economic Cooperation and Development.

Wolfe, Barbara, and Sam Zuvekas (1997). Non-market effects of education. *International Journal of Education Research* 27(6): 491–502.

Wood, Adrian (1994). *North-South Trade, Employment and Inequality: Changing Economic Fortunes in a Skill Driven World*. Oxford: Clarendon Press.

World Bank (2005). Indicators of world development. Washington, DC: The World Bank.

World Bank (1993). The east Asian miracle: Economic growth and public policy. Policy Research Paper, Policy Research Department. Washington, DC: The World Bank.

Wright, David (2007, 2004). State higher education finance. SHEEO 2004 Professional Development Conference. Boulder: State Higher Education Executive Officers.

Note: Page numbers in *italics* refer to figures and tables.

Bowen, Howard, 35, 254
Breton, Theodore, 227, 243, 246, 251–52, 254
Brinkman, Paul, 36, 94, 184, 202, 213, 237, 252, 254, 288
Burd, Stephen, 325
Bush, George W., 303
business management field, 266
Butcher, Kristin, 334
Byner, John, 207, 209

Caffrey, J., 184
California State at Long Beach, 300, 304
campus-level policies: differences by discipline, 313–14; differences in mission, 314–15; overview of, 312–13; specific rates of return, 317–19; tracer studies, 319–20; value-added, 315–17, 317
campus management. *See* university management
Canada, 9, 17–18, 237–38
capital markets: imperfect, 178–80; private, 15–16
Card, David, 334
Carniero-Heckman analysis, 92, 98n
Carter, Alan, 272
Case, Anne, 203, 334
Chambers, Jay, 149
chemistry field, 273
child education: as social benefit, 139–40; value of, 168–69
child health: as social benefit, 138–39; value of, 168
civic institutions, contributions to: democracy and, 34–35, 130, 206, 207; quality of life and, 46–47
Clague, Christopher, 205
Clotfelter, Charles, 322
Cohn, Elchanan, 258
college earnings differential, 95, 95–96
community colleges, 32, 67–68, 283, 300
competition among institutions, 45
compromise approach to increasing enrollments, 305–6
conditional convergence, 106, 107
consumption benefits, 151–52, 171–72

cooperation within higher education community, 25–26, 306, 310
Cornwell, Christopher, 215
cost disease, 63, 84
cost-effectiveness of publications by academic field, 272–73, 274–79, 280–82
costs: of failed experiments, 267, 268, 269; opportunity, 85; of prisons and welfare, 220–22; of public health care, 220–22, 238; of R&D, returns relative to costs, 268–70, 269
costs of higher education: accountability and, 59–63; affordability of, 57–58; definition of, 85–87, 86, 87, 88, 89, 90–91; in European Union, 99; foregone earnings, 6–7, 59–60, 85, 89, 319; institutional, 291, 319; social rates of return to, 89, 92–102
crime rates, 127–28, 150, 217–20, 238
Curs, Bradley, 302

Dale, Stacy Berg, 345
Deaton, A., 137–38
Dee, Thomas, 207
de facto privatization, 2, 11, 64
deforestation, 223
degree completion, 60, 215
De Groot, Hans, 258
democracy: behaviors contributing to, 206–7, 207; education and, 34–35, 130–31, 202–6; human rights and, 208–9; per capita income and, 367; political stability and, 366; rule of law and, 265–66, 313; value of, 231, 236
Denison, E. F., 182
developed countries: economic growth in, 105; higher education in, 20–24; high school graduation rates in, 304–5; inequality in, 248; privatization in, 326; research in, 195, 262, 263, 265; social rates of return in, 98–99; value of social benefits in, 241–44, 242. *See also* European Union; Organization for Economic Cooperation and Development (OECD) countries; United Kingdom; *specific countries*
developing countries: education policy in, 9; happiness in, 144; investment in

equity: continuum of, 216–17; definition of, 216; privatization and, 327; public support and, 181–82. *See also* inequality

Erbsland, M., 165

Ermisch, John, 139

European Commission, 31, 36

European Union: access in, 57; admissions in, 237; costs in, 99; increasing enrollments in, 303–4; investment in education in, 117; lifelong learning in, 33; modern human capital approach and, 9; public support in, 54–55; wage inequality in, 23

expenditure, total: on higher education, 17–20; per student, 3n; trends in, 89, 90–91

external efficiency: accountability and, 61–62; definition of, 12

externalities (external benefits): definition of, 193–94; development process and, 197–98; dynamic growth process and, 192–201; dynamic model and, 347–50; economic growth and, 103–4; in endogenous growth theory, 196; overview of, 293; in relation to private and social benefits, 49, 49–54; research and, 256–57; skeptics and, 252–54; social benefits as, 181

extracurricular activities, 151–52

Faggio, Giulia, 248

failed experiments, cost of, 267, 268, 269

fertility rates/family size: as social benefit, 141–42; value of, 169–70

financial aid. *See* loans for education; merit-based aid; need-based aid; Pell Grants

financing strategies, 329–30

Florida, 237, 311

foregone earnings costs, 6–7, 59–60, 85, 89–92, 319

Francesconi, M., 139

Frank, John, 139

Freeman, Richard, 71, 288–89

freer trade, 22, 33–34, 103, 365

Friedman, Thomas, 24

Fuchs, Victor, 135

full method of reporting rates of return, 94, 186, 187–88, 189

future-oriented behavior, 134–35, 148

Georgia, 237, 311

Geske, T., 216

GI Bill, 32, 104, 303, 305

Glaeser, Edward, 34, 204

globalizing economies, higher education in, 20–24. *See also* developed countries

Gottschalk, Peter, 248

graduate education: degrees completed by field, 264, 265–67; policy strategies for states, 282–83

graduates: contributions and attitudes of, 130; demand for, 16, 72, 114, 294–95; starting salaries of, 98, 318

graduation rates, high school, 22, 304–5, 306

Great Britain. *See* United Kingdom

Greece, 3, 214

Green, Andy, 28, 30

Griliches, Zvi, 28, 29, 94, 183, 191, 225, 259, 270, 284, 334

Grossman, Michael, 50–51, 119, 126, 127, 133, 134, 135, 136, 137, 138–39, 161, 165, 166, 167, 169, 173, 296

gross non-market outcomes, 122–23

growth. *See* economic growth; endogenous growth

growth accounting approach, 182–83

guaranteed loans, 178–80

Hallock, Kevin, 335, 337, 339, 342, 343

Hansen, Lee, 213, 215

happiness: economics of, 19; factors contributing to, 145–47; income and, 119, 126–27, 143–45; levels of, 147; measurement of, 30–31; as social benefit, 223–24; value of, 170–71

Hatch Act, 32

Haveman, Robert, 6, 133, 168–69, 171, 173–75, 202, 254

Haveman-Wolfe method: dynamic simulations and, 230; equations for, 160–61; new social rates of return and, 249; private non-market benefits and,

119; research and, 270; social benefits and, 49, 53, 227; strengths and weaknesses of, 228; tables based on, 369, 372; valuation of social benefits using, 230–31, 232–35, 236–40, 323

health benefits of education: as social benefit, 20, 127, 133–36; value of, 165–66

health care aides, 77, 81

Healy, Tom, 100

Heckman, James, 92, 96, 97, 98, 101, 131, 183, 186, 187, 189, 229, 245

Helliwell, John, 145, 146, 170, 224, 239

Hettich, Walter, 148

Hicks, J. R., 143

Higher Education Act, 32–33

higher education policy: as asleep at switch, ix–xii; federal matching grants, 298–301; financing strategies, 329–30; gaps in, 321–24; increasing enrollment rates, 301–6; modern human capital approach to, 5–10; national gaps in, 294–95; need-based aid, 297–98; need for new, 287–94; paying for changes in, 307–8; problems with, 1–4; providing better information, 295–97; public funding for, 10–11; school finance reform, 306–7; solutions needed for, 24–32; universal entitlement approach, 305; value of social benefits and, 53–54. *See also* campus-level policies; states, policy strategies for

high school graduation rates, 22, 304–5, 306

Hodgkinson, V., 206

Hong Kong, 33–34

household management efficiency, 147–48

household production function: happiness and, 146; home economics field and, 28; human capital and, 41; non-market outcomes and, 123–26, 348–49

Huber, Evelyne, 204

human capital: definition of, 41–42; diminishing returns to, 92–93, 347–50; economic growth and, 92–93, 102–9, 226; obsolescence of, 47–49,

259–60, 323; U.S. comparative advantage in, 26, 66; vintages of, 47–49, 260–61, 323. *See also* modern human capital approach

human rights, 208–9, 236

Hunt, James B., 325

Ikenberry, Stanley, 297

Illinois, 217

immigration: backlash against, 23; earnings and, 51, 73, 76; skill levels and, 22

impact studies, 183–85

income equivalent approach to valuing social benefits, 230–31, 232–35, 236–40, 370–73, 372

India, 204

indirect benefits, and public support, 55

indirect effects: definition of, 193; dynamic simulations and, 240–44; estimation of, 194; externalities in relation to private and social benefits, 49, 49–54; market returns and, 253; non-market benefits and, 280, 281–82

Indonesia, 204, 210

inequality: access and, 16, 56–57; economic, and education, 213–14; endogenous growth models and, 103; happiness and, 19; in OECD countries, 368; Pell Grants and, 131; reduction in, as social benefit, 237–38; trends in, 214–16; underinvestment and, 15–16; wage, in developed countries, 248. *See also* equity

infant mortality, 138–39

information available to investors: about child education, 140, 169; about health benefits, 136; about social benefits, 13–15; increasing, 329; market failure and, 45, 120–21, 175–78; poor, policy implications of, 2–3, 175–80; providing better, to enable markets to work, 295–97; valuing benefits and, 162

innovation and research, 260

Inside Higher Education website, 286

institutional costs, 291, 319

instructional units, 62, 320

internal efficiency: accountability and,

public support: access and, 56–57; decline in, 7, 10–24, 54–56, 66–68; equity and, 181–82; social rates of return and, 329–30
Putnam, Robert, 224
putty to clay analogy, 48, 149–50, 260–61

quality of life, 46–47, 280–81

rates of return. *See* full method of reporting rates of return; private rates of return; social rates of return
Rauch, J., 199, 247
replacement investment, 28, 42, 48, 49, 261
research and development (R&D): academic, investment in, 262, 263, 265; cost-effectiveness of investment in, by field, 271–73, 274–79, 280–82; developed countries and, 195; dissemination of new knowledge and, 225–26, 239; on economic growth, 70–71; failed experiments, cost of, 267, 268, 269; federal support for, 299; impact studies, 20; investment in by developed countries, 102–4; on non-market private and social benefits, 27–31; patenting and, 17, 257, 266, 285; privatization and, 17, 64, 282; profit-oriented, 55; returns relative to costs, 268–70, 269; social benefits of, 256–59; state support for, 282–83, 311–12
research funding, 1–2
research units, 62, 320
research universities, contribution of, 21–22
residual, 183, 192–93
Robbins, Lionel, 43
Romer, Paul, 27, 29, 52, 102–3, 195, 254, 258, 259, 323
Rosen, Sherwin, 28
Rosenzweig, Mark, 95, 334, 335n
Ross, C. E., 165
Rothstein, Richard, 114
Rouse, Celia, 95, 202, 219, 333, 334, 339
rule of law, 265–66, 313

Sala-I-Martin, Xavier, 27, 93, 212, 237, 265
salaries, starting, 98, 318
Sarbates, Ricardo, 217
saving: economic value of, 171–72; growth and, 31; as private benefit, 148
Schkade, David, 170
school finance reform, 131, 306–7, 309–10
Schultz, T. W., 27, 35–36, 182, 201–2, 254
screening hypothesis, 111–13, 253
self-selection bias. *See* ability bias
Sell, K. R., 10, 36, 40, 54, 329
SEOP grant programs, 325
service occupations, 80–81, 81
Shakotko, R. A., 168
Shapiro, Morton, 301
sheepskin effect, 318
short-term dynamics: definition of, 197; model of, 347–50
Sidgwick, Henry, 19, 143
Singapore, 33–34
skill levels: access and, 57; earnings and, 22–24, 72–76, 75; federal government and, 301; immigration and, 280; privatization and, 64–65; Spellings Report and, 325; stagnation of tax base and, 67–68
Slaughter, Sheila, 36, 64, 328–29
Smart, John, 36, 286
Smeeding, Timothy, 248
Smith, V. Kerry, 222
social benefits of education: crime rates, 217–20; democratization, 202–7; dissemination of new knowledge, 224–27; dynamic development process and, 198–201, 200; economic equality, 213–17, 237–38; environmental, 222–23; estimations of, 182–85, 227–30; evidence of, 201–2; externalities in relation to, 49, 49–54, 181; happiness and social capital, 223–24; human rights, 208–9; knowledge of, 14; life expectancy and net population growth rates, 212–13; lower welfare, medical, and prison costs for states, 220–22; market failure and, 46–47;

The True Genius of America at Risk
(Lyall and Sell), 10, 36
tuition and fee costs, trends in, *86, 86–87, 87, 88*

underinvestment in education: graduation rate and, 3; market failure and,
15–16, 46; poor information and, 13;
price of, 330
unemployment, 152–54, *153*, 218
United Kingdom: enrollments in, 303–4;
institutional research productivity in,
29–30; literacy in, 280; modern
human capital approach and, 9;
National Committee of Inquiry Into
Higher Education, 27; Research
Assessment Exercises, 271; Robbins
Commission, 32, 113; screening
hypothesis and, 112–13
United States: access in, compared to
other countries, 26; economic growth
in, 26, 106; education, government
investment in, 298–301; enrollments
in, 11, 35; research, government
investment in, 262, 263; southern
states of, 117. *See also* states, policy
strategies for; *specific states*
universal entitlement approach to college education, 305
university management: accountability
and, 59–63; decline in public support
and, 56; education policy and, 25;
inefficiency in, 293; privatization and,
17
University of Illinois at Urbana
Champaign, 269, 272, 274–79, 318
University of Phoenix, 16, 293
university research, benefits from,
256–59
U.S. Department of Education: fields for
national interest, 209; information for
investors and, 177, 296–97; special

analyses of, 296; website of, 61, 121.
See also Spellings Commission Report
U.S. National Commission on the Cost
of Higher Education, 27

valuation: explanatory variables and
units of measurement, *356–62*; methods and sources, *351–52*; of non-market benefits, 155, *156–59*, *160–62*,
353–54, *355*; of social benefits, 369–
73, *372–81*; of social benefits by
aggregate methods, 244–47; of social
benefits by dynamic simulation, 240–
44; of social benefits by income equivalent approach, 230–31, *232–35*,
236–40
value-added, 177–78, 191, 315–17, *317*
Vedder, Richard, 325
vintages of human capital, 47–49, 260–
61, 323
vocationalism, 12–13, 16, 113–14

Wagstaff, A., 136
Warren, David, 325
water pollution, 222
Weisbrod, Burt, 213, 215, 254
Weitzman, M., 206
welfare costs, 220–22
Willis, R. J., 169–70
Wise, David, 151
Witte, Ann Dryden, 218, 296
Witter, Robert, 146
Wolfe, Barbara, 6, 119, 133, 160, 168–
69, 171, 173–75, 202, 254. *See also*
Haveman-Wolfe method
women: education of, 141–42; labor
force participation rates, 154–55, *155*
World Bank, 26

Zimmerman, David, 334
Zuvekas, Sam, 119, 160